P9-CMB-970
DISCARD
LIBRARY

THE MMPI

THE MMPI
A Practical Guide

Second Edition

John R. Graham, Ph.D.
Professor of Psychology
Kent State University

New York Oxford
OXFORD UNIVERSITY PRESS
1987

Oxford University Press

Oxford New York Toronto
Delhi Bombay Calcutta Madras Karachi
Petaling Jaya Singapore Hong Kong Tokyo
Nairobi Dar es Salaam Cape Town
Melbourne Auckland

and associated companies in
Beirut Berlin Ibadan Nicosia

Published by Oxford University Press, Inc.,
200 Madison Avenue, New York, New York 10016

Library of Congress Cataloging-in-Publication Data
Graham, John R. (John Robert), 1940–
The MMPI: a practical guide.
Bibliography: p.
Includes index.
1. Minnesota Multiphasic Personality Inventory.
I. Title. [DNLM: 1. MMPI. WM 145 G739m]
BF698.8.M5G72 1987 155.2′83 86-33284
ISBN 0-19-504263-8

10 9 8 7 6 5 4 3 2 1

Printed in the United States of America
on acid-free paper

TO
BECKY, JOHN, MARY, AND DAVID

Foreword

The first edition of this outstanding MMPI textbook made a substantial contribution to clinical psychology by providing an introduction to MMPI concepts in a clear, interesting, and readable manner. The intervening ten years since the first publication of Graham's *The MMPI: A Practical Guide* produced many changes in the MMPI. Extensive research and broadened clinical applications expanded the MMPI's use greatly.

Dr. Graham is in the forefront of these developments with the MMPI. His accomplishments range from expanding the empirical base of the instrument through research, broadening the clinical utility of the test through applications in novel settings, such as the courtroom, and through teaching the MMPI to hundreds of psychologists in MMPI workshops and graduate classes. The publisher of the MMPI, the University of Minnesota Press, recognized Graham's expertise by appointing him as one of the consultants to help direct the restandardization of the MMPI, a project now nearing completion. Graham's participation in that project assures his continued prominence in new developments in the MMPI during the next ten years as well.

Graham's revision of this classic introductory textbook on the MMPI incorporates his broad experience and comprehensive understanding of the MMPI. The second edition of his practical guide is an even more refined and up-to-date version of the original work. Graham critically appraises the current literature and incorporates a considerable amount of new and useful MMPI research, while sharpening the relevance of his approach by eliminating information that has become obsolete or dated. This book provides summaries of the extensive research base of the MMPI in a manner that clinicians can easily use in their practices. I have recommended the book as essential to clinicians attending my workshops if their practice includes interpreting MMPIs.

The First Edition of the *The MMPI: A Practical Guide* quickly became an integral part of my graduate course in psychological assessment. Graham's thorough approach to introducing students to the MMPI is a sound one, providing an extensive amount of useful clinical information, as well as an effective, pragmatic strategy for interpreting profiles. One important quality of the first edition of the book is its accuracy. The only error I ever found was rather esoteric, concerning a mislabeling of a figure. This error became the center of an extra-credit assignment for my classes. Every year on the first day of class, I informed the students that there was one error in the book that if they learned the material well they might be able to detect. They were told if they discovered the error it would be worth *extra credit* points on the feared and dreaded final examination. The search for the error became quite a competition, with each succeeding class hoping to find it. Attesting to the rarity of the error, no student ever earned the extra credit points! Furthermore, no other errors were ever discovered, despite, I might add, considerable searching on the part of many students.

With the comprehensive and high quality revision of this book, I anticipate that Graham's *The MMPI: A Practical Guide (Second Edition)* will be as influential in introducing the next generation of MMPI'ers into the field as the first edition was with the present generation.

Minneapolis
April 9, 1987

James N. Butcher

Preface

As its title suggests, this book is intended for anyone who uses or is interested in learning to use the MMPI. For students in psychology, medicine, counseling, social work, and related fields, it represents an efficient way to become acquainted with a vast amount of information about the MMPI, its methodology, and its uses. For practicing clinicians it can serve as a source book to which continuing reference can be made as MMPIs are interpreted in clinical work. It is likely to be especially useful in preparing written reports which are based, at least in part, on the MMPI.

In Chapter 1 the rationale underlying the MMPI is discussed, and the methodology utilized in constructing the basic scales is presented. Chapter 2 contains detailed information about administering and scoring the MMPI and about coding profiles. Chapter 3 is devoted to consideration of the validity scales. In addition to discussion of the construction of each validity scale, information relevant to the identification of response sets and to the interpretation of the validity scales singly and in configuration is presented. Each of the ten standard clinical scales is discussed in Chapter 4, and interpretive information is presented for high and low scores on each scale. In Chapter 5 psychometric characteristics of the MMPI (e.g., reliability and validity) are examined and the MMPI's use with special populations (e.g., adolescents, medical patients) is discussed. The interpretation of two- and three-point code types and other profile configurations is covered in Chapter 6. Chapter 7 presents several different approaches to interpretation of MMPI content. The approaches include content scales (Wiggins, Harris and Lingoes, Serkownek) and critical items. Chapter 8 covers some of the more frequently used MMPI supplementary scales. For each scale, construction procedures, reliability, validity, and interpretation of high and low scores are discussed. Chapter 9 presents the author's general strategy for interpreting MMPIs, and the strategy is illustrated with a case. This chapter should be especially beneficial to beginning MMPI users who have not yet developed their own interpretive strategies. In Chapter 10 computerized administration, scoring, and interpretation are examined. A major focus of this chapter is consideration of professional and ethical issues involved in computerized approaches to MMPI use.

A guiding principle throughout the preparation of this book was that material should be presented in a way that will be most directly useful to clinicians. Thus, no attempt was made to include all of the technical information and research data concerning the MMPI. Other sources, such as the MMPI *Manual* (Hathaway & McKinley, 1983) and the two-volume *MMPI Handbook* (Dahlstrom, Welsh, & Dahlstrom, 1972, 1975), are readily available to those who require these kinds of information. In order to present material in the most useful way, specific sources are not cited for individual interpretive statements. Instead, the sources consulted in formulating the intepretive material are listed at the ends of the appropriate chapters.

The MMPI is becoming more and more widely used in this country and around the world. It is this author's opinion that the MMPI is the best personality assessment instrument currently available. If used appropriately the MMPI is a tool that can make assessment tasks more efficient and more fruitful. It is hoped that this book will help clinicians better understand and utilize the MMPI in clinical assessment.

Kent, Ohio
April 1987

J. R. G.

Acknowledgments

Many persons have supported the revision of this book. I am indebted to the authors and publishers who granted permission to reproduce their works. I am especially appreciative of the assistance provided by Professional Assessment Services and the University of Minnesota Press. The Department of Psychology at Kent State University provided clerical support.

Contents

THE MMPI

1

Introduction

GENERAL DESCRIPTION OF THE MMPI

The Minnesota Multiphasic Personality Inventory (MMPI) consists of 566 self-reference statements. People taking the test respond to each statement as true as applied to them, as false as applied to them, or as not applying to them. The relatively unambiguous stimuli and the structured response format qualify the MMPI for classification as an objective technique of personality assessment. Traditionally, great importance has been placed on the differences between objective and projective assessment procedures. In addition to the differences in stimulus ambiguity and the extent to which response format is structured, it also has been suggested that objective and projective techniques differ in terms of the involvement of a skilled clinician in the interpretation of test results. It has been suggested that whereas a skilled clinician is an integral part of the interpretation of projective test protocols, objective test results can be interpreted by less skilled individuals by reference to appropriate norms. In clinical practice, this distinction does not exist. As Matarazzo (1972) stated, interpretation of both objective and projective techniques is "a highly subjective art which requires a well-trained and experienced practitioner to give such 'scores' predictive meaning in the life of any given human being" (p. 11).

After administration of the test, an individual's responses are scored objectively either by hand or with automated scoring equipment. The scoring procedures yield scores for four validity scales and 10 basic clinical or personality scales. Numerous additional scales and indices also have been developed, and some of these are discussed later in this *Guide*. The raw scores from the standard validity and clinical scales are transformed to linear T-scores (mean = 50; *SD* = 10) using data provided in the *Manual* (Hathaway & McKinley, 1983). The responses of the Minnesota normal group provide the basis for the T-score conversions. Separate norms are available for males and females. The T-scores are utilized to construct a profile on a standard profile sheet. This profile serves as the basis for generating inferences about the individual who was examined.

ORIGINAL PURPOSE

The MMPI was first published in 1943. The test authors, Starke Hathaway, PhD, and J. Charnley McKinley, MD, were working in the University of Minnesota Hospitals and hoped that the MMPI would be useful for routine diagnostic assessments. During the late 1930s and early 1940s a primary goal of the clinical psychologist and the psychiatrist was to assign appropriate psychodiagnostic labels to individual cases. An individual interview or mental status examination and individual psychological testing usually were done of each patient. It was hoped that a group-administered paper-and-pencil personality inventory would provide a more efficient way of arriving at appropriate psychodiagnostic evaluation.

RATIONALE

Hathaway and McKinley utilized the empirical keying approach in the construction of the various MMPI scales. This approach, which requires that one empirically determine items that differentiate between groups of subjects, is a common technique today. However, it represented a significant innovation at the time of the MMPI construction. Most prior personality inventories had been constructed according to a logical keying approach. With this earlier approach, test items were selected or generated rationally according to face validity, and responses were keyed according to the subjective judgment of the test author concerning what kinds of responses were likely to be indicative of the attributes being measured. Both clinical experience and research data seriously questioned the adequacy of this logical keying approach. Increasingly, it became apparent that subjects could falsify or distort their responses to items in order to present themselves in any particular way they chose. Further, empirical studies indicated that the subjectively keyed responses often were not consistent with differences actually observed between groups of subjects. In the newly introduced empirical keying procedure, responses to individual test items are treated as unknowns, and empirical item analysis is utilized to identify test items that differentiate between criterion groups. Such an approach to the item responses overcomes many of the difficulties associated with the earlier, subjective approaches.

CLINICAL SCALE DEVELOPMENT

The first step in the construction of the basic MMPI scales was to collect a large pool of potential inventory items.[1] Hathaway and McKinley selected a wide

1. Information concerning clinical and validity scale development is abstracted from a series of articles by Hathaway (1956, 1965), Hathaway and McKinley (1940, 1942), McKinley and Hathaway (1940, 1944), McKinley, Hathaway, and Meehl (1948), and Meehl and Hathaway (1946).

variety of personality-type statements from such sources as psychological and psychiatric case histories and reports, textbooks, and earlier published scales of personal and social attitudes. From an initial pool of about 1000 statements the test authors selected a pool of 504 statements that they judged to be reasonably independent of each other.

The next step was to select appropriate criterion groups. One criterion group, hereafter referred to as the Minnesota normals, consisted primarily of relatives and visitors of patients in the University of Minnesota Hospitals. This group was augmented by several other groups of normal subjects. These included a group of recent high school graduates who were attending pre-college conferences at the University of Minnesota, a group of Work Progress Administration workers, and some medical patients at the University of Minnesota Hospitals. The second major group of subjects, hereafter referred to as clinical subjects, was made up of psychiatric patients at the University of Minnesota Hospitals. This second group included patients representing all of the major psychiatric diagnostic categories being utilized clinically at the time of the test construction. Clinical subjects were divided into subgroups of discrete diagnostic samples according to their clinically arrived at diagnostic labels. Whenever there was any doubt about a patient's clinical diagnosis or when more than one diagnosis was present, the patient was not included in this clinical reference group. The different subgroups of clinical subjects formed were: hypochondriasis, depression, hysteria, psychopathic deviate, paranoia, psychasthenia, schizophrenia, and hypomania.

The next step in scale construction was to administer the original 504 test items to the Minnesota normals and to the patients in each of the clinical groups. For each of the clinical groups, separately, an item analysis was conducted to identify those items in the pool of 504 that differentiated significantly between the specific clinical group, other clinical groups, and a group of normal subjects. Individual MMPI items that were identified by this procedure were included in the resulting MMPI scale for that clinical group.

In an attempt to cross-validate such a clinical scale (e.g., the depression scale), new groups of normal subjects and clinical subjects with that particular clinical diagnosis were selected and the scale was administered to each. If significant differences were found between scores for the normal group and the clinical group in question, the clinical scale was considered to have been adequately cross-validated and thus was ready for use in the differential diagnosis of new patients whose diagnostic features were unknown.

At a somewhat later time, two additional clinical scales were constructed. First, the Masculinity-Femininity (Mf) scale originally was intended to distinguish between homosexual males and heterosexual males. Because of difficulty in identifying adequate numbers of items that differentiated between these two groups, Hathaway and McKinley subsequently broadened their approach in the construction of the Mf scale. In addition to the all too few items that did discriminate between homosexual and heterosexual males, other items were identified that were differentially endorsed by normal male and female subjects. Also, a number of items from the Terman and Miles I scale (1936) were added to the original item pool and included in the Mf scale. Second, the Social Introversion (Si) scale was developed by Drake (1946) and has come to be included as one of the basic MMPI scales. Although this scale initially was constructed by identifying items from the original item pool that differentiated successfully between female college students who tended to participate in many extracurricular activities and female college students who were not very socially participative, its use now has been extended to men as well as women.

VALIDITY SCALE DEVELOPMENT

Hathaway and McKinley at the outset also developed four scales, hereafter referred to as the validity scales, whose purpose was to detect deviant test-taking attitudes. The "Cannot Say" scale or category is simply the total number of items in the MMPI omitted or responded to as both true and false by the individual taking the test. Obviously, the omission of large numbers of items, which tends to lower the scores on the clinical scales, calls into question the interpretability of the whole resulting profile.

The L scale, originally called the "Lie" scale of the MMPI, was designed to detect rather unsophisticated and naïve attempts on the part of the individuals to present themselves in an overly favorable light. The L scale items were rationally derived and cover everyday situations in order to assess the strength of the person's unwillingness to admit even very minor weaknesses in character or personality. An example of an L scale item is: "I do not read every editorial in the newspaper every day." Most people would be quite willing to admit that they do not read every editorial every day, but persons determined to present themselves in a very favorable light might not be willing to admit to such a perceived shortcoming.

The F scale of the MMPI was designed to detect individuals who are approaching the test-taking task in a way different from that intended by the test authors. F scale items were selected by examining for each item the endorsement frequency of the Minnesota normal group and identifying those items endorsed in a particular direction by fewer than 10 percent of the normals. Obviously, because few normal people endorse an item in that direction, a person who does endorse the item in that direction is exhibiting a deviant response.

The K scale of the MMPI was designed to identify clinical defensiveness. Items in the K scale were selected empirically by comparing the responses of a group of patients who were known to be clinically deviant but who produced normal MMPI profiles with a group of people producing normal MMPI profiles and for whom there was no indication of psychopathology. It was intended that a high K score be indicative of defensiveness and call into question the person's responses to all of the other items. The K scale also was later utilized to develop a correction factor for some of the clinical scales. Hathaway and

McKinley reasoned that, if the effect of a defensive test-taking attitude as reflected by a high K score is to lower scores on the clinical scales, perhaps one might be able to determine the extent to which the scores on the clinical scales should be raised in order to reflect more accurately a person's behavior. By comparing the efficiency of each clinical scale with various portions of the K scale added as a correction factor, McKinley et al. determined the appropriate weighting of the K scale score for each clinical scale to correct for the defensiveness indicated by the K scale. Some clinical scales are not K-corrected at all, because the simple raw score on those clinical scales seemed to produce the most accurate prediction about a person's clinical condition. Other scales have proportions of K, ranging from .2 to 1.0, added in order to elevate appropriately the clinical scales.

CURRENT APPROACH TO MMPI UTILIZATION

After a decade of clinical use and additional validity studies it became apparent that the MMPI was not adequately successful for the purpose for which it originally was developed, namely, the valid psychodiagnosis of a new patient. Although patients in any particular clinical category (e.g., depression) were likely to obtain high scores on the corresponding clinical scale, they also often obtained high scores on other clinical scales. Also, many normal subjects also obtained high scores on one or more of the clinical scales. Clearly, the clinical scales are not pure measures of the symptom syndromes suggested by the scale names.

A number of different reasons have been suggested for the MMPI's failure to fulfill completely its original purpose. From further research it became apparent that many of the clinical scales of the MMPI are highly intercorrelated, making it highly unlikely that only a single scale would be elevated for an individual. Also, the unreliability of specific psychiatric diagnoses themselves contributes to the failure of the MMPI scales to differentiate among clinical groups.

Although the limited success of the MMPI scales to differentiate among clinical groups might have been bothersome in the 1940s, this limitation is not particularly critical today. Currently, practicing clinicians place less emphasis on diagnostic labels per se. Accumulating evidence suggests that psychiatric nosology is not as useful as is medical diagnosis. Information in a psychiatric chart that a patient's diagnosis is schizophrenia, for example, does not tell us much about the etiology of the disorder for that individual or about recommended therapeutic procedures.

For this reason, the MMPI currently is used in a way quite different from the way in which it originally was intended to be used. It is assumed that the clinical scales are measuring something, because reliable differences in scores are found among individuals from different clinical reference groups. The new approach treats each MMPI scale as an unknown and, through clinical experience and empirical research, the correlates of each scale are identified. When a person obtains a score on a particular scale, the clinician attributes to that person the characteristics and behaviors that through previous research and experience have been identified for other individuals with similar scores on that scale. To lessen the likelihood that excess meaning will be attributed because of the clinical scale names, the following scale numbers have been assigned to the original clinical scales, and today they replace the clinical labels:

Present Scale Number	*Discarded Scale Name*
1	Hypochondriasis
2	Depression
3	Hysteria
4	Psychopathic Deviate
5	Masculinity-Femininity
6	Paranoia
7	Psychasthenia
8	Schizophrenia
9	Hypomania
0	Social Introversion

Thus, for example, when discussing a patient among themselves, MMPI experts will refer to him or her as a "four-nine" or a "one-two-three," descriptive phrases in shorthand which communicate to the listener the particular behavior descriptions associated with the "4-9" or "1-2-3" syndrome.

In addition to identifying empirical correlates of high scores on each of the above numbered scales, it also is possible to identify empirical correlates for low scores and for various combinations of scores on the scales (e.g., highest scale in the profile, two highest scales in the profile). Some investigators have developed very complex rules for classifying individual MMPI profiles and have identified behavioral-empirical correlates of profiles that meet these criteria. Thus, even though the MMPI has not been successful in terms of its original purpose (differential diagnosis of clinical group believed in the 1930s to be discrete psychiatric types), it has proved possible subsequently to use the test to generate descriptions of and inferences about individuals (normals and patients) on the basis of their own MMPI profiles. It is this new behavioral description approach to the utilization of the MMPI in everyday practice that has led to the instrument's great popularity among practicing clinicians. Lubin, Larsen, and Matarazzo (1984) reported that the MMPI is the most widely used personality test in the United States.

2

Administration and Scoring

One appealing feature of the MMPI is that although it takes an experienced clinician to interpret it, it can be administered easily to individual subjects or groups of subjects by nonprofessional examiners. The availability of a number of different MMPI test forms increases the number and range of potential subjects. In addition, the test can be scored objectively by hand or by machine. Because of these factors, MMPI users sometimes become careless in the administration and scoring of the test. It must be emphasized that the same caution and attention to standardized procedures that are appropriate for other psychological tests also must be followed with the MMPI. Persons who administer the test should be familiar with all of the material presented in the *Manual* (Hathaway & McKinley, 1983). Also, Chapter 1 of *An MMPI Handbook,* Volume I (Dahlstrom, Welsh, & Dahlstrom, 1972) discusses additional administrative problems and considerations.

The *Manual* indicates that individuals 16 years of age or older with at least six years of schooling should be able to complete the MMPI satisfactorily. Experience suggests that if they are properly motivated and carefully supervised, and if appropriate forms of the test are employed, people with even less than six years of education may be able to take the test. Reading level seems to be the primary consideration in determining who can take the test. Some examiners have individuals read aloud some of the MMPI items to determine whether they can read well enough to take the test. Other test users have found it useful to administer some brief measure of reading ability, such as the Kent Emergency Scales (Kent, 1946), before administering the MMPI.

Age is another important factor in determining who can take the MMPI. As long as visual handicaps or other physical problems do not interfere, there is no upper age limit on who can take the test. There are, however, several considerations in determining the youngest age for which the test is appropriate. Although the *Manual* (Hathaway & McKinley, 1983) indicates 16 as the youngest age for which the test is appropriate, the MMPI has been administered successfully to persons as young as 13 or 14 years of age. Younger individuals, even if they can read well enough and can maintain their attention and motivation long enough to complete the test, may not have a range of experience wide enough to make the content of many items meaningful to them. Separate norms for adolescents are presented in Appendix C of this *Guide.* Whereas specialized norms may be useful in comparing the level of a person's scores with his or her specific reference group, the generating by a practicing clinician of inferences from profiles constructed from such norms is questionable, because most interpretative data are based on profiles derived from the adult norms.

Clinical condition of potential examinees is another important consideration. Completion of the entire MMPI is a lengthy and tedious task for most subjects. Persons who are very anxious or agitated often find the task almost unbearable. It frequently is possible to break the testing session into several shorter periods for such individuals. Persons who are very confused may not be able to understand or to follow the standard instructions. Such individuals sometimes can complete the test satisfactorily if it is administered individually using either the box or auditory tape form in contrast to the booklet form. Some examiners find it useful to read the items to the subject, with either the examiner or the subject recording the responses.

For most individuals the test can be administered either individually or in groups, using the forms of the test and answer sheet most convenient for the examiner. For persons of average or above average intelligence, without complicating factors, the testing time typically is between 1 and 1½ hours. For less intelligent individuals, or those with other complicating factors, the testing time may exceed 2 hours. Although it sometimes is more convenient to have the subject take the MMPI home to complete and return to the examiner, whenever possible it is preferable to have the MMPI completed in the professional atmosphere of the clinician's office.

It is important when administering the MMPI to any individuals in any setting to communicate clearly to them the purposes for which the test is being given and to assure them of the confidentiality of the test results. Persons who know why they are taking the test, who will see the test results, and who know how the results will be used on their behalf are more likely to be cooperative and to approach the task in a manner that will make the resulting data meaningful.

TEST FORMS

The availability of several basic forms of the MMPI ensures that the test can be administered to a broad spectrum of people in a manner that is most convenient to both subjects and examiner. Forms are available for individual administrations, for group administrations, for blind individuals or others who cannot read the printed items, and for subjects who have limited facility with the English language. Researchers also have developed experimental forms of the test in which reading difficulty has been reduced, in which items are presented in an oral interrogative form, in which items are presented in the second person, and so forth. In this section, only those forms most often utilized by the practicing clinician are discussed. For other forms the reader is referred to Chapters 2 and 3 of the *Handbook,* Volume I (Dahlstrom et al., 1972).[1]

Individual (Box) Form

In the box form, each of the 550 items[2] is printed on a small card. The cards are presented in random order in a box that includes instructions inside the cover. The box also contains 3 dividers labeled True, False, and Cannot Say. Examinees are instructed to read each item and to decide whether it is true as applied to them or false as applied to them and to place the card behind either the True or False divider. For items that do not apply to them or that deal with something that they do not know about, the cards are placed behind the Cannot Say divider. The instructions indicate that fewer than 10 cards should be placed behind the Cannot Say divider.

The box form is especially useful for individuals of limited ability or education who might have difficulty completing the booklet forms. It also is easier than the booklet forms for disturbed or confused persons who might get mixed up in marking answers on a separate sheet.

It is a good idea to place at the front of the box a few items that have easy vocabulary and that are free of content that might be especially upsetting to the person taking the test. Also, many examiners include instructions to limit the use of the Cannot Say category even more than is indicated in the standard instructions. If examinees place many items in the Cannot Say category, they should be encouraged to reconsider the items and to try to place them in either the True or False category. With this prodding, most people will leave no items or only a few items in the Cannot Say category.

The first step in scoring the box form is for the examiner to transfer the responses to the box form answer sheet. This answer sheet has 550 blanks arranged in columns labeled A through J and rows numbered 1 through 55. Each card is identified by a column letter and a row number. Cannot Say responses are entered as question marks in the appropriate blanks of the answer sheet. The examiner next identifies those cards in the True category that have the lower right-hand corner cut off. For these items a red X is placed in the appropriate blanks of the answer sheet. Cards in the False category with the lower left-hand corner cut off are identified, and each is recorded as a red X in the appropriate blank of the answer sheet. It should be noted that items in the True and False categories that have been recorded on the answer sheet indicate infrequent responses and not necessarily abnormal ones.

After the appropriate entries are made on the answer sheet, the responses

1. MMPI materials are available only from National Computer Systems, Inc., P.O. Box 1416, Minneapolis, Minnesota 55440.

2. Although the original MMPI item pool consisted of 504 items, 46 items were added when the Mf scale was constructed, bringing the total number of items to 550.

are scored for the four validity indicators and the 10 basic clinical scales. The Cannot Say score simply is the number of question marks on the record form. The L score is obtained by counting the number of red X's among the last 15 items (numbers J41 through J55). For the F and K scales and for the 10 clinical scales, transparent scoring templates are used for hand scoring. For each of these scales the appropriate template is placed over the record form. The raw score is determined by counting the number of blanks that contain a red X next to an X on the scoring template, plus the number of blank cells on the record form that correspond to the O's on the template. The raw scores are recorded in the appropriate blanks along the right edge of the record form.

Group (Booklet) Form

The group form consists of 566 items printed in a reusable paper booklet. To obtain a more economical method of scoring the answer sheets, 16 items are duplicated in the booklet and on the answer sheet. Instructions, which are printed on the front of the booklet, direct persons being examined to read each statement and to decide whether it is true as applied to them or false as applied to them and to mark their answers on a separate answer sheet. Although they are told to make no mark for a statement that does not apply to them or that is something that they do not know about, they are cautioned not to leave any blank spaces if they can avoid it.

Several different types of answer sheets are available for use with the group form. The hand-scored group form answer sheet has true and false circles numbered 1 to 566. The person being examined blackens in the circle corresponding to the desired response. In hand scoring, the Cannot Say score is determined by counting the number of items left blank or marked as both True and False. No scoring key is available for the L scale. The L score is the number of False responses to the following items: 15, 30, 45, 60, 75, 90, 105, 120, 135, 150, 165, 195, 225, 255, 285. It should be noted that these items are easily identified by their location on the answer sheet. Raw scores for the F and K scales, for the 10 basic clinical scales, and for four special scales (A, R, Es, MAC) are determined by placing appropriate templates over the answer sheet and counting the number of blackened spaces. For some of the scales two templates are necessary, and the raw score for each is the total of the two part scores. There are different scoring keys for male and female subjects for the Mf scale.

Computerized scoring and interpretive services are available through National Computer Systems and other companies. To utilize these computerized services, special computer-scoring answer sheets must be used. The companies should be consulted concerning appropriate answer sheets before the MMPI is administered.

Form R

In Form R the 566 items contained in the booklet form are printed in a hard cover, spiral-bound booklet with stepdown pages. Instructions appear on the first page of the booklet. A Form R answer sheet is inserted over two pegs in the back of the booklet. As a person works through the booklet, each item is aligned with the appropriate space on the answer sheet. A response is indicated by blackening in an oval containing either T or F.

A major advantage of Form R is that the hard cover permits the test to be completed even when a desk or table space is not available. Also, for many persons the alignment of items and appropriate spaces on the answer sheet makes the task easier than with the group form. A further advantage is that the items have been rearranged from the group form order in such a way that all items required for scoring the standard validity and clinical scales appear in the first 399 items. After Item 366, the order of some items will be different in Form R and the group form. The *Manual* (Hathaway & McKinely, 1983) includes tables for converting group form item numbers to Form R item numbers and vice versa.

The Form R answer sheet must be hand-scored with a special set of scoring templates. The Cannot Say score is determined by counting the number of items left blank or answered as both True and False. Raw scores for the L, F, and K scales, for the 10 basic clinical scales, and for four special scales (A, R, Es, MAC) are obtained by placing the transparent templates over the answer sheet and counting the number of blackened ovals that appear in the boxes on the template. Because all 566 item responses appear on one side of the answer sheet, only one template is needed for each scale, with the exception of the Mf scale, which has different templates for male and female subjects.

Tape Recording Form

There is a standard tape recording of MMPI items available for administration to semiliterates and persons with other disabilities that make completion of other forms difficult or impossible. The tape is played to the person, and during a pause after each item, the response is recorded either by the person being examined or by the examiner. The items appear on the tape in the same order as in the group form; therefore, the same answer sheets and scoring procedures utilized for the group form also are appropriate for the tape form.

Short Forms

Because the length of time required to complete the MMPI is sometimes prohibitive, numerous efforts have been made to develop short or abbreviated forms of the test. The utilization of short forms always leads to a loss of information. Many of the additional scales that were subsequently developed cannot be scored if all of the MMPI items are not administered. Before deciding to utilize a short form, the examiner should carefully think about whose time is being saved. Because the MMPI typically is not administered by the clinician personally, the time saved by utilizing a short form is that of the person being examined and/or of a clerical worker. In most situations, there is no compelling reason to shorten the time of test administration. However, it is recognized that in some instances where testing time is quite limited, the examiner may have to consider using a short form of the test.

The only acceptable abbreviated form involves the administration of only those items that are scored for the validity scales and the basic clinical scales. With the group form of the test, a person is instructed to complete the first 366 items and 33 additional items that are scattered throughout the remainder of the test booklet. The booklet form numbers for these additional items are: 371, 374, 377, 383, 391, 397, 398, 400, 406, 411, 415, 427, 436, 440, 446, 449, 450, 451, 455, 461, 462, 469, 473, 479, 481, 482, 487, 502, 505, 521, 547, 549, 564. Some individuals become confused with these directions, so some examiners type the 33 additional items on a separate sheet, number them consecutively, and insert the sheet into a standard test booklet. Such a procedure requires that the scoring templates for scales K and Si be modified appropriately. In the Form R test booklet, all of the items scored on the validity and basic clinical scales appear as the first 399 items in the booklet. Thus, a person can be instructed simply to complete only the first 399 items in the booklet.

Other abbreviated MMPI forms (e.g., one with only 71 items) have been proposed (Dean, 1972; Faschingbauer, 1974; Kincannon, 1968; Overall & Gomez-Mont, 1974). Although it is sometimes tempting to use one of these forms of the test, existing research data do not support the use of any of them as a substitute for the standard MMPI (Butcher, Kendall, & Hoffman, 1980; Dahlstrom, 1980).

CONSTRUCTING THE PROFILE

For the box form and for Form R, the reverse side of the record form contains profiles for males and females. For the hand-scored group form answer sheet, a separate profile sheet, with a male profile on one side and a female profile on the other side, is used.

A first step in constructing the profile is to transfer the raw scores from the answer sheet or record form to appropriate blanks at the bottom of the profile form, making sure that the profile is the appropriate one for the person's sex. At this time it also is important to be certain that identifying data (name, age, date, education, etc.) are recorded on the profile sheet.

At this point a K-correction is added to the raw scores for the Hs, Pd, Pt, Sc, and Ma scales. The proportion of a person's K scale raw score that is to be added to each of these scales is indicated on the profile form. There has been some discussion in the literature concerning the possibility that profiles without the K-correction added might be more appropriate in some settings. However, because the standard profile form is based on K-corrected scores and because virtually all of the data concerning interpretation of scores are derived from K-corrected scores, it is recommended that the K-correction be used routinely.[3]

For each scale the examiner then should refer to the numbers in the column above the scale label. The number in the column corresponding to the raw score (K-corrected if appropriate) on the scale is marked by the examiner either with a small x or a small dot. Standard procedure calls for raw scores of less than 30 on the Cannot Say (?) scale to be plotted as 30. Many examiners find it less confusing if raw scores less than 30 are indicated in the appropriate blank but are not plotted as part of the profile. After a dot or x has been entered in the column above each scale label, the MMPI profile for the person examined is completed by connecting the plotted dots or x's with each other. Traditionally, the three validity scales are joined to each other but are not connected with the 10 clinical scale scores. The four special scales (A, R, Es, MAC) are joined to each other.

Because a T-score scale is printed on each side of the profile sheet, by plotting the scores in the above manner on the profile sheet, the raw scores for each scale can be converted visually to T-scores. A T-score has a mean of 50 and a standard deviation of 10. The T-score conversions provided on the profile sheet are based on the responses of the Minnesota normal standardization group which was described in Chapter 1 of this *Guide*. Thus, a T-score of 50 for any particular scale indicates that a person's score is equal to the average or mean score for the normal standardization group examined by Hathaway and McKinley. Scores greater than 50 indicate scores higher than the average for the standardization group, and scores below 50 indicate scores lower than average for the standardization group.

CODING THE PROFILE

Although it is possible to derive some useful information by interpreting an examinee's T-score on a single scale in isolation, much of the information relevant to interpretation of MMPI protocols is *configural* in nature. In addition to interpreting individual scales, it is necessary to consider the pattern of the

3. One exception is when using the Marks, Seeman, and Haller codebook for adolescents (1974). This codebook utilizes noncorrected scores that must be converted to T-scores with special tables provided by the authors.

scales in relation to each other. To facilitate profile interpretation, coding is a procedure for recording most of the essential information about a profile in a concise form and for reducing the possible number of different profiles to a manageable size. Coding conveys information about the scores on scales relative to each other and also indicates an absolute range within which scores fall. Coding also permits easy grouping of similar profiles, using all or only part of the code.

Two major coding systems have been utilized in the MMPI literature: Hathaway's (1947) original system and a more complete system developed by Welsh (1948). Because the Hathaway system is rarely used any more, only the Welsh system will be described here.

Welsh Code

Step 1

Utilize the number instead of the name of each clinical scale:

Hs–1	Pa–6
D–2	Pt–7
Hy–3	Sc–8
Pd–4	Ma–9
Mf–5	Si–0

Step 2

Record the 10 numbers of the clinical scales in order of T-scores, from the highest on the left to the lowest on the right.

Step 3

To the right of and separated from the clinical scales, record the three validity scales (L, F, K) in order of T-scores with the highest on the left and the lowest on the right. Do not include the ? scale unless its T-score is equal to or greater than 30. The set of clinical scales and the set of validity scales are coded separately. The four special scales are not included in the coding.

Step 4

When adjacent scales are within one T-score point, they are underlined. When adjacent scales have the same T-score, place in the ordinal sequence found on the profile sheet and underline.

Step 5

To indicate scale elevations, appropriate symbols are inserted after scale numbers as follows:

90 & greater	*
80–89	"
70–79	'
60–69	–
50–59	/
40–49	:
30–39	#
29 & less	to the right of #

If a 10-point T-score range does not contain any scale, the appropriate symbol for that elevation must be included. It is not necessary to include a symbol to the left of the scale with the highest score or to the right of the scale with the lowest score.

Step 6

Repeat steps 4 and 5 for the validity scales. An example of the Welsh code is presented in Table 2.1. As a practice exercise, the reader might wish to cover the code at the bottom of Table 2.1 and code the T-scores into the Welsh code using the instructions given above.

Table 2.1 Example of Welsh code

Scale name	Scale no.	Raw score	T-score
Cannot Say		5	—
L		7	60
F		13	73
K		7	40
Hypochondriasis	1	20	64
Depression	2	41	92
Hysteria	3	21	54
Psychopathic Deviate	4	16	43
Masculinity-Femininity	5	23	57
Paranoia	6	3	35
Psychasthenia	7	46	84
Schizophrenia	8	44	83
Hypomania	9	8	28
Social Introversion	0	4	28
Welsh code:	2*78"'1–53/4:6#90 F'L–/K		

3

The Validity Scales

For the MMPI to yield maximally accurate and useful information, it is necessary that the person examined approach the test-taking task in the manner intended by the test authors. After carefully reading each item and considering its content, he or she should give a direct and, as far as possible, honest response utilizing the response format provided. To the extent that deviations from this procedure occur, the resulting profile either should be considered invalid and not interpreted further or should be interpreted in the context of the test-taking attitude of the person. Early inventories were criticized for being susceptible to distortion and for not including any index of test-taking attitude. Although it was hoped that the empirical keying procedure utilized in developing the MMPI would make such distortions less likely, subsequently four validity indicators were developed specifically to detect deviant test-taking attitudes. In addition to providing important information about test-taking attitudes, in common with the clinical scales, the validity scales themselves have come to be used as sources of inferences about extratest behaviors. Both aspects of the validity scales will be considered in this chapter. The items included in each validity scale and the keyed response for each item are presented in Appendix A of this *Guide*.[1]

CANNOT SAY (?) SCALE

The Cannot Say score simply is the number of omitted items (including items answered both true and false). There are a number of reasons why people omit items on the MMPI. Occasionally, items are omitted because of carelessness or confusion. Omitted items also can reflect an attempt to avoid admitting undesirable things about oneself without directly lying. Indecisive people, who cannot decide between the two response alternatives, may leave many items unanswered. Some items are omitted because of a lack of information or experience

Sources consulted in preparing Chapter 3: Carson (1969); Dahlstrom, Welsh, & Dahlstrom (1972); Duckworth & Duckworth (1975); Lachar (1974b).

1. Item numbers in Appendix A and elsewhere in this *Guide* are for the booklet (group) form of the MMPI.

necessary for a meaningful response. For example, an individual who has never read *Alice in Wonderland* may not feel able to respond meaningfully to the item "I liked *Alice in Wonderland* by Lewis Carroll."

Regardless of the reasons for omitting items, a large number of such items can lead to lowered scores on other scales. Therefore, the validity of a resulting protocol with many omitted items should be questioned. Traditionally, Cannot Say raw scores greater than 30 have been interpreted as indicating profile invalidity. As indicated in Chapter 2, however, the best procedure probably is to ensure that few or no items are omitted. If encouraged before beginning the MMPI to answer all items, most people usually will use the Cannot Say response category infrequently. Also, if the examiner scans answer sheets at the time that the test is completed and encourages individuals to try to answer previously omitted items, most people will complete all or most of the items. If it is not possible to return protocols with instructions to try to answer omitted items, protocols with more than 30 items omitted should not be interpreted further.

L SCALE

As indicated in Chapter 1, the L scale originally was constructed to detect a deliberate and rather unsophisticated attempt on the part of subjects to present themselves in a favorable light (Meehl & Hathaway, 1946). The 15 rationally derived L scale items deal with rather minor flaws and weaknesses to which most people are willing to admit. However, individuals who deliberately are trying to present themselves in a very favorable way are not willing to admit even such minor shortcomings. The result is that such people produce high L scale scores.

Although most L scale items are not answered in the scored direction (false) by most people, many normal individuals do endorse several of the items in the scored direction. The average raw score for the MMPI standardization group was 4. However, subsequent research revealed that scores on the L scale are related to educational level, intelligence, socioeconomic status, and psychological sophistication. Better educated, brighter, more sophisticated people from higher social classes score lower on the L scale. The typical L scale raw score for college students, for example, is 0 or 1.

High Scores on L Scale

Because of the relationship between L scale scores and demographic variables, such variables must be taken into account when deciding if a score should be considered high. Whereas a raw score of 4 or 5 on the L scale would be about average for a lower middle class laborer of average or below average intelligence, such a score would be considered as moderately high for a college-educated person from an upper middle class background.

When the L scale score is higher than would be expected when appropriate demographic variables are taken into account, one should entertain the possibility that the person is not being honest and frank in answering all of the other MMPI items. The result of such a test-taking attitude is, inferentially, that the individual's scores on most or all of the clinical scales have been lowered (distorted) in the direction of appearing better adjusted psychologically.

In addition to suggesting a defensive test-taking attitude, high L scale scores have been found empirically to be associated with some other important extra-test attitudes and behaviors. Thus, high scorers tend to be overly conventional and socially conforming. They are unoriginal in their thinking and inflexible in their approaches to problems. In addition, they have a poor tolerance for stress and pressure. They are rigid and moralistic and overevaluate their own worth. They utilize repression and denial excessively, and they appear to have little or no insight into their own motivations. Also, they have little awareness of the consequences to other people of their behavior. In some rare cases, an extremely high L scale score may be suggestive of a full blown clinical confusion that may be either organic or functional in nature.

Low Scores on L Scale

On the other hand, low scores on the L scale suggest that the person responded frankly to the items and was confident enough to be able to admit to minor personal faults and shortcomings. Low scorers were described by Gough, McKee, and Yandell (1955) as perceptive, socially responsive, self-reliant, and independent. They also appear to be strong, natural, and relaxed, and they function effectively in leadership roles. They are able to communicate their ideas effectively, although at times they impress others as somewhat cynical and sarcastic.

Summary of Descriptors[2]

A high L scale score is indicative of an individual who (is):

1. trying to create a favorable impression by not being honest in responding to the items

2. The reader should recognize that the descriptors listed in this and subsequent summaries are *modal* ones and that all descriptors will not apply necessarily to all individuals with a given score or configuration of scores. The descriptors should be viewed as hypotheses to be validated by reference to history, behavior, and performance on other psychological tests.

2. conventional; socially conforming
3. unoriginal in thinking; inflexible in problem solving
4. has poor tolerance for stress and pressure
5. rigid, moralistic
6. overevaluates own worth
7. utilizes repression and denial excessively
8. manifests little or no insight into own motivations
9. shows little awareness of consequences to other people of his/her own behavior
10. may be confused

A low L scale score is indicative of a person who (is):

1. responded frankly to the items
2. confident enough about self to be able to admit minor faults and shortcomings
3. perceptive, socially reliant
4. self-reliant, independent
5. strong, natural, relaxed
6. functions effectively in leadership role
7. communicates ideas effectively
8. described by others as cynical, sarcastic

F SCALE

The F scale originally was developed to detect deviant or atypical ways of responding to the test items (Meehl & Hathaway, 1946). The 64 items in the F scale are ones that were answered in the scored direction by fewer than 10 percent of adult normal subjects. Thus, a person who on examination endorses many F scale items in the scored direction is said to be not responding as most normal people do. A subsequent factor analysis of the 64 F scale items by Comrey (1958a) identified 19 content dimensions, tapping such diverse characteristics as paranoid thinking, antisocial attitudes or behavior, hostility, and poor physical health. A person can obtain a high F scale score by endorsing items in some, but not necessarily all, of these 19 content areas. In general, and because the scales of the MMPI are intercorrelated, high scores on the F scale are associated with elevated clinical scales, especially scales 6 and 8. Scores on the F scale also have been found to correlate with age and with race, with adolescents and blacks scoring approximately 10 T-score points higher on the F scale than other groups.

As used by the practicing clinician, the F scale serves three important functions. First, it is an index of test-taking attitude and is useful in detecting deviant response sets. Second, if one can rule out profile invalidity, the F scale is a good indicator of degree of psychopathology, with higher scores suggesting greater psychopathology. Finally, scores on the F scale allow inferences about extratest behaviors.

High Scores on F Scale

When T-scores on the F scale are equal to or greater than 100 (raw score ≥ 26), a deviant response set that can invalidate the profile should be considered. For example, random responding, all true responding, and deliberate attempts to fake bad responses all result in F scale scores in this 100 range (see discussion of profile invalidity below for details about these deviant response sets). Seriously disturbed persons rarely produce such elevated F scale scores. However, Gynther, Altman, and Warbin (1973) have demonstrated reliable and potentially important correlates for psychiatric patients who do have F scale T-scores equal to or greater than 100. Such patients display delusions of reference, visual and auditory hallucinations, reduced speech, withdrawal, and poor judgment. In addition, they are likely to be monosyllabic, to have a short attention span, and to be disoriented for place. They may not know why they are in the hospital; they are likely to be diagnosed as psychotic; and there may be evidence of organic etiology.

In a T-score range of 80 to 99 (raw score = 16 to 25), F scale scores may be indicative of all false responding or of malingering (see discussion of profile invalidity below for details about these two response sets). It also is possible that the person is using the test to exaggerate problems as a plea for help. Also, some individuals who are very resistant to the testing procedure produce scores in this range. If a deviant response set can be ruled out, F scale scores in this range are suggestive of very serious psychopathology. Many clearly psychotic individuals earn F scale scores at this level.

Psychotic persons and those labeled as severe neurotics often have F scale scores in a T-score range of 65 to 79 (raw score = 10 to 15). Also, individuals with very deviant social, political, or religious convictions have been found to score at this level. In such cases, examination of the actual items may be useful in detecting such convictions. Gough et al. (1955) demonstrated that among people who are relatively free of serious psychopathology, scores in this range may indicate moodiness, restlessness, and dissatisfaction. In addition, such people may be changeable, unstable, curious, complex, opinionated, and opportunistic.

When F scale scores fall within a T-score range of 50 to 64 (raw score = 3 to 9), the person usually has endorsed items relevant to some particular content area (e.g., relationship with family, sexual concerns, health concerns, antisocial beliefs). Although such individuals may be experiencing difficulties in a specific area, they may be functioning effectively in other aspects of their life situations. The clinical practitioner who is interested in knowing such information about an examinee need simply write out on a sheet of paper each F scale item endorsed and scan these items for the content categories or information.

Low Scores on F Scale

T-scores in the 45 to 49 range (raw score = 0 to 2) indicate that the individual is answering items as most normal people do and thus is likely to be socially conforming in everyday, extratest behavior. Low scores obtained from subjects known to have significant psychopathology indicate that they are denying turmoil and psychological problems. Scores in this range also are found for people who deliberately are faking good responses on the test (see discussion of profile invalidity below for details about the faking good response set).

Summary of Descriptors

High F Scale Scores

A T-score equal to or greater than 100 (raw score ≥ 26) is indicative of a person who (is):

1. may have responded to the MMPI items in a random way
2. may have answered all of the MMPI items true
3. may have been faking bad responses when taking the MMPI
4. if a hospitalized psychiatric patient, may manifest
   a. delusions of reference
   b. visual and/or auditory hallucinations
   c. reduced speech
   d. withdrawal
   e. poor judgment
   f. monosyllabic speech
   g. short attention span
   h. lack of knowledge of reasons for hospitalization
   i. a clinically arrived at diagnosis of psychosis
   j. some extratest signs of organic etiology

A T-score in a range of 80 to 99 (raw score = 16 to 25) is indicative of a person who (is):

1. may have answered all MMPI items false
2. may be malingering
3. exaggerates symptoms as a plea for help
4. may be quite resistant to testing procedure
5. may be clearly psychotic by the usual criteria

A T-score in a range of 65 to 79 (raw score = 10 to 15) is indicative of a person who (is):

1. has very deviant social, political, or religious convictions
2. may manifest clinically a severe neurotic or psychotic condition
3. if relatively free of serious psychopathology, is described as:
   a. moody
   b. restless
   c. dissatisfied
   d. changeable, unstable
   e. curious
   f. complex
   g. opinionated
   h. opportunistic

A T-score in a range of 50 to 64 (raw score = 3 to 9) is indicative of an individual who (is):

1. has endorsed items relevant to some particular problem area
2. typically functions effectively in most aspects of his/her life situation

Low F Scale Scores

A T-score in a range of 45 to 49 (raw score = 0 to 2) is indicative of an individual who (is):

1. answered items as most normal people do
2. socially conforming
3. free of disabling psychopathology
4. may have tried to fake a good profile

K SCALE

When early experience with the MMPI indicated that the L scale was quite insensitive to several kinds of test distortion, the K scale was developed as a more subtle and more effective index of attempts by examinees to deny psychopathology and to present themselves in a favorable light or, conversely, to exaggerate psychopathology and to try to appear in a very unfavorable light (Meehl & Hathaway, 1946; McKinley et al., 1948). High scores on the K scale thus were thought to be associated with a defensive approach to the test, whereas low scores were indicative of unusual frankness and self-criticality. In addition to identifying these deviations in test-taking attitudes, a statistical procedure also was developed for correcting scores on some of the clinical scales (see discussion of the K-correction in Chapter 2). The K scale was developed empirically by contrasting specific item responses of abnormal individuals who produced normal profiles with responses to the same items of a group of normals.

Subsequent research and experience with the MMPI have indicated that the K scale is much more complex than was originally believed. Scores on the K scale are related to clinical defensiveness, but they also are related to educational level and socioeconomic status, with better educated and higher socioeconomic level subjects scoring higher on the scale. In addition, moderate elevations on the K scale sometimes reflect ego strength and psychological resources. There is no definitive way to determine when elevated K scores indicate clinical defensiveness and when they indicate ego strength. However, if elevated K scores are found for persons who do not seem to be disturbed psychologically and who appear to be functioning reasonably well, the possibility that the K score is reflecting positive characteristics rather than defensiveness must be considered.

There has not been a great deal of research to support the routine use of the K-correction to the clinical scales. Although the K-correction may lead to better discriminative power for each clinical scale, it does not necessarily improve the accuracy of the overall profile configuration. However, because the K-correction was adopted as a standard part of the MMPI scoring, and because virtually all information about profile interpretation is based on K-corrected scores, it is recommended that the K-correction be used routinely unless separate norms and interpretive data are available for uncorrected scores. Marks et al. (1974) have used such an approach in utilizing uncorrected scores in their codebook for adolescents, but they are a notable exception within the ranks of users of the MMPI.

The 30 items in the K scale cover several different content areas in which a person can deny problems (e.g., hostility, suspiciousness about motivations of other people, family dissension, lack of self-confidence, excessive worry). The K scale items tend to be much more subtle than items in the L scale; therefore, it is less likely that a defensive person will recognize the purpose of the items and will be able to avoid detection.

In interpreting K scale scores, it is essential that a person's socioeconomic status be taken into account. For college students and college-educated people, K scale scores in a T-score range of 55 to 70 should be considered average. Thus, scores must be greater than 70 to be considered high and less than 55 to be considered low for such people. For lower middle and upper lower class individuals, T-scores typically range from 40 to 60. Thus, for a score to be treated as a high score, it must exceed 60, whereas a score must be below 40 to be considered as a low score for such individuals.

High Scores on K Scale

When a K scale score is higher than is typically expected for a person's socioeconomic status, the possibility of a deliberate attempt to deny problems and psychopathology and thereby to appear in a favorable light or the possibility of all false responding should be considered (see discussion of profile invalidity below for details about these two response sets). High K scale scorers may be trying to maintain an appearance of adequacy, control, and effectiveness. High scorers tend to be shy and inhibited, and they are hesitant about becoming involved emotionally with other people. In addition, they are intolerant and unaccepting of unconventional beliefs and behavior in other people. They lack self-insight and self-understanding. Delinquency is unlikely among people with high scores on the K scale. When high K scale scores are accompanied by marked elevations on the clinical scales, it is likely that the person is quite seriously disturbed psychologically but has little or no awareness of such problems. When moderately high scores are found for persons who do not seem to be disturbed psychologically and who appear to function reasonably well, they may be reflecting ego strength and other positive characteristics.

Average Scores on K Scale

When K scale scores fall within the range that is expected for a person's socioeconomic status, they suggest a healthy balance between positive self-evaluation and self-criticism. Such people tend to be well adjusted psychologically and to manifest few signs of emotional disturbance. They are independent, self-reliant, and capable of dealing with problems in their daily lives. They tend to have high intellectual abilities, to have wide interests, and to be ingenious, enterprising, versatile, and resourceful. They are clear thinking, and they approach problems in a reasonable and systematic way. In social situations, they mix well with other people, are enthusiastic and verbally fluent, and tend to take an ascendant role.

Low Scores on K Scale

When K scale scores are lower than are expected for socioeconomic status, the possibility of all true responding or a deliberate attempt to present oneself in an unfavorable light should be considered (see discussion of profile invalidity below for details about these two response sets). Low scores also may indicate that subjects are exaggerating problems as a plea for help or that they are experiencing confusion that may be either organic or functional in nature.

Low scorers tend to be very critical of themselves and of others and to be quite self-dissatisfied. They may be quite ineffective in dealing with problems in their daily lives, and they tend to have little insight into their own motives and behavior. They are socially conforming and tend to be overly compliant with authority. They are inhibited, retiring, and shallow, and they have a slow personal tempo. They tend to be rather awkward socially and to be blunt and harsh in social interactions. Their outlook toward life is characterized as cynical, skeptical, caustic, and disbelieving, and they tend to be quite suspicious about the motivations of other people.

Summary of Descriptors

A high K scale score is indicative of an individual who (is):

1. may have tried to fake a good profile
2. may have responded false to most of the MMPI items
3. trying to give an appearance of adequacy, control, and effectiveness
4. shy, inhibited
5. hesitant about becoming emotionally involved with other people
6. intolerant, unaccepting of unconventional attitudes and beliefs in other people
7. lacks self-insight and self-understanding
8. not likely to display overt delinquent behavior
9. if clinical scales also are elevated, may be seriously disturbed psychologically but has little awareness of this
10. if not seriously disturbed psychologically, may have above-average ego strength and other positive characteristics

An average K scale score is indicative of an individual who (is):

1. maintained a healthy balance between positive self-evaluation and self-criticism in responding to the MMPI items
2. psychologically well adjusted
3. shows few overt signs of emotional disturbance
4. independent, self-reliant
5. capable of dealing with problems in daily life
6. has high intellectual ability
7. exhibits wide interests
8. ingenious, enterprising, versatile, resourceful
9. clear thinking, approaches problems in reasonable and systematic way
10. a good mixer
11. enthusiastic, verbally fluent
12. takes ascendant role

A low K scale score is indicative of an individual who (is):

1. may have responded true to most of the MMPI items
2. trying to fake a bad profile
3. may be exaggerating problems as a plea for help
4. exhibits either overt acute psychotic or organic confusion
5. critical of self and others, self-dissatisfied

6. ineffective in dealing with problems of daily life
7. shows little insight into own motives and behavior
8. socially conforming
9. overly compliant with authority
10. inhibited, retiring, shallow
11. has a slow personal tempo
12. socially awkward
13. blunt, harsh in social situations
14. cynical, skeptical, caustic, disbelieving
15. suspicious about motivations of other people

PROFILE INVALIDITY

Some MMPI users label as invalid and uninterpretable any protocol with more than 30 omitted items or with a T-score greater than 70 on one or more of the validity scales (L, F, K). Although this practice is a very conservative one and is not likely to result in labeling as valid profiles that are in fact invalid, it represents an oversimplified view of profile validity and causes many valid profiles to be discarded. For example, Dahlstrom and Welsh (1960) indicated that F scores in a T-score range of 65 to 80 are more likely to be produced by psychotic and severely neurotic persons than by others. Gynther et al. (1973) demonstrated that profiles with F scale scores equal to or greater than 100 can have reliable extratest personality and behavioral correlates (e.g., disorientation, hallucinations, delusions, short attention span, etc.). In addition, the experienced clinician is not very surprised to encounter a K scale score greater than 70 among college-educated persons. Thus, it appears that a more sophisticated approach to profile validity is indicated.

Deviant Response Sets

To produce a valid protocol a person must read and consider the content of each MMPI item and respond to the item as true or false. Occasionally individuals respond in a stylistic way (e.g., false to *each* item) without reference to item content. Such behavior usually occurs among people who lack adequate reading skills, who are too confused to follow directions, or who have a very negativistic attitude toward the assessment procedure. Obviously, the examiner should try to be aware of such factors before administering the test, but sometimes, particularly in situations where large numbers of people are tested at once, such individuals do complete the test.

Random Responding

One deviant response set involves a random or near random response to the test items. A person may respond in a clearly random manner, or may adopt an

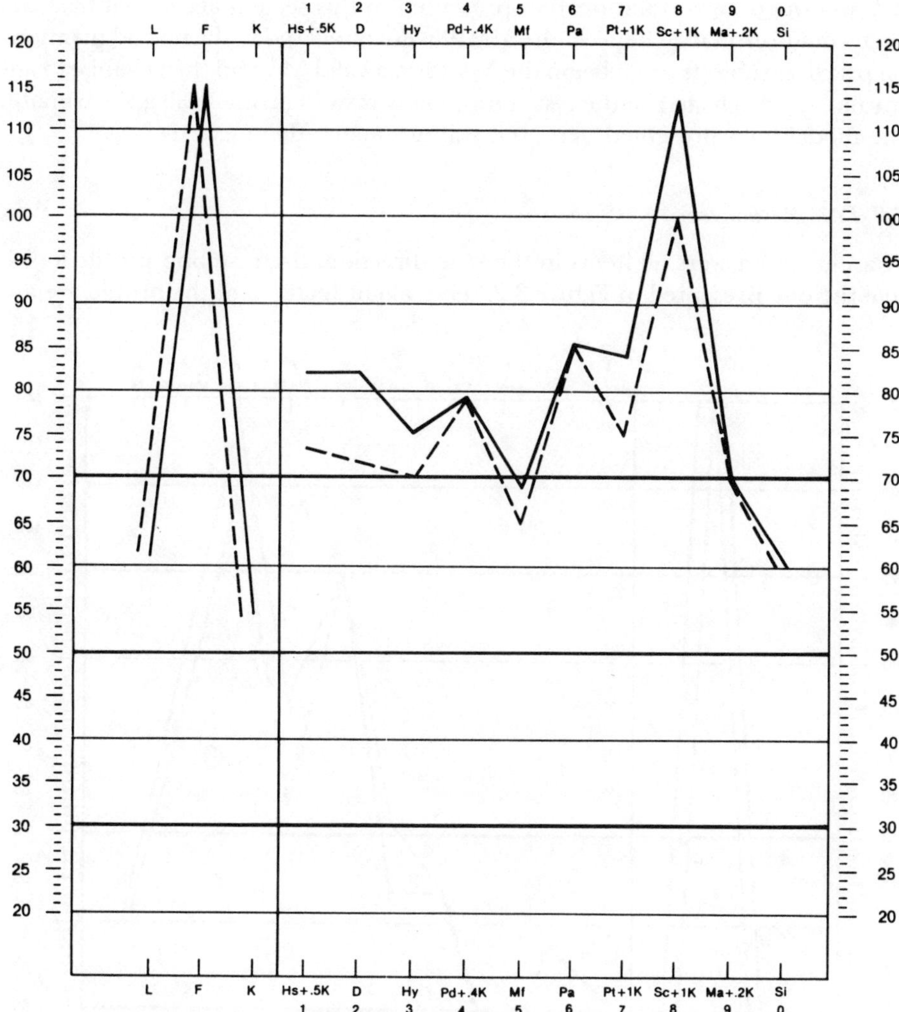

Fig. 3.1. K-corrected profiles indicative of random response set for males (——) and females (----).

idiosyncratic response pattern such as marking every block of eight items as true, true, false, false, true, true, false, false, or every block of six items as true, false, true, false, true, false, and repeating this with each such subsequent block. Because the responses are made without regard to item content, the resulting protocol must be considered invalid. The profile configuration resulting from a completely random response set is shown in Figure 3.1. In the random response profile, the F scale is greater than 100 and scales L and K are both at or slightly above 50. The clinical scales are characterized by a *psychotic slope*, usually with a spike on scale 8 and a subspike on scale 6. Scales 5 and 0 remain below 70. It should be understood that the random profiles in Figure

3.1 and the other invalid profiles presented in this section are modal profiles that would result if all items in the MMPI were answered in the invalid manner. In practice, subjects often begin the MMPI in a valid way and then change to an invalid approach later in the test. Thus, many invalid profiles will approximate the modal ones presented here, but will not match them exactly.

All True Responding

If a person answers all items in the true direction, the resulting profile looks like the one presented in Figure 3.2. The salient features of the profile are an

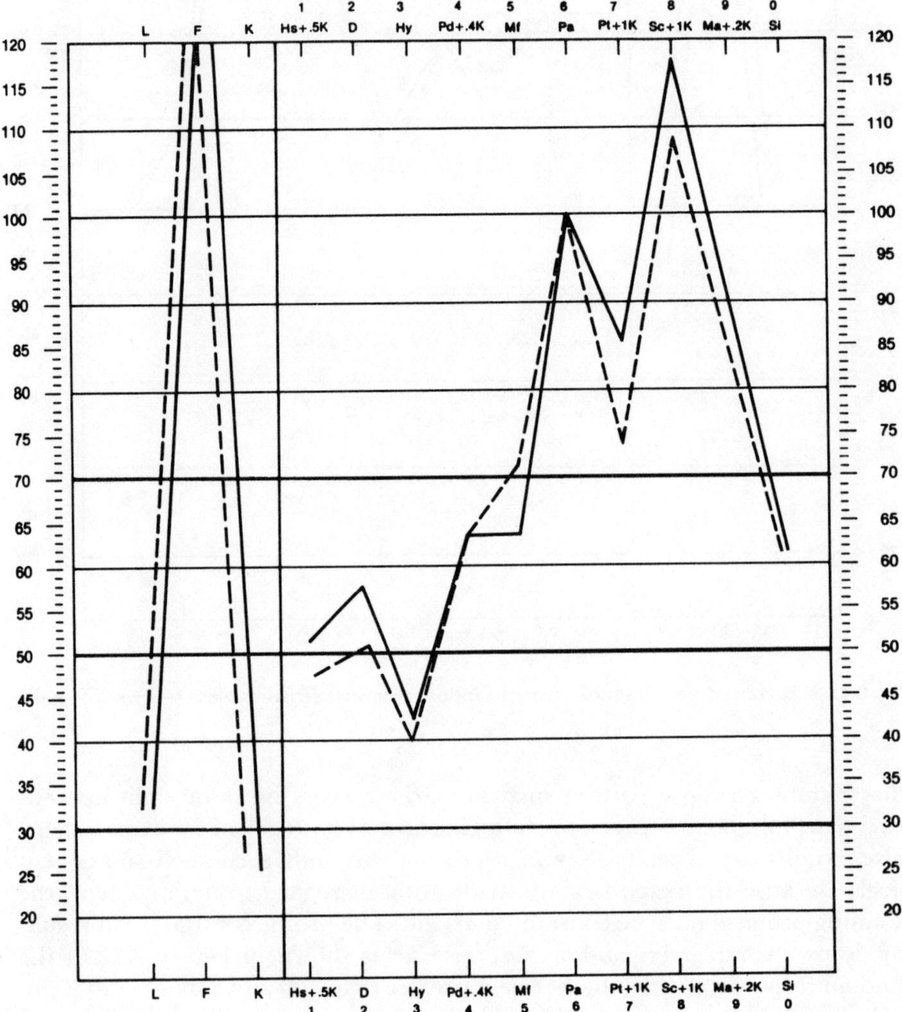

Fig. 3.2. K-corrected profiles indicative of all true response set for males (——) and females (----).

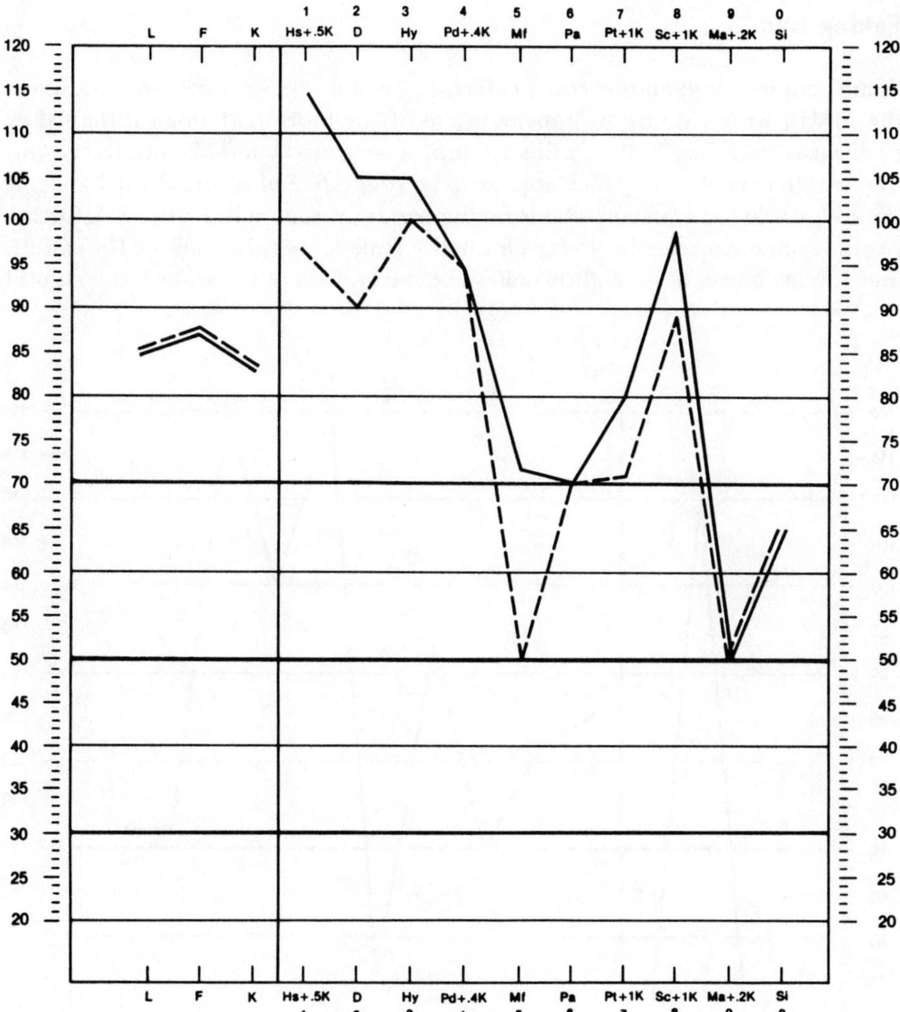

Fig. 3.3. K-corrected profiles indicative of all false response set for males (——) and females (----).

extremely elevated F scale score (usually off the top of the profile sheet), scales L and K well below 50, a positive (psychotic) slope, a spike on scale 8, and a subspike on scale 6.

All False Responding

The person who responds false to all items will produce a profile like the one shown in Figure 3.3. Note the simultaneous elevations on scales L, F, and K and the *neurotic-like slope* of the clinical scales.

Faking Bad

Some people (for example, court referrals, involuntary draftees, etc.) complete the MMPI with a desire to appear worse off or more pathological than they really are ("fake bad"). When this attempt is very direct and blatant, the resulting profile may at first glance appear to be suggestive of severe disturbance. A typical profile for a person who is faking bad is presented in Figure 3.4. Such a profile is characterized by a very elevated F scale score (often above 100) and L and K scale scores at or slightly below the mean. Except for scale 5, the clinical

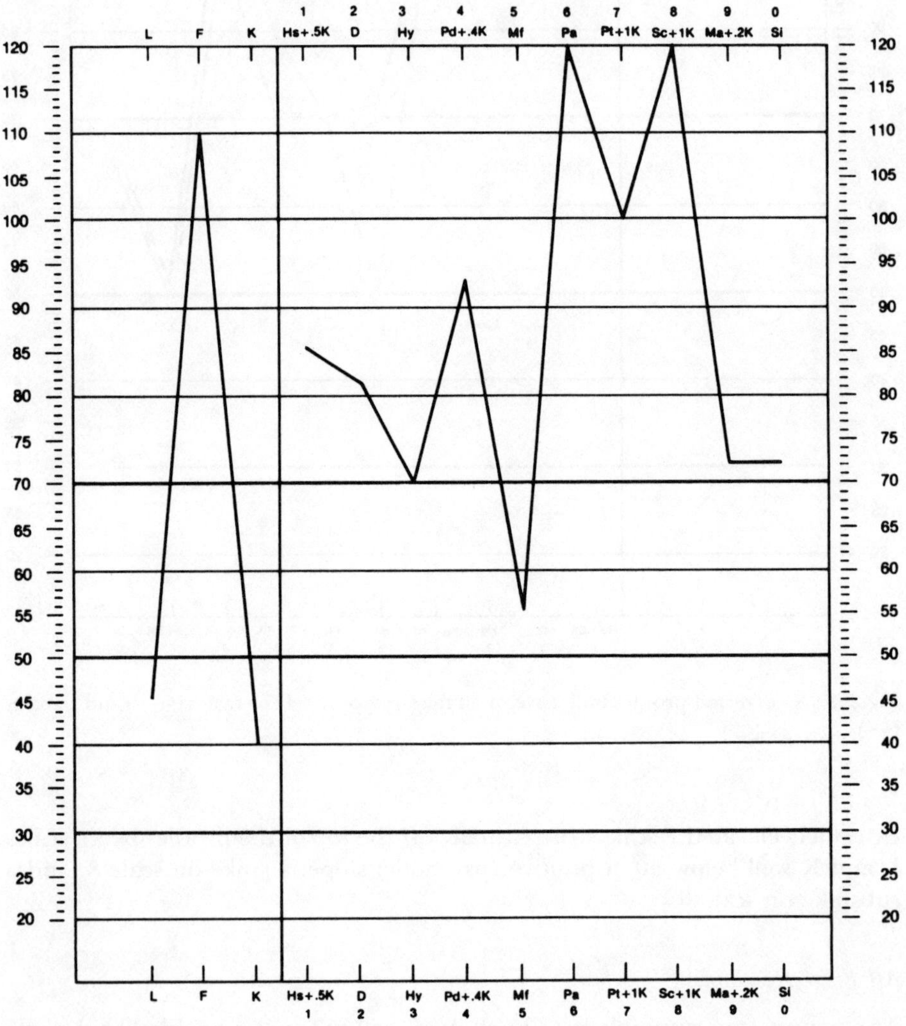

Fig. 3.4. Typical K-corrected profile produced by subject who is deliberately faking bad.

scales usually are quite elevated, with scales 6 and 8 as the highest two in the profile.

Gough (1950) found that people who are trying to create the impression of severe psychopathology score considerably higher on the F scale than on the K scale. He suggested that the difference between the F scale *raw score* and the K scale *raw score* can serve as a useful index for detecting fake bad profiles. Gough (1950) and Meehl (1951) indicated that when such an index number is positive and is greater than 9, it indicates that a profile should be considered as a fake bad profile. Carson (1969) has suggested that a cutoff score of +11 yields a more accurate identification of fake bad profiles. Although a single cutoff score cannot be established for all settings, whenever the F scale raw score is greater than the K scale raw score the possibility of faking bad should be considered, and as the difference becomes greater the likelihood of a fake bad profile becomes greater.

The fake bad profile can be differentiated from that of a severely disturbed person in several ways. First, the F scale score is usually higher for the fake bad profile. The usual range of F scale scores in an individual who has been clinically diagnosed as psychotic is 70 to 90, whereas in the fake bad profile the F scale score usually is well above 100. In addition, in a valid profile from a disturbed person, the L and K scales typically are elevated along with the F scale. Finally, in a fake bad profile the clinical scales tend to be more extremely elevated than in a valid profile from a disturbed person.

Fake bad profiles can be differentiated from those resulting from random responding because in the fake bad profile the L and K scales usually are below the mean whereas in the random response profile they are somewhat above the mean. In addition, the random response profile usually has a spike on scale 8, whereas the fake bad profile shows simultaneous extreme elevations on scales 6 and 8.

If one compares the fake bad profile with the profile resulting from an all true response set, several differences are obvious. First, in the all true profile, the F scale score is much more elevated (greater than 120) and the L and K scale scores are lower than in the fake bad profile. Although both types of profiles show elevations for scales 6 and 8, in the all true profile the slope of the profile is more clearly psychotic-like, with scales 1, 2, and 3 at or near T-scores of 50.

The fake bad profile is easily differentiated from the profile resulting from an all false response set. Whereas the F scale is considerably higher than the L and K scales for the fake bad profile, in the all false profile all three scales are elevated simultaneously. In addition, the all false profile has a clearly negative slope.

If a person tends to exaggerate symptoms but does not blatantly fake bad responses (malingering), the resulting profile is harder to differentiate from a valid one from a disturbed person. However, in the malingering profile, the F scale is not as extremely elevated as in the fake bad profile, and scales L and K are usually near 50. The most salient feature of the malingering profile is its

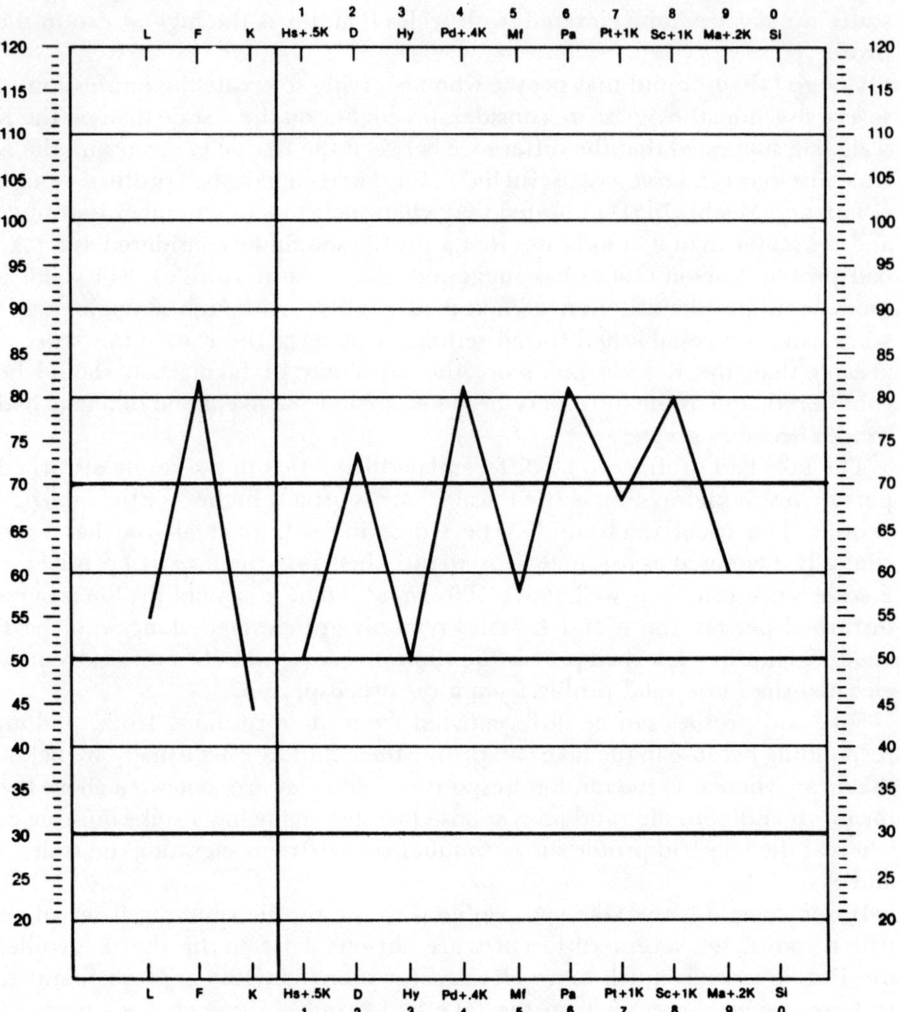

Fig. 3.5. K-corrected saw-toothed profile indicative of malingering. (From W. G. Dahlstrom & G. S. Welsh, *An MMPI Handbook: A Guide to Use in Clinical Practice and Research.* The University of Minnesota Press, Minneapolis. Copyright 1960 by the University of Minnesota. Reprinted with permission.)

saw-toothed appearance (Fig. 3.5). This results because the person who is malingering tends to endorse a wide array of the obviously pathological items which appear on scales 2, 4, 6, and 8.

Faking Good

Sometimes people completing the MMPI, including a surprising number of patients voluntarily seeking professional help, are motivated to deny problems and to appear better off psychologically than is in fact the case. In its most blatant form this tendency is referred to as "faking good." A typical profile resulting from such a test-taking attitude is presented in Figure 3.6. The clearest indication of a fake good profile is a *V-shaped* validity scale configuration with elevations on scales L and K and an F scale score in a T-score range of 40 to 50. Most of the clinical scales will be in a T-score range of 30 to 50, with scales 3, 5 and 9 often the highest of the clinical scales.

Because of the rather obvious nature of the L scale items, individuals who are bright, well educated, and psychologically sophisticated may detect the purpose of the items and will obtain a lower score on the L scale. However, because the

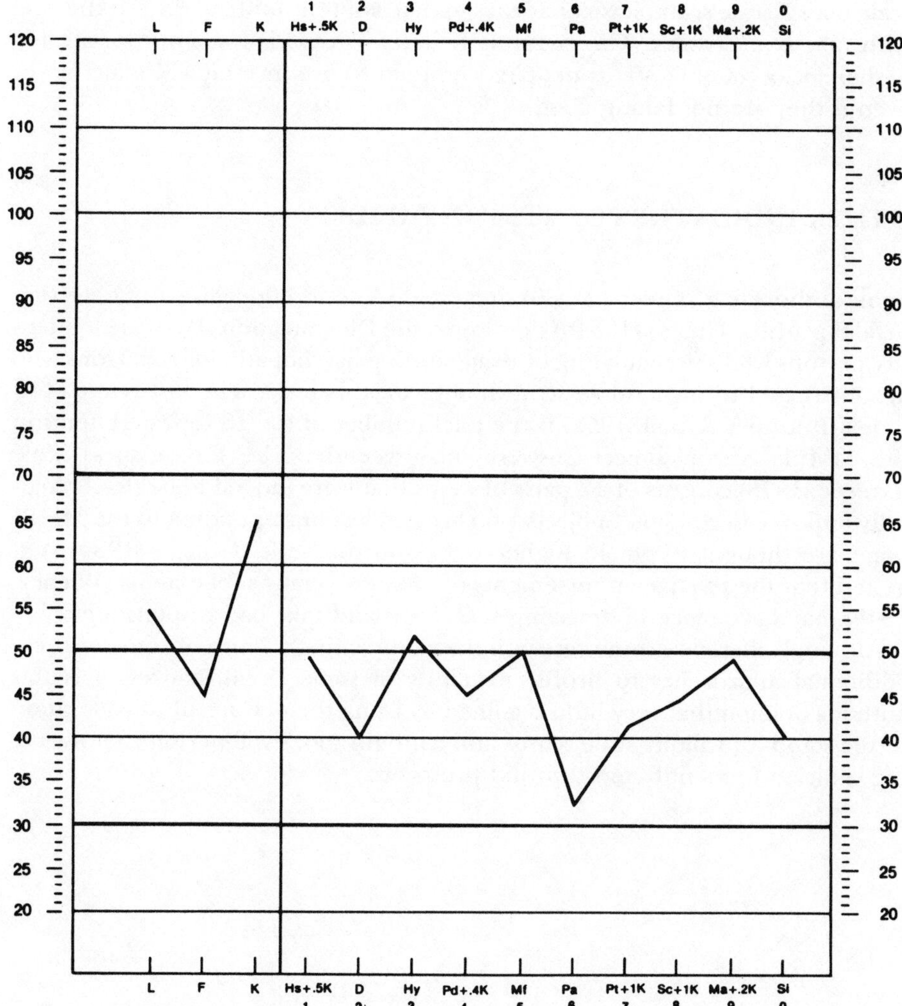

Fig. 3.6. Typical K-corrected profile produced by subject who is deliberately faking good.

K scale items are not as obvious as those in the L scale, even bright, well-educated, and psychologically sophisticated people produce very elevated scores on the K scale if they adopt a fake good attitude toward the test. Before concluding that a high K scale score is indicative of a fake good strategy, the socioeconomic status of the person should be considered. Higher socioeconomic status individuals tend to score higher on the K scale than do lower socioeconomic status individuals, and scores in a T-score range of 60 to 70 do not necessarily imply faking for the higher socioeconomic status individuals.

Some clinicians tend to use the F minus K index to identify fake good profiles as well as fake bad profiles. If the F scale *raw score* minus the K scale *raw score* is negative (K greater than F) and large, it may be that a fake good attitude is present. Whereas it is clear that a fake good profile does have a higher K scale than F scale score, it is not as easy to determine a cutoff score as is the case with fake bad profiles. The F minus K index is especially inappropriate for higher socioeconomic status people, who tend to produce high K scale scores even if they are not faking good.

OTHER INDICATORS OF TEST INVALIDITY

Some authors (e.g., Greene, 1980) suggested some additional ways of detecting invalid profiles. Gough (1954b) developed the Dissimulation (Ds) scale to identify persons who are simulating or exaggerating psychopathology. Persons who are instructed to dissimulate score higher on this scale. The test-retest (TR) index (Buechley & Ball, 1952) is the total number of the 16 repeated items in the MMPI that a subject answers inconsistently. The Carelessness scale (Greene, 1978) consists of 12 pairs of items that were judged to be psychologically opposite in content. Subjects who are careless in responding to the MMPI items are thought to obtain higher scores on this scale. Greene (1980) suggested that the relative endorsements of obvious versus subtle items (Wiener, 1948) may have merit in detecting fake good and fake bad response sets.

Although there are some research data supporting the use of some of these additional approaches to profile invalidity in some circumstances, it is this author's opinion that very little is gained by using them. Careful consideration of the standard validity scale scores and configurations will permit the practicing clinician to identify most invalid protocols.

4

The Clinical Scales

A primary goal of this chapter is to discuss the nature of each clinical scale in an attempt to help the MMPI user understand the dimensions being assessed by the scale. In addition, descriptive material is presented for high scorers and low scorers on each scale. In order to present information in a way that is most directly useful to the clinician, sources are not cited for each descriptor. The general approach utilized has been to examine all previously reported descriptive data for each scale, to augment these data from the author's own research and experience, and to present a meaningful synthesis of all data. The sources consulted in preparing this chapter are indicated in the footnote on this page. The items included in each clinical scale and the keyed response for each item are presented in Appendix A of this *Guide*.

The definition of a high score on the clinical scales has varied considerably in the literature. Some writers consider a T-score above 70 as a high score. Others have defined high scores in terms of the upper quartile in a distribution. Still others have presented descriptors for several T-score levels. Another approach has been to identify the highest scale in the profile (high point) irrespective of its T-score value. A careful examination of the literature suggests that basically the same general picture of high scoring individuals emerges regardless of which of the above definitions is utilized.

Some adjustments are required to take into account a particular examinee's actual T-score level on a scale. In general, the higher the scores, the more likely it is that the descriptors discussed below will apply to an examinee. In addition, for most scales very high scores ($T > 80$) suggest serious psychopathology and incapacitating symptoms as well as the personality characteristics presented for the scale. More moderate elevations suggest the personality characteristics presented for the scale, but the incapacitating symptoms are less likely than for the extreme scores. Whenever the data clearly indicate that different descriptors are appropriate for different levels of scores, the differences are discussed.

Limited information is available concerning the meaning of low scores on the

Sources consulted in preparing Chapter 4: Boerger, Graham, & Lilly (1974); Carkhuff, Barnette, & McCall (1965); Carson (1969); Dahlstrom, Welsh, & Dahlstrom (1972); Drake & Oetting (1959); Gilberstadt & Duker (1965); Gough (1954a); Graham & McCord (1985); Hedlund (1977); Hovey & Lewis (1967); Lachar (1974a); Marks, Seeman, & Haller (1974); Schubert (1973); Tisdale (1982); Welsh & Dahlstrom (1956).

clinical scales. Although it often has been assumed that low scorers on a scale are characterized by the absence of traits and/or behaviors that are present for high scorers, this is not always the case. Although low scores have been defined in several different ways in the literature, it generally is acceptable to consider T-scores below 45 as low scores. Whenever a low score is understood differently in this chapter, specific notation to that effect is made.

SCALE 1 (HYPOCHONDRIASIS)

Scale 1 originally was developed to identify patients who manifested a pattern of symptoms associated with the label of hypochondriasis. The syndrome is characterized in clinical terms by preoccupation with the body and concomitant fears of illness and disease. Although such fears are not of delusional quality, they are quite persistent.

Of all the clinical scales of the MMPI, scale 1 seems to be the most clearly unidimensional in nature. All of the 33 items in the scale deal with somatic concerns or with general physical competence. Factor analytic studies have indicated that much of the variance in scale 1 scores is accounted for by a single factor, one that is characterized by the denial of good health and the admission of a variety of somatic symptoms.

High Scores on Scale 1

As might be expected, high scorers are characterized by excessive bodily concern. For persons with very high scores ($T > 80$), bizarre somatic concerns, perhaps even somatic delusions, should be suspected. Persons with more moderate elevations tend to have generally vague, nonspecific complaints. When specific symptoms are elicited, they tend to be epigastric in nature. Chronic fatigue, pain, and weakness also tend to be characteristic of high scorers. Medical patients with bona fide physical problems generally show somewhat elevated scores on scale 1 (T approximately 60). When medical patients produce T-scores much above 60, one should suspect a strong psychological component to the illness. High scores on scale 1 tend to be associated with diagnoses such as somatoform disorders, anxiety disorders, and depressive disorders. Psychopathic acting out is rare among high scale 1 scorers.

High scale 1 scorers in both psychiatric and nonpsychiatric samples tend to be characterized by a rather distinct set of personality attributes. They are likely to be selfish, self-centered, and narcissistic. Their outlook toward life tends to be pessimistic, defeatist, and cynical. They are generally dissatisfied and unhappy and are likely to make those around them miserable. They complain a great deal and communicate in a whiny manner. They are demanding of others and are very critical of what others do. Hostility is likely to be expressed in rather indirect ways. Scores on scale 1 seem to correlate negatively with intellectual ability, and high scorers often are described as dull, unenthusiastic, unambitious, and lacking ease in oral expression.

High scorers generally do not exhibit much manifest anxiety, and in general they do not show signs of major incapacity. Rather, they appear to be functioning at a reduced level of efficiency. Problems are much more likely to be long-standing than situational or transient in nature.

High scorers typically see themselves as physically ill, and they are seeking medical explanations and treatment for their symptoms. They tend to lack insight and to resist psychological interpretations of their problems. These tendencies, coupled with their generally cynical outlook, suggest that they are not very good candidates for psychotherapy or counseling. They tend to be very critical of their therapists and to terminate a relationship if the therapist is perceived as not giving them enough support and attention.

Low Scores on Scale 1

Because scale 1 is unidimensional in nature, low scorers tend to be very much the opposite of high scorers. In addition to being free of somatic preoccupation, they seem to be optimistic, alert, sensitive, insightful, and generally effective in their daily lives.

Summary of Descriptors for Scale 1

A high scale 1 score indicates an individual who (is):

1. has excessive bodily concern
2. could have somatic delusions (if T > 80)
3. has somatic symptoms that generally are vague, but if specific are likely to be epigastric in nature
4. complains of chronic fatigue, pain, and weakness
5. likely to have been given a diagnosis of somatoform, depression, or anxiety disorder
6. lacks manifest anxiety
7. selfish, self-centered, narcissistic
8. has pessimistic, defeatist, cynical outlook
9. dissatisfied, unhappy
10. makes others miserable
11. complains
12. whiny
13. demanding and critical of others
14. expresses hostility indirectly
15. rarely acts out in psychopathic manner

16. dull, unenthusiastic, unambitious
17. ineffective in oral expression
18. has long-standing problems
19. in extratest behavioral adjustment gives no indication of major incapacity but rather seems to be functioning at a reduced level of efficiency
20. seeking medical explanations and treatment for symptoms
21. not very responsive in psychotherapy or counseling because of lack of insight and cynical outlook
22. critical of therapist
23. tends to terminate therapy when therapist is perceived as not giving enough attention and support

A low scale 1 score indicates an individual who (is):

1. free of somatic preoccupation
2. optimistic
3. sensitive
4. insightful
5. generally effective in daily life

SCALE 2 (DEPRESSION)

Scale 2 was developed originally to assess symptomatic depression. The primary characteristics of symptomatic depression are poor morale, lack of hope in the future, and a general dissatisfaction with one's own life situation. Many of the 60 items in the scale deal with various aspects of depression such as denial of happiness and personal worth, psychomotor retardation and withdrawal, and lack of interest in one's surroundings. Other items in the scale cover a variety of other symptoms and behaviors, including physical complaints, worry or tension, denial of impulses, difficulty in controlling one's own thought processes, and religious fervor. Scale 2 seems to be an excellent index of examinees' discomfort and dissatisfaction with their life situations. Whereas very elevated scores on this scale may be suggestive of clinical depression, more moderate scores tend to be indicative of a general attitude or life-style characterized by poor morale and lack of involvement. Scale 2 scores seem to be related to age, with adolescent subjects scoring 5 to 10 T-score points lower than the standardization sample mean and elderly subjects scoring 5 to 10 T-score points higher than the standardization sample mean.

High Scores on Scale 2

High scorers on this scale (particularly if the T-scores exceed 80) often display depressive symptoms. They may report feeling depressed, blue, unhappy, or dysphoric. They tend to be quite pessimistic about the future in general and more specifically about the likelihood of overcoming their problems and making a better adjustment. Self-depreciation and guilt feelings are common. Behavioral manifestations may include refusal to speak, crying, and psychomotor retardation. Patients with high scores often receive depressive diagnoses. Other symptoms often found in high scorers include physical complaints, weakness, fatigue or loss of energy, agitation, and tension. They also are described as irritable, high-strung, and prone to worry.

High scorers also show a marked lack of self-confidence. They report feelings of uselessness and inability to function in a variety of situations. They see themselves as having failed to achieve adequately in school and at their jobs.

A life-style characterized by withdrawal and lack of intimate involvement with other people is common. High scorers tend to be described as introverted, shy, retiring, timid, seclusive, and secretive. Also, they tend to be aloof and to maintain psychological distance from other people. They often have a severely restricted range of interests and may withdraw from activities in which they previously have participated. They are very cautious and conventional in their activities.

High scorers may have great difficulty in making even simple decisions, and they may be overwhelmed when faced with major life decisions such as vocation, marriage, etc. They tend to be very overcontrolled and to deny their own impulses. They are likely to try to avoid unpleasantness and will make concessions in order to avoid confrontations.

Because a high scale 2 score is suggestive of great personal distress, it may indicate a good prognosis for psychotherapy or counseling. There is some evidence, however, that high scorers may tend to terminate treatment when the immediate crisis passes.

Low Scores on Scale 2

Low scorers on Scale 2 tend to be much more comfortable than high scorers. They indicate that they do not experience tension, anxiety, guilt, and depression and that they feel relaxed and at ease. They tend to be self-confident and generally are emotionally stable and capable of effective functioning in most situations. They are cheerful and optimistic and have little difficulty in verbal expression. They are alert, active, and energetic. They tend to seek out additional responsibilities and are seen as quite competitive by others.

Low scorers feel at ease in social situations and are rather quick to assume a leadership role. They appear to be clever, witty, and colorful, and they generally create very favorable first impressions.

Low scorers also tend to be somewhat impulsive and undercontrolled. Their lack of inhibitions leads them to be somewhat show-offish and exhibitionistic, and they may arouse hostility and resentment in other people. Also, they often find themselves in conflict with authority figures.

Summary of Descriptors for Scale 2

A high scale 2 score indicates a person who (is):

1. feels blue, unhappy, dysphoric
2. pessimistic about the future
3. self-depreciatory
4. harbors guilt feelings
5. refuses to speak
6. cries
7. slow moving, sluggish
8. has been given a depressive diagnosis
9. has somatic complaints
10. complains of weakness, fatigue, loss of energy
11. agitated, tense
12. irritable, high-strung
13. prone to worry
14. lacks self-confidence
15. feels useless and unable to function
16. feels like a failure at school or on the job
17. introverted, shy, retiring, timid, seclusive, secretive
18. aloof
19. maintains psychological distance; avoids interpersonal involvement
20. cautious, conventional
21. difficulty in making decisions
22. nonaggressive
23. overcontrolled, denies impulses
24. avoids unpleasantness
25. makes concessions in order to avoid confrontations
26. because of discomfort, likely to be motivated for psychotherapy
27. may terminate treatment when immediate stress subsides

A low scale 2 score indicates a person who (is):

1. free of tension, anxiety, guilt, and depression
2. feels relaxed and at ease
3. self-confident
4. emotionally stable
5. functions effectively in most situations
6. cheerful, optimistic
7. has little difficulty in verbal expression
8. alert, active, energetic
9. competitive
10. seeks out responsibilities
11. at ease in social situations

12. assumes leadership role
13. clever, witty, colorful
14. creates favorable first impression
15. impulsive, undercontrolled
16. uninhibited, show-offish, exhibitionistic
17. arouses hostility and resentment in others
18. has conflict with authority figures

SCALE 3 (HYSTERIA)

This scale was developed to identify patients who were utilizing hysterical reactions to stress situations. The hysterical syndrome is characterized by involuntary psychogenic loss or disorder of function.

The 60 items comprising scale 3 are of two general types. Some of the items deal with a general denial of physical health and a variety of rather specific somatic complaints, including heart or chest pain, nausea and vomiting, fitful sleep, and headaches. Another group of items involves a rather general denial of psychological or emotional problems and of discomfort in social situations. Although these two clusters of items are reasonably independent in normal subjects, subjects utilizing hysterical defenses seem to score high on both clusters. In fact, it is not possible to obtain a T-score above 70 on scale 3 without endorsing both kinds of items.

Scores on scale 3 are related to intellectual ability, educational background, and social class. Brighter, better educated, and higher social class subjects tend to score higher on the scale. In addition, high scores, particularly when scale 3 is the highest point in the profile, are much more common for women than for men in both normal and psychiatric populations.

As an exception to the general statement made earlier in this chapter, it is important to take into account the level of scores on scale 3. Whereas marked elevations ($T > 80$) suggest a pathological condition characterized by classical hysterical symptomatology, moderate levels are associated with a number of characteristics that are consistent with hysterical disorders but which do not include the classical hysterical symptoms.

High Scores on Scale 3

Marked elevations on scale 3 ($T > 80$) may be suggestive of persons who react to stress and avoid responsibility by developing physical symptoms. The extratest symptoms usually do not fit the pattern of any known organic disorder. They may include, in some combination, headaches, chest pains, weakness, tachycardia, and acute anxiety attacks. Nevertheless, such persons may be symptom free most of the time, but under stress the symptoms appear suddenly; and they are likely to disappear just as suddenly when the stress subsides.

Except for the physical symptoms, high scorers tend to be relatively free of other symptoms. Although they sometimes describe themselves as prone to worry, they are not likely to report anxiety, tension, or depression. Hallucinations, delusions, and suspiciousness are rare. In fact, a psychotic diagnosis is almost never found among high scorers on scale 3. The most frequent diagnosis among psychiatric patients is conversion disorder.

A salient feature of the day-to-day functioning of high scorers is a marked lack of insight concerning the possible underlying causes of their symptoms. In addition, they show little insight concerning their own motives and feelings.

High scorers are often described as extremely immature psychologically, and at times even childish or infantile. They are quite self-centered, narcissistic, and egocentric, and they expect a great deal of attention and affection from others. They often use indirect and devious means to get the attention and affection they crave. When others do not respond appropriately, they may become hostile and resentful, but these feelings are likely to be denied and not expressed openly or directly.

High scale 3 scorers tend to be emotionally involved, friendly, talkative, enthusiastic, and alert. Although their needs for affection and attention drive them into social interactions, their interpersonal relationships tend to be rather superficial and immature. They are interested in other people primarily because of what they can get from them rather than because of a sincere interest in others.

Occasionally high scorers will act out in a sexual or aggressive manner with little apparent attention to or understanding of what they are doing. When confronted with the realities of their behavior, they may act surprised and feel resentful and persecuted.

Because of their needs for acceptance and affection, high scorers may initially be quite enthusiastic about counseling or psychotherapy. They often respond quite well to direct suggestion and advice. However, they are slow to gain insight into the underlying causes of their behavior, and they are quite resistant to psychological interpretations. Problems presented by high scorers frequently include worry about failure in school or work, marital unhappiness, lack of acceptance by their social groups, and problems with authority figures. Histories often include a rejecting father to whom females reacted with somatic complaints and males reacted with rebellion or overt hostility.

Low Scores on Scale 3

Low scorers on scale 3 tend to be rather constricted, conventional, and conforming in their everyday behaviors. They are described by others as unadventurous, as lacking industriousness, and as having a narrow range of interests.

They are cold and aloof and may display blunted affect. They are very limited in social interests and participation, and they tend to avoid leadership responsibilities. They often are seen as unfriendly and tough minded, and they are hard to get to know. They may have difficulties trusting other people, and in general they seem to be rather suspicious.

They are realistic, logical, and level-headed in their approach to problems and are not likely to make impulsive decisions. They seem to be content with what others would judge to be a rather dull, uneventful life situation.

Summary of Descriptors for Scale 3

A high scale 3 score indicates an individual who (is):

1. reacts to stress and avoids responsibility through development of physical symptoms
2. has headaches, chest pains, weakness, tachycardia, anxiety attacks
3. has symptoms which appear and disappear suddenly
4. lacks insight concerning causes of symptoms
5. lacks insight concerning own motives and feelings
6. prone to worry
7. lacks anxiety, tension, and depression
8. rarely reports delusions, hallucinations, and suspiciousness
9. unlikely to be given a psychotic diagnosis
10. if a psychiatric patient, most frequently diagnosed as conversion disorder
11. psychologically immature, childish, infantile
12. self-centered, narcissistic, egocentric
13. expects attention and affection from others
14. uses indirect and devious means to get attention and affection
15. does not openly express hostility and resentment
16. socially involved
17. friendly, talkative, enthusiastic, alert
18. has superficial and immature interpersonal relationships
19. interested in what other people can do for him/her
20. occasionally acts out in sexual and aggressive manner with little apparent insight into his/her actions
21. initially enthusiastic about treatment
22. responds well to direct advice or suggestion
23. slow to gain insight into causes of own behavior
24. resistant to psychological interpretations and treatment
25. worries about failure in school or at work
26. experiences marital unhappiness
27. feels unaccepted by social group
28. has problems with authority figures
29. has a history of a rejecting father

A low scale 3 score indicates a person who (is):

1. constricted, conventional, conforming
2. unadventurous; lacks industriousness
3. has a narrow range of interests
4. has limited social participation
5. avoids leadership role
6. unfriendly, tough minded, hard to get to know
7. suspicious, has difficulty trusting other people
8. realistic, logical, and level-headed in approach to problems
9. seems content with dull, uneventful life situation

SCALE 4 (PSYCHOPATHIC DEVIATE)

Scale 4 was developed to identify patients diagnosed as psychopathic personality, asocial or amoral type. Whereas subjects included in the original criterion group were characterized in their everyday behavior by such delinquent acts as lying, stealing, sexual promiscuity, excessive drinking, and the like, no major criminal types were included. The 50 items in this scale cover a wide array of topics including absence of satisfaction in life, family problems, delinquency, sexual problems, and difficulties with authorities. Interestingly, the keyed responses include both admissions of social maladjustment and assertions of social poise and confidence.

Scores on scale 4 tend to be related to age. Adolescents and college students often score in a T-score range of 55 to 65. It also has been reported that black subjects tend to score higher than white subjects on scale 4. This latter finding may reflect the tendency of blacks to view many social regulations as unfair and therefore as less important in influencing their behavior.

High Scores on Scale 4

High scorers on scale 4 have great difficulty in incorporating the values and standards of society, and they are likely to engage in a wide array of asocial or antisocial behaviors. These behaviors may include lying, cheating, and stealing. Sexual acting out and excessive use of alcohol and/or drugs are not uncommon. High scorers tend to be rebellious toward authority figures and often are in conflict with authorities of one kind or another. They often have stormy relations with their families, and parents tend to be blamed for their difficulties. Underachievement in school, poor work history, and marital problems are characteristic of high scorers.

High scorers are very impulsive individuals who strive for immediate gratification of their impulses. They often do not plan their behavior very well, and they may act without considering the consequences of their actions. They are very impatient and have a limited frustration tolerance. Their behavior may involve poor judgment and considerable risk taking. They tend not to profit from experiences and may find themselves in the same difficulties time and time again.

High scorers are described by others as immature and childish. They are narcissistic, self-centered, selfish, and egocentric. Their behavior often is ostentatious and exhibitionistic. They are insensitive to the needs and feelings of other people and are interested in others in terms of how they can be used. Although they tend to be seen as likable and generally create a good impression, their relationships with other people tend to be shallow and superficial. This may be in part due to rejection on the part of the people they mistreat, but it also seems to reflect their own inability to form warm attachments with others.

In addition, high scorers typically are very extroverted and outgoing. They are talkative, active, adventurous, energetic, and spontaneous. They are judged by others to be intelligent and self-confident. Although they have a wide range of interests and may become involved in many activities, they lack definite goals and their behavior lacks clear direction.

High scorers tend to be very hostile and aggressive. Their attitude is characterized by sarcasm and cynicism. They are very resentful and rebellious and are prone to act out their aggressive impulses. They also are described as antagonistic and refractory. Aggressive outbursts, sometimes accompanied by assaultive behavior, are common, and often such behavior is not accompanied by guilt. Whereas the high scorers may feign guilt and remorse when their behaviors get them into trouble, such responses are short-lived, disappearing when the immediate crisis passes.

Generally, high scorers are free from disabling felt anxiety and depression. Likewise, psychotic symptoms are uncommon. Among psychiatric patients, a personality disorder diagnosis is most common, with antisocial personality or passive-aggressive personality occurring most frequently. However, beneath the facade of a carefree and comfortable person, one is likely to find evidence of worry and dissatisfaction. There may be an absence of deep emotional response, and this lack may produce feelings of boredom and emptiness.

Because of their verbal facility, outgoing manner, and apparent intellectual resources, high scorers often are perceived as good candidates for psychotherapy or counseling. Unfortunately, the prognosis for change is poor. Although they may agree to treatment to avoid something more unpleasant (e.g., jail or divorce), they generally are unable to accept blame for their own problems, and terminate treatment as soon as possible. They tend to utilize intellectualization and to blame others for their difficulties.

Low Scores on Scale 4

Low scorers on scale 4 tend to be very conventional, conforming, and accepting of authority. They are rather passive, submissive, and unassertive. They are concerned about how others will react to them, and they tend to be sincere and trusting in their interpersonal relationships.

Low scorers are characterized by a low level of drive. Although they are concerned about status and security, they do not tend to be very competitive. They have a narrow range of interests, and although they are not creative or spontaneous in their approach to problems, they tend to be very persistent. Low scorers also are seen as moralistic and rigid in their views. Males do not seem to be very much interested in sex, and they may actually be afraid of women.

Low scorers tend to be very critical of themselves, and unwarranted self-dissatisfaction is common. They are accepting of advice and suggestion. Although they may initially respond well to psychotherapy or counseling, they tend to become very dependent on treatment and often are afraid to accept responsibility for their own behavior.

Summary of Descriptors for Scale 4

A high scale 4 score indicates a person who (is):

1. has difficulty in incorporating values and standards of society
2. engages in asocial or antisocial behavior
   a. lying, cheating, stealing
   b. sexual acting out
   c. excessive use of alcohol and/or drugs
3. rebellious toward authority figures
4. has stormy family relationships
5. blames parents for problems
6. has a history of underachievement in school
7. has a poor work history
8. experiences marital problems
9. impulsive; strives for immediate gratification of impulses
10. does not plan well
11. acts without considering consequences of actions
12. impatient, has limited frustration tolerance
13. shows poor judgment, takes risks
14. does not profit from experience
15. immature, childish
16. narcissistic, self-centered, selfish, egocentric
17. ostentatious, exhibitionistic
18. insensitive to others
19. interested in others in terms of how they can be used
20. likable, creates a good first impression

21. has shallow, superficial relationships
22. unable to form warm attachments
23. extroverted, outgoing
24. talkative, active, adventurous, energetic, spontaneous
25. intelligent, self-confident
26. has a wide range of interests
27. lacks definite goals
28. hostile, aggressive
29. sarcastic, cynical
30. resentful, rebellious
31. acts out
32. antagonistic, refractory
33. has aggressive outbursts, assaultive behavior
34. experiences little guilt over behavior
35. may feign guilt and remorse when in trouble
36. free from disabling anxiety, depression, and psychotic symptoms
37. likely to receive a personality disorder diagnosis (antisocial personality or passive-aggressive personality)
38. prone to worry, dissatisfied
39. has an absence of deep emotional response
40. feels bored, empty
41. has a poor prognosis for change in psychotherapy or counseling
42. tends to blame others for problems
43. uses intellectualization
44. may agree to treatment to avoid jail or some other unpleasant experience but is likely to terminate prematurely

A low scale 4 score indicates a person who (is):

1. conventional, conforming
2. accepting of authority
3. passive, submissive, unassertive
4. concerned about how others will react
5. sincere, trusting
6. has low drive, not competitive
7. concerned about status and security
8. has a narrow range of interests
9. not creative or spontaneous
10. persistent
11. moralistic, rigid
12. if a male, not very interested in sex; afraid of women
13. critical of self, self-dissatisfaction
14. accepting of advice and suggestion

15. may become very dependent in treatment
16. afraid to accept responsibility for own behavior

SCALE 5 (MASCULINITY-FEMININITY)

Scale 5 originally was developed by Hathaway and McKinley to identify homosexual invert males. Because of the heterogeneity of the homosexual sample, the test authors could identify only a very small number of cases characterized by sexual inversion and relatively free of neurotic, psychotic, and psychopathic tendencies. Thus, items also were added to this scale if they differentiated between high and low scoring males on the Terman and Miles Attitude Interest Test or if they were endorsed differentially by normal males and females. Although Hathaway and McKinley considered this scale as a preliminary one, it has come to be used in its original form as a standard clinical scale.

The test authors attempted unsuccessfully to develop a corresponding scale for identifying sexual inversion in females. As a result, the standard procedure is to use scale 5 for both male and female subjects. Fifty-five of the items are keyed in the same direction for both sexes, whereas five of the items, all dealing with frankly sexual material, are keyed in opposite directions for males and females. After obtaining raw scores, T-score conversions are reversed for the sexes, so that a high raw score for males automatically is transformed by means of the profile sheet itself to a high T-score whereas a high raw score for females is transformed to a low T-score. The result is that a high T-score for both sexes is indicative of deviation from one's own sex.

Although some of the 60 items in scale 5 deal with frankly sexual material, most items are not sexual in nature and cover a diversity of topics, including interests in work, hobbies and pastimes, worries, fears, and sensitivities, social activities, religious preferences, and family relationships.

Scores on scale 5 are related to intelligence, education, and socioeconomic level. It is not uncommon for male college students and other college-educated males to obtain T-scores in the 60 to 70 range. These expected elevations are particularly important in determining whether scores should be considered to be extremely elevated. Although a T-score of 80 would be considered extreme for a male with limited formal education and from a lower social class, it would be only a moderate elevation for a better educated male from a middle or upper middle class. Female college students and other college-educated females usually score somewhat below 50 on scale 5. Women with graduate or professional level educations often score between 40 and 50 on scale 5.

Because of the reversal of scoring with scale 5, high T-scores have different meanings for males and females. Some writers have suggested that high scores for males are equivalent to low scores for females and that both indicate feminine interests and attitudes. A careful analysis of the data for high scoring males and females indicates that such an understanding is a great oversimplification. Thus, high scores and low scores are discussed separately for males and females.

High Scores on Scale 5 (Males)

Although there has been a great reluctance to infer homosexuality from high scores on scale 5, the possibility of homoerotic trends or homosexual behavior must be considered when extreme elevations are obtained, particularly if the scores deviate markedly from what is expected based on the subject's intelligence, education, and social class. Of course, one would want other confirming data before concluding that a subject was homosexual. High scores also may be indicative of conflicts in sexual identity and insecurity in one's masculine role, and high scorers may display clearly effeminate behavior.

High scores for males on scale 5 are indicative of a lack of stereotyped masculine interests. High scoring males tend to have aesthetic and artistic interests, and they are likely to participate in housekeeping and childrearing activities to a greater extent than do most men.

High scoring males are intelligent, capable persons who value cognitive pursuits. They are characterized as ambitious, competitive and persevering. They are clever, clear-thinking, organized, and logical, and they show good judgment and common sense. They are very curious and may be creative, imaginative, and individualistic in their approach to problems.

Sociability and sensitivity to others are also characteristic of high scoring males. They are quite tolerant of other people and are capable of expressing warm feelings toward them. In interpersonal situations high scoring males tend to be very passive, dependent, and submissive. They are peace loving and will make many concessions to avoid confrontations.

There is some evidence that high scores for males are indicative of good self-control. Acting out behavior is quite rare among high scorers. Even in subgroups with a high degree of delinquency, high scoring males on scale 5 are not likely to display delinquent behavior.

High Scores on Scale 5 (Females)

High scale 5 scores are very uncommon among female subjects. When they are encountered, they generally indicate rejection of the traditional female role. Females having high scale 5 scores are interested in sports, hobbies, and other activities that tend to be stereotypically more masculine than feminine. They are described as active, vigorous, and assertive. They also tend to be very competitive, aggressive, and dominating, and they are seen by others as rather coarse, rough, and tough.

High scoring females are very outgoing, uninhibited, and self-confident. They are easygoing, relaxed, and balanced. They are rather logical and calculated in their behavior and may be rather unemotional. They are seen as unfriendly by many people.

Among hospitalized psychiatric patients, high scoring females tend to be diagnosed as psychotic. They may exhibit hallucinations, delusions, and suspiciousness, but acting out behavior is uncommon.

Low Scores on Scale 5 (Males)

Males who score low on scale 5 are presenting themselves as extremely masculine. They clearly have stereotypically masculine preferences in work, hobbies, and other activities. They place an overemphasis on physical strength and prowess. They also are described as aggressive, thrill-seeking, adventurous, and reckless. Coarse, crude, and vulgar talk and behavior are not uncommon. The exaggerated nature of their attitudes and behaviors suggests that they may be covering up basic doubts about their own masculinity.

Low scoring males are seen by others as having limited intellectual ability. They have a narrow range of interests and are rather inflexible and unoriginal in their approach to problems. They prefer action to thought and are practical and nontheoretical.

Other people see low scoring males as easy going, leisurely, and relaxed. They also are described as cheerful, jolly, and humorous. They seem to be reasonably contented and are willing to settle down. However, they seem to be unaware of their social stimulus values and lack insight into their own motives.

Low Scores on Scale 5 (Females)

Comparatively little information is available concerning women who score low on scale 5. However, it is clear that different interpretations should be made for low 5 scores depending on educational level. Low scale 5 women with limited education (high school degree or less) are presenting themselves in terms of a stereotyped female role. Again, as with the low scoring males, the exaggerated nature of their attitudes and behaviors suggests that they may be covering up doubts about their own adequacy as women. They tend to be very passive, submissive, and yielding. They are likely to defer to men in decision making. They may be self-pitying, complaining, and fault finding. Other people describe these women as constricted, sensitive, modest, and idealistic.

A somewhat different interpretation should be made for low scale 5 women who have college degrees or professional training. The general picture of these low scale 5 women is much more positive, and they seem to have a more balanced view of gender role behavior. Although they do not present themselves as stereotypically feminine, they have many interests, attitudes, and behaviors that are traditionally feminine. In addition, they see themselves as capable, competent, and conscientious. They also may describe themselves as cynical, unimaginative, and unenthusiastic. Others see the more educated low scale 5 women in very favorable terms. They are described as intelligent, capable, conscientious, and forceful. In addition, they are seen as considerate, easygoing, insightful, and unprejudiced.

Summary of Descriptors for Scale 5

A high scale 5 score for males indicates a person who (is):

1. conflicted about his sexual identity
2. insecure in masculine role
3. effeminate
4. has aesthetic and artistic interests
5. intelligent, capable; values cognitive pursuits
6. ambitious, competitive, persevering
7. clever, clear-thinking, organized, logical
8. shows good judgment, common sense
9. curious
10. creative, imaginative, and individualistic in approach to problems
11. sociable; sensitive to others
12. tolerant
13. capable of expressing warm feelings toward others
14. passive, dependent, submissive in interpersonal relationships
15. peaceloving; makes concessions to avoid confrontations
16. has good self-control; rarely acts out
17. may display homoerotic trends or overt homosexual behavior

A high scale 5 score for females indicates a person who (is):

1. rejects the traditional female role
2. has stereotypic masculine interests in work, sports, hobbies
3. active, vigorous, assertive
4. competitive, aggressive, dominating
5. coarse, rough, tough
6. outgoing, uninhibited; self-confident
7. easygoing, relaxed, balanced
8. logical, calculated
9. unemotional
10. unfriendly

A low scale 5 score for males indicates a person who (is):

1. presents himself as extremely masculine
2. overemphasizes strength and physical prowess

3. aggressive, thrill-seeking, adventurous, reckless
4. coarse, crude, vulgar
5. harbors doubts about his own masculinity
6. has limited intellectual ability
7. has a narrow range of interests
8. inflexible and unoriginal approach to problems
9. prefers action to thought
10. practical, nontheoretical
11. easygoing, leisurely, relaxed
12. cheerful, jolly, humorous
13. contented; willing to settle down
14. unaware of social stimulus value
15. lacks insight into own motives

A low scale 5 score for females with relatively less education indicates a person who (is):

1. presenting herself in terms of stereotyped female role
2. may be covering up doubts about her own femininity
3. passive, submissive, yielding
4. self-pitying, complaining, faultfinding
5. seen by others as constricted, sensitive, modest, idealistic

A low scale 5 score for females with relatively more education indicates a person who (is):

1. has a balanced view of gender role behavior
2. although not stereotypically feminine, has many traditionally feminine interests
3. sees herself as capable, competent, conscientious
4. describes herself as cynical, unimaginative, unenthusiastic
5. described by others as intelligent, capable, conscientious, forceful, considerate, easygoing, insightful, unprejudiced

SCALE 6 (PARANOIA)

Scale 6 originally was developed to identify patients who were judged to have paranoid symptoms such as ideas of reference, feelings of persecution, grandiose self-concepts, suspiciousness, excessive sensitivity, and rigid opinions and attitudes. Although the scale was considered as preliminary because of problems in cross-validation, a major reason for its retention was that it produces relatively few false positives. Persons who score high on the scale usually have paranoid symptoms. However, some patients with clearly paranoid symptoms are able to achieve average scores on scale 6.

Although some of the 40 items in the scale deal with frankly psychotic behaviors (suspiciousness, ideas of reference, delusions of persecution, grandiosity, etc.), many items cover such diverse topics as sensitivity, cynicism, asocial behavior, excessive moral virtue, rigidity, and complaints about other people. It is quite possible to obtain a T-score greater than 70 without endorsing any of the frankly psychotic items.

Although scores on scale 6 are reasonably independent of age, education, and intelligence, black subjects score consistently higher than white subjects. Rather than suggesting gross psychopathology, these elevated scores may reflect the views of many blacks that they are getting a raw deal in life and their generally suspicious attitudes concerning the motives of whites.

Interpretation of scores on scale 6 is very complicated because the scale clearly is not bipolar in nature. Very high scores (T > 75) generally are suggestive of frank paranoid or psychotic behavior. More moderate elevations (T = 65 to 75) are associated with a paranoid predisposition. Mild elevations (T = 55 to 65) for nonclinical subjects generally are indicative of fairly positive characteristics, but for clinical subjects they suggest more negative characteristics. Moderately low scores (T = 35 to 45) also have different meanings for normal and disturbed groups. The former are seen in generally positive terms, whereas the latter are described more negatively. When scores on scale 6 are extremely low (T < 35), especially if the scale is the lowest one in the profile, one suspects paranoid or psychotic behavior, but it may not be as obvious as with extreme elevations. Because of the complexity of scale 6, a simple dichotomization into high scores and low scores would be a vast oversimplification.

High Scores on Scale 6

Extreme Elevations

When scale 6 is elevated above a T-score of 75, and especially when it also is the highest scale in the profile, subjects may exhibit frankly psychotic behavior. Their thinking may be disturbed, and they may have delusions of persecution and/or grandeur. Ideas of reference also are common. They may feel mistreated and picked on; they may be angry and resentful; and they may harbor grudges. Projection is a common defense mechanism. Diagnoses of paranoid schizophrenia or paranoid state are most frequent.

Moderate Elevations

When scale 6 scores are within a T-score range of 65 to 75, frankly psychotic symptoms are not as common. However, subjects within this range are characterized by a variety of traits and behaviors that may suggest a paranoid predisposition. They tend to be excessively sensitive and overly responsive to the opinions of others. They feel that they are getting a raw deal out of life and tend to rationalize and to blame others for their own difficulties. Also, they are seen as suspicious and guarded. Hostility, resentment, and an argumentative manner are common. They tend to be very moralistic and rigid in their opinions and attitudes. Rationality is likely to be overemphasized greatly. Prognosis for psychotherapy is poor, because these subjects do not like to talk about emotional problems and are likely to rationalize most of the time. They have great difficulty in establishing rapport with therapists. In therapy, they are likely to reveal hostility and resentment toward family members.

Mild Elevations

When subjects who are not psychiatric patients score in a T-score range of 55 to 65, they generally are seen in rather positive ways. They are described as kind, affectionate, generous, sentimental, softhearted, and peaceable. They also tend to be sensitive to what is going on around them and to be trusting of other people. Although they are cooperative, they tend to be rather frank. They have a wide range of interests and seem to be energetic and industrious. They display much initiative and become ego-involved in work and activities. They are seen as poised, intelligent, fair-minded, rational, clear-thinking, and insightful. On the more negative side, they are submissive and dependent in interpersonal relationships, and they tend to lack self-confidence. They describe themselves as high-strung and prone to worry.

When mild elevations are obtained by psychiatric patients, the interpretation is much more negative. Such scorers tend to have a rather paranoid orientation toward life. They see the environment as demanding and not particularly supportive. They tend to be very sensitive to what other people think of them, and they are suspicious of the motives of others. Anger and resentment are common.

Low Scores on Scale 6

Moderately low scores on scale 6 (T = 34 to 45) seem to have somewhat different meanings for normal subjects and for subjects who are psychiatric patients or for whom there is other evidence of maladjustment. For normal subjects, particularly if they are above average in intelligence and/or education, rather positive adjectives, such as cheerful, balanced, serious, orderly, mature, and reasonable, are suggested. They tend to be seen as wise, decisive, and persevering. They are socially interested and tend to face life situations adequately. They are trustful and loyal. They tend to be cautious, conventional, and self-controlled in their approach to problems. Scores in this same range, if obtained by disturbed subjects, are suggestive of negative traits and behaviors. Such subjects are seen as stubborn, evasive, and guarded. They are likely to be self-centered and to show little concern for things that do not affect them directly. Self-dissatisfaction and oversensitivity to the reactions of others are common. These subjects are rather uninsightful and lack social interest and social skills. They have a narrow range of interests and tend to be inflexible in their approach to problems. They do not have very strong consciences and have little regard for principles. Other adjectives applied to such subjects are rough, awkward, undependable, touchy, antagonistic, and underachieving. Among hospitalized psychiatric patients, psychotic symptoms or diagnoses are not common.

Extremely low scores (T < 35) should alert the clinician to the possibility of a frank paranoid disorder. Whereas subjects with scores in this range may have delusions, suspiciousness, and ideas of reference, these may be less obvious to others than is true for extremely high scorers. They tend to be very evasive, defensive, and guarded. Rather than being openly hostile, aggressive, and abrasive, they seem more shy, secretive, and withdrawn.

Summary of Descriptors for Scale 6

An extreme scale 6 elevation (T > 75) indicates an individual who (is):

1. manifests frankly psychotic behavior
2. has disturbed thinking
3. has delusions of persecution and/or grandeur
4. has ideas of reference
5. feels mistreated or picked on
6. angry, resentful; harbors grudges
7. uses projection as a defense mechanism
8. most frequently is given a diagnosis of schizophrenic disorder or paranoid disorder

A moderate scale 6 elevation (T = 65 to 75) indicates an individual who (is):

1. has a paranoid predisposition
2. sensitive; overly responsive to reactions of others
3. feels he/she is getting a raw deal from life
4. rationalizes; blames others for own difficulties
5. suspicious, guarded
6. hostile, resentful, argumentative
7. moralistic, rigid
8. overemphasizes rationality
9. has a poor prognosis for psychotherapy

10. does not like to talk about emotional problems
11. has difficulty in establishing rapport with therapist
12. expresses hostility and resentment toward family members

A mild scale 6 elevation (T = 55 to 65) indicates an individual who (is):

1. if not a psychiatric patient and with no other evidence of maladjustment:
   a. kind, affectionate, generous
   b. sentimental, softhearted, peaceable
   c. sensitive
   d. trusting
   e. cooperative
   f. frank
   g. has a wide range of interests
   h. energetic, industrious
   i. shows initiative, becomes ego-involved in work and other activities
   j. poised, intelligent, fair-minded, rational, clear-thinking, insightful
   k. submissive
   l. lacks self-confidence
   m. high-strung, prone to worry
2. if a psychiatric patient or with other evidence of maladjustment:
   a. has a rather paranoid orientation toward life
   b. sees environment as demanding and not particularly supportive
   c. tends to be very sensitive to what other people think
   d. suspicious of motives of others
   e. shows anger and resentment

A moderately low scale 6 elevation (T = 35 to 45) indicates an individual who (is):

1. if not a psychiatric patient and with no other evidence of maladjustment:
   a. cheerful
   b. balanced
   c. orderly
   d. serious, mature, reasonable
   e. wise, decisive, persevering
   f. socially interested
   g. faces life situations adequately
   h. trustful, loyal
   i. cautious, conventional, self-controlled
2. if a psychiatric patient or with other evidence of maladjustment:
   a. stubborn, evasive, guarded
   b. self-centered
   c. shows little concern for things that do not affect him/her directly
   d. self-dissatisfied

e. overly sensitive to reactions of others
f. uninsightful
g. lacks social interests and social skills
h. has weak conscience, little regard for principles
i. rough, awkward
j. undependable
k. underachieving
l. touchy, antagonistic
m. not likely to manifest psychotic symptoms; not commonly diagnosed as psychotic

An extremely low scale 6 elevation (T < 35) indicates an individual who (is):

1. may have a frankly paranoid disorder
2. may have delusions, exhibits suspiciousness, ideas of reference
3. has symptoms that are less obvious than those of extremely high scorers
4. evasive, defensive, guarded
5. shy, secretive, withdrawn

SCALE 7 (PSYCHASTHENIA)

Scale 7 originally was developed to measure the general symptomatic pattern labeled psychasthenia. Although this label is not used commonly today, it was popular when the scale was developed. Among currently popular diagnostic categories, the obsessive-compulsive disorder probably is closest to the original psychasthenia label. Persons diagnosed as psychasthenic had thinking characterized by excessive doubts, compulsions, obsessions, and unreasonable fears. This symptom pattern was much more common among outpatients than among hospitalized patients, so the number of cases available for scale construction was small.

The 48 items in scale 7 cover a variety of symptoms and behaviors. Many of the items deal with uncontrollable or obsessive thoughts, feelings of fear and/or anxiety, and doubts about one's own ability. Unhappiness, physical complaints, and difficulties in concentration also are represented in the scale.

High Scores on Scale 7

Scale 7 is a good index of psychological turmoil and discomfort. High scorers tend to be very anxious, tense, and agitated. They worry a great deal, even over very small problems, and are fearful and apprehensive. They are high-strung and jumpy and report difficulties in concentrating. The most common diagnosis for high 7 scorers is anxiety disorder.

High scorers tend to be very introspective; obsessive thinking, compulsive and ritualistic behavior, and ruminations are common among very high scorers. The obsessions and ruminations often center around feelings of insecurity and inferiority. They lack self-confidence, are self-critical, self-conscious, and self-degrading, and are plagued by self-doubts. High scorers tend to be very rigid and moralistic and to have high standards of behavior and performance for themselves and others. They are likely to be quite perfectionistic and conscientious; they may feel guilty about not living up to their own standards and depressed about falling short of goals.

In general, high scorers are neat, orderly, organized, and meticulous. They are persistent and reliable, but they lack ingenuity and originality in their approach to problems. They are seen by others as dull and formal. They have great difficulties in decision making, and they may vacillate and be indecisive over very small, routine decisions. In addition, they are likely to distort the importance of problems and to be quite overreactive to stressful situations.

High scorers tend to be shy and do not interact well socially. They are described as hard to get to know, and they worry a great deal about popularity and social acceptance. Other people see them as sentimental, peaceable, soft-hearted, trustful, sensitive, and kind. Other adjectives used to describe them include dependent, individualistic, verbal, emotional, and immature.

Some high scorers express physical complaints. These may center around the heart, the gastrointestinal system, or the genitourinary system. Complaints of fatigue, exhaustion, and insomnia are not uncommon.

Although high scorers may be uncomfortable and miserable, they are not very responsive in brief psychotherapy or counseling. In spite of some insight into their problems, they tend to rationalize and to intellectualize a great deal. They often are resistant to interpretations and may express much hostility toward the therapist. However, they tend to remain in therapy longer than most patients, and they may show very slow but steady progress. Problems presented in therapy may include difficulties with authority figures, poor work or study habits, or concern about homosexual impulses.

Low Scores on Scale 7

Low scorers on scale 7 are free of disabling fears and anxieties and are very self-confident. They are perceived as warm, cheerful, and friendly. They have a wide range of interests and are responsible, efficient, realistic, and adaptable. Success, status, and recognition are important to them.

Summary of Descriptors for Scale 7

A high scale 7 score indicates an individual who (is):

1. experiences turmoil and discomfort

2. anxious, tense, agitated
3. worried, apprehensive
4. high-strung, jumpy
5. has difficulties in concentrating
6. frequently given a diagnosis of anxiety disorder
7. introspective, ruminative
8. obsessive in his/her thinking
9. has compulsive behaviors
10. feels insecure and inferior
11. lacks self-confidence
12. has self-doubts; self-critical; self-conscious; self-derogatory
13. rigid, moralistic
14. has high standards for himself/herself and others
15. perfectionistic, conscientious
16. guilty, depressed
17. neat, orderly, organized, meticulous
18. persistent
19. reliable
20. lacks ingenuity and originality in approach to problems
21. dull, formal
22. vacillates, is indecisive
23. distorts importance of problems; overreacts
24. shy
25. does not interact well socially
26. hard to get to know
27. worries about popularity and acceptance
28. sentimental, peaceable, softhearted, trustful, sensitive, kind
29. dependent
30. individualistic
31. unemotional
32. immature
33. has physical complaints
    a. heart
    b. genitourinary
    c. gastrointestinal
    d. fatigue, exhaustion, insomnia
34. not responsive to brief psychotherapy
35. shows some insight into problems
36. intellectualizes, rationalizes
37. resistant to interpretations in psychotherapy
38. expresses hostility toward therapist
39. remains in psychotherapy longer than most patients
40. makes slow but steady progress in psychotherapy
41. discusses in therapy problems including difficulties with authority figures, poor work or study habits, and concern about homosexual impulses

A low scale 7 score indicates an individual who (is):

1. free of disabling fears and anxiety
2. self-confident
3. has a wide range of interests
4. responsible, efficient, realistic, adaptable
5. values success, status, and recognition

SCALE 8 (SCHIZOPHRENIA)

Scale 8 was developed to identify patients diagnosed as schizophrenic. This category included a heterogeneous group of disorders characterized by disturbances of thinking, mood, and behavior. Misinterpretations of reality, delusions, and hallucinations may be present. Ambivalent or constricted emotional responsiveness is common. Behavior may be withdrawn, aggressive, or bizarre.

The 78 items in scale 8 cover a wide array of behaviors. Some of the items deal with such frankly psychotic symptoms as bizarre mentation, peculiarities of perception, delusions of persecution, and hallucinations. Other topics covered include social alienation, poor family relationships, sexual concerns, difficulties in impulse control and concentration, and fears, worries, and dissatisfactions.

Scores on scale 8 are related to age and to race. Adolescents and college students often obtain T-scores in a range of 55 to 65, perhaps reflecting the turmoil associated with that period in life. Black subjects, particularly males, tend to score higher than white subjects. The elevated scores for blacks do not necessarily suggest greater overt psychopathology. They may simply be indicative of the alienation and social estrangement experienced by many blacks. Some elevations of scale 8 can be accounted for by subjects who are reporting a large number of unusual experiences, feelings, and perceptions related to the use of drugs.

High Scores on Scale 8

Although one should be cautious about concluding that a subject is schizophrenic on the basis of only the score on scale 8, T-scores in a range of 80 to 90 suggest the possibility of an extratest psychotic condition. Confusion, disorganization, and disorientation may be present. Unusual thoughts or attitudes, perhaps even delusional in nature, hallucinations, and extremely poor judgment may be evident. Extreme scores on scale 8 ($T > 100$) usually are not produced by psychotic subjects. They are more likely to be indicative of an individual who is in acute psychological turmoil or of a less disturbed individual who is endorsing many deviant items as a cry for help.

High scores on scale 8 may suggest a schizoid life-style. High scorers tend to feel as if they are not part of their social environments. They feel isolated, alienated, misunderstood, and unaccepted by their peers. They are withdrawn, seclusive, secretive, and inaccessible. They may avoid dealing with people and with new situations. They are described by others as shy, aloof, and uninvolved.

High scorers experience a great deal of very generalized anxiety. They may feel very resentful, hostile, and aggressive, but they are unable to express such feelings. A typical response to stress is withdrawal into daydreams and fantasies, and some subjects may have a difficult time in separating reality and fantasy.

High scorers may be plagued by self-doubts. They feel inferior, incompetent, and dissatisfied. Sexual preoccupation and sex role confusion are not uncommon. Their behavior often is characterized by others as nonconforming, unusual, unconventional, and eccentric. Physical complaints may be present, and they usually are vague and long-standing in nature.

High scorers may at times be very stubborn, moody, and opinionated. At other times they are seen as generous, peaceable, and sentimental. Other adjectives used to describe high scorers include immature, impulsive, adventurous, sharp-witted, conscientious, and high-strung. Although they may have a wide range of interests and may be creative and imaginative in approaching problems, their goals generally are abstract and vague, and they seem to lack basic information that is required for problem solving.

The prognosis for psychotherapy is not good because of the long-standing nature of high scorers' problems and their reluctance to relate in a meaningful way to the therapist. However, high scorers tend to stay in therapy longer than most patients, and eventually they may come to trust the therapist. Medical consultation to evaluate appropriateness of chemotherapy may be indicated.

Low Scores on Scale 8

Low scorers on scale 8 tend to be friendly, cheerful, good-natured, sensitive, and trustful. They are seen as well-balanced and adaptable, and they are responsible and dependable. However, low scorers tend to be somewhat restrained in their relationships, and they avoid deep, emotional involvement with other people. In interpersonal relationships they are submissive and compliant, and they are overly accepting of authority. Low scorers tend to be cautious, conventional, conservative, and unimaginative in their approach to problems, and they tend to be very practical and concrete in their thinking. They are concerned about success, status, and power, but they are so overcontrolled that they are reluctant to place themselves in clearly competitive situations.

Summary of Descriptors for Scale 8

A high scale 8 score indicates an individual who (is):

1. may manifest blatantly psychotic behavior (especially if T = 80 to 100)
2. confused, disorganized, disoriented
3. has unusual thoughts or attitudes; delusions
4. has hallucinations
5. shows poor judgment
6. has a schizoid life-style
7. does not feel a part of social environment
8. feels isolated, alienated, misunderstood
9. feels unaccepted by peers
10. withdrawn, seclusive, secretive, inaccessible
11. avoids dealing with people and new situations
12. shy, aloof, uninvolved
13. experiences generalized anxiety
14. feels resentful, hostile, aggressive
15. unable to express feelings
16. reacts to stress by withdrawing into daydreams and fantasies
17. has difficulty separating reality and fantasy
18. plagued by self-doubts
19. feels inferior, incompetent, dissatisfied
20. has sexual preoccupation, sex role confusion
21. nonconforming, unusual, unconventional, eccentric
22. vague, long-standing physical complaints
23. stubborn, moody, opinionated
24. generous, peaceable, sentimental
25. immature, impulsive
26. adventurous
27. sharp-witted
28. conscientious
29. high-strung
30. has a wide range of interests
31. creative and imaginative
32. has abstract, vague goals
33. lacks basic information required for problem solving
34. has a poor prognosis for psychotherapy
35. reluctant to relate in meaningful way to therapist
36. stays in psychotherapy longer than most patients
37. may eventually come to trust the therapist
38. may benefit from medical consultation and chemotherapy

A low scale 8 score indicates an individual who (is):

1. friendly, cheerful, good-natured, sensitive, trustful

2. well-balanced, adaptable
3. responsible, dependable
4. restrained in relationships; avoids deep emotional involvement
5. submissive, compliant, overly accepting of authority
6. cautious, conventional, conservative, unimaginative in approach to problems
7. practical, concrete in thinking
8. concerned about success, status, power
9. reluctant to become involved in clearly competitive situations

SCALE 9 (HYPOMANIA)

Scale 9 originally was developed to identify psychiatric patients manifesting hypomanic symptoms. Hypomania is characterized by elevated mood, accelerated speech and motor activity, irritability, flights of ideas, and brief periods of depression.

Some of the 46 items in scale 9 deal specifically with features of the hypomanic disturbance (e.g., activity level, excitability, irritability, grandiosity). Other items cover topics such as family relationships, moral values and attitudes, and physical or bodily concerns. No single dimension accounts for much of the variance in scores, and the sources of variance represented in the scale are not duplicated in other clinical scales.

Scores on scale 9 clearly are related to age and to race. Younger subjects (e.g., adolescents and college students) typically obtain scores in a T-score range of 55 to 65, and for elderly subjects scale 9 scores below a T-score of 50 are not uncommon. Black subjects typically score higher than white subjects on the scale; scores in a T-score range of 60 to 70 are not uncommon for black subjects.

High Scores on Scale 9

Extreme elevations ($T > 90$) may be suggestive of a manic episode. Patients with such scores are likely to show excessive, purposeless activity and accelerated speech; they may have hallucinations and/or delusions of grandeur; and they are very emotionally labile. Some confusion may be present, and flight of ideas is not uncommon.

Subjects with more moderate elevations are not likely to exhibit frankly psychotic symptoms, but there is a definite tendency toward overactivity and unrealistic self-appraisal. High scores are energetic and talkative, and they prefer action to thought. They have a wide range of interests and they are likely to have many projects going at once. However, they do not utilize energy very wisely and often do not see projects through to completion. They may be creative, enterprising, and ingenious, but they have little interest in routine or in details. High scorers tend to become bored and restless very easily, and their frustration tolerance is quite low. They have great difficulty in inhibiting expression of impulses, and periodic episodes of irritability, hostility, and aggressive outbursts are not uncommon. An unrealistic and unqualified optimism is also characteristic of high scorers. They seem to think that nothing is impossible, and they have grandiose aspirations. Also, they have an exaggerated appraisal of their own self-worth and self-importance and are not able to see their own limitations.

High scorers are very outgoing, sociable, and gregarious. They like to be around other people and generally create good first impressions. They impress others as being friendly, pleasant, enthusiastic, poised, and self-confident. Their relationships with other people are usually quite superficial, and as others get to know them better they become aware of their manipulations, deceptions, and unreliability.

In spite of the outward picture of confidence and poise, high scorers are likely to harbor feelings of dissatisfaction concerning what they are getting out of life. They may feel upset, tense, nervous, anxious, and agitated, and they describe themselves as prone to worry. Periodic episodes of depression may occur.

In psychotherapy, high scorers may reveal negative feelings toward domineering parents, may report difficulties in school or at work, and may admit to a variety of delinquent behaviors. Female subjects may be rebelling against the stereotyped female role, and some male subjects may be concerned about homosexual impulses. The prognosis for psychotherapy is poor. High scorers are resistant to interpretations, are irregular in their attendance, and are likely to terminate therapy prematurely. They engage in a great deal of intellectualization and may repeat problems in a stereotyped manner. They do not become dependent on the therapist, who may be a target for hostility and aggression.

Low Scores on Scale 9

Low scorers on scale 9, particularly if the scale is the lowest one in the profile, are characterized by low energy and activity levels. They appear to be lethargic, listless, apathetic, and phlegmatic, and they are difficult to motivate. Chronic fatigue and physical exhaustion are not uncommon. Depression, accompanied by tension and anxiety, may be present.

Low scorers are reliable, responsible, and dependable. They approach problems in a conventional, practical, and reasonable way, and they are conscientious and persevering. They may lack self-confidence, and they are seen by others as sincere, quiet, modest, and humble. They also tend to be somewhat withdrawn and seclusive, and they see themselves as not being very popular. They tend to be overcontrolled and are not likely to express their feelings directly or openly.

Low scoring males have home and family interests and seem willing to settle down. For hospitalized psychiatric patients, low scale 9 scores have favorable prognostic implications.

Summary of Descriptors for Scale 9

A high scale 9 score indicates an individual who (is):

1. may be having a manic episode
2. manifests excessive, purposeless activity
3. has accelerated speech
4. may have hallucinations, delusions of grandeur
5. emotionally labile
6. may be confused
7. displays flight of ideas
8. energetic, talkative
9. prefers action to thought
10. has a wide range of interests; involved in many activities
11. does not utilize energy wisely, does not see projects through to completion
12. creative, enterprising, ingenious
13. has little interest in routine or details
14. easily bored, restless; has low frustration tolerance
15. has difficulty in inhibiting expression of impulses
16. has episodes of irritability, hostility, aggressive outbursts
17. unrealistic, unqualified optimism
18. has grandiose aspirations
19. exaggerates self-worth and self-importance
20. unable to see own limitations
21. outgoing, sociable, gregarious
22. likes to be around other people
23. creates good first impression
24. friendly, pleasant, enthusiastic
25. poised, self-confident
26. has superficial relationships
27. manipulative, deceptive, unreliable
28. harbors feelings of dissatisfaction
29. feels upset, tense, nervous, anxious
30. agitated, prone to worry
31. may have periodic episodes of depression
32. has negative feelings toward domineering parents
33. has difficulties at school or work; exhibits delinquent behaviors
34. if female, may be rejecting stereotyped female role
35. if male, may be concerned about homosexual impulses
36. has a poor prognosis for therapy
37. resistant to interpretations in psychotherapy

38. attends psychotherapy irregularly
39. may terminate psychotherapy prematurely
40. repeats problems in a stereotyped manner
41. not likely to become dependent on therapist
42. becomes hostile and aggressive toward therapist

A low scale 9 score indicates an individual who (is):

1. has low energy level, low activity level
2. lethargic, listless, apathetic, phlegmatic
3. difficult to motivate
4. reports chronic fatigue, physical exhaustion
5. depressed, anxious, tense
6. reliable, responsible, dependable
7. approaches problems in conventional, practical, and reasonable way
8. lacks self-confidence
9. sincere, quiet, modest, humble
10. withdrawn, seclusive
11. unpopular
12. overcontrolled; unlikely to express feelings openly
13. if male, has home and family interests; willing to settle down
14. if a hospitalized psychiatric patient, has favorable prognosis

SCALE 0 (SOCIAL INTROVERSION)

Although scale 0 was developed later than the other clinical scales, it has come to be treated as a standard clinical scale. The scale was designed to assess a subject's tendency to withdraw from social contacts and responsibilities. Items were selected by contrasting high and low scorers on the Social Introversion-Extroversion scale of the Minnesota T-S-E Inventory.

The 70 items of this scale are of two general types. One group of items deals with social participation, whereas the other group deals with general neurotic maladjustment and self-depreciation. High scores can be obtained by endorsing either kind of item, or both.

High Scores on Scale 0

The most salient characteristic of high scorers on scale 0 is social introversion. High scorers are very insecure and uncomfortable in social situations. They tend to be shy, reserved, timid, and retiring. They feel more comfortable when alone or with a few close friends, and they do not participate in many social activities. They may be especially uncomfortable around members of the opposite sex.

High scorers lack self-confidence, and they tend to be self-effacing. They are hard to get to know and are described by others as cold and distant. They are sensitive to what others think of them, and they are likely to be troubled by their lack of involvement with other people. They are quite overcontrolled and are not likely to display their feelings directly. They are submissive and compliant in interpersonal relationships, and they are overly accepting of authority.

High scorers also are described as serious and as having a slow personal tempo. Although they are reliable and dependable, their approach to problems tends to be cautious, conventional, and unoriginal. They are somewhat rigid and inflexible in their attitudes and opinions. They also have great difficulty in making even minor decisions. They seem to enjoy their work and get pleasure from productive personal achievement.

High scorers tend to worry, to be irritable, and to feel anxious. They are described by others as being very moody. Guilt feelings and episodes of depression may occur.

Low Scores on Scale 0

Low scorers on scale 0 tend to be sociable and extroverted. They are outgoing, gregarious, friendly, and talkative. They have a strong need to be around other people, and they mix well with other people. They are seen as intelligent, verbally fluent, and expressive. They are active, energetic, and vigorous. They are interested in power, status, and recognition and they tend to seek out competitive situations.

Low scorers have problems with impulse control, and they may act out without considering the consequences of their actions. They are somewhat immature and self-indulgent. Relationships with other people may be superficial and insincere. A tendency to manipulate other people and to be opportunistic may be evident. Their exhibitionistic and ostentatious styles may arouse resentment and hostility in others.

Summary of Descriptors for Scale 0

A high scale 0 score indicates an individual who (is):

1. socially introverted
2. more comfortable alone or with a few close friends
3. reserved, timid, shy, retiring
4. uncomfortable around members of the opposite sex
5. lacks self-confidence, is self-effacing
6. hard to get to know
7. sensitive to what others think
8. troubled by lack of involvement with other people
9. overcontrolled; not likely to display feelings openly

10. submissive, compliant
11. overly accepting of authority
12. serious, has slow personal tempo
13. reliable, dependable
14. cautious, conventional, unoriginal in approach to problems
15. rigid and inflexible in attitudes and opinions
16. has difficulty making even minor decisions
17. enjoys work; gains pleasure from productive personal achievement
18. tends to worry; is irritable, anxious
19. moody
20. experiences guilt feelings, episodes of depression

A low scale 0 score indicates an individual who (is):

1. sociable, extroverted
2. outgoing, gregarious, friendly, talkative
3. has a strong need to be around other people
4. mixes well
5. intelligent, expressive, verbally fluent
6. active, energetic, vigorous
7. interested in power, status, recognition
8. seeks out competitive situations
9. has problems with impulse control
10. may act without considering consequences of actions
11. immature, self-indulgent
12. has superficial, insincere relationships
13. manipulative, opportunistic
14. arouses resentment and hostility in others

5

Psychometric Considerations and Use with Special Groups

Although the major purpose of this book is to help students and clinicians learn to use and interpret the MMPI clinically, it also is very important for MMPI users to understand the strengths and weaknesses of the instrument. This chapter is intended as a brief summary of information concerning the psychometric properties of the MMPI and its use with subjects different from those on whom it was standardized. Coverage will not be exhaustive, and readers requiring more information concerning topics covered here should consult other references such as *An MMPI Handbook,* Volumes I and II (Dahlstrom, Welsh, & Dahlstrom, 1972, 1975) or Chapter 10 of *Psychological Testing* (Graham & Lilly, 1984).

The MMPI is the most widely used psychological test in the United States (Lubin, Larsen, & Matarazzo, 1984). Far more research articles have been published about the MMPI than about any other personality inventory (Graham & Lilly, 1984). Reviewers of the MMPI have been generally positive about its utility. Alker (1978) concluded that the MMPI can provide reliable indications of psychological treatments that will or will not work for specific patients. King (1978) concluded his review of the MMPI by stating: "The MMPI remains matchless as the objective instrument for the assessment of psychopathology . . . and still holds the place as the sine qua non in the psychologist's armamentarium of psychometric aids" (p. 938). This author agrees that the MMPI is the most useful and valid personality test currently available. He is aware of its limitations, and he encourages others to work to improve the psychometric adequacy of the instrument.

STANDARDIZATION

Unlike many of the projective techniques, the MMPI is well standardized in terms of materials, administration, and scoring. Essentially the same items, scales, and profile sheets have been used since the test's inception in the 1930s. Although there are some variations in the ways in which scores are interpreted, most users base interpretations on the sizable research literature that has accumulated since the MMPI's publication. This standardization of materials and procedures has ensured that data collected in diverse settings are comparable and has led to the accumulation of a significant data base for interpreting results.

SCALE CONSTRUCTION

As was discussed briefly in Chapter 1, the clinical scales of the MMPI were constructed according to empirical keying procedures. Items were selected for inclusion in a scale if groups of subjects known to differ on the characteristic in question (e.g., hypochondriasis, depression) responded differentially to the items. The reader interested in details concerning scale construction should consult a series of articles by Hathaway and his associates in *Basic Readings on the MMPI* (Dahlstrom & Dahlstrom, 1980).

Although the empirical keying approach was an improvement over the face-valid approach used in earlier personality inventories, the scale construction procedures were rather unsophisticated by current psychometric standards. The clinical samples were often very small. For example, only 20 criterion subjects were used to select items for scale 7. Although the test authors stressed that they tried to identify criterion groups composed of patients with only one kind of psychopathology, no data were presented concerning the reliability of the criterion placements. For most scales, cross-validation procedures were employed. The statistical analyses were not very sophisticated, and often only descriptive statistics were presented.

Because no attempt was made to ensure that items appeared on only one scale, there is considerable item overlap for some of the scales. For example, 13 of the 40 items in scale 6 also appear in scale 8. This item overlap contributes to high intercorrelations among the scales and limits the extent to which scores on a single scale contribute uniquely to prediction of appropriate criterion measures.

The empirical keying approach used with the MMPI precluded attention to item content and scale homogeneity. Hathaway and McKinley (1940) noted that the MMPI item content was heterogeneous, but they did not give attention to the homogeneity of the individual scales. As a result, the internal consistency of the scales is not very high. More information about internal consistency will be presented later in this chapter.

NORMS

The norms of a test provide a summary of results obtained when the test is given to a sample of individuals. The sample is referred to as the *normative sample* or *standardization sample.* A person's score on a test typically has meaning only when it is compared with a standardization sample.

The normal subjects used in constructing the original scales of the MMPI included 724 persons who were visiting friends or relatives at the University of Minnesota Hospitals. Only persons who reported that they were under the care of a physician were excluded from the sample. Other normal subjects used in various phases of scale development were 265 high school graduates who came to the University of Minnesota Testing Bureau for precollege guidance, 265 skilled workers involved with local Work Progress Administration projects, and 243 medical patients who did not report psychiatric problems.

Only the 724 hospital visitors were included in the sample that was used to determine T-score values employed on the standard MMPI profile sheet. All of the subjects in the standardization sample were white, and the typical person was about 35 years of age, married, residing in a small town or rural area, working in a skilled or semiskilled trade (or married to a man of this occupational level), and having about eight years of formal education (Dahlstrom, Welsh, & Dahlstrom, 1972). Hathaway and Briggs (1957) later refined this sample by eliminating persons with incomplete records or faulty background information. The refined sample is the one typically used for converting raw scores on supplementary MMPI scales to T-scores.

Although some data collected on nonclinical subjects in a variety of research projects have suggested that the original MMPI norms may still be appropriate, there is concern that the norms may be out of date. Colligan, Osborne, and Offord (1980) collected contemporary data from normal subjects in the same geographical area where the original MMPI norms were collected. These investigators found that on some MMPI scales contemporary subjects endorsed more items in the scored direction than did Hathaway's normal subjects. Unfortunately, the meaning of these differences is not clear. Subjects in Hathaway's research were encouraged to omit items and did so to a greater extent than did the Colligan et al. subjects. The higher scores for the Colligan et al. subjects may reflect, at least to some degree, the differential use of the Cannot Say category. By current standards the Colligan et al. data are unacceptable because they are limited geographically and demographically. Finally, the Colligan et al. data are presented as normalized T-scores, whereas the original MMPI norms were presented as linear T-scores. Although Colligan et al. argued that the normalized scores are more appropriate, Hsu (1984) offered some convincing arguments to the contrary, and Graham and Lilly (1986) demonstrated that the use of normalized T-scores led to underdiagnosis of psychopathology of psychiatric inpatients.

For the past several years a project has been under way to update and restandardize the MMPI. Sponsored by the test publisher, the University of Minnesota Press, the project involves collection of normative data for adult and adolescent subjects. In various parts of the United States, adult subjects are being randomly solicited from community directories to participate in the project. The goal is to develop a new normative sample that will resemble the U.S.

census data on major demographic variables such as age, race, marital status, education, occupation, and urban versus rural residence. Data also are being collected from normal adolescent subjects throughout the United States. The adolescent sample will include male and female subjects between the ages of 13 and 18 years. The normative data from adult and adolescent samples will be analyzed to determine the extent to which existing normative data are still appropriate. If changes in norms are indicated, the data will be used to develop new T-score conversion tables.

TEMPORAL STABILITY

That scores on tests of ability, interest, and aptitude should have high temporal stability is quite accepted by most psychologists. What should be expected from personality tests is not as clear. Although personality test scores should not be influenced by sources of error variance, such as room temperature, lack of sleep, and the like, it must be recognized that many personality attributes change over relatively short periods of time. Dahlstrom (1972) pointed out that many of the inferences that we make from personality test data involve current emotional status, whereas others deal with personality structure. Scales assessing personality structure should have high temporal stability, but those designed to measure current emotional status should be sensitive to rather short-term fluctuations.

From the MMPI's inception there has been an awareness of the importance of scale stability. Dahlstrom, Welsh, and Dahlstrom (1972), Graham (1977a), and Schwartz (1977) summarized temporal stability data for the individual validity and clinical scales of the MMPI. Table 5.1 reports ranges and typical values of test-retest correlations for various samples and varying test-retest intervals. For normal subjects the test-retest coefficients for relatively short intervals are relatively high and comparable to coefficients for other person-

Table 5.1 Summary of test-retest reliability coefficients for standard MMPI scales

	One day or less[a]		One to two weeks[a]		One year or more[a]	
Samples	Actual range	Typical values	Actual range	Typical values	Actual range	Typical values
Normal	.49–.96	.80–.85	.29–.92	.70–.80	.13–.73	.35–.45
Psychiatric	.61–.94	.80–.85	.43–.86	.80–.85	.22–.72	.50–.60
Criminal	.40–.86	.70–.80	.21–.84	.60–.70	—	—

Source: G. F. Schwartz, *An Investigation of the Stability of Single Scale and Two-Point MMPI Code Types for Psychiatric Patients.* Unpublished doctoral dissertation, Kent State University, Kent, OH, 1977. Reproduced with permission.

[a]Test-retest interval.

ality tests. For longer intervals the coefficients are considerably lower. The data for psychiatric patients are very similar to those for normals. For criminal samples the short-term coefficients are a bit lower than for the normal and psychiatric samples. No long-term coefficients have been reported for criminal subjects. Schwartz (1977) concluded that temporal stability does not seem to be related systematically to gender of subjects or to MMPI form used. Further, no MMPI scale appears to be consistently more stable than other scales. In summary, the temporal stability of individual MMPI scales over short periods of time compares favorably with that of scores from other personality instruments.

Because current MMPI interpretive strategies emphasize configural aspects of profiles, it is important to consider the stability of such configurations. Many clinicians assume that because the individual scales of the MMPI have reasonably good temporal stability, the configurations based on the scales also have good temporal stability. Only limited data are available concerning the stability of MMPI configurations. Canter (1951) and Warman and Hannum (1965) demonstrated that mean profiles for some groups of subjects are temporally stable. Lichtenstein and Bryan (1966) and Pauker (1966) demonstrated the similarity of individual pairs of test-retest profiles.

Table 5.2 summarizes the results of studies that have reported stability of high-point, two-point, and three-point codes. Although the kinds of subjects and test-retest intervals have differed across studies, the results have been rather consistent. About one half of subjects have had the same high-point

Table 5.2. Percentages of high-point, two-point, and three-point MMPI codes remaining the same on retest

Source	Sample	*N*	Sex	Test-retest interval	High-point	Two-point[a]	Three-point[a]
Graham (1977a)	College student	43	M	1 week	51	35	23
Graham (1977a)	College student	36	F	1 week	50	31	28
Faschingbauer (1974)	College student & psychiatric	61	M/F	1 day	63	41	23
Lichtenstein & Bryan (1966)	Volunteer & psychiatric	82	M/F	1–2 days	50	—	—
Kincannon (1968)	Psychiatric	60	M/F	1–2 days	61	—	—
Pauker (1966)	Psychiatric	107	F	13–176 days	44	25	—
Sivanich (1960)[b]	Psychiatric	202	F	2–2230 days	48	20	—
Graham, Smith, & Schwartz (1986)	Psychiatric	405	M/F	29–222 days	43	28	—
Uecker (1969)	Organic	30	M	1 week	—	23	—
Lauber & Dahlstrom (1953)	Delinquent	19	F	?	90	95	—

Source: J. R. Graham, R. L. Smith, & G. F. Schartz, Stability of MMPI configurations for psychiatric inpatients, *Journal of Consulting and Clinical Psychology, 54,* 375–380. Copyright 1986 by American Psychological Association. Adapted with permission.

[a]For two-point and three-point codes, scales are used interchangeably.

[b]Used only four two-point codes (4–6, 4–2, 6–8, 2–7).

code on two administrations; about one fourth to one third had the same two-point code; and about one fourth had the same three-point code.

Graham, Smith, and Schwartz (1986) reported that no particular high-point code or two-point code was significantly more stable than any other codes. Graham et al. (1986) also found that configurations tended to be more stable when the scales in the code types were more elevated initially and when there was a greater difference between these scales and other scales in the profile.

When code types of subjects changed from test to retest administrations, the second code type often was in the same diagnostic grouping (neurotic, psychotic, characterological) as was the first code type (Graham, Smith, & Schwartz, 1986). From one half to two thirds of subjects had code types in the same diagnostic grouping on test and retest. When the code types were from different diagnostic groupings on test and retest, the most frequent change was from psychotic on the initial test to characterological on the retest. The implication of these data is that many of the inferences that would be made would be the same even though the patients did not have exactly the same two-point code on the two occasions.

What about subjects whose code types changed from one major diagnostic grouping on the initial test to another major grouping on the retest? Were these changes due to the unreliability of the MMPI, or do they reflect significant changes in the status of the patients? Graham, Smith, and Schwartz (1986) addressed this issue to a limited extent. They studied psychiatric inpatients who produced psychotic two-point codes at the time of the initial testing and nonpsychotic codes at the time of retesting. They compared these patients with patients who had psychotic codes for both administrations or for neither administration. External psychiatric ratings of psychotic behaviors were available for the patients. Patients who changed from psychotic to nonpsychotic code types showed concomitant changes in psychiatric ratings. Patients who had nonpsychotic codes on both administrations were given relatively low psychosis ratings on both occasions. Complicating the results of the study was the finding that patients who had psychotic codes on both test and retest were given lower psychosis ratings at retest than at test. The psychiatrists who did the ratings also were case managers for the patients they rated. It may be that they were reluctant to indicate that patients that they were treating, and perhaps were about ready to discharge from the hospital, had not shown decreases in psychotic behaviors.

Several summary statements can be made about the temporal stability of MMPI scores. Individual MMPI scales seem to be as reliable temporally as other personality measures. Code types tend to be more stable when their scales are more elevated and when they are significantly more elevated than other scales in the profile. Although MMPI configurations probably are not as stable as often assumed by clinicians, subjects often produce the same code types on different administrations of the test. When the code types change from one administration to another, they tend to remain in the same diagnostic grouping. When the code types change dramatically, there often are concomitant behavioral changes.

INTERNAL CONSISTENCY

Because of the empirical keying procedures used in constructing the basic validity and clinical scales, little or no attention was given by the test authors to internal consistency of scales. Dahlstrom, Welsh, and Dahlstrom (1975) summarized internal consistency data for a variety of samples. Estimates of internal consistency varied considerably (from −.05 to +.96), with typical values ranging from .60 to .90. Internal consistency seems to be lower for college students than for psychiatric patients. Scales 3, 5, and 9 appear to be the least consistent ones, whereas scales 1, 7, and 8 appear to be the most internally consistent. Factor analyses of items within each standard scale indicate that most of the scales are not unidimensional (Comrey, 1957abc, 1958abcde; Comrey & Margraff, 1958; Graham, Schroeder, & Lilly, 1971). The one exception seems to be scale 1, where most of the variance is associated with a single dimension: concern about health and bodily functioning. Because no attention was given to internal consistency when the MMPI scales were constructed, it is not surprising that the scales are not as internally consistent as some other personality scales that were developed according to internal consistency procedures.

FACTOR STRUCTURE

Two basic dimensions have emerged whenever scores on the basic validity and clinical scales have been factor-analyzed (Block, 1965; Eichman, 1961, 1962; Welsh, 1956). Factor I has high positive loadings on scales 7 and 8 and a high negative loading on the K scale. Welsh and Eichman both labeled this factor "Anxiety," whereas Block scored it in the opposite direction and called it "Ego Resiliency." Welsh developed the Anxiety (A) scale to assess this dimension. This scale is discussed in some detail in Chapter 8. Factor I seems to be assessing a general maladjustment dimension.

Factor II has high positive loadings on scales 1, 2, and 3 and a moderately high negative loading on scale 9. Welsh and Eichman labeled this dimension "Repression," and Block called it "Ego Control." Welsh developed the Repression (R) scale to assess this dimension. This scale is discussed in some detail in Chapter 8. This second factor seems to be assessing denial, rationalization, lack of insight, and overcontrol of needs and impulses.

Some investigators have factor- or cluster-analyzed responses to the entire MMPI item pool (Barker, Fowler, & Peterson, 1971; Chu, 1966; Johnson, Null,

Butcher, & Johnson, 1984; Lushene, 1967; Stein, 1968; Tryon, 1966; Tryon & Bailey, 1965). Most of these early studies were limited by small sample sizes or analyses based on subsets of the total MMPI item pool. Only the study of Johnson et al. (1984) utilized a very large sample (more than 11,000 subjects) and analyzed the entire item pool in a single computational pass.

Using replication procedures, Johnson et al. identified the following 21 factors in the MMPI item pool: Neuroticism–General Anxiety and Worry; Psychoticism–Peculiar Thinking; Cynicism–Normal Paranoia; Denial of Somatic Problems; Social Extroversion; Stereotypic Femininity; Aggressive Hostility; Psychotic Paranoia; Depression; Delinquency; Inner Directedness; Assertiveness; Stereotypic Masculinity; Neurasthenic Somatization; Phobias; Family Attachment; Well-being–Health; Intellectual Interests; Rebellious Fundamentalism; Sexual Adjustment; and Dreaming. The authors noted the similarity of these factors to the content dimensions represented in the Wiggins scales and in the original content categories presented by Hathaway and McKinley. They also commented that the item pool seems to be measuring more aspects of personality than merely emotional stability.

Studies of the factor structure of MMPI item responses offer some interesting insights into the psychometric properties of the MMPI and suggest the basis for new and potentially useful scales. Barker et al. (1971) and Tryon, Stein, and Chu (Stein, 1968) developed scales to assess their factor dimensions and demonstrated them to be as reliable as the standard MMPI scales and as good or better than the standard scales in discriminating among diagnostic groups. The Tryon, Stein, and Chu scales are frequently scored by computer services. No information has yet been published concerning scales based on the Johnson et al. analyses. The limited amount of data concerning the utility of scales based on factor analyses precludes recommending their routine clinical use at this time.

RESPONSE SETS

Over the years some critics, such as Messick and Jackson (1961) and Edwards (1957, 1964) argued that the MMPI scales are of limited utility because most of the variance in their scores can be attributed to response sets or styles. Jackson and Messick argued that subjects who get high scores on the scales do so only because of an acquiescence response style (i.e., a tendency for subjects to agree passively with inventory statements). In support of their argument, Messick and Jackson pointed out that the standard MMPI scales are not balanced for proportion of items keyed as true or false. Further, it was shown that scores on Welsh's Anxiety scale (a measure of the major source of variance in MMPI responses) correlated positively with an acquiescence measure.

Edwards maintained that scores on the standard scales of the MMPI are grossly confounded with a social desirability response set (i.e., a tendency for test subjects to be willing to admit to socially undesirable traits and behaviors). Major support for this position came from data indicating that scores on the standard MMPI scales and on Welsh's Anxiety scale were highly correlated with a social desirability scale.

Although a number of persons have argued against the acquiescence and social desirability interpretations of the MMPI scales, Block (1965) reviewed most thoroughly the arguments in support of acquiescence and social desirability and pointed out some statistical and methodological problems. He also presented some new evidence that clearly rebutted the supportive positions. Block modified the standard MMPI scales, balancing the number of true and false items within each scale. Contrary to the prediction of Messick and Jackson, the factor structure of the MMPI with these modified scales was essentially the same as with the standard scales. Block also developed a measure of Welsh's Anxiety factor that was free of social desirability influences. Correlations between his modified Anxiety scale and standard MMPI scales were essentially the same as for Welsh's scale. Finally, Block demonstrated that MMPI scales have reliable correlates with important nontest behaviors even when the effects of social desirability and acquiescence have been removed.

In summary, the criticisms directed at the MMPI from critics such as Messick and Jackson and Block were severe. However, the MMPI withstood their challenges.

VALIDITY

In Volume II of *An MMPI Handbook,* Dahlstrom, Welsh, and Dalhstrom (1975) cited over 6000 studies involving the MMPI. In trying to reach some conclusions about the validity of the MMPI from these studies, it seems helpful to group them into three general categories. First, there have been studies that have compared the MMPI profiles of relevant criterion groups. Most of these studies have identified significant differences on one or more of the MMPI scales among groups formed on the basis of diagnosis, severity of disturbance, treatment regimes, and numerous other criteria. Lanyon (1968) published average or typical profiles for many of these criterion groups. Efforts to develop classification rules to discriminate among groups also are included in this category (Goldberg, 1965; Henrichs, 1964, 1966; Meehl & Dahlstrom, 1960; Peterson, 1954; Taulbee & Sisson, 1957). Most of these classification studies have indicated that rules can be developed to discriminate among groups of interest.

A second category of studies includes efforts to identify reliable behavioral correlates of MMPI scales and configurations. Nontest correlates of high or low scores on individual clinical scales have been identified for adolescents (Hathaway & Monachesi, 1963; Marks, Seeman, & Haller, 1974), normal college students (Black, 1953; Graham & McCord, 1985), student nurses (Hovey,

1953), normal Air Force officers (Block & Bailey, 1955; Gough, McKee, & Yandell, 1955), medical patients (Guthrie, 1949), and psychiatric patients (Boerger, Graham, & Lilly, 1974; Hedlund, 1977). Correlates for configurations of two or more MMPI scales were reported for normal adults (Hathaway & Meehl, 1952), normal college students (Black, 1953), medical patients (Guthrie, 1949), and psychiatric patients (Boerger, Graham, & Lilly, 1974; Gilberstadt & Duker, 1965; Gynther, Altman, & Sletten, 1973; Lewandowski & Graham, 1972; Marks, Seeman, & Haller, 1974; Meehl, 1951). The results of these numerous empirical studies are synthesized in Chapters 4 and 6 of this book and have been summarized previously by Dahlstrom, Welsh, & Dahlstrom (1972) and Greene (1980). Clinicians draw heavily on the results of these studies in making inferences about MMPI scores and configurations. These data suggest some consistent nontest correlates for MMPI scores and configurations, but they also indicate that exactly the same correlates may not always be found for subjects of differing demographic backgrounds.

A third category of studies considers the MMPI scores and the person interpreting them as an integral unit and examines the accuracy of inferences based on the MMPI. In an early study of this type, Little and Shneidman (1959) asked expert test interpreters to provide diagnoses, ratings, and descriptions of subjects from test data [MMPI, Rorschach, Thematic Apperception Test (TAT), and Make a Picture Story (MAPS)]. The accuracy of these judgments was determined by comparing them with judgments based on extensive case history data. The average correlations between judges' descriptions of subjects based on the MMPI, Rorschach, TAT, and MAPS were .28, .16, .17, and .11, respectively. Kostlan (1954) reported data suggesting that the MMPI leads to the most accurate inferences when it is used in conjunction with social case history data. Sines (1959) reported a mean correlation of .378 between judgments based on MMPI and interview data and criterion ratings provided by patients' therapists. In a study limited to MMPI data, Graham (1967) reported correlations between MMPI-based descriptions and criterion descriptions of .31, .37, and .29 for judges of high, medium, and low experience, respectively.

Reviewing clinical judgment research, of which the above cited studies are a part, Goldberg (1968) concluded that, in general, clinical judgments tend to be rather unreliable, only minimally related to the confidence and to the amount of experience of test judges, relatively unaffected by the amount of information available to judges, and rather low in validity on an absolute basis. In a more recent review of the clinical judgment literature, Garb (1984) was more optimistic, concluding that adding MMPI data to demographic information led to increases in validity of inferences. Graham and Lilly (1984) pointed out that compared with Rorschach and other projective techniques, personality descriptions based on the MMPI are relatively more accurate. Also, descriptions based on MMPI data are more accurate than descriptions based on judges' stereotypes of typical patients. When MMPI data are used in conjunction with social history and/or interview data, the resulting descriptions are more valid than when the MMPI data are used alone.

Although research data concerning validity of the MMPI are considerable, differences in subjects, settings, criterion measures, methodologies, and statistical analyses make it difficult to reach precise conclusions concerning the MMPI's validity. Almost all of the research data are concurrent rather than predictive in nature. However, existing data indicate that judgments, inferences, and decisions based on MMPI data are likely to be more accurate than judgments based on no assessment data or on projective data. Accuracy is likely to be enhanced greatly if MMPI data are used in conjunction with social history and interview data.

USE OF MMPI WITH SPECIAL GROUPS

The MMPI was developed for use with adult psychiatric patients. Its norms were based on white adult normals in cities and towns surrounding the University of Minnesota. Considerable caution is indicated when the test is used with subjects whose demographic characteristics are different from those of the standardization sample or when it is used in other than traditional psychiatric settings. This section will review briefly some information concerning the use of the MMPI with special groups.

Adolescents

Although the MMPI was developed for use with adults, it was administered to large groups of adolescents in Minnesota as early as 1947 (Hathaway & Monachesi, 1963). These early data and those of subsequent researchers (e.g., Ball, 1962; Baughman & Dahlstrom, 1968; Marks, Seeman, & Haller, 1974) indicated that on some MMPI scales normal adolescents obtain higher scores than the adult standardization sample. More specifically, mean profiles for groups of normal adolescents typically have T-scores of approximately 60 on the F scale and on scales 4, 8, and 9. In several samples the mean profiles also show moderate elevation on scale 7.

The meaning of these elevated scores is not clear. They could be suggestive of the turmoil and instability that some believe even normal adolescents experience. They could be indicative of more frequent psychopathology in adolescents, although this may be unlikely, given the results of studies that have found only a slightly higher prevalence rate of psychiatric disorders in adolescence compared with middle childhood (e.g., Rutter, Graham, Chadwick, & Yule, 1976). They could result from experiences that are unique to adolescent subjects but which are not particularly disturbing nor pathological but part of normal adolescent development. They could be due, at least in part, to differences in sampling and administration procedures in the adult and adolescent studies. However, it is clear that these differences between normal adult and normal adolescent scores create some problems when we try to interpret the profiles of adolescent subjects.

Ehrenworth and Archer (1985) reported that adolescent psychiatric patients produce different code types depending on whether adult or adolescent norms are used. Only 25 percent of the adolescent patients had the same two-point code for both adult and adolescent norms. When adult norms are used with adolescent patients, psychotic code types are much more likely to emerge than when adolescent norms are used (Chase, Chaffin, & Morrison, 1975; Ehrenworth, 1984).

Given that differences exist in scores and code types depending on which norms are used for adolescents, which norms lead to the most accurate judgments and inferences about adolescents? Both Archer (in press) and Williams (1986) concluded that adolescent norms are more appropriate than adult norms for adolescent subjects. For example, Ehrenworth (1984) found that adolescent norms led to a lower false positive rate for psychotic diagnoses for adolescent patients. Moore and Handal (1980) found that clinical scale elevations obtained when MMPIs of normal adolescents were scored on adult norms were not accompanied by indications of pathology on the Affect checklist. Newmark, Gentry, and Whitt (1983) indicated that MMPIs scored on adult norms were not very effective in identifying schizophrenia in adolescents. Archer, Ball, and Hunter (1985) found that adolescent MMPIs scored on adolescent norms were useful in identifying borderline personality disorders in an inpatient psychiatric sample.

Another important issue in the use of the MMPI with adolescents centers on the source of descriptors to be used in generating inferences about profiles, whether they result from adolescent or adult norms. Should one use adult descriptors, such as those reported in other chapters of this book, or should one use descriptors developed specifically for adolescents? Marks, Seeman, and Haller (1974) determined empirical correlates of two-point codes for adolescent psychiatric patients. These correlates were based on a sample of adolescents who were literate, white, 12 to 18 years old, living with natural or adoptive parents, did not have organic brain syndrome, but who did have emotional problems and were in treatment for them. Although Marks and his colleagues are to be commended for conducting the only adequate research to date concerning empirical correlates of adolescent code types, there has not been subsequent research to try to replicate the findings and to determine whether they are generalizable to other kinds of clinical settings. Therefore, at this time it is not known to what extent the correlates apply to subjects different from those studied by Marks et al. (e.g., a black adolescent living in a group home for runaways).

Several studies have addressed the issue of whether adolescent profiles should be interpreted using descriptors based on adults or those based on adolescents. Lachar, Klinge, and Grisell (1976) found that computer interpretations generated from adolescent norms and adult-based descriptors were more accurate than those generated from adult norms and adult-based descriptors. However, these investigators did not examine the accuracy of descriptions generated from adolescent norms and adolescent-based descriptors. Ehrenworth and Archer (1985) examined the accuracy of interpretations of adolescent MMPIs under three conditions: adult norms and adult-based descriptors; adolescent norms and adolescent-based descriptors; and adolescent norms and adult-based descriptors. Accuracy of interpretations were rated by therapists of the adolescent inpatients. Although accuracy for all conditions was less than the investigators had expected, the interpretations generated from adolescent norms and adolescent-based descriptors were less accurate than in the other conditions. Wimbish (1984) reached a different conclusion about this matter. Her data indicated that the most accurate inferences about adolescent subjects came from the use of adolescent norms and adolescent-based descriptors.

Archer (in press) has suggested that a "common-sense compromise" appears to be most appropriate in interpreting profiles of adolescent subjects. He recommended using adolescent norms to convert raw scores to T-scores and subsequently interpreting the resulting profiles by combining information from both adolescent samples (e.g., Marks, Seeman, & Haller, 1974) and adult samples (e.g., Graham, 1977b; Lachar, 1974a). Although this compromise has much to recommend it, the clinician is still in a difficult position when the adolescent and adult descriptors lead to significantly different impressions of adolescent subjects. In these circumstances, other data sources (interview, history, observations, etc.) must be utilized in determining which kinds of descriptors are likely to be most accurate for a given subject.

Clearly, several kinds of additional research are needed. First, more up-to-date and representative normative data are needed for adolescent subjects. The adolescent norms presented in Dahlstrom et al. (1972), utilized by Marks et al. (1974), and reprinted in Appendix C of this book are limited. Some of the data were collected by Hathaway in Minnesota as early as 1947. All of the subjects were in the ninth grade, which makes the older and younger ones atypical. The Hathaway data were supplemented by data collected by Briggs in 1964 and 1965 in Alabama, California, Kansas, Missouri, North Carolina, and Ohio. There are serious reservations about how representative the samples are. We know that they included almost exclusively white subjects. Clearly, there is a pressing need for new normative data based on census representative samples of adolescents. The publisher of the MMPI, the University of Minnesota Press, is sponsoring collection of such data. Another pressing need is for more empirical research to establish empirical correlates of scores and configurations for adolescent subjects. Replication and extension of the Marks et al. study would be very helpful.

There are some practical suggestions that can be made concerning the use of the MMPI with adolescents. Archer (in press) and Williams (1986) have offered practical advise for those who use the MMPI with adolescents. Williams suggested that in addition to the adolescent's reading level, his or her developmental level must also be considered. A fifth- or sixth-grade reading level is needed, and Williams suggested screening for reading problems prior to administering the MMPI. The adolescent must be willing to stick to the task of answering the items, and he or she must have a wide enough range of experience to make the content of the items psychologically and semantically meaningful. In deciding to administer the MMPI to an adolescent, the examiner must decide if the task is appropriate to his or her cognitive, social, and emotional stage of development.

Once the MMPI is administered to adolescents and the raw scores are determined, two profiles should be plotted, one for adult norms and one for adolescent norms. The adult profile can be plotted on a standard MMPI answer sheet. To plot an adolescent profile the examiner must consult adolescent norm tables, such as those found in Appendix C of this book. Separate tables are available for male and female subjects between the ages of 14 and below and 17 and 18. The appropriate tables are entered using raw scores that are *not K-corrected.* T-scores are then plotted on a standard profile sheet. It may be helpful to plot both profiles for a subject on a single profile sheet.

For some adolescent subjects the profiles based on the two kinds of normative data will be quite similar and will yield the same code type. For others there will be significant differences in the two profile types. Typically, the adult norms will yield scores for adolescents that make them appear to be more psychopathological than when the adolescent norms are used. As stated earlier, it often is difficult to decide which profile better reflects the adolescent's adjustment level. A good rule of thumb is that in nonclinical settings, where the MMPI is being used for screening purposes, the profile based on adult norms is likely to lead to overestimates of psychopathology. However, in clinical settings, where subjects are known to have significant psychopathology, the adult norms may more accurately reflect the level of pathology. Often, when MMPI scores of very disturbed adolescents are plotted on adolescent norms, the resulting profiles fall within "normal limits." Archer (in press) recommended that if adolescent norms are used clinicians should interpret scores below 70 as clinically significant. He suggested a cutoff score of $T > 65$ in these instances.

The next step is to identify the two-point code for each profile. Marks et al. (1974) suggested that if an adolescent's code type does not appear in their book the third highest score should be used instead of the second highest score to define a two-point code. For the adult profile, procedures for defining code types described in Chapter 6 of this book should be used. Consider both the adolescent-based and adult-based descriptors. Descriptors that are congruent for both profiles for the subject should be accepted with some confidence. Descriptors that are not consistent for the two profiles should be viewed more cautiously, and reference to data other than the MMPI profile may help to make decisions between incongruent descriptors. Williams (1986) provided suggestions for learning more about adolescent clients by discussing their MMPI interpretations with them.

Except for the MacAndrew Alcoholism (MAC) scale, no adolescent normative or interpretive data are available for MMPI supplementary scales, so they should not be used. Available data suggest that the MAC can be interpreted for adolescents similarly to how it is interpreted for adults (Wisniewski, Glenwick, & Graham, 1985; Wolfson & Erbaugh, 1984; refer to Chapter 8).

Blacks

Because the standardization sample did not include any black subjects, much has been said and written about the appropriateness of using the MMPI with black subjects. There appear to be two important questions that we can try to answer concerning the use of the MMPI with black subjects. First, do black and white subjects respond differently to MMPI items? Second, to the extent that differences in responding occur, how are they to be interpreted?

Most studies that have compared mean T-scores for groups of black and white subjects have found significant differences on some of the MMPI scales. Greene (1980), Gynther and Green (1980), and Pritchard and Rosenblatt (1980) reviewed numerous studies that compared means for black and white samples. The general finding was that, when differences are found, blacks tend to score higher than whites on scales F, 8, and 9. Differences between blacks and whites on these scales tend to be approximately 5 T-score points (1 or 2 raw points). When black and white groups are comparable on age, education, and other demographic characteristics, the differences are smaller and often not significant (Dahlstrom, Lachar, & Dahlstrom, 1986).

Differing interpretations of these mean differences have been offered. Greene (1980) concluded that the small differences between blacks and whites probably are of very limited clinical significance. Gynther and Green (1980) suggested that these differences mean that normal blacks are more likely than normal whites to be incorrectly identified as being abnormal. Pritchard and Rosenblatt (1980) maintained that the meaning of these differences cannot be determined in most studies. One cannot assume that the higher scores for blacks mean that the MMPI is biased against black subjects. The higher scores for blacks could mean that the blacks have more psychopathology than the whites. Unfortunately, most studies have not included reliable and unbiased measures of psychopathology for black or white subjects.

Pritchard and Rosenblatt suggested that the only meaningful way of analyzing racial differences on the MMPI is to use what they call the "accuracy test." This approach involves determining if inferences made from MMPI scores are differentially accurate for different racial groups. Pritchard and Rosenblatt noted the lack of well-designed studies that address the accuracy test. Butcher, Braswell, and Raney (1983) reported that MMPI differences between black and white psychiatric inpatients were meaningfully associated with actual symptomatic differences between the groups. Dahlstrom, Lachar, and Dahlstrom (1986) reported analyses suggesting that MMPI scores based on the standard test norms were not differentially related to psychopathology for black and white psychiatric patients. Additionally, Dahlstrom et al. reported that the use of special norms based exclusively on black subjects overcorrected deviations and failed to identify many black subjects who had serious emotional problems and were in need of professional intervention.

In summary, it would appear that groups of black subjects often obtain slightly higher scores on some MMPI scales. Although the meaning of these differences is not completely clear at this time, there are data suggesting that the differences are related to important differences in personality and behavior and cannot be attributed simply to test bias. Dahlstrom et al. (1986) suggested that the more elevated MMPI scores of black subjects, especially young males, may be reflecting the various coping and defense mechanisms to which some minority subjects may resort in their efforts to deal with the special circumstances that they all too often encounter in America today. Dahlstrom et al. made some very reasonable recommendations concerning the interpretation of MMPIs from black subjects. They felt that the best procedure is to accept the pattern of MMPI scores that results from the use of the standard profile sheet and, when the profile is markedly deviant, to take special pains to explore in detail the life circumstances of the test subject to understand as fully as possible the nature and degree of his or her problems and demands. Special attention should be given to the adequacy of the subject's efforts to deal with what are too often extremely difficult life circumstances.

Special comment is necessary concerning the use of the MacAndrew Alcoholism (MAC) scale with black subjects. As indicated in Chapter 8, where the MAC is discussed in some detail, several studies have suggested caution in using the MAC with black subjects (Graham & Mayo, 1985; Walters, Greene, & Jeffrey, 1984; Walters, Green, Jeffrey, Kruzich, & Haskin, 1983). Black alcoholics tend to obtain relatively high scores on the MAC, but classification rates for black subjects are not very good because nonalcoholic black psychiatric patients also tend to obtain rather high MAC scores.

Other Ethnic Groups

There are few empirical studies concerning MMPI performances of ethnic subjects other than blacks. Greene (in press) identified only 10 studies comparing Hispanic and white subjects on the MMPI. Although there were some significant differences between Hispanic and white subjects in these studies, Greene concluded that there was no pattern to the differences. The data did not support Greene's earlier contention (Greene, 1980) that Hispanics frequently score higher on the L scale and lower on scale 5. It also appeared that there were fewer differences between Hispanics and whites on the MMPI than between black and white subjects.

Greene (in press) identified only seven studies that compared MMPI performance of American Indians and whites. Although the American Indians tended to score higher than whites on some clinical scales, there was no clear pattern to these differences across the studies. Uecker, Boutilier, and Richardson (1980) reported no differences between American Indian and white alcoholics on the MacAndrew Alcoholism scale (MAC). However, these results are difficult to interpret because no data were presented for nonalcoholic American Indians and whites on the MAC.

Greene (in press) reported only three studies comparing MMPI performance of Asian-American and white subjects. Sue and Sue (1974) reported that male Asian-American college student counselees obtained higher scores than white counselees on most of the MMPI scales. However, other studies of Asian-Americans, which utilized normal persons and medical patients as subjects, reported many fewer differences between Asian-Americans and whites. In summary, little is known about using the MMPI with Asian-American subjects, and clinicians should be cautious when the test is used with such subjects.

Medical Patients

The MMPI is being used increasingly often in medical settings. Osborne (1979) and Henrichs (1981) presented overviews of the use of the MMPI in such settings. Swenson, Pearson, and Osborne (1973) reported item, scale, and pattern data for 50,000 medical patients at the Mayo Clinic. Swenson, Rome, Pearson, and Brannick (1965) reported data indicating that most medical patients (89.2%) readily agreed to take the MMPI and completed and returned the test booklet. Swenson et al. (1965) also surveyed 158 physicians who had used the MMPI routinely for at least four months. For all 14 items on the questionnaire, 70 to 85 percent of the physicians indicated that the MMPI was useful with their patients.

It will not be possible in this chapter to review even briefly the voluminous research literature concerning the relationship between MMPI data and characteristics of medical patients. Rather, an attempt will be made to indicate the general purposes for which the MMPI can be used in medical settings.

One important use of the MMPI with medical patients is to screen for serious psychopathology that might be present but that has not been reported or that has been minimized by patients. The indicators of serious psychopathology discussed elsewhere in this book (e.g., F scale level; overall profile elevation; profile slope) should be considered when examining the profiles of medical patients.

Many clinicians seem to assume that medical problems are going to be upsetting to patients and that this upset will be reflected in very deviant scores on the MMPI. It is important to develop some expectations concerning typical MMPI scores and profiles produced by medical patients. Swenson, Pearson, and Osborne (1973) reported summary MMPI data for approximately 25,000 male and 25,000 female patients at the Mayo Clinic. Figure 5.1 summarizes these data. Note that for both male and female patients all scores are basically within normal limits. The validity scales suggest a slightly defensive test-taking attitude. T-scores on scales 1, 2, and 3 are near 60. Apparently, the medical

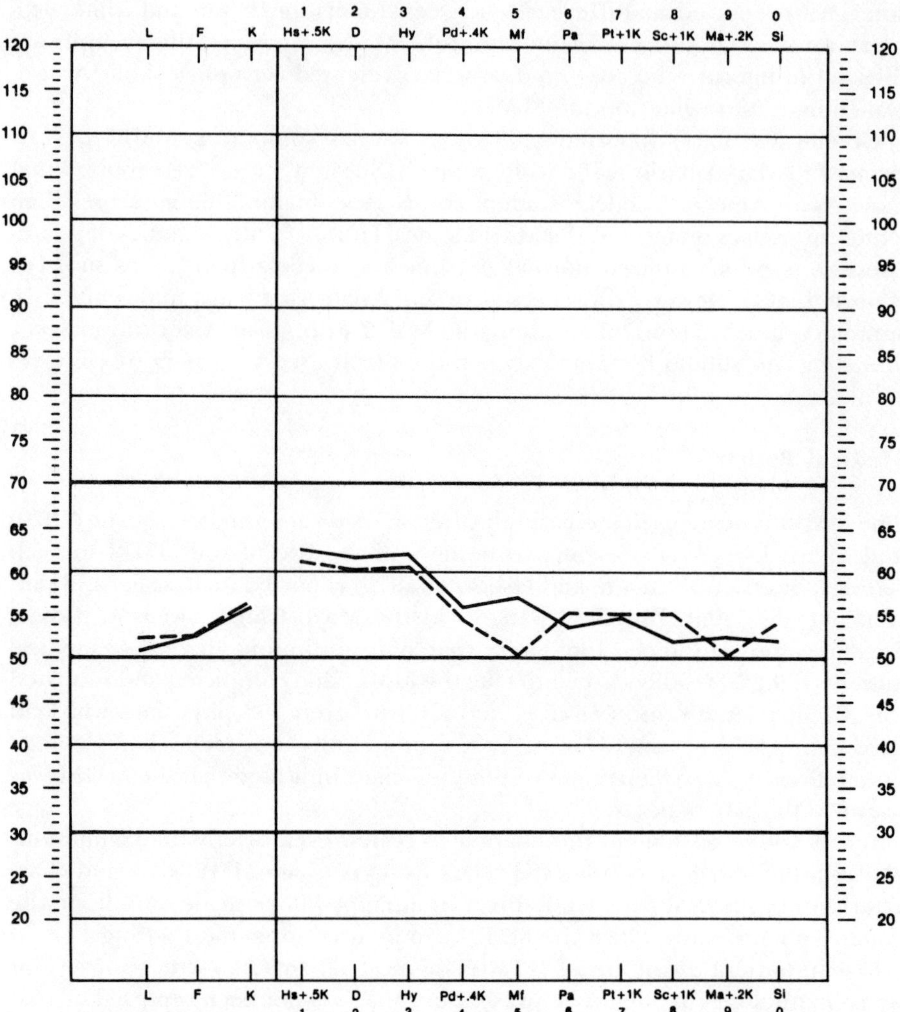

Fig. 5.1. K-corrected mean profiles for 25,723 male (——) and 24,277 female (----) medical patients. (Based on data from W. M. Swenson, J. S. Pearson, & D. Osborne, *An MMPI Source Book: Basic Item, Scale, and Pattern Data on 50,000 Medical Patients.* The University of Minnesota Press, Minneapolis. Copyright 1973 by the University of Minnesota. Data used with permission.)

problems of these patients were not psychologically distressing enough to lead to grossly elevated MMPI scale scores.

The MMPI can be useful in alerting clinicians to the possibility of substance abuse problems among medical patients. Some patients develop physical symptoms because of chronic substance abuse; some patients develop substance abuse problems because of their medical problems; and some patients have substance abuse problems that are not directly related to their physical symptoms. Regardless of the relationship between substance abuse problems and medical problems, early awareness of the substance abuse problems facilitates treatment planning.

There is not a single pattern of MMPI scales associated with substance abuse problems. However, there is convincing evidence that scale 4 typically is elevated among groups of persons who abuse substances. Scale 4 typically is not significantly elevated among medical patient groups. Thus, when a person is presenting primarily physical symptoms in a medical setting and has significant scale 4 elevation, the possibility of some abuse of substances should be considered carefully.

Fordyce (1979) suggested that chronic pain patients can easily become addicted to narcotics, barbiturates, or muscle relaxants. He reported that such persons often obtain elevations on scales 2 and 9. When both of these scales are elevated above T = 70, the possibility of addiction to prescription medications should be considered.

The 24/42 two-point code type is the most typical pattern found among male alcoholics in treatment, and the 46/64 code type is the most common one for female alcoholics in treatment. Neither of these code types is very common among medical patients who do not abuse alcohol. Thus, when these code types are encountered in medical patients (particularly when the scores are greater than T = 70), the possibility of alcohol abuse should be explored carefully.

In Chapter 8, the MacAndrew Alcoholism scale (MAC) will be considered in some detail. Although this scale was developed by comparing item responses of male alcoholic outpatients and male psychiatric outpatients, subsequent research has indicated that the scale is a very useful one for identifying substance abuse problems of various kinds for men and women in a variety of settings. If significant elevation is found on the MAC for patients in a medical setting, careful consideration should be given to the possibility that the person is abusing substances. As discussed in Chapter 8, MAC raw scores of 28 or above strongly suggest substance abuse. Scores between 24 and 27 are somewhat suggestive of such abuse. Scores below 24 strongly contraindicate a substance abuse problem. It should be emphasized that research concerning the MAC has emphasized abuse of alcohol and other nonprescribed drugs. Little is known about the extent to which the MAC is sensitive to the abuse of prescribed drugs, such as those used by chronic pain patients.

The MMPI often has been used to try to determine if the physical symptoms presented by patients are organic or functional in origin. It is never appropriate to use the MMPI alone to diagnose an organic condition or to rule out such a condition. The most that the MMPI can do is to give some information concerning the underlying personality characteristics of the patient. This information can then be used, along with all other available information, to make inferences concerning the compatibility of the personality characteristics and a functional explanation of symptoms.

Osborne (1979) summarized studies that have tried to determine if patients' symptoms are functional or organic. The symptoms studied have included low back pain, sexual impotence, neurologic-like complaints, and others. In general, the research has indicated that patients with symptoms that are exclusively or primarily psychological in origin tend to score higher on scales 1, 2, and 3 than patients with similar symptoms that are organic in origin. Particularly common among groups of patients with symptoms of psychological origin is the 13/31 two-point code. When this code type is found and when scales 1 and 3 are elevated above T = 70 and are considerably higher than scale 2, the likelihood of functional origin increases. However, Osborne pointed out that the differences between functional and organic groups typically have been small enough that prediction from the MMPI alone is not very accurate.

Several MMPI supplementary scales have been developed specifically to try to determine if physical symptoms are of functional or organic origin. Although none of these scales should be used alone in making this differentiation, two of the most commonly used scales will be discussed briefly.

The Low Back Pain (Lb) scale (Hanvik, 1949, 1951) is discussed in detail in Chapter 8. It was developed to differentiate between patients with chronic low back pain but with no evidence of organic disease and patients with similar pain but with clear evidence of organic disease. The scale is scored in such a way that higher scores are thought to be more indicative of functional problems. Hanvik suggested that a raw score cutoff of 11 be used to discriminate between patients with functional versus organic low back pain. Subsequent research has indicated that differences between functional and organic groups are so small that scores on the scale alone are not particularly effective in differentiating the groups. However, when patients are presenting low back pain in the absence of clear organic basis for the complaints, an elevation on the Lb scale can be considered as one bit of information, to be added to other information, in trying to understand the etiology of the complaints.

The Caudality (Ca) scale also is described in some detail in Chapter 8. It was developed to differentiate between patients with frontal lobe and parietal lobe brain damage (Williams, 1952). The scale is scored in such a way that higher scores are thought to be suggestive of nonfrontal damage. The Ca scale is of no utility whatsoever in screening for the presence of organic brain pathology. However, when there already is clear evidence of organic pathology, the Ca scale may be helpful in understanding behaviors and emotions associated with various kinds of organic brain damage. Brain-damaged persons who are scoring higher on the Ca scale are indicating that they feel anxious and depressed, that they worry excessively, that they are socially extroverted, that they are having problems in controlling emotional expression, and that they fear that they are losing control of their thought processes.

The MMPI has been used to understand how persons with medical problems of clearly organic origin are affected psychologically by the physical problems (Osborne, 1979). When used for this purpose, the clinician should use traditional MMPI indicators of emotional disturbance. For example, significant elevation on scale 2 suggests that the medical patient is experiencing dysphoria/depression, and elevated scores on scale 7 and/or Welsh's Anxiety scale would indicate that the medical patient is anxious, worried, and tense. Empirically determined correlates of various MMPI code types for patients of an internist were given by Guthrie (1949), and Henrichs (1981) provided a useful summary table describing characteristics associated with MMPI profile patterns of medical patients.

The MMPI also can provide important information concerning how medical patients are likely to respond psychologically to medical interventions. Several examples can be given to illustrate this potential use. Henrichs and Waters (1972) investigated the extent to which MMPIs administered preoperatively to cardiac patients could predict emotional or behavioral reactions to the surgery. Based on prior literature concerning cardiac patients, five types were conceptualized and rules for classifying MMPI profiles into these types were developed. The rules were able to classify 97 percent of MMPIs given to patients preoperatively. Postoperative course was recorded for all patients to determine if they had behavioral or emotional problems. The occurrence of such postoperative problems was significantly different for the different MMPI types. Only 6 percent of patients who were in the well-adjusted MMPI type preoperatively had postoperative emotional or behavioral problems. By contrast, 44 percent of persons having seriously disturbed preoperative MMPIs had postoperative behavioral or emotional problems. Henrichs and Waters pointed out that different types of preoperative interventions could be developed to address anticipated postoperative problems.

Sobel and Worden (1979) demonstrated that the MMPI was useful in predicting psychosocial adjustment of patients who had been diagnosed as having cancer. The MMPI typically was administered following cancer surgery, and patients were studied for six months following this intervention. Patients were classified as having high distress or low distress at follow-up on the basis of multiple measures of emotional turmoil, physical symptoms, and effectiveness of coping with the demands of patients' life situations. Using multiple regression analyses of MMPI scores, 75 percent of patients were correctly classified as having high distress or low distress. The authors pointed out that interventions could be developed to assist cancer patients who are considered to be high-risk for psychosocial problems.

A general finding in the literature seems to be that persons who are well adjusted emotionally before they develop serious medical problems and/or before they are treated for such problems seem to handle the illness-related stress better than persons who are emotionally less well adjusted. Additionally, better adjusted persons seem to have better postoperative courses than do less well adjusted persons. However, not all studies have found positive relationships between MMPI results and response to medical interventions. Although the MMPI seems to have a great deal of potential in predicting response to medical interventions, there is a need for additional rigorous research to establish more clearly the extent to which the MMPI can and should be used for this purpose.

Correctional Subjects

Dahlstrom, Welsh, and Dahlstrom (1975) briefly reviewed the major ways in which the MMPI is used with correctional subjects and presented lists of references concerning the use of the MMPI with these subjects. Dahlstrom et al. indicated that the MMPI profiles of prisoners are remarkably homogeneous. Numerous studies have documented that scale 4 usually is the most elevated scale in mean profiles of groups of prisoners. The 4-2 and 4-9 profiles are the most frequently occurring two-point codes for prisoners.

A major use of the MMPI in correctional settings is to classify prisoners. Accurate classification permits correctional administrators to make more efficient use of limited resources and to avoid providing resources for offenders who do not require them. Early work by Panton and his associates in North Carolina (e.g., Panton, 1958) and by Fox and his associates in California (e.g., Fox, Gould, & André, 1965) indicated moderate success in using the MMPI to classify prisoners in meaningful ways when they entered the correctional system.

A comprehensive and useful system of classifying criminal offenders based on the MMPI was developed by Megargee and his associates (Megargee, Bohn, Meyer, & Sink, 1979). These investigators used hierarchical profile analysis to identify clusters among the MMPIs of offenders. Classification rules were developed for placing offenders into the groups defined by the cluster analyses. Following some use of the system with other samples of offenders, the original classification rules were refined and expanded.

The resulting classification system involves 10 types of offender MMPIs and explicit rules for classifying offenders into the type to which they are most similar. Megargee (1979) reported that in a variety of correctional settings mechanical application of the rules classifies about two thirds of offender profiles. Most of the remaining one third of the profiles can be classified by clinicians using published guidelines and additional data. Overall, 85 to 95 percent of offender profiles can be classified using rules for the 10 profile types. Although the derivational work for the Megargee system took place in a federal facility and involved primarily young, male offenders, subsequent data indicated that the classification system also works well in other settings (e.g., state prisons, county jails) and with other kinds of offenders (e.g., women, older persons) (Megargee, 1979).

If a classification system for offender MMPIs is to be useful, the groups identified using the system must differ from each other on important non-MMPI variables. Accumulating data suggest that there are important non-MMPI differences between the groups in the Megargee system. Megargee et al. (1979) found significant differences between the Megargee types on demographic characteristics, criminal behavior patterns, rated personality characteristics, measures of institutional adjustment (including frequency of disciplinary infractions, incidence of reports to sick call, interpersonal relations, and work performance), and recidivism rates. It is not possible to describe in this book the rules for classifying profiles in the Megargee system or to discuss the important ways in which the Megargee types differ from each other. The interested reader should consult the book by Megargee et al. (1979) for more information.

In summary, although high scale 4 scores are extremely common among offenders, there are important differences in other aspects of their MMPI profiles. These MMPI differences can be very useful in understanding offenders and making important decisions about them.

Subjects in Nonclinical Settings

The MMPI was developed in a psychiatric hospital setting, and most of the research done with the instrument has been with subjects in clinical settings. However, the use of the MMPI with nonclinical subjects is increasing dramatically (Graham & McCord, 1985). The most obvious nonclinical use of the MMPI is in the selection of persons for jobs or for training programs. The MMPI has been used in two basic ways in relation to selection of employees or students (Butcher, 1979, 1985b). First, the test has been used to screen for psychopathology among applicants. Second, the MMPI has been used to try to predict quality of job performance by matching individuals with certain personal characteristics to jobs or positions that are believed to require such characteristics.

Using the MMPI to screen for psychopathology among applicants is most justified when individuals are being considered for employment in occupations involving susceptibility to occupational stress, personal risk, and personal responsibility. Such sensitive occupations include air traffic controller, airline pilot, police officer, and nuclear power plant operator. Routine use of the MMPI for personnel selection is not recommended. For many jobs the primary requirements for the job are appropriate training and ability, and personality factors may be unimportant or irrelevant.

Research data are accumulating suggesting that the MMPI can be used effectively to screen for psychopathology in normal groups. Lachar (1974c) demonstrated that the MMPI could predict serious psychopathology leading to dropouts among Air Force Academy cadets. Strupp and Bloxom (1975) found that men with certain MMPI code types were likely to have difficulty with personal adjustment, graduating from college, finding a job, and deciding on a career.

There also are data suggesting that the MMPI can be used to predict effective hotline workers (Evans, 1977), competent clergymen (Jansen & Garvey, 1973), and successful businessmen (Harrell & Harrell, 1973). The success of police applicant selection is well documented (e.g., Bernstein, 1980; Costello, Schoenfeld, & Kobos, 1982). The MMPI also has been used successfully in selecting physicians' assistants (Crovitz, Huse, & Lewis, 1973), medical assistants (Stone, Basset, Brosseau, Demers, & Stiening, 1972), psychiatric residents (Garetz & Anderson, 1973), clinical psychology graduate students

(Butcher, 1979), nurses (Kelly, 1974), fire fighters (Avery, Mussio, & Payne, 1972), probation officers (Solway, Hays, & Zieben, 1976), and nuclear power plant personnel (Dunnette, Bownas, & Bosshardt, 1981). In virtually all of these studies the most useful way to use the MMPI has been to exclude persons with very elevated scales on one or more of the clinical scales.

There is far less information available about using the MMPI to match persons with certain personality characteristics with jobs requiring those characteristics. There are several problems with using the MMPI in this manner. First, there is only limited information concerning the personality characteristics of normal persons with particular MMPI scores and profiles. Graham and McCord (1985) suggested a strategy for generating inferences about personality characteristics of normal persons who do not have extremely elevated MMPI scores. For such persons clinicians are advised to use the descriptive information that has been generated for clinical subjects but to eliminate those inferences that deal with serious psychopathology. For example, a normal person with a 68 two-point code and no T-scores above 70 might be described as suspicious and distrustful of others, as deficient in social skills, and as avoiding deep emotional ties. However, a normal person with this kind of profile would not be seen as having confused thinking, delusions, or hallucinations. Although Graham and McCord presented some data indicating that this approach is justified, much more research data are needed before it can be recommended that such interpretations should be made on a routine basis. Another problem in using the MMPI to match persons with certain personality characteristics with jobs requiring such characteristics is that for most jobs there is not a clear understanding of the kinds of personality characteristics associated with successful performance.

There are several important considerations in using the MMPI for personnel selection purposes. It has been suggested that requiring applicants for jobs to complete the MMPI is an invasion of privacy (Brayfield, 1965). Many persons feel that items dealing with sex, religious beliefs, family relationships, or bowel and bladder functioning are inappropriate for job applicants because there is not likely to be any relationship between these items and job success (Butcher & Tellegen, 1966). It can be argued that such an invasion of privacy is justified when evaluating applicants for psychologically sensitive or stress-vulnerable occupations. Applicants are less likely to object to the content of test items if they are given an explanation of how the items were selected and why they are included in the MMPI.

Because job applicants understandably are motivated to present themselves in the best possible light, they frequently produce defensive MMPI profiles (Butcher, 1979). If a profile is considered to be invalid because of defensiveness, the profile should not be interpreted, and the applicant should be evaluated by other means (e.g., interview). Butcher (1985a) suggested some guidelines for interpreting defensive profiles that are not considered to be invalid. If there are T-scores above 70 on any of the clinical scales, the elevations probably accurately reflect important problems, because they were obtained when the person was presenting a very favorable view of himself/herself. Since the person was trying to present an overly favorable view of himself/herself, T-scores in the 65 to 70 range on the clinical scales should also be interpreted as indicating significant problems. If all clinical scale T-scores are below 65, the profile will not provide much useful information about the person. It is not possible to determine if such a profile indicates a person who is not functioning very well and is being defensive or if it indicates a person who is functioning within normal limits.

6

Profile Configurations

From the MMPI's inception, Hathaway and McKinley made clear that *configural* interpretation of an examinee's scores was diagnostically richer and thus more useful than was an interpretation that utilized examination of single scales without regard for relationships among the scales. Meehl (1951), Meehl and Dahlstrom (1960), Taulbee and Sisson (1957), and others also stressed configural approaches to MMPI interpretation. Thus, some of the earliest MMPI validity studies (e.g., Black, 1953; Guthrie, 1952; Meehl, 1951) grouped profiles according to the two highest clinical scales in the profile and tried to identify reliable extratest behaviors that were uniquely related to each such profile type. Other investigators (e.g., Gilberstadt & Duker, 1965; Marks & Seeman, 1963) developed complex rules for classifying profiles into homogeneous groups and tried to identify extratest correlates for each such group. For example, the following criteria must be met in order for a profile to be classified as a 4-9 type in the Gilberstadt and Duker system: (1) Pt and Ma greater than T-score 70; (2) no other scales greater than T-score 70; (3) L less than T-score 60; (4) Ma 15 or more T-scores greater than Sc; and (5) Pd 7 or more T-scores greater than Mf. Although clinicians initially were quite enthusiastic about this complex approach to profile classification, they became disenchanted as accumulating research and clinical evidence indicated that only a small proportion of the MMPI protocols encountered in a typical psychiatric setting could be classified using the complex types currently available (Fowler & Coyle, 1968; Huff, 1965; Meikle & Gerritse, 1970).

Currently, there seems to be a departure from interest in complex rules for classifying profiles and a resurgence of interest in the simpler two-scale approach to classification of MMPI profiles. Gynther and his colleagues (Gynther, Altman, & Sletten, 1973) and Lewandowski and Graham (1972) demonstrated that reliable extratest correlates can be identified for profiles that are classified according to their two highest clinical scales. An obvious advantage of the two-point code approach is that a large proportion of the

Sources consulted in preparing Chapter 6: Carson (1969); Dahlstrom, Welsh, & Dahlstrom (1972); Davis & Sines (1971); Drake & Oetting (1959); Duckworth & Duckworth (1975); Gilberstadt & Duker (1965); Good & Brantner (1961); Gynther, Altman, & Sletten (1973); Hovey & Lewis (1967); Lachar (1974a); Lewandowski & Graham (1972); Marks, Seeman, & Haller (1974); Persons & Marks (1971); Schubert (1973).

profiles encountered in most settings can be classified into a reasonably small number of two-point codes. Marks, Seeman, and Haller (1974), in their revision and extension of the earlier work by Marks and Seeman (1963), acknowledged that no appreciable loss in accuracy of extratest descriptions resulted when they used two-point codes instead of their more complex rules for classifying MMPI profiles.

This chapter presents interpretive data for some configurations of MMPI scales. As in the earlier chapters, the approach is to examine existing literature concerning extratest behavioral correlates for various configurations, to augment these data from the author's research and clinical experience, and to present a meaningful synthesis of all data. Although references are not cited for each descriptor presented, the sources consulted in preparing this chapter are listed on the chapter title page.

DEFINING CODE TYPES

Described very simply, code types are ways of classifying MMPI profiles that take into account more than a single clinical scale at a time. The simplest code types are high-points and low-points. A high-point code (e.g., high-point 2) simply tells us that the scale, in this example scale 2, is higher than any other clinical scale in the profile. The high-point code does not tell us anything about the absolute level of the highest scale. We simply know that, relative to other scales in the profile, this particular one is highest. A low-point code (e.g., low-point 7) simply tells us that the scale, in this example scale 7, is lower than any other clinical scale in the profile. Again, the low-point code does not tell us anything about the absolute level of the lowest scale. We simply know that, relative to other scales in the profile, this particular one is the lowest.

There can only be one high-point code or low-point code for any particular profile. In an earlier chapter, we defined high and low scores in terms of absolute T-score levels and not in relation to other scales in the profile. In this earlier conceptualization a subject could have several or more high or low scores. A careful examination of the MMPI literature suggests that basically the same general picture of high scoring or low scoring individuals emerges regardless of whether we are dealing with high or low scores or with high-point or low-point code types. Thus, no additional interpretive information will be presented in this chapter for high-point codes or low-point codes.

Two-point code types tell us which two clinical scales are the highest ones in the profile. Thus, a 27 two-point code tells us that scale 2 is the highest clinical scale in the profile and scale 7 is the second highest clinical scale in the profile. For most two-point codes the scales are interchangeable. For example, we often talk about code types such as 27/72, and we make basically the same interpretations for the 27 code as we do for the 72 code. When order of the scales in the two-point code makes a difference in interpretation, specific mention to that effect is made in the descriptive data for those particular codes in this chapter. As is true with high point codes, two-point codes tell us nothing about the absolute level of scores for the two scales in the code type. In general, the descriptors presented for a particular code type are more likely to fit a subject with that code type if the two scales in the code type are elevated above T = 70 and if the two scores are significantly higher than other clinical scales in the profile.

Three-point code types tell us which three clinical scales are the highest ones in the profile. For example, a 278 code type is one in which scale 2 is the highest in the profile, scale 7 is the second highest, and scale 8 is the third highest. For most three-point codes the order of scales is interchangeable. When order is important in terms of the interpretation of code types, specific mention to that effect is made when the descriptive data for those codes are presented in this chapter. Again, a three-point code tells us nothing about the absolute level of scores for the three scales in the code. As with two point codes, descriptors are more likely to find a particular subject with the three-point code when the three scales are elevated above T = 70 and are significantly higher than the rest of the clinical scales in the profile.

TWO-POINT CODE TYPES

If two-point codes are used interchangeably, there are 40 possible two-point combinations of the 10 clinical scales. The two-point codes included in this chapter are those that occur reasonably frequently in a variety of settings and for which an adequate amount of interpretive information is available in the literature.[1] The reader will note that few codes including scales 5 and 0 are presented in this chapter. The reason is that in many research studies with two-point codes, scales 5 and 0 have been excluded because these two scales were added after the original publication of the MMPI and thus were not available for some subjects in some of the early studies. The descriptions provided below represent *modal* patterns and obviously do not describe unfailingly each and every such person. For profiles that do not fit any of the two-point codes presented here, the clinician will have to rely on interpretation of high and low scores on individual scales (see Chapter 4).

12/21

The most prominent features of the 12/21 code are somatic discomfort and pain. Individuals with this code present themselves as physically ill, although

1. Although useful interpretive data concerning two-point codes for adolescents have been published by Marks et al. (1974), their data are not included in this chapter because their classification of profiles is not based on K-corrected scores and utilizes specialized adolescent norms. The reader who is interested in interpretive information for two-point codes for adolescents should consult their book.

there may be no clinical evidence of an organic basis for their symptoms. They are very concerned about health and bodily functions, and they are likely to overreact to minor physical dysfunction. They may present multiple somatic complaints, or the symptoms may be restricted to one particular system. Although headaches and cardiac complaints may occur, the digestive system is more likely to be involved. Ulcers, particularly of the upper gastrointestinal tract, are common, and anorexia, nausea, and vomiting may be present. Individuals with the 12/21 code also may complain of dizziness, insomnia, weakness, fatigue, and tiredness. They tend to react to stress, including responsibility, with physical symptoms, and they resist attempts to explain their symptoms in terms of emotional or psychological factors.

12/21 individuals are generally anxious, tense, and nervous. Also, they are high-strung and tend to worry about many things, and they tend to be restless and irritable. Although pronounced clinical depression is not common for persons with the 12/21 code, they do report feelings of unhappiness or dysphoria, brooding, and loss of initiative.

Persons with the 12/21 code report feeling very self-conscious. They are introverted and shy in social situations, particularly with members of the opposite sex, and they tend to be somewhat withdrawn and seclusive. They harbor many doubts about their own abilities, and they show vacillation and indecision about even minor, everyday matters. They are hypersensitive concerning what other people think about them, and they may be somewhat suspicious and untrusting in interpersonal relations. They also tend to be passive-dependent in their relationships, and they may harbor hostility toward people who are perceived as not offering enough attention and support.

Excessive use of alcohol may be a problem for 12/21 individuals, especially among psychiatric patients. Their histories may include blackouts, job loss, arrests, and family problems associated with alcohol abuse. Persons with the 12/21 code most often are given diagnoses of anxiety disorder, depressive disorder, or somatoform disorder, although a small proportion of individuals with this code may be diagnosed as schizophrenic. In this latter group (schizophrenic), scale 8 usually also is elevated along with scales 1 and 2.

Individuals with the 12/21 code are not seen as good risks for traditional psychotherapy. They can tolerate high levels of discomfort before becoming motivated to change. They utilize repression and somatization excessively, and they lack insight and self-understanding. In addition, their passive-dependent life-styles make it difficult for them to accept responsibility for their own behavior. Although long-term change after psychotherapy is not very likely, short-lived symptomatic changes often occur.

13/31

The 13/31 code is more common among women and older persons than among men and younger persons. Psychiatric patients with the 13/31 code usually receive a somatoform disorder diagnosis. Classical conversion symptoms may be present, particularly if scale 2 is considerably lower than scales 1 and 3 (i.e., the so-called conversion V pattern). Whereas some tension may be reported by 13/31 persons, severe anxiety and depression usually are absent, as are clearly psychotic symptoms. Rather than being grossly incapacitated in functioning, the 13/31 individual is likely to continue functioning but at a reduced level of efficiency.

The somatic complaints presented by 13/31 persons include headaches, chest pain, back pain, and numbness or tremors of the extremities. Eating problems, including anorexia, nausea, vomiting, and obesity, are common. Other physical complaints include weakness, fatigue, dizziness, and sleep disturbance. The physical symptoms increase in times of stress, and often there is clear secondary gain associated with the symptoms.

Individuals with the 13/31 code present themselves as normal, responsible, and without fault. They make excessive use of denial, projection, and rationalization, and they blame others for their difficulties. They prefer medical explanations for their symptoms, and they lack insight into psychological factors underlying their symptoms. They manifest an overly optimistic and Pollyannaish view of their situations and of the world in general, and they do not show appropriate concern about their symptoms and problems.

13/31 persons tend to be rather immature, egocentric, and selfish. They are insecure and have a strong need for attention, affection, and sympathy. They are very dependent, but they are uncomfortable with the dependency and experience conflict because of it. Although they are outgoing and socially extroverted, their social relationships tend to be shallow and superficial, and they lack genuine emotional involvement with other people. They tend to exploit social relationships in an attempt to fulfill their own needs. They lack skills in dealing with the opposite sex, and they may be deficient in heterosexual drive.

13/31 individuals harbor resentment and hostility toward other people, particularly those who are perceived as not fulfilling their needs for attention. Most of the time they are overcontrolled and likely to express their negative feelings in indirect, passive ways, but they occasionally lose their tempers and express themselves in angry, but not violent, ways. Behaving in a socially acceptable manner is important to 13/31 persons. They need to convince other people that they are logical and reasonable, and they are conventional and conforming in their attitudes and values.

Because of their unwillingness to acknowledge psychological factors underlying their symptoms, 13/31 persons are difficult to motivate in traditional psychotherapy. They expect the psychotherapist to provide definite answers and solutions to their problems, and they may terminate psychotherapy prematurely when the therapist fails to respond to their demands.

14/41

The 14/41 code is not encountered frequently in clinical practice and is much more likely to be found for males than for females. Persons with the 14/41 code frequently report severe hypochondriacal symptoms, particularly nonspecific headaches. They also may appear to be indecisive and anxious. Although they are socially extroverted, they lack skills with members of the opposite sex. They may feel rebellious toward home and parents, but direct expression of these feelings is not likely. Excessive use of alcohol may be a problem, and 14/41 persons may have a history of alcoholic benders, job loss, and family problems associated with their drinking behavior. In school or on the job, the 14/41 persons lack drive and do not have well-defined goals. They are dissatisfied and pessimistic in their outlook toward life, and they are demanding, grouchy, and referred to as bitchy in interpersonal relationships. Because they are likely to deny psychological problems, they tend to be resistant to traditional psychotherapy.

18/81

Persons with the 18/81 code harbor many feelings of hostility and aggression, and they are not able to express these feelings in a modulated, adaptive manner. Either they inhibit expression almost completely, which results in the feeling of being "bottled up," or they are overly belligerent and abrasive.

18/81 persons feel socially inadequate, especially around members of the opposite sex. They lack trust in other people, keep other people at a distance, and feel generally isolated and alienated. A nomadic life-style and a poor work history are common.

Psychiatric patients with the 18/81 code most often are diagnosed on strictly clinical criteria as schizophrenic, although diagnoses of anxiety disorder and schizoid personality are sometimes given to them. 18/81 individuals tend to be unhappy and depressed, and they may display flat affect. They present somatic concerns (including headaches and insomnia) which at times are so intense that they border on being delusional. 18/81 individuals also may be confused in their thinking, and they are very distractible.

19/91

Persons with the 19/91 code are likely to be experiencing a great deal of distress and turmoil. They tend to be very anxious, tense, and restless. Somatic complaints, including gastrointestinal problems, headaches, and exhaustion, are common, and these people are reluctant to accept psychological explanations of their symptoms. Although on the surface 19/91 individuals appear to be verbal, socially extroverted, aggressive, and belligerent, they are basically passive-dependent persons who are trying to deny this aspect of their personalities.

19/91 persons have a great deal of ambition. They expect a high level of achievement from themselves, but they lack clear and definite goals. They are frustrated by their inability to achieve at a high level. The 19/91 code is sometimes found for brain-damaged individuals who are experiencing difficulty in coping with their limitations and deficits.

23/32

Although persons with the 23/32 code typically do not experience disabling anxiety, they do report feeling nervous, agitated, tense, and worried. They also report feeling sad, unhappy, and depressed; fatigue, exhaustion, and weakness are common. They lack interest and involvement in their life situations, and they have difficulty in getting started on a project. Decreased physical activity is likely, and somatic complaints, usually gastrointestinal in nature, may occur.

23/32 individuals are rather passive, docile, and dependent. They are plagued by self-doubts, and they harbor feelings of inadequacy, insecurity, and helplessness. They tend to elicit nurturant and helpful attitudes from other people. Persons with the 23/32 code are very interested in achievement, status, and power. They may appear to be competitive, industrious, and driven, but they do not really place themselves in directly competitive situations where they might experience failure. They seek increased responsibility, but they dread the stress and pressure associated with it. They often feel that they do not get adequate recognition for their accomplishments, and they are easily hurt by even mild criticism.

23/32 persons are extremely overcontrolled. They have difficulty expressing their feelings, and they may feel bottled up much of the time. They tend to deny unacceptable impulses, and when denial fails they feel anxious and guilty. Persons with the 23/32 code feel socially inadequate, and they tend to avoid social involvement. They are especially uncomfortable with members of the opposite sex, and sexual maladjustment, including frigidity and impotence, is common.

The 23/32 code is much more common for women than for men. Rather than indicating incapacitating symptoms, it suggests a lowered level of efficiency for prolonged periods. Problems are long-standing, and the 23/32 persons have learned to tolerate a great deal of unhappiness. Among psychiatric patients, the diagnosis most frequently assigned to persons with the 23/32 code is depressive disorder. Antisocial personality disorder diagnoses are very rare among persons with this code type.

Response to traditional psychotherapy is likely to be poor for the 23/32 persons. They are not introspective; they lack insight into their own behavior; they resist psychological formulations of their problems; and they tolerate a great deal of unhappiness before becoming motivated to change.

24/42

When persons with the 24/42 code come to the attention of professionals, it usually is after they have been in trouble with the law or with their families.

24/42 individuals are impulsive and unable to delay gratification of their impulses. They have little respect for social standards and often find themselves in direct conflict with societal values. Their acting out behavior is likely to involve excessive use of alcohol, and their histories include alcoholic benders, arrests, job loss, and family discord associated with drinking.

24/42 persons feel frustrated by their own lack of accomplishment and are resentful of demands placed on them by other people. They may react to stress by drinking excessively or by using addictive drugs. After periods of acting out, they express a great deal of remorse and guilt about their misdeeds. They may report feeling depressed, anxious, and worthless, but their expressions do not seem to be sincere. In spite of their resolutions to turn over a new leaf, they are likely to act out again in the future. It has been noted in the literature that when both scales 2 and 4 are grossly elevated, suicidal ideation and attempts are quite possible. Often the suicide attempts are directed at making other people feel guilty.

When they are not in trouble, 24/42 individuals tend to be energetic, sociable, and outgoing. They create favorable first impressions, but their tendencies to manipulate others produce feelings of resentment in long-term relationships. Beneath the outer facade of competent, comfortable persons, 24/42 individuals tend to be introverted, self-conscious, and passive-dependent. They harbor feelings of inadequacy and self-dissatisfaction, and they are uncomfortable in social interactions, particularly ones involving members of the opposite sex.

Although persons with the 24/42 code may express the need for help and the desire to change, the prognosis for traditional psychotherapy is not good. They are likely to terminate psychotherapy prematurely when the situational stress subsides or when they have extracted themselves from their legal difficulties.

27/72

27/72 individuals tend to be anxious, nervous, tense, high-strung, and jumpy. They worry excessively, and they are vulnerable to real and imagined threat. They tend to anticipate problems before they occur and to overreact to minor stress. Somatic symptoms are common among 27/72 individuals. They usually involve rather vague complaints of fatigue, tiredness, and exhaustion, but insomnia, anorexia, and cardiac pain may be reported. Depression also is an important feature of the 27/72 code. Although 27/72 persons may not report feeling especially sad or unhappy, they show symptoms of clinical depression, including weight loss, slow personal tempo, slowed speech, and retarded thought processes. They are extremely pessimistic about the world in general and more specifically about the likelihood of overcoming their problems, and they brood and ruminate about their problems much of the time.

Individuals with the 27/72 code have a strong need for achievement and for recognition for their accomplishments. They have high expectations for themselves, and they feel guilty when they fall short of their goals. They tend to be rather indecisive, and they harbor feelings of inadequacy, insecurity, and inferiority. They are intropunitive, blaming themselves for all problems in their life situations. 27/72 individuals are rigid in their thinking and problem solving, and they are meticulous and perfectionistic in daily activities. They also may be excessively religious and extremely moralistic.

Persons with the 27/72 code tend to be rather docile and passive-dependent in their relationships with other people. In fact, they often find it difficult to be even appropriately assertive. They have the capacity for forming deep, emotional ties, and in times of stress they become overly clinging and dependent. They are not aggressive or belligerent, and they tend to elicit nurturance and helping behavior from other people. Because of the intense discomfort they experience, they are motivated for psychotherapy. They tend to remain in psychotherapy longer than many patients, and considerable improvement is likely.

Psychiatric patients with the 27/72 code are likely to receive a diagnosis of anxiety disorder, depressive disorder, or obsessive-compulsive disorder. Antisocial personality disorder diagnoses are very rare among persons with this code type.

28/82

Persons with the 28/82 code report feeling anxious, agitated, tense, and jumpy. Sleep disturbance, inability to concentrate, confused thinking, and forgetfulness also are characteristic of 28/82 people. Such persons are quite inefficient in carrying out their responsibilities, and they tend to be unoriginal in their thinking and stereotyped in problem solving. They are likely to present themselves as physically ill, and somatic complaints include dizziness, blackout spells, nausea, and vomiting. They resist psychological interpretations of their problems, and they are resistant to change. They underestimate the seriousness of their problems, and they tend to be unrealistic about their own capabilities.

28/82 individuals are basically dependent and ineffective, and they have problems in being assertive. They are irritable and resentful much of the time; they fear loss of control and do not express themselves directly. They attempt to deny undesirable impulses, and cognitive dissociative periods during which they act out may occur. Such periods are followed by guilt and depression. 28/82 persons are rather sensitive to the reactions of others, and they are quite suspicious of the motivations of others. They may have a history of being hurt emotionally, and they fear being hurt more. They avoid close interpersonal relationships, and they keep people at a distance emotionally. This lack of meaningful involvement with other people increases their feelings of despair and worthlessness.

If both scales 2 and 8 are very elevated, the 28/82 code is suggestive of serious psychopathology. The most common diagnoses given to psychiatric patients with this code are bipolar disorder and schizoaffective disorder. 28/82 individuals have chronic, incapacitating symptomatology. They are guilt-ridden and appear to be clinically depressed. Withdrawal, soft and reduced speech, retarded stream of thought, and tearfulness are characteristic of 28/82 persons. Apathy, indifference, and feelings of worthlessness also are common. Psychiatric patients with the 28/82 code may be preoccupied with suicidal thoughts, and they are likely to have a specific plan for doing away with themselves.

29/92

29/92 persons tend to be self-centered and narcissistic, and they ruminate excessively about self-worth. Although they may express concern about achieving at a high level, it often appears that they set themselves up for failure. In younger persons, the 29/92 code may be suggestive of an identity crisis characterized by lack of personal and vocational direction.

29/92 persons report feeling tense and anxious, and somatic complaints, often centering in the upper gastrointestinal tract, are common. Although they may not appear to be clinically depressed at the time that they are examined, their histories typically suggest periods of serious depression. Excessive use of alcohol may be employed as an escape from stress and pressure.

The 29/92 code is found primarily among individuals who are denying underlying feelings of inadequacy and worthlessness and defending against depression through excessive activity. Alternating periods of increased activity and fatigue may occur. Whereas the most common diagnosis for psychiatric patients with the 29/92 code is bipolar disorder, it sometimes is found for patients with brain damage who have lost control or who are trying to cope with deficits through excessive activity.

34/43

The most salient characteristic of 34/43 persons is chronic, intense anger. They harbor hostile and aggressive impulses, but they are unable to express their negative feelings appropriately. If scale 3 is higher than scale 4, passive, indirect expression of anger is likely. Persons with scale 4 higher than scale 3 appear to be overcontrolled most of the time, but brief episodes of aggressive, violent acting out may occur. Prisoners with the 43 code have histories of assaultive, violent crimes. In some rare instances, individuals with the 34/43 code successfully dissociate themselves from their aggressive acting out behavior. 34/43 individuals lack insight into the origins and consequences of their behavior. They tend to be extrapunitive and to blame other people for their difficulties. Other people may define the 34/43 person's behavior as problematic, but he or she is not likely to view it in the same way.

Persons with the 34/43 code are reasonably free of disabling anxiety and depression, but complaints of headaches, upper gastrointestinal discomfort, blackout spells, and eye problems may occur. Although these people may feel upset at times, the upset does not seem to be related directly to external stress.

Most of the 34/43 person's difficulties stem from deep, chronic feelings of hostility toward family members. They demand attention and approval from others. They are very sensitive to rejection, and they become hostile when criticized. Although they appear outwardly to be socially conforming, inwardly they are quite rebellious. They may be sexually maladjusted, and marital instability and sexual promiscuity are common. Suicidal thoughts and attempts are characteristic of 34/43 individuals; these are most likely to follow episodes of excessive drinking and acting out behavior. Personality disorder diagnoses are most commonly associated with the 34/43 code, with passive-aggressive personality being most common.

36/63

Individuals with the 36/63 code may report moderate tension and anxiety and may have physical complaints, including headaches and gastrointestinal discomfort, but their problems do not seem to be acute or incapacitating. Most of their difficulties stem from deep, chronic feelings of hostility toward family members. They do not express these feelings directly, and much of the time they may not even recognize the hostile feelings within themselves. When they do become aware of their anger, they try to justify it in terms of the behavior of others. In general, 36/63 individuals are defiant, uncooperative, and hard to get along with. They may express mild suspiciousness and resentment about others, and they are very self-centered and narcissistic. They deny serious psychological problems and express a very naive, Pollyannaish attitude toward the world.

38/83

Persons with the 38/83 code appear to be in a great deal of psychological turmoil. They report feeling anxious, tense, and nervous. Also, they are fearful and worried, and phobias may be present. Depression and feelings of hopelessness are common among 38/83 individuals, and they have difficulties in making even minor decisions. A wide variety of physical complaints (gastrointestinal and musculoskeletal discomfort, dizziness, blurred vision, chest pain, genital pain, headaches, insomnia) may be presented. 38/83 persons tend to be quite vague and evasive when talking about their complaints and difficulties.

38/83 persons are rather immature and dependent, and they have strong needs for attention and affection. They display intropunitive reactions to frustration. They are not involved actively in their life situations, and they are apathetic and pessimistic. They approach problems in an unoriginal, stereotyped manner. Although response to insight-oriented psychotherapy is not likely to be good for 38/83 persons, they often benefit from a supportive psychotherapeutic relationship.

The 38/83 code suggests the presence of disturbed thinking. Individuals with this code complain of not being able to think clearly, of problems in concentration, and of lapses of memory. They express unusual, unconventional ideas, and their ideational associations may be rather loose. Obsessive ruminations, blatant delusions and/or hallucinations, and irrelevant, incoherent speech may be present. The most common diagnosis for psychiatric patients with the 38/83 code is schizophrenia, but they are sometimes diagnosed as somatoform disorders.

45/54

Persons with the 45/54 code tend to be rather immature and narcissistic. They are emotionally passive, and they harbor very strong unrecognized dependency needs. They have difficulty in incorporating societal values into their own personalities. They are nonconforming, and they seem to be defying convention through their dress, speech, and behavior. In the 45/54 configuration, scale 5 indicates that these individuals have adequate control and are not likely to act out in obviously delinquent ways. However, a low frustration tolerance, coupled with intense feelings of anger and resentment, can lead to brief periods of aggressive acting out. Temporary remorse and guilt may follow the acting out behavior, but 45/54 persons are not likely to be able to inhibit similar episodes in the future. The modal diagnosis for psychiatric patients with the 45/54 code is passive-aggressive personality disorder.

45/54 persons are likely to be experiencing great difficulty with sex role identity. They are rebelling against stereotyped sex roles, and overt homosexuality is a definite possibility, particularly if both scales 4 and 5 are markedly elevated. Males with the 45/54 code fear being dominated by females, and they are extremely sensitive to the demands of females.

46/64

Persons with the 46/64 code are immature, narcissistic, and self-indulgent. They are passive-dependent individuals who make excessive demands on others for attention and sympathy, but they are resentful of even the most mild demands made on them by others. Females with the 46/64 code seem overly identified with the traditional female role and are very dependent on males. Both 46/64 males and females do not get along well with others in social situations, and they are especially uncomfortable around members of the opposite sex. They are suspicious of the motivations of others and avoid deep emotional involvement. They generally have poor work histories, and marital problems are quite common. Repressed hostility and anger are characteristic of 46/64 persons. They appear to be irritable, sullen, argumentative, and generally obnoxious. They seem to be especially resentful of authority and may derogate authority figures.

Individuals with the 46/64 code tend to deny serious psychological problems. They rationalize and transfer blame to others, and they accept no responsibility for their own behavior. They are somewhat unrealistic and grandiose in their self-appraisals. Because they deny serious emotional problems, they generally are not receptive to traditional counseling or psychotherapy.

Among psychiatric patients, diagnoses associated with the 46/64 code are about equally divided between passive-aggressive personality disorder and schizophrenia, paranoid type. In general, as the elevation of scales 4 and 6 increases and as scale 6 becomes higher than scale 4, a prepsychotic or psychotic disorder becomes more likely. 46/64 individuals present vague emotional and physical complaints. They report feeling moderately nervous and depressed, and they are indecisive and insecure. Physical symptoms may include asthma, hay fever, hypertension, headaches, blackout spells, and cardiac complaints.

47/74

Persons with the 47/74 code may alternate between periods of gross insensitivity to the consequences of their actions and excessive concern about the effects of their behavior. Episodes of acting out, which may include excessive drinking and sexual promiscuity, may be followed by temporary expressions of guilt and self-condemnation. However, the remorse does not inhibit further episodes of acting out. 47/74 individuals may present vague somatic complaints, including headaches and stomach pain. They also may report feeling tense, fatigued, and exhausted. They are rather dependent, insecure individuals who require almost constant reassurance of their self-worth. In psychotherapy they tend to respond symptomatically to support and reassurance, but long-term changes in personality are unlikely.

48/84

48/84 individuals do not seem to fit into their environments. They are seen by others as odd, peculiar, and queer. They are nonconforming and resentful of authority, and they often espouse radical religious or political views. Their behavior is erratic and unpredictable, and they have marked problems with impulse control. They tend to be angry, irritable, and resentful, and they act out in asocial ways. When crimes are committed by 48/84 persons, they tend to be vicious and assaultive and often appear to be senseless, poorly planned, and poorly executed. Prostitution, promiscuity, and sexual deviation are fairly common among 48/84 individuals. Excessive drinking and drug abuse (particularly involving hallucinogens) may also occur. Histories of 48/84 individuals usually indicate underachievement, uneven performance, and marginal adjustment.

Persons with the 48/84 code harbor deep feelings of insecurity, and they have exaggerated needs for attention and affection. They have poor self-concepts, and it seems as if they set themselves up for rejection and failure. They may have periods during which they become obsessed with suicidal ideation. 48/84 persons are quite distrustful of other people, and they avoid close relationships. When they are involved interpersonally, they have impaired empathy and try to manipulate others into satisfying their needs. They lack basic social skills and tend to be socially withdrawn and isolated. The world is seen as a threatening and rejecting place, and their response is to withdraw or to strike out in anger as a defense against being hurt. They accept little responsibility for their own behavior, and they rationalize excessively, blaming their difficulties on other people. 48/84 persons tend to harbor serious concerns about their masculinity or femininity. They may be obsessed with sexual thoughts, but they are afraid that they cannot perform adequately in sexual situations. They may indulge in antisocial sexual acts in an attempt to demonstrate sexual adequacy.

Psychiatric patients with the 48/84 code tend to be diagnosed as schizophrenia (paranoid type), antisocial personality, schizoid personality, or paranoid personality. If both scales 4 and 8 are very elevated, and particularly if scale 8 is much higher than scale 4, the likelihood of psychosis and bizarre symptomatology, including unusual thinking and paranoid suspiciousness, increases.

49/94

The most salient characteristic of 49/94 individuals is a marked disregard for social standards and values. They frequently get into trouble with the authorities because of antisocial behavior. They have poorly developed consciences, easy morals, and fluctuating ethical values. Alcoholism, fighting, marital problems, sexual acting out, and a wide array of delinquent acts are among the difficulties in which they may be involved.

49/94 individuals are narcissistic, selfish, and self-indulgent. They are quite impulsive and are unable to delay gratification of their impulses. They show poor judgment, often acting without considering the consequences of their acts, and they fail to learn from experience. They are not willing to accept responsibility for their own behavior, rationalizing shortcomings and failures and blaming difficulties on other people. They have a low tolerance for frustration, and they often appear to be moody, irritable, and caustic. They harbor intense feelings of anger and hostility, and these feelings get expressed in occasional emotional outbursts.

49/94 persons tend to be ambitious and energetic, and they are restless and overactive. They are likely to seek out emotional stimulation and excitement. In social situations they tend to be uninhibited, extroverted, and talkative, and they create a good first impression. However, because of their self-centeredness and distrust of people, their relationships are likely to be superficial and not particularly rewarding. They seem to be incapable of deep emotional ties, and they keep others at an emotional distance. Beneath the facade of self-confidence and security, the 49/94 individuals are immature, insecure, and dependent persons who are trying to deny these feelings. A diagnosis of antisocial personality disorder is usually associated with the 49/94 code, although patients with the code occasionally are diagnosed as having a bipolar disorder.

68/86

Persons with the 68/86 code harbor intense feelings of inferiority and insecurity. They lack self-confidence and self-esteem, and they feel guilty about perceived failures. Withdrawal from everyday activities and emotional apathy are common, and suicidal ideation may be present. 68/86 persons are not emotionally involved with other people. They are suspicious and distrustful of others, and they avoid deep emotional ties. They are seriously deficient in social skills, and they are most comfortable when alone. They are quite resentful of demands placed on them, and other people see them as moody, irritable, unfriendly, and negativistic. In general, their life-styles can be characterized as schizoid.

Although some persons with the 68/86 code are diagnosed as paranoid personality or schizoid personality, among psychiatric patients this configuration usually is associated with a diganosis of schizophrenia, paranoid type, particularly if scales 6 and 8 are very elevated and both are considerably higher than scale 7. 68/86 individuals are likely to manifest clearly psychotic behavior. Thinking is described as autistic, fragmented, tangential, and circumstantial, and thought content is likely to be bizarre. Difficulties in concentrating and attending, deficits in memory, and poor judgment are common. Delusions of persecution and/or grandeur and hallucinations may be present, and feelings of unreality may be reported. Persons with the 68/86 code often are preoccupied with abstract or theoretical matters to the exclusion of specific, concrete aspects of their life situations. Affect may be blunted, and speech may be rapid and at times incoherent. Effective defenses seem to be lacking, and these persons respond to stress and pressure by withdrawing into fantasy and daydreaming. Often it is difficult for the 68/86 person to differentiate between fantasy and reality. Medical consultation to determine appropriateness of psychotrophic medication should be considered.

69/96

69/96 individuals are rather dependent and have strong needs for affection. They are vulnerable to real or imagined threat, and they feel anxious and tense much of the time. In addition, they may appear to be tearful and trembling. A marked overreaction to minor stress also is characteristic of persons with the 69/96 code. A typical response to severe stress is withdrawal into fantasy. 69/96 individuals are unable to express emotions in an adaptive, modulated way, and they may alternate between overcontrol and direct, uncontrolled emotional outbursts.

Psychiatric patients with the 69/96 code almost always receive a diagnosis of schizophrenia, paranoid type, and they are likely to show signs of a thought disorder. They complain of difficulties in thinking and concentrating, and their stream of thought is retarded. They are ruminative, overideational, and obsessional. They may have delusions and hallucinations, and their speech seems to be irrelevant and incoherent. They appear to be disoriented and perplexed, and they may show poor judgment.

78/87

78/87 individuals typically are in a great deal of turmoil. They are not hesitant to admit to psychological problems, and they seem to lack adequate defenses to keep them reasonably comfortable. They report feeling depressed, worried, tense, and nervous. When first seen professionally, they may appear to be confused and in a state of panic. They show poor judgment and do not seem to profit from experience. They are introspective and are characterized as ruminative and overideational.

Persons with the 78/87 code harbor chronic feelings of insecurity, inadequacy, and inferiority, and they tend to be quite indecisive. They lack even an average number of socialization experiences, and they are not socially poised or confident. As a result, they withdraw from social interactions. They are passive-dependent individuals who are unable to take a dominant role in interpersonal relationships. Mature heterosexual relationships are especially difficult for the 78/87 persons. They feel quite inadequate in the traditional sex role, and sexual performance may be poor. In an apparent attempt to compensate for these deficits, they engage in rich sexual fantasies.

Schizophrenic, depressive, obsessive-compulsive, and personality disorders are all represented among individuals with the 78/87 code. Schizoid is the most common personality disorder diagnosis found. The relative elevations of scales 7 and 8 are important in differentiating psychotic from nonpsychotic disorders. As scale 8 becomes greater than scale 7, the likelihood of a psychotic disorder increases. Even when a psychotic label is applied, blatant psychotic symptoms may not be present.

89/98

Persons with the 89/98 code tend to be rather self-centered and infantile in their expectations of other people. They demand a great deal of attention and may become resentful and hostile when their demands are not met. Because they fear emotional involvement, they avoid close relationships and tend to be socially withdrawn and isolated. They seem especially uncomfortable in heterosexual relationships, and poor sexual adjustment is common.

89/98 persons also are characterized as hyperactive and emotionally labile. They appear to be agitated and excited, and they may talk excessively in a loud voice. They are unrealistic in self-appraisal, and they impress others as grandiose, boastful, and fickle. They are vague, evasive, and denying in talking about their difficulties, and they may state that they do not need professional help.

Although 89/98 persons have a high need to achieve and may feel pressured to do so, their actual performance tends to be mediocre. Their feelings of inferiority and inadequacy and their low self-esteem limit the extent to which they involve themselves in competitive or achievement-oriented situations.

The 89/98 code is suggestive of serious psychological disturbance, particularly if scales 8 and 9 are grossly elevated. The modal diagnosis for 89/98 persons is schizophrenia. Severe disturbance in thinking is likely. 89/98 individuals are confused, perplexed, and disoriented, and they report feelings of unreality. They have difficulty concentrating and thinking, and they are unable to focalize on issues. Thinking also may appear to be odd, unusual, autistic, and circumstantial. Speech may be bizarre and may include clang associations, neologisms, and echolalia. Delusions and hallucinations may be present. The 89/98 code frequently is found among adolescents who are using drugs.

THREE-POINT CODE TYPES

As stated earlier in this chapter, three-point code types tell us which three clinical scales are the highest ones in the profile. Far less research has been conducted concerning three-point codes than concerning two-point codes or single-scale scores. The three-point codes included in this section are those that occur reasonably frequently in a variety of clinical settings and for which some research data are available. Because profiles classified according to three-point codes result in rather homogeneous groupings, the descriptors presented for any particular code are likely to fit many individuals with that code rather well. However, it must again be emphasized that the descriptions provided represent modal patterns. Not every descriptor will apply to every person with a particular three-point code.

123/213/231

Persons with this code usually are diagnosed as somatoform disorder, anxiety disorder, or depressive disorder. Somatic complaints, particularly those associated with the gastrointestinal system, are common, and often there appears to be clear secondary gain associated with the symptoms. Sleep disturbance, perplexity, despondency, and feelings of hopelessness occur. Persons with this code are in conflict about dependency and self-assertion, and they often keep other people at an emotional distance. They tend to have a low energy level, and they are lacking in sex drive. Such persons often show good work and marital adjustment, but they rarely take risks in their lives.

132/312

This configuration, in which scales 1 and 3 often are significantly higher than scale 2, has been referred to as the "conversion valley." Persons with this code type may show classic conversion symptoms, and diagnoses of conversion disorder or psychogenic pain disorder are common. Stress is often converted into physical complaints. Persons with this code use denial and repression excessively; they lack insight into the causes of their symptoms; and they resist psychological explanations of their problems. Although these individuals tend to be rather sociable, they tend to be passive-dependent in relationships. It is important for them to be liked by and approved of by others, and their behavior typically is conforming and conventional.

138

Persons with this code usually are diagnosed as schizophrenic disorder (paranoid type) or paranoid personality disorder. They are likely to have rather bizarre somatic symptoms that may be delusional in nature. Depressive episodes and suicidal preoccupation may occur. Sexual and religious preoccupation may be present. Clear evidence of thought disorder may be observed. These individuals are agitated, excitable, loud, and short-tempered. They often have histories of excessive use of alcohol. They feel restless and bored much of the time. They are ambivalent about forming close relationships, and they often feel suspicious and jealous.

139

Persons with this code type often are diagnosed as somatoform disorder or organic brain syndrome. If they have the latter diagnosis, they may show spells of irritation, assaultiveness, and temper outbursts.

247/274/472

The modal diagnosis for persons with this code is passive-aggressive personality disorder, and symptoms of depression and anxiety may be present. This is a very common code type among males who abuse alcohol and/or other substances. Family and marital problems are common. They may feel fearful, worried, and high-strung. They overreact to stress and undercontrol impulses. They tend to be angry, hostile, and immature. They have strong unfilled needs for attention and support. They are in conflict about dependency and sexuality. They tend to be phobic, ruminative, and overideational. They experience guilt associated with anger. Although they often have strong achievement needs, they are afraid to compete for fear of failing. They have difficulty enduring anxiety during treatment, and they may respond best to directive, goal-oriented treatment.

278/728

Persons with this code often present a mixed-picture diagnostically. They are experiencing a great deal of emotional turmoil, and they tend to have a rather schizoid life-style. Brief, acute psychotic epidodes may occur. They tend to feel tense, nervous, and fearful, and they have problems in concentrating and attending. They feel depressed, despondent, and hopeless, and they often ruminate about suicide. Affect appears blunted or otherwise inappropriate. These persons lack basic social skills and are shy, withdrawn, introverted, and socially isolated. They feel inadequate and inferior. They tend to set high standards for themselves and to feel guilty when the standards are not met. They tend to show interest in obscure, esoteric subjects.

687/867

This code type, in which scales 6 and 8 typically are much more elevated than scale 7, has been referred to as the "psychotic valley." It suggests very serious psychopathology, and the most common diagnosis for persons with the code type is schizophrenic disorder, paranoid type. Hallucinations, delusions, and extreme suspiciousness are common. Affect tends to be blunted. Persons with this code tend to be shy, introverted, and socially withdrawn, but they may become quite aggressive when drinking. They tend to have problems with memory and concentration.

OTHER CONFIGURAL ASPECTS

Regardless of their absolute elevations and whether or not they are the highest scales in the profile, the relative elevations of scales 1, 2, and 3 provide important interpretive information. When scales 1 and 3 are 10 or more T-score points higher than scale 2, individuals probably are using denial and repression excessively. They tend to have little or no insight into their own needs, conflicts, or symptoms. They are reasonably free of depression, anxiety, and other emotional turmoil, but somatic symptoms are likely. These persons want medical explanations for their problems, and they resist psychological explanations. When scale 2 is equal to or higher than scales 1 and 3, the individuals are not likely to be so well defended, and they may report a wide variety of symptoms and complaints.

The relationship between scales 3 and 4 gives important information about impulse control. Even when these two scales are not the most elevated ones in the profile, their relative positions are meaningful. When scale 4 is 10 or more T-score points higher than scale 3, we expect problems with impulse control. Such persons tend to act without adequately considering the consequences of their actions. When scale 3 is 10 or more T-score points higher than scale 4, we expect persons to have adequate control and not to act impulsively. When scores on scales 3 and 4 are about equal, and especially when they are both above T-scores of 70, persons may be overly controlled and not even appropriately assertive most of the time, but periods of impulsive acting out may occur.

Scale 5's position in the profile also tells us something about control. Regardless of the scores on other scales in the profile, elevation on scale 5 suggests an element of control. High scale 5 persons are not likely to act out impulsively. Hathaway and Monachesi (1953) found that even in environments where the base rate for delinquency was very high, adolescents who scored high on scale 5 did not become involved in delinquent acts.

A profile configuration in which scales 4 and 6 are at above average levels and scale 5 is below average suggests rather intense anger that is expressed in passive-aggressive ways. This configuration occurs for both men and women, but is more common for women. Patients with this configuration often have mislabeled their feelings and present themselves as depressed rather than as angry. Women with this configuration often feel trapped in a role (e.g., housewife, mother) that is not very satisfying to them.

The relationship between scales 7 and 8 gives important information concerning the likelihood of thought disorder. When scale 7 is 10 or more T-score points greater than scale 8, the likelihood of a thought disorder is not great. As scale 8 becomes higher than scale 7, the likelihood of a thought disorder increases. When both scales 7 and 8 are elevated, persons may be rather confused, but a well-developed delusional system is not to be expected.

7

Content Interpretation

As pointed out in the introductory chapters, empirical keying procedures were employed by Hathaway and McKinley in the construction of the original MMPI scales. Items were included in a scale if they empirically differentiated between external criterion groups. No emphasis was placed on the content of the items identified in this manner, and no attempts were made to ensure that the resulting scales were homogeneous or internally consistent. In fact, some early clinicians seemed to believe that examination of content of items endorsed by subjects would spoil the empirical approach to assessment.

More recently, clinicians and researchers have become increasingly aware that consideration of item content adds significantly to MMPI interpretation. The purpose of this chapter is to discuss some approaches to the interpretation of content dimensions in the MMPI. It should be emphasized that these approaches are viewed as supplementary to interpretation of the standard MMPI scales and should not be used instead of these standard scales.

THE HARRIS SUBSCALES FOR THE MMPI

Subscale Development

As mentioned above, the standard MMPI clinical scales were constructed by empirical keying procedures. Because no attention was given by Hathaway and McKinley to scale homogeneity, the standard clinical scales are quite heterogeneous in terms of item content. The same total raw score on a clinical scale can be achieved by individuals endorsing combinations of quite different kinds of items. A number of investigators have suggested that systematic analysis of these subgroups of items within the standard clinical scales can add significantly to the interpretation of MMPI protocols (e.g., Comrey, 1957abc, 1958bcde; Comrey & Marggraff, 1958; Graham, Schroeder, & Lilly, 1971; Harris & Lingoes, 1955, 1968; Pepper & Strong, 1958). The subscales developed by Harris represent the most comprehensive effort of this kind. His scales have come to be widely used clinically and are routinely scored and reported by some of the automated MMPI scoring and interpretation services.

Harris and Lingoes (1955, 1968) reported the construction of subscales for 6 of the 10 standard clinical scales (scales 2, 3, 4, 6, 8, 9). They did not develop subscales for scales 1, 5, 7, and 0. Each subscale was constructed logically by examining the content of items within a standard clinical scale and grouping together items that seemed similar in content or were judged to reflect a single attitude or trait. A new label was assigned to each subscale on the basis of Harris and Lingoes's clinical judgment of the content of items in that subscale. Although it was assumed that the resulting subscales would be more homogeneous than their parent scales, no statistical estimates of subscale homogeneity were provided by Harris and Lingoes. Although 31 subscales were developed, three subscales that are obtained by summing scores on other subscales generally are not used in clinical interpretation. The other 28 Harris subscales are listed in Table 7.1, and the numbers of the items included in each subscale, along with the scored response for each item, are presented in Appendix D of this *Guide.*[1] No scoring keys or profile sheets are available from the test publisher for use with the Harris subscales. However, scoring templates can be constructed using the information in Appendix D. If a profile sheet for plotting the Harris subscales is desired, one can be constructed from the data in Appendix E.

No attempt was made by Harris to avoid placing an item in more than one subscale. Thus, item overlap among the subscales is considerable and may account for the high correlations among subscale scores. Table 7.2 summarizes these intercorrelations as presented by Harris and Lingoes (1968).

Subscale Norms

Harris and Lingoes (1955) presented no normative data for their subscales when they were first described, but a later paper (Harris & Lingoes, 1968) reported means and standard deviations for psychiatric patients at the Langley Porter Clinic. Gocka and Holloway (1963) presented means and standard deviations for 68 male Veterans Administration psychiatric patients. Dahlstrom, Welsh, and Dahlstrom (1972) developed tables for converting raw scores on the Harris subscales to T-scores based on the scores of normal adult male and female subjects who were used in the original MMPI derivational work. These Dahlstrom et al. norms for normal subjects, which are the ones that should be used for general clinical interpretation of the Harris subscales, are reproduced in Appendix E of this *Guide.*

1. In their 1968 paper, Harris and Lingoes presented corrections to their earlier paper in terms of items included in some of the subscales. These corrected scale compositions are the ones presented in Appendix D and throughout the discussion of the Harris subscales.

Table 7.1. Internal consistency values (Kuder-Richardson 21) and test-retest coefficients for the Harris subscales of the MMPI

Scale	Subscale		Kuder-Richardson reliability[a]	Test-retest reliability[b] Male	Test-retest reliability[b] Female
1–Hypochondriasis		None			
2–Depression	D1	Subjective Depression	.82	.80	.76
	D2	Psychomotor Retardation	.11	.70	.57
	D3	Physical Malfunctioning	.24	.51	.62
	D4	Mental Dullness	.80	.80	.75
	D5	Brooding	.73	.78	.79
3–Hysteria	Hy1	Denial of Social Anxiety	.72	.80	.80
	Hy2	Need for Affection	.65	.77	.64
	Hy3	Lassitude-Malaise	.85	.81	.63
	Hy4	Somatic Complaints	.84	.71	.80
	Hy5	Inhibition of Aggression	.31	.53	.62
4–Psychopathic Deviate	Pd1	Familial Discord	.67	.83	.80
	Pd2	Authority Problems	.04	.70	.57
	Pd3	Social Imperturbability	.67	.86	.84
	Pd4A	Social Alienation	.71	.72	.70
	Pd4B	Self-Alienation	.78	.76	.71

5–Masculinity-Femininity		None			
6–Paranoia	Pa1	Persecutory Ideas	.85	.59	.53
	Pa2	Poignancy	.48	.62	.72
	Pa3	Naiveté	.70	.73	.76
7–Psychasthenia		None			
8–Schizophrenia	Sc1A	Social Alienation	.71	.66	.79
	Sc1B	Emotional Alienation	.37	.46	.63
	Sc2A	Lack of Ego Mastery, Cognitive	.82	.71	.79
	Sc2B	Lack of Ego Mastery, Conative	.76	.76	.67
	Sc2C	Lack of Ego Mastery, Defective Inhibition	.74	.70	.64
	Sc3	Bizarre Sensory Experiences	.80	.51	.64
9–Hypomania	Ma1	Amorality	.46	.75	.73
	Ma2	Psychomotor Acceleration	.19	.70	.72
	Ma3	Imperturbability	.51	.68	.63
	Ma4	Ego Inflation	.50	.58	.63
0–Social Introversion		None			

[a]From Gocka (1965).

[b]From Moreland (1985b).

Table 7.2. Intercorrelations for Harris subscales

	D	D1	D2	D3	D4
D1	.92				
D2	.70	.65			
D3	.64	.60	.18		
D4	.86	.91	.63	.50	
D5	.70	.85	.45	.42	.83

	Hy	Hy1	Hy2	Hy3	Hy4
Hy1	.25				
Hy2	.31	.28			
Hy3	.67	−.26	−.19		
Hy4	.71	−.13	−.15	.55	
Hy5	.38	.25	.36	−.06	−.01

	Pd	Pd1	Pd2	Pd3	Pd4A
Pd1	.58				
Pd2	.48	.12			
Pd3	−.33	−.39	−.03		
Pd4A	.72	.44	.25	−.53	
Pd4B	.77	.37	.29	−.56	.74

	Pa	Pa1	Pa2
Pa1	.68		
Pa2	.67	.53	
Pa3	.31	−.29	−.24

	Sc	Sc1A	Sc1B	Sc2A	Sc2B	Sc2C
Sc1A	.87					
Sc1B	.78	.63				
Sc2A	.74	.52	.58			
Sc2B	.80	.63	.85	.76		
Sc2C	.79	.87	.53	.45	.55	
Sc3	.72	.47	.40	.44	.44	.68

	Ma	Ma1	Ma2	Ma3
Ma1	.66			
Ma2	.75	.40		
Ma3	−.14	−.14	−.46	
Ma4	.77	.40	.56	−.30

Source: R. Harris and J. Lingoes, *Subscales for the Minnesota Multiphasic Personality Inventory*. Mimeographed materials, The Langley Porter Clinic. Reproduced with permission.

Subscale Reliability

Gocka (1965) presented reliability data for the Harris subscales. He calculated Kuder-Richardson 21 values (internal consistency) for the subscales based on 220 male admissions to a Veterans Administration Hospital. These values are reported in Table 7.1. Although several of the Harris subscales have rather low coefficients, most of the subscales have a high degree of internal consistency. Table 7.1 also reports test-retest reliability coefficients for 95 male and 108 female college students with a six-week test-retest interval (Moreland, 1985b).

Subscale Validity

Although the Harris subscales have been in existence for about 30 years and have come to gain fairly wide usage among clinicians (partly because they are scored routinely by some automated scoring and interpretation services), disappointingly little empirical research concerning the subscales has been published. The factor analytic work of Comrey (1957abc, 1958bcde; Comrey & Marggraff, 1958) indirectly offers some support for the construct validity of the Harris subscales. Comrey reported factor analyses of the intercorrelations of items *within* each scale, separately for each of the clinical scales of the MMPI (excluding scales 5 and 0). Although there are some significant differences between the logically derived Harris subscales and the corresponding factor-analytically derived Comrey factors, in general the Comrey studies revealed factors within each clinical scale that are similar to the Harris subscales and supported Harris' notion that the clinical scales are not homogeneous and unidimensional.

Lingoes (1960) factor-analyzed scores on the Harris subscales and on the Wiener subtle-obvious subscales of the MMPI (Wiener, 1948) in an attempt to determine the statistical factor structure of the MMPI. He concluded that the dimensionality of the MMPI is more complex than the six standard scales from which the various subscales were derived, but simpler than the 36 subscales (Harris, Wiener) included in his own factor analysis. Harris and Lingoes (1955) reasoned intuitively that the subscales should be more homogeneous than the parent scales from which they were drawn, but they did not offer any evidence in this regard. Calvin (1974) statistically examined the homogeneity of the five Harris subscales for scale 2 (Depression). He separately factor-analyzed inter-item correlations for each of the five subscales, and he concluded that four of the subscales appeared to be unidimensional, whereas one subscale (Psychomotor Retardation) was two-dimensional (loss of interest in life activities and inhibition of hostility).

Harris and Christiansen (1946) studied pretherapy MMPI differences between neurotic patients who were judged to have been successful in psychotherapy and similar patients who were judged to have been unsuccessful in psychotherapy. They found that the successful patients scored lower on scales

4, 6, 8, and 9 of the MMPI, suggesting that they had more ego strength. Significant differences between successful and unsuccessful patients also were identified for eight Harris subscales. Successful patients scored lower on the Pd1 (Familial Discord), Pd2 (Authority Problems), and Pd4A (Social Alienation) subscales, on the Pa1 (Persecutory Ideas) subscale, on the Sc2C (Defective Inhibition) and Sc3 (Bizarre Sensory Experiences) subscales. Harris and Christiansen did not address themselves to the question of whether greater accuracy of prediction of psychotherapy outcome was possible with the subscales than with only the standard clinical scales. They felt, however, that the subscale information could lead to a better understanding of how successful therapy patients view themselves and the environments in which they live.

Gocka and Holloway (1963) correlated scores of psychiatric patients on the Harris subscales with other MMPI scales assessing social desirability, introversion-extroversion, and dissimulation, with a number of demographic variables (intelligence, occupational level, marital status), with legal competency status at the time of hospital admission, and with number of days of hospitalization. Most Harris subscales were related to the social desirability scale, and some Harris subscales were related to the introversion-extroversion and dissimulation scales. Few significant correlations were found between Harris subscale scores and demographic variables. Two Harris subscale scores correlated significantly with competency status, and no Harris subscale correlated significantly with length of hospitalization.

Panton (1959) compared the Harris subscale scores of black and white prison inmates. He found that whites scored higher on Pd2 (Authority Problems), suggesting that whites had more authority problems and aggressive tendencies than blacks. Blacks scored higher on Pa1 (Persecutory Ideas), Sc1A (Social Alienation), and Ma4 (Ego Inflation), suggesting more psychotic trends for blacks than for whites. Panton also compared the Harris subscale scores of prison inmates with the psychiatric norms presented by Harris and Lingoes (1968). He found that prison inmates were higher than the psychiatric patients on Pd4A (Social Alienation), Pd4B (Self-Alienation), and Ma1 (Amorality). Prisoners were lower than the psychiatric patients on D1 (Subjective Depression), D2 (Psychomotor Retardation), D4 (Mental Dullness), Hy2 (Need for Affection), Hy3 (Lassitude-Malaise), Hy5 (Inhibition of Aggression), Sc2A (Lack of Cognitive Ego Mastery), Sc2B (Lack of Conative Ego Mastery), and Ma2 (Psychomotor Acceleration).

Calvin (1975) attempted to identify empirical behavioral correlates for the Harris subscales for a sample of hospitalized psychiatric patients. He compared high scores on each Harris subscale with other scores on that subscale on a number of extratest variables, including psychiatric diagnosis, reasons for hospitalization, nurses' ratings, and psychiatrists' ratings. Although 10 of the 28 Harris subscales were determined to have reliable behavioral correlates, Calvin concluded that in most cases the Harris subscales are not likely to add significantly to protocol analysis based on the standard clinical scales for psychiatric patients. The results of Calvin's study are included in the interpretive descriptions that are presented in the following section.

Interpretation of Subscales

Scores on the Harris subscales provide information concerning the kinds of items that subjects endorsed in the scored direction in obtaining a particular score on a clinical scale. Although such information is generally useful, there are two circumstances in which it seems to be especially helpful. First, it can help to explain why a subject receives an elevated score on a clinical scale when that elevation was not expected from history and other information available to the clinician. For example, a patient whose primary symptom is depression could produce a profile with elevations on scales 2, 7, and 8. The scale 2 and 7 elevations are consistent with history and clinical observation. However, the scale 8 elevation is somewhat troublesome. Why does this patient, for whom there is no history or clinical indication of schizophrenia or thought disorder, score relatively high on scale 8? Reference to the Harris subscale scores might reveal that most of the scale 8 elevation is coming from items in the Lack of Ego Mastery, Conative (Sc2B) subscale. This subscale assesses feelings of depression and despair and that life is a strain much of the time. These characteristics are very consistent with those based on the rest of the profile and with the patient's history. Second, the Harris subscales can be very useful in interpreting clinical scale scores that are marginally elevated (T=65 to 75). Often it does not seem that many of the interpretations suggested for a high score on a scale are appropriate for the less elevated scores. For example, a subject might receive a T-score of 72 on scale 4, and there would be some reluctance to attribute to that subject the antisocial characteristics suggested for high scale 4. The Harris subscales could be very helpful in this instance. A high score on Pd1 (Familial Discord), for example, could explain the moderately elevated score on scale 4 without requiring inferences about more deviant asocial or antisocial behaviors.

As with the other scales previously discussed, it is not possible to establish absolutely firm cutoff scores to define high and low scorers on the subscales. As clinicians gain experience with the subscales, they will come to establish specific cutoff scores for the settings in which the MMPI is used. The individual who is just beginning to use the subscales for MMPI interpretation should find it useful to consider T-scores greater than 70 as high scores and T-scores less than 40 as low scores.

The descriptions that follow for high and low scorers on each of the subscales are based on the descriptions provided by Harris and Lingoes (1955, 1968), on the validity studies reviewed in the previous section, on the author's own clinical experience, and on examination of the content of the items in each subscale. The resulting descriptions should be viewed as preliminary. As the subscales are used more frequently and as more empirical research is conducted to determine extratest correlates for the subscales, more comprehensive, and perhaps more accurate, descriptions can be developed. The descriptions presented are *modal* ones, and as such they will not apply completely to every examinee who achieves high or low scores on the subscales. It should be emphasized again that the Harris subscales should be used to *supplement* the standard validity and clinical scales and should not replace them.

Subjective Depression (D1)

A high score on the D1 subscale is indicative of an individual who (is):

1. feels unhappy, blue, or depressed much of the time
2. lacks energy for coping with problems of his/her everyday life
3. not interested in what goes on around him/her
4. feels nervous or tense much of the time
5. has difficulties in concentrating and attending
6. has a poor appetite and trouble sleeping
7. broods and cries frequently
8. lacks self-confidence
9. feels inferior and useless
10. easily hurt by criticism
11. feels uneasy, shy, and embarrassed in social situations
12. tends to avoid interactions with other people, except for relatives and close friends
13. if a hospitalized psychiatric patient, likely to receive a clinical diagnosis of depressive disorder

A low score on the D1 subscale is indicative of an individual who (is):

1. feels happy and satisfied
2. interested in and stimulated by his/her environment
3. denies tension, difficulties in concentration and attendance, poor appetite, sleep disturbances, and frequent brooding or crying
4. self-confident
5. socially extroverted
6. likes to be around other people
7. at ease in social situations

Psychomotor Retardation (D2)

A high score on the D2 subscale is indicative of an individual who (is):

1. characterized as immobilized and withdrawn
2. lacks energy to cope with everyday activities

3. avoids other people
4. denies hostile or aggressive impulses or actions

A low score on the D2 subscale is indicative of an individual who (is):

1. describes himself/herself as active and involved
2. has no difficulty getting started on things
3. views everyday life as interesting and rewarding
4. admits to having hostile and aggressive impulses at times

Physical Malfunctioning (D3)

A high score on the D3 subscale is indicative of an individual who (is):

1. preoccupied with his/her own physical functioning
2. denies good health
3. reports a wide variety of specific somatic symptoms that may include weakness, hay fever or asthma, poor appetite, constipation, nausea or vomiting, and convulsions

A low score on the D3 subscale is indicative of an individual who (is):

1. presents himself/herself as being in good physical health
2. does not report the wide variety of specific somatic symptoms characteristic of high scorers on this subscale

Mental Dullness (D4)

A high score on the D4 subscale is indicative of an individual who (is):

1. lacks energy to cope with the problems of everyday life
2. feels tense
3. complains of difficulties in concentrating
4. complains of poor memory and judgment
5. lacks self-confidence
6. feels inferior to others
7. gets little enjoyment out of life
8. appears to have concluded that life is no longer worthwhile

A low score on the D4 subscale is indicative of an individual who (is):

1. views life as interesting and worthwhile
2. feels capable of coping with everyday problems
3. denies tension
4. denies difficulties in concentrating

5. claims that memory and judgment are satisfactory
6. self-confident
7. compares himself/herself favorably with other people

Brooding (D5)

A high score on the D5 subscale is indicative of an individual who (is):

1. broods, ruminates, and cries much of the time
2. lacks energy to cope with problems
3. seems to have concluded that life is no longer worthwhile
4. feels inferior, unhappy, and useless
5. easily hurt by criticism
6. feels that he/she is losing control of his/her thought processes

A low score on the D5 subscale is indicative of an individual who (is):

1. feels happy most of the time
2. feels that life is worthwhile
3. denies lack of energy, brooding, and frequent crying
4. self-confident
5. not excessively sensitive to criticism

Denial of Social Anxiety (Hy1)

A high score on the Hy1 subscale is indicative of an individual who (is):

1. socially extroverted
2. feels quite comfortable in interacting with other people
3. finds it easy to talk with other people
4. not easily influenced by social standards and customs

A low score on the Hy1 subscale is indicative of an individual who (is):

1. socially introverted
2. shy and bashful in social situations
3. finds it difficult to talk with other people
4. greatly influenced by social standards and customs

Need for Affection (Hy2)

A high score on the Hy2 subscale is indicative of an individual who (is):

1. expresses naively optimistic and trusting attitudes toward other people
2. sees others as honest, sensitive, and reasonable
3. denies having negative feelings about other people

4. tries to avoid unpleasant confrontations whenever possible
5. has strong needs for attention and affection from others and fears that these needs will not be met if he/she is more honest about his/her feelings and attitudes

A low score on the Hy2 subscale is indicative of an individual who (is):

1. has very negative, critical, and suspicious attitudes toward other people
2. sees others as dishonest, selfish, and unreasonable
3. admits to negative feelings toward other people who are perceived as treating him/her badly

Lassitude-Malaise (Hy3)

A high score on the Hy3 subscale is indicative of an individual who (is):

1. feels uncomfortable and not in good health
2. feels weak, fatigued, or tired
3. does not present specific somatic complaints
4. reports difficulties in concentrating, poor appetite, and sleep disturbance
5. feels unhappy and blue
6. describes home environment as unpleasant and uninteresting.

A low score on the Hy3 subscale is indicative of an individual who (is):

1. comfortable and in good health
2. does not have difficulties in concentrating, poor appetite, or disturbed sleep
3. feels happy and satisfied with his/her life situation

Somatic Complaints (Hy4)

A high score on the Hy4 subscale is indicative of an individual who (is):

1. presents multiple somatic complaints
2. complains of pain in head and/or chest
3. complains of fainting spells, dizziness, or balance problems
4. complains of nausea and vomiting, poor vision, shakiness, and feeling too hot or too cold
5. utilizes repression and conversion of affect
6. expresses little or no hostility toward other people

A low score on the Hy4 subscale is indicative of an individual who (is):

1. does not report the multiple somatic symptoms characteristic of high scorers on this subscale

Inhibition of Aggression (Hy5)

A high score on the Hy5 subscale is indicative of an individual who (is):

1. denies hostile and aggressive impulses
2. says he/she is not interested in reading about crime and violence
3. sensitive about how others respond to him/her
4. says he/she is decisive

A low score on the Hy5 subscale is indicative of an individual who (is):

1. admits to hostile and aggressive impulses
2. expresses an interest in reading about crime and violence
3. sees himself/herself as indecisive
4. says he/she is not very concerned about how other people view him/her

Familial Discord (Pd1)

A high score on the Pd1 subscale is indicative of an individual who (is):

1. describes his/her home and family situation as quite unpleasant
2. has felt like leaving the home situation
3. describes his/her home as lacking in love, understanding, and support
4. describes his/her family as critical, quarrelsome, and refusing to permit adequate freedom and independence

A low score on the Pd1 subscale is indicative of an individual who (is):

1. describes his/her home and family situation in very positive terms
2. sees his/her family as offering love, understanding, and support
3. describes his/her family as not being overly controlling or domineering

Authority Problems (Pd2)

A high score on the Pd2 subscale is indicative of an individual who (is):

1. resentful of societal and parental standards and customs
2. admits to having been in trouble in school or with the law
3. has definite opinions about what is right and wrong
4. stands up for what he/she believes
5. not greatly influenced by the values and standards of others

A low score on the Pd2 subscale is indicative of an individual who (is):

1. tends to be very socially conforming and accepting of authority
2. does not express personal opinions or beliefs openly

3. easily influenced by other people
4. denies having been in trouble in school or with the law

Social Imperturbability (Pd3)

A high score on the Pd3 subscale is indicative of an individual who (is):

1. presents himself/herself as comfortable and confident in social situations
2. likes to interact with other people
3. experiences no difficulty in talking with other people
4. tends to be somewhat exhibitionistic and "show-offish"
5. has strong opinions about many things and is not reluctant to defend his/her opinions vigorously

A low score on the Pd3 subscale is indicative of an individual who (is):

1. experiences a great deal of discomfort and anxiety in social situations
2. does not like to meet new people
3. finds it difficult to talk in interpersonal situations
4. is socially conforming
5. does not express personal opinions or attitudes

Social Alienation (Pd4A)

A high score on the Pd4A subscale is indicative of an individual who (is):

1. feels alienated, isolated, and estranged
2. believes that other people do not understand him/her
3. feels lonely, unhappy, and unloved
4. feels that he/she gets a raw deal from life
5. blames other people for his/her problems and shortcomings
6. concerned about how other people react to him/her
7. self-centered and insensitive to the needs and feelings of others
8. acts in inconsiderate ways toward other people
9. verbalizes regret and remorse for his/her actions

A low score on the Pd4A subscale is indicative of an individual who (is):

1. feels that he/she belongs in his/her social environment
2. sees other people as loving, understanding, and supportive
3. finds interpersonal relationships gratifying
4. not overly influenced by the values and attitudes of others
5. willing to settle down; finds security in routine

Self-Alienation (Pd4B)

A high score on the Pd4B subscale is indicative of an individual who (is):

1. describes himself/herself as uncomfortable and unhappy
2. has problems in concentrating
3. does not find daily life interesting or rewarding
4. verbalizes regret, guilt, and remorse for past deeds but is vague about the nature of this misbehavior
5. finds it hard to settle down
6. may use alcohol excessively

A low score on the Pd4B subscale is indicative of an individual who (is):

1. presents himself/herself as comfortable and happy
2. finds daily life stimulating and rewarding
3. willing to settle down
4. denies excessive use of alcohol
5. does not express regret, remorse, or guilt about past misdeeds

Persecutory Ideas (Pa1)

A high score on the Pa1 subscale is indicative of an individual who (is):

1. views the world as a threatening place
2. feels that he/she is getting a raw deal from life
3. feels misunderstood
4. feels that others have unfairly blamed or punished him/her
5. suspicious and untrusting of other people
6. blames others for his/her problems and shortcomings
7. in extreme cases may have delusions of persecution

A low score on the Pa1 subscale is indicative of an individual who (is):

1. feels that he/she is understood and fairly treated
2. able to trust other people
3. does not project blame for problems and shortcomings
4. denies the persecutory ideas expressed by high scorers on this subscale

Poignancy (Pa2)

A high score on the Pa2 subscale is indicative of an individual who (is):

1. sees himself/herself as more high-strung and more sensitive than other people

2. says that he/she feels more intensely than others
3. feels lonely and misunderstood
4. looks for risky or exciting activities to make him/her feel better

A low score on the Pa2 subscale is indicative of an individual who (is):

1. feels understood and accepted
2. does not present himself/herself as more sensitive than others
3. avoids risky or dangerous activities

Naiveté (Pa3)

A high score on the Pa3 subscale is indicative of an individual who (is):

1. expresses extremely naive and optimistic attitudes about other people
2. sees others as honest, unselfish, generous, and altruistic
3. presents himself/herself as trusting
4. says he/she has high moral standards
5. denies hostility and negative impulses

A low score on the Pa3 subscale is indicative of an individual who (is):

1. has rather negative and suspicious attitudes toward other people
2. sees others as dishonest, selfish, and untrustworthy
3. admits to some hostility and resentment toward people who make demands on or take advantage of him/her

Social Alienation (Sc1A)

A high score on the Sc1A subscale is indicative of an individual who (is):

1. feels that he/she is getting a raw deal from life
2. feels that other people do not understand him/her
3. feels that other people have it in for him/her
4. feels that other people are trying to harm him/her
5. describes family situation as lacking in love and support
6. feels that family treats him/her more as a child than an adult
7. feels lonely and empty
8. admits that he/she has never had a love relationship with anyone
9. reports hostility and hatred toward family members
10. avoids social situations and interpersonal relationships whenever possible

A low score on the Sc1A subscale is indicative of an individual who (is):

1. feels understood and loved

2. reports having rewarding emotional involvements with other people
3. describes his/her family situation in positive terms
4. denies feelings of hatred and resentment toward family members

Emotional Alienation (Sc1B)

A high score on the Sc1B subscale is indicative of an individual who (is):

1. reports feelings of depression and despair; wishes he/she were dead
2. is apathetic and frightened
3. may exhibit sadistic and/or masochistic needs

A low score on the Sc1B subscale is indicative of an individual who (is):

1. denies feelings of depression and despair
2. not apathetic and frightened
3. feels that life is worth living
4. denies sadistic or masochistic needs

Lack of Ego Mastery, Cognitive (Sc2A)

A high score on the Sc2A subscale is indicative of an individual who (is):

1. feels that he/she might be losing his/her mind
2. reports strange thought processes and/or feelings of unreality
3. reports difficulties in concentration and memory

A low score on the Sc2A subscale is indicative of an individual who (is):

1. denies concern about loss of control of thought processes
2. does not admit to strange or unusual thought processes
3. does not admit to feelings of unreality
4. does not admit difficulties in concentration and memory

Lack of Ego Mastery, Conative (Sc2B)

A high score on the Sc2B subscale is indicative of an individual who (is):

1. feels that life is a strain; admits feelings of depression and despair
2. has difficulty in coping with everyday problems; worries excessively
3. responds to stress by withdrawing into fantasy and daydreaming
4. does not find his/her daily activities interesting and rewarding
5. has given up hope of things getting better
6. may wish that he/she were dead

A low score on the Sc2B subscale is indicative of an individual who (is):

1. feels that life is interesting and very much worthwhile
2. has the energy to cope with everyday problems
3. denies feelings of depression, excessive worry, suicidal ideation

Lack of Ego Mastery, Defective Inhibition (Sc2C)

A high score on the Sc2C subscale is indicative of an individual who (is):

1. feels that he/she is not in control of his/her emotions and impulses and is frightened by this perceived loss of control
2. tends to be restless, hyperactive, and irritable
3. may have periods of laughing and crying that he/she cannot control
4. may report episodes during which he/she did not know what was being done and later could not remember what had been done

A low score on the Sc2C subscale is indicative of an individual who (is):

1. denies concern about loss of control of impulses and emotions
2. does not admit to restlessness, hyperactivity, or irritability
3. does not admit to periods of activity that he/she could not control or could not later remember

Bizarre Sensory Experiences (Sc3)

A high score on the Sc3 subscale is indicative of an individual who (is):

1. experiences feeling that his/her body is changing in strange or unusual ways
2. reports skin sensitivity, feeling hot or cold, voice changes, muscle twitching, clumsiness, problems in balance, ringing or buzzing in the ears, paralysis, weakness
3. admits to hallucinations, unusual thought content, ideas of external influence

A low score on the Sc3 subscale is indicative of an individual who (is):

1. denies bodily changes, feelings of depersonalization, and other strange experiences characteristic of high scorers on this scale

Amorality (Ma1)

A high score on the Ma1 subscale is indicative of an individual who (is):

1. perceives other people as selfish, dishonest, and opportunistic, and because of these perceptions feels justified in behaving in similar ways
2. seems to derive vicarious satisfaction from the manipulative exploits of others

A low score on the Ma1 subscale is indicative of an individual who (is):

1. denies that other people are selfish, dishonest, or opportunistic and finds such behaviors unacceptable in himself/herself
2. denies receiving vicarious gratification from the manipulative exploits of others

Psychomotor Acceleration (Ma2)

A high score on the Ma2 subscale is indicative of an individual who (is):

1. experiences acceleration of speech, thought processes, and motor activity
2. feels tense and restless
3. feels excited or elated without cause
4. becomes bored easily and seeks out risk, excitement, or danger as a way of overcoming the boredom
5. admits to impulses to do something harmful or shocking

A low score on the Ma2 subscale is indicative of an individual who (is):

1. calm and placid
2. denies hyperactivity, restlessness, or tension
3. satisfied with a life situation that many other people might judge to be dull or boring
4. avoids situations or activities involving risk or danger

Imperturbability (Ma3)

A high score on the Ma3 subscale is indicative of an individual who (is):

1. denies social anxiety
2. feels comfortable around other people
3. has no problem in talking with others
4. professes little concern about or sensitivity to the opinions, values, and attitudes of other people
5. feels impatient and irritable toward others

A low score on the Ma3 subscale is indicative of an individual who (is):

1. quite uncomfortable around other people

2. has problem in talking with others
3. easily influenced by the opinions, values, and attitudes of those around him/her
4. denies resentment, impatience, irritability toward others

Ego Inflation (Ma4)

A high score on the Ma4 subscale is indicative of an individual who (is):

1. has an unrealistic evaluation of his/her own abilities and self-worth
2. resentful and opportunistic when others make demands on him/her, particularly if the persons making those demands are perceived as less capable

A low score on the Ma4 subscale is indicative of an individual who (is):

1. has a realistic notion of his/her own self worth or may even be extremely self-critical
2. denies resentment toward others who make demands on him/her

SUBSCALES FOR SCALES 5 AND 0

Development of the Subscales

As stated in the previous section, Harris and Lingoes (1955, 1968) did not develop subscales for scales 5 (Masculinity-Femininity) and 0 (Social Introversion) of the MMPI. Their omission of these scales was consistent with other early research efforts that did not consider scales 5 and 0 as standard clinical scales. In recent years there has been an increasing awareness of the importance of scales 5 and 0 in the clinical interpretation of MMPI protocols.

An early effort by Pepper and Strong (1958), who used clinical judgment in forming subgroups of items for scale 5, received little attention among MMPI users. Factor analyses of scales 5 and 0 by Graham et al. in 1971 provided the basis for the construction of subscales for these two scales. The factor analyses were conducted on scale 5 and 0 item responses of psychiatric inpatients, psychiatric outpatients, and normal subjects. For each of the two scales seven factors emerged, one of which represented demographic variables included in the analysis.

Serkownek (1975) utilized the data from Graham et al.'s factor analyses to develop subscales for scales 5 and 0. Items that loaded higher than .30 on a factor were selected for the scale to assess that factor dimension. Labels were assigned to the subscales on the basis of an examination of the content of the items included in the scale. Whereas most of the items in the subscales are scored in the same direction as for the parent scales, 14 items from the scale 5

Table 7.3. Subscales for scales 5 and 0 of the MMPI

Scale	Subscale		Test-retest reliability[a] Male	Female
5–Masculinity-Femininity	Mf1	Narcissism-Hypersensitivity	.83	.77
	Mf2	Stereotypic Feminine Interests	.80	.79
	Mf3	Denial of Stereotypic Masculine Interests	.82	.83
	Mf4	Heterosexual Discomfort-Passivity	.67	.69
	Mf5	Introspective-Critical	.76	.77
	Mf6	Socially Retiring	.80	.74
0–Social Introversion	Si1	Inferiority-Personal Discomfort	.89	.87
	Si2	Discomfort with Others	.68	.75
	Si3	Staid-Personal Rigidity	.87	.83
	Si4	Hypersensitivity	.79	.72
	Si5	Distrust	.82	.76
	Si6	Physical-Somatic Concerns	.58	.63

[a]From Moreland (1985b).

subscales and 7 items from the scale 0 subscales are scored in the opposite direction from the parent scales, to be consistent with their factor loadings. The scale 5 and scale 0 subscales are listed in Table 7.3. Item composition and scoring directions for each subscale are presented in Appendix F of this *Guide*. Although scoring keys for the scale 5 and scale 0 subscales are not available commercially, they can be constructed from the data presented in Appendix F.

Subscale Norms

Separate T-score conversion tables for males and females are presented in Appendix G of this *Guide*. If a profile sheet for plotting the subscales is desired, one can be constructed from the data in Appendix G.

Subscale Reliability and Validity

Only very limited data are available concerning the reliability and validity of the scale 5 and scale 0 subscales. Test-retest reliability coefficients (with a six-week interval) are presented in Table 7.3. Although no internal consistency data are available, one can assume that the subscales possess a high level of internal consistency because of the factor analytic basis for scale construction.

Interpretation of Scores on the Subscales

Because the scale 5 and scale 0 subscales only recently have been made available for general clinical use, no tradition exists concerning cutoffs for high and low scores on the subscales. Until additional data become available, the best procedure is to use the same cutoff scores as for the Harris subscales. Subscale T-scores greater than 70 should be considered as high scores, and subscale T-scores less than 40 should be considered as low scores. Because no validity data and only limited clinical experience are available for the subscales, the interpretive descriptions that follow are based on an examination of the content of items included in each subscale. The descriptions should be considered as preliminary, and should be expanded and/or modified on the basis of future research data and clinical experience with the subscales.

Narcissism-Hypersensitivity (Mf1)

A high score on the Mf1 subscale is indicative of an individual who (is):

1. self-centered, narcissistic
2. concerned about his/her physical appearance
3. sees himself/herself as extremely sensitive and easily hurt
4. lacks self-confidence
5. preoccupied with sexual matters
6. expresses resentment and hostility toward his/her family
7. characterizes other people as insensitive, unreasonable, and dishonest

A low score on the Mf1 subscale is indicative of an individual who (is):

1. self-confident
2. free of worry
3. denies concern about sexual matters
4. not very sensitive to the reactions of others
5. denies negative feelings about his/her family
6. characterizes other people as sensitive, reasonable, and honest

Stereotypic Feminine Interests (Mf2)[2]

A high score on the Mf2 subscale is indicative of an individual who (is):

1. expresses interest in stereotypically feminine occupations (e.g., nurse, librarian, etc.)
2. enjoys stereotypically feminine activities and pastimes (e.g., reading poetry or love stories, growing plants, cooking, etc.)
3. as a child liked stereotypically feminine play activities (e.g., dolls, hopscotch, etc.)

2. Empirical data (Graham et al., 1971) suggest that scores on the Mf2 subscale (Stereotypic Feminine Interests) and the Mf3 subscale (Denial of Stereotypic Masculine Interests) are relatively independent of each other. Thus, an individual can score high on both, low on both, or high on one and low on the other. For example, although a high score on Mf2 indicates interest in stereotypically feminine activities, it does not necessarily indicate a lack of interest in masculine activities.

A low score on the Mf2 subscale is indicative of an individual who (is):

1. denies interest in stereotypically feminine occupations (e.g., nurse, librarian, etc.)
2. does not enjoy stereotypically feminine activities and pastimes (e.g., reading poetry or love stories, growing plants, cooking, etc.)
3. as a child did not like stereotypically feminine play activities (e.g., dolls)

Denial of Stereotypic Masculine Interests (Mf3)

A high score on the Mf3 subscale is indicative of an individual who (is):

1. not interested in stereotypically masculine occupations (e.g., forest ranger, soldier, building contractor, etc.)
2. does not enjoy stereotypically masculine activities or interests (e.g., science, hunting, reading mechanics magazines, etc.)

A low score on the Mf3 subscale is indicative of an individual who (is):

1. interested in stereotypically masculine occupations (e.g., forest ranger, soldier, building contractor, etc.)
2. enjoys stereotypically masculine activities and interests (e.g., science, hunting, reading mechanics magazines, etc.)

Heterosexual Discomfort–Passivity (Mf4)

A high score on the Mf4 subscale is indicative of an individual who (is):

1. attracted by members of his/her own sex
2. uncomfortable talking about sex
3. passive
4. unaspiring

A low score on the Mf4 subscale is indicative of an individual who (is):

1. denies being attracted by members of his/her own sex
2. comfortable talking about sex
3. assertive
4. aspiring

Introspective-Critical (Mf5)

A high score on the Mf5 subscale is indicative of an individual who (is):

1. introverted
2. dislikes crowds

3. lacks self-confidence
4. does not subscribe to some fundamentalist religious beliefs (e.g., devil, hell, afterlife)

A low score on the Mf5 subscale is indicative of an individual who (is):

1. extroverted
2. enjoys and feels comfortable in loud, active social gatherings
3. self-confident
4. subscribes to some fundamentalist religious beliefs (e.g., devil, hell, afterlife)

Socially Retiring (Mf6)

A high score on the Mf6 subscale is indicative of an individual who (is)

1. socially introverted
2. tries to avoid being the center of attention
3. does not stand up for his/her own rights or argue in support of his/her opinions
4. does not seek out excitement, danger, or risk

A low score on the Mf6 subscale is indicative of an individual who (is):

1. socially extroverted
2. exhibitionistic; enjoys being the center of attention
3. stands up for his/her rights; argues in support of his/her opinions
4. seeks out excitement, risk, or danger

Inferiority–Personal Discomfort (Si1)

A high score on the Si1 subscale is indicative of an individual who (is):

1. lacks social skills
2. shy, easily embarrassed in social situations
3. finds it difficult to talk in social situations
4. does not make friends easily
5. avoids social interactions whenever possible
6. sensitive to criticism
7. socially suggestible
8. feels unhappy; views himself/herself as failure
9. indecisive; obsessive
10. impatient
11. has problems in concentrating
12. does not face up to problems

A low score on the Si1 subscale is indicative of an individual who (is):

1. socially extroverted; comfortable in social situations
2. makes friends easily
3. finds it easy to talk in social situations
4. not overly sensitive to criticism
5. feels happy and successful
6. patient, decisive
7. faces up to problems
8. denies problems in concentrating

Discomfort with Others (Si2)

A high score on the Si2 subscale is indicative of an individual who (is):

1. uncomfortable around most other people
2. dislikes crowds and large social gatherings
3. withdraws from social interactions whenever possible
4. lacks self-confidence; gives up easily

A low score on the Si2 subscale is indicative of an individual who (is):

1. enjoys being around other people
2. feels comfortable around most other people
3. seeks out excitement
4. self-confident; does not give up easily

Staid–Personal Rigidity (Si3)

A high score on the Si3 subscale is indicative of an individual who (is):

1. dislikes social groups (clubs, etc.) and parties
2. does not seek out excitement
3. avoids placing himself/herself in risky or competitive situations
4. has no desire to assume leadership role

A low score on the Si3 subscale is indicatve of an individual who (is):

1. enjoys social groups (clubs, etc.) and parties
2. seeks out excitement, risk, and competition
3. has periods of hyperactivity
4. blames others for his/her failure to accomplish great things

Hypersensitivity (Si4)

A high score on the Si4 subscale is indicative of an individual who (is):

1. overly sensitive to reactions of others; easily hurt
2. enjoys being the center of attention
3. broods; has problems in concentrating
4. does not face up to problems; gives up easily

A low score on the Si4 subscale is indicative of an individual who (is):

1. avoids being the center of attention
2. not especially sensitive to reactions of others
3. denies problems in concentrating
4. faces up to problems; does not give up easily

Distrust (Si5)

A high score on the Si5 subscale is indicative of an individual who (is):

1. has generally negative perception of other people
2. sees others as selfish, dishonest, insensitive, and untrustworthy
3. feels overwhelmed by problems and responsibilities
4. indecisive; obsessive
5. lacks self-confidence

A low score on the Si5 subscale is indicative of an individual who (is):

1. has naively optimistic perception of other people
2. sees others as trustworthy, honest, unselfish, and sensitive
3. faces up to problems; responsible
4. self-confident

Physical-Somatic Concerns (Si6)

A high score on the Si6 subscale is indicative of an individual who (is):

1. reports somatic symptoms including changes in speech and hearing, hay fever, or asthma
2. concerned about his/her physical appearance
3. broods; worries
4. socially introverted

A low score on the Si6 subscale is indicative of an individual who (is):

1. denies somatic symptoms such as changes in speech or hearing and hay fever or asthma
2. not especially concerned about physical appearance
3. does not brood or worry excessively
4. socially extroverted

WIGGINS CONTENT SCALES

Wiggins Content Scale Development

Although Hathaway and McKinley (1940) presented 26 categories for classifying the content of the MMPI item pool, they did so only to demonstrate that the items sampled a wide array of behaviors. The empirical keying procedure used in developing the original MMPI scales did not necessitate consideration of the content of individual items. Items were selected for inclusion in the original scales because they *empirically* differentiated criterion groups, and the content of the items was of no concern. With the exceptions discussed earlier in this chapter, among many MMPI users a tradition has developed that consideration of the *content* of an examinee's individual item responses might interfere with the empirical nature of the test.

In the 1960s and 1970s, some investigators suggested that the content of responses to items on the MMPI and other structured personality assessment techniques could add significantly to the understanding of an examinee's personality and behavior (e.g., Goldberg, 1972; Hase & Goldberg, 1967; Jackson, 1971; Koss & Butcher, 1973). Whereas a number of efforts had been made to construct MMPI scales on the basis of item content, Wiggins and his associates accomplished the most complete investigation of the content dimensions of the MMPI and developed psychometrically sound scales for assessing the content dimensions (Wiggins, 1966, 1969; Wiggins, Goldberg, & Applebaum, 1971; Wiggins & Vollmar, 1959).

Wiggins (1969) pointed out that two examinees with exactly the same profile based on the standard four validity and 10 clinical scales can have quite different patterns of scores on his content scales, which are listed in Table 7.4. He argued that consideration of the content scales in addition to the standard profile could add significantly to the understanding of the examinee. In common with what was stated above, he did not suggest that the content scales be used instead of the standard scales, but in addition to them.

Wiggins (1969) discussed in some detail the procedures utilized in developing the content scales. Hathaway and McKinley (1940) had suggested that the original MMPI item pool could be clustered on the basis of content into 26 categories. Initially, Wiggins treated each of these 26 categories as a scale, and a score was obtained for each scale by keying items in the scale in the deviant direction (i.e., the infrequent response of the Minnesota normal group). The internal consistency of these 26 scales was determined by analyzing the scores of 500 college students. Because the internal consistency of some of these 26 scales left much to be desired, Wiggins revised the scales based on the 26 categories suggested by Hathaway and McKinley by collapsing several categories into a single one, by reassigning items from one category to another, by eliminating some original categories, and by adding new categories. The inter-

Table 7.4. The Wiggins content scales

Scale symbol	Scale name	Test-retest reliability[a] Male	Female
SOC	Social Maladjustment	.90	.88
DEP	Depression	.83	.86
FEM	Feminine Interests	.85	.83
MOR	Poor Morale	.87	.85
REL	Religious Fundamentalism	.95	.93
AUT	Authority Conflict	.81	.83
PSY	Psychoticism	.81	.84
ORG	Organic Symptoms	.74	.77
FAM	Family Problems	.83	.85
HOS	Manifest Hostility	.85	.76
PHO	Phobias	.84	.83
HYP	Hypomania	.79	.78
HEA	Poor Health	.74	.73

[a]From Moreland (1985b).

nal consistencies of the revised content scales were determined for a number of different samples, and several more scales were eliminated because of lack of homogeneity. This series of revisions yielded a final set of 13 content scales (see Table 7.4) that are mutually exclusive, internally consistent, moderately independent, and representative of the major content dimensions of the MMPI. Cohler, Weiss, and Grunebaum, (1974) demonstrated that the content scales could be scored from a shortened (400-item) version of the MMPI. The abbreviated content scales were internally consistent and showed high correspondence with the longer scales.

The item composition and scoring directions for the content scales are presented in Appendix H of this *Guide.* Scoring keys and profile sheets for use with the content scales are available from the test distributor.

Norms for the Wiggins Content Scales

Normative data for the Wiggins content scales have been reported for college students (Fowler & Coyle, 1969; Wiggins et al., 1971) and Air Force enlisted men (Gilberstadt, 1970). Wiggins constructed tables for converting raw scores on his content scales to T-scores based on the Minnesota normative sample. Because the Minnesota normative sample did not respond to most of the items on the Feminine Interests scale, norms for that scale are based on college student data. Tables for converting raw scores on the Wiggins content scales to T-scores are presented in Appendix I of this *Guide.* These same data were used by the test distributor in preparing profile sheets for the content scales.

Table 7.5. Coefficient alpha internal consistency estimates for MMPI content scales in seven normal samples

Content scale	Air Force enlisted men	University of Minnesota Men (*n* = 96)	University of Minnesota Women (*n* = 125)	University of Oregon Men (*n* = 95)	University of Oregon Women (*n* = 108)	University of Illinois Men (*n* = 100)	University of Illinois Women (*n* = 83)
SOC	.829	.856	.835	.830	.862	.856	.843
DEP	.872	.860	.831	.821	.756	.842	.854
FEM	.585	.523	.505	.594	.566	.650	.542
MOR	.857	.866	.825	.804	.753	.867	.804
REL	.674	.892	.861	.842	.756	.817	.793
AUT	.681	.794	.772	.743	.669	.766	.698
PSY	.877	.794	.687	.738	.662	.763	.806
ORG	.863	.772	.645	.662	.695	.749	.731
FAM	.707	.712	.789	.712	.694	.806	.643
HOS	.764	.819	.794	.788	.651	.776	.765
PHO	.765	.663	.721	.568	.701	.705	.770
HYP	.671	.701	.715	.682	.632	.679	.667
HEA	.743	.557	.713	.555	.537	.673	.651

Source: J. S. Wiggins, Content dimensions in the MMPI. In J. N. Butcher (Ed.), *MMPI: Research Developments and Clinical Applications.* New York: McGraw-Hill, 1969. Copyright 1969 by McGraw-Hill Book Company. Reproduced with permission.

Wiggins Content Scale Reliability

Wiggins (1969) reported internal consistency estimates (Cronbach's coefficient alpha) for the content scales. These estimates for seven samples are presented in Table 7.5. An examination of these values indicates that most of the content scales have a high degree of internal consistency. Table 7.4 reports test-retest reliability coefficients (six-week interval) for 95 male and 108 female college students. The temporal stability of the content scales seems to be at least as great as that of the standard MMPI clinical scales.

Wiggins Content Scale Validity

Some evidence concerning concurrent validity of the content scales is available from studies that have related scores on the content scales to other measures of the same or similar characteristics. Wiggins et al. (1971) correlated scores on the Wiggins content scales with a variety of other MMPI scales, with scales from the Edwards Personal Preference Schedule, the California Psychological Inventory, and the Adjective Check List, and with scales assessing masculinity and femininity from the Strong Vocational Interest Blank. They obtained numerous significant correlations and concluded that their data offered evidence for the concurrent validity of the Wiggins content scales. Of special interest in the Wiggins et al. study are correlations between the content scales and the standard MMPI scales (see Table 7.6). Some of the content scales correlate so highly with corresponding standard scales that they can be interpreted in similar ways. The Social Maladjustment and Social Introversion scales seem to be measuring very similar characteristics, as are the Poor Health and Hypochondriasis scales. Other scales have high correlations with corresponding standard scales (e.g., Depression and Depression, Feminine Interests and Masculinity-Femininity, Psychoticism and Schizophrenia, Organic Symptoms and Hypochondriasis, Hypomania and Hypomania), but the correlations are low enough that one suspects that each scale is assessing some unique characteristics as well as some common ones. Other content scales have only moderate correlations with the standard MMPI scales and seem to be measuring unique characteristics.

Hoffman and Jackson (1976) found factor analytic convergence for the Wiggins content scales and scales from the Differential Personality Inventory in the areas of health problems, interpersonal conflict, depression and withdrawal, and familial problems. Taylor, Ptacek, Carithers, Griffin, and Coyne (1972) compared scores of psychiatric patients on the Wiggins content scales with other scales and self-ratings judged to be assessing the same or similar characteristics. They found generally good agreement between content scale scores and the other measures of corresponding characteristics. Lachar and Alexander (1978) reported replicated correlates of the Wiggins content scales for Air Force personnel and their dependents who had received psychiatric evaluations.

Boerger (1975) was able to identify empirical extratest correlates for some of the Wiggins content scales. In general, the correlates reflected closely the content of the Wiggins scales. Although many fewer extratest correlates were identified for the Wiggins content scales than for the standard clinical scales, as many correlates were identified for the content scales as for two different sets of factor analytically derived MMPI scales.

Payne and Wiggins (1972) examined the self-report of psychiatric patients whose profiles had been classified according to scores and configurations of scores on the standard MMPI validity and clinical scales. They found that when more complex rules were utilized for classification, the self-report of patients within a given profile type was more homogeneous. In addition, descriptions of the profile types based on self-report (the Wiggins content scales) were similar to descriptions based on empirical extratest correlates for the same types.

A number of studies have demonstrated that scores on the Wiggins content scales differ for various kinds of criterion groups. Wiggins (1969) compared his content scale scores of seven groups: normal Air Force males, male psychiatric inpatients, female psychiatric inpatients, male psychiatric outpatients, female psychiatric outpatients, college males, and college females. He found differences among the groups on many of his content scales. The largest differences were between college students and psychiatric patients, but substantial

Table 7.6. Correlations between Wiggins content scales and standard MMPI validity and clinical scales

Content scale	Standard MMPI scales												
	L	F	K	1	2	3	4	5	6	7	8	9	0
Males													
SOC	−001	325	−472	335	481	−180	083	305	132	598	488	−192	899
DEP	−282	561	−708	618	557	−027	438	444	315	877	788	257	685
FEM	013	203	−158	275	206	131	144	684	237	317	295	079	231
MOR	−256	460	−711	524	479	−136	314	384	197	847	700	200	725
REL	036	−264	055	−009	−165	−089	−139	−137	084	019	−073	−152	037
AUT	−349	388	−632	294	038	−385	301	−049	−273	422	440	531	243
PSY	−193	535	−577	449	223	−148	344	345	359	694	725	499	367
ORG	−153	520	−442	772	399	247	408	345	328	599	665	360	386
FAM	−139	449	−432	412	328	062	584	295	129	427	517	399	362
HOS	−375	408	−719	388	092	−348	277	143	−001	571	592	548	321
PHO	−236	283	−466	418	311	−092	169	270	176	561	471	115	491
HYP	−368	313	−601	323	021	−150	175	169	030	535	515	617	145
HEA	−207	457	−413	800	437	176	379	371	247	597	561	252	417
Females													
SOC	013	336	−356	177	485	−249	−021	188	171	456	352	−260	894
DEP	−267	501	−642	530	611	077	476	241	363	879	774	305	570
FEM	−141	−140	058	105	051	123	−055	587	131	073	−065	−079	−033
MOR	−307	460	−686	467	550	−063	336	237	267	851	689	232	663
REL	120	−265	142	−059	−212	023	−093	−062	020	−050	−088	−067	−055
AUT	−381	364	−597	214	021	−319	222	−268	−302	350	466	490	126
PSY	−245	566	−590	441	217	−023	363	112	361	694	765	530	301
ORG	−186	451	−403	738	328	339	312	120	244	560	643	379	233
FAM	−099	360	−462	274	225	028	551	151	143	446	534	404	190
HOS	−385	458	−698	292	045	−253	277	−098	038	560	645	585	215
PHO	−182	180	−385	321	273	043	072	181	123	487	354	040	385
HYP	−333	287	−563	334	019	−011	216	036	097	510	531	688	−060
HEA	−163	407	−305	835	408	394	311	285	188	527	484	280	248

Source: Unpublished materials provided by Lewis Goldberg, Oregon Research Institute.

differences also were found between college males and Air Force males and between male and female psychiatric outpatients. Wiggins (1969) also reported data concerning the ordering of means on his content scales for groups differing in degree of psychopathology. He concluded that his content scales do not provide measures of pathology that are consistent with the conventional meaning of the term.

Wiggins (1969) used his 13 content scales as predictors of diagnostic classification for six categories of psychiatric patients. The diagnostic groups used were brain disorders, personality disorders, sociopathic disorders, affective psychoses, schizophrenic psychoses, and psychoneurotic disorders. His content scales were related significantly to diagnostic classification for both male and female patients. The Authority Conflict, Poor Morale, Hostility, Psychoticism, and Depression scales were the most important contributors to group discrimination, but the Family Problems, Organic Symptoms, and Hypomania scales also were related to diagnostic classification.

Cohler et al. (1974) compared women hospitalized for psychiatric treatment after childbirth with an appropriate control group and found that the two groups differed for 11 of the 13 Wiggins content scales. Mezzich, Damarin, and Erickson (1974) reported significant relationships between psychiatric diagnosis of depression and 8 of the 13 Wiggins content scales. Comprehensive study of the protocols of 25 males, who were given the MMPI while in college and many years later were found to be alcoholics, indicated that the prealcoholic males and a control group of male college students who did not become alcoholic differed significantly on 2 of the 13 Wiggins content scales (Loper, Kammeier, & Hoffman, 1973). In addition, the scores of the college males who later became alcoholics showed changes for 5 of the 13 Wiggins content scales when they were retested while in treatment for their alcoholism (Hoffman, Loper, & Kammeier, 1974; Kammeier, Hoffman, & Loper, 1973).

A factor analysis of scores on the 13 Wiggins content scales (Wiggins, 1969) identified five important factor dimensions. Factor I, Anxiety Proneness versus Ego Resiliency, is similar to Welsh's first factor (Anxiety) and to Block's Ego Resiliency dimension. It has high loadings for the Poor Morale, Social Maladjustment, and Depression scales. Factor II, Impulsivity versus Control, is similar to Welsh's second factor (Repression) and to Block's Control dimension. It has high loadings for the Hypomania scale for males and for the Manifest Hostility and Authority Conflict scales for females. Factor III, Health Concern, is identified by the Organic Symptoms and Poor Health scales. Factor IV, Social Desirability Role Playing, is defined by a special social desirability scale included in the factor analysis and by the Religious Fundamentalism scale. Factor V, Feminine Interests, is virtually identical to the Feminine Interests scale.

It may be concluded that whereas validity studies of the Wiggins content scales currently available are limited, they do support the notion that scores on the content scales are related to important aspects of extratest behavior for a variety of populations. More empirical research is needed to specify more clearly how the content scales can be used in understanding an examinee's behavior and personality.

Interpretation of Wiggins Content Scale Scores

Most suggestions for interpreting scores on the content scales have been based on examination of the content of items in each scale. Wiggins (1966, 1969) provided the most complete interpretive information for the content scales, and the descriptions that follow are based to a large extent on his information. Also, inferences based on the data from the validity studies described above are included in the descriptions that are presented below.

Although some limited information is available about low scores on the content scales, most interpretive efforts to date have dealt only with high scores. In the absence of descriptive information about low scores on a content scale, it may be inferred that low scorers are not reporting the behaviors, feelings, ideas, and so forth characteristic of high scorers on that scale. However, it should not be assumed that low scorers on a content scale necessarily are the opposite of high scorers.

Because the use of the Wiggins content scales as part of routine MMPI interpretation is relatively new and infrequent, no strong tradition exists concerning cutoff scores for considering scores on the content scales as high or low. Boerger (1975) defined high scores on the content scales as those falling within the top 25 percent of his sample of psychiatric patients and low scores as those falling within the bottom 25 percent for the same sample. Using Wiggins's norms, these cutoffs for the most part ranged from T-scores of 60 to 70 for high scores and from 40 to 50 for low scores. Lachar and Alexander (1978) used a T-score cutoff of 70 to define high scores for some content scales and 60 for others. Low scores were defined as those of 40 or below. As with other scales discussed in earlier chapters of this *Guide,* the higher the scores are, the most likely it is that interpretive material presented for high scores will apply, and the lower the scores are, the more likely it is that interpretive information presented for low scores will apply. Although practicing clinicians will come to establish their own cutoff scores as they gain experience with the content scales, persons who are just beginning to use the content scales will find it useful to consider T-scores above 70 as high and T-scores below 40 as low. It should be understood that the descriptions that follow are based on limited empirical data and thus should be viewed as preliminary and tentative. The content scales are most useful for clinical assessment if used along with other MMPI scales and extratest information.

Social Maladjustment (SOC)

A high score on the SOC scale is indicative of an individual who (is):

1. self-conscious, introverted, and withdrawn

2. feels bashful, embarrassed, and shy in social situations
3. feels inadequate and inferior
4. tends to be reserved, reticent, and apathetic
5. if a psychiatric patient, may show depressive symptoms such as psychomotor retardation
6. if a psychiatric patient, is less grandiose than other patients

A low score on the SOC scale is indicative of an individual who (is):

1. outgoing and extroverted
2. gregarious and fun-loving
3. assertive
4. relates easily to other people
5. experiences no difficulty in speaking before groups
6. if a psychiatric patient, is less depressed, fearful, perplexed, and withdrawn than other patients

Depression (DEP)

A high score on the DEP scale is indicative of an individual who (is):

1. clinically depressed
2. experiences guilt, regret, worry, and unhappiness
3. feels inadequate and inferior
4. convinced of his/her unworthiness and believes that he/she deserves to be punished
5. feels that life has lost its zest
6. has little motivation to pursue interests or activities
7. has decreased sex drive
8. has difficulty in concentrating
9. anxious and apprehensive about the future
10. feels misunderstood
11. if a psychiatric patient, is more likely than other patients to show evidence of thinking disturbance, to talk or mutter to self, and to be slow-moving and sluggish

A low score on the DEP scale is indicative of an individual who (is):

1. presents himself/herself as happy and satisfied with his/her life situation
2. stimulated by his/her everyday activities
3. optimistic about the future
4. denies anxiety, worry, and depression
5. has a high degree of self-esteem
6. if a psychiatric patient, is more likely than other patients to be irritable, impatient, and grouchy

7. if a psychiatric patient, is less likely than other patients to feel anxious, depressed, or guilty, or to show motor retardation

Feminine Interests (FEM)

A high score on the FEM scale is indicative of an individual who (is):

1. expresses more interest in activities, games, and occupations that are stereotypically feminine than most members of his/her sex
2. as a child, liked stereotypically feminine games
3. likes activities such as cooking and growing flowers
4. says he/she would like occupations such as florist, nurse, or dressmaker
5. has romantic outlook on life
6. identifies with females
7. denies liking stereotypically masculine activities such as hunting, fishing, or auto racing
8. says that he/she would not like occupations such as forest ranger or building contractor
9. has cultural and aesthetic interests such as poetry, literature, theater, etc.
10. if male, is more likely to come from higher socioeconomic class
11. feels perplexed
12. has difficulty in concentration

A low score on the FEM scale is indicative of an individual who (is):

1. denies liking stereotypically feminine activities, games, and interests
2. professes interest in and liking of stereotypically masculine activities and occupations
3. not likely to have strong cultural or aesthetic interests
4. if male, has a strong traditional masculine identification
5. if female, is rejecting the traditional female role

Authority Conflict (AUT)

A high score on the AUT scale is indicative of an individual who (is):

1. sees the world as a jungle in which everyone must fight to exist
2. characterizes other people as dishonest, untrustworthy, and motivated primarily by selfish needs
3. expresses little respect for laws or for authority figures
4. may have been in trouble with the law
5. feels that it is acceptable to lie to keep out of trouble
6. enjoys excitement and risk
7. obtains vicarious gratification from the activities of other people who engage in asocial or antisocial behavior

8. because of his/her negative perceptions of other people, feels justified in behaving in selfish, insensitive ways

A low score on the AUT scale is indicative of an individual who (is):

1. has a trusting attitude toward the world
2. sees other people as sensitive, honest, and law-abiding
3. respects the law, social standards, and authority figures
4. feels that it is best to be honest, even if honesty gets him/her into trouble
5. denies having been in trouble with the law
6. does not seek out excitement and risk
7. if a psychiatric patient, less likely than other patients to hallucinate, to talk or mutter to self, or to have conceptual disorganization

Psychoticism (PSY)

A high score on the PSY scale is indicative of an individual who (is):

1. admits to a wide variety of clearly psychotic symptoms, including:
   a. hallucinations
   b. confused thinking; unusual thought content
   c. mannerisms or posturing
   d. clearly paranoid orientation
   e. loss of control of thinking and behavior
2. feels misunderstood, mistreated, and persecuted
3. feels that other people are trying to influence his/her behavior
4. responds to a threatening and hostile world by withdrawing into fantasy and daydreaming
5. has unrealistic self-appraisal
6. sees self as important, sensitive, and dutiful person who could be of great benefit to the world if given a fair chance

A low score on the PSY scale is indicative of an individual who (is):

1. does not admit to the wide variety of psychotic symptoms characteristic of high scorers on this scale
2. does not have exaggerated appraisal of his/her own worth
3. does not tend to withdraw from people
4. does not engage in excessive fantasy or daydreaming

Organic Symptoms (ORG)

A high score on the ORG scale is indicative of an individual who (is):

1. reports symptoms that could be suggestive of a neurological disorder (e.g.,

fits or convulsions, paralysis, clumsiness, loss of balance, double vision, etc.)

2. reports many somatic symptoms that could be functional in origin:
   a. nausea, vomiting, anorexia
   b. back pain, head pain, joint pain
   c. skin sensitivity or numbness
   d. dizziness
   e. shaky hands; twitching muscles
   f. problems with speech, hearing, or vision
   g. weakness, fatigue
3. has difficulties in memory and concentration
4. has decreased sex drive
5. experiences insomnia
6. shows poor judgment
7. admits having periods during which he/she carried out activities without awareness of what he/she was doing
8. if a psychiatric patient, more likely than other patients to be anxious and to experience conceptual disorganization

A low score on the ORG scale is indicative of an individual who (is):

1. presents few, if any, somatic complaints
2. denies difficulties in conentration, attention, or memory

Family Problems (FAM)[3]

A high score on the FAM scale is indicative of an individual who (is):

1. describes his/her home and family situation as unpleasant[4]
2. says his/her home situation is lacking in love and understanding
3. admits to having had the desire to run away from the home situation
4. sees his/her parents as nervous, critical, quick-tempered, and quarrelsome
5. feels that his/her parents object to his/her friends and acquaintances
6. reports that his/her family does frightening and irritating things
7. feels that his/her family treats him/her more like a child than like an adult
8. has decreased sex drive
9. is having significant marital conflicts
10. if a psychiatric patient, more likely than other patients to have been given clinical diagnosis of personality disorder or adjustment disorder

3. This scale seems to assess the same characteristics as the Pd1 Harris subscale (Familial Discord) discussed earlier in this chapter.

4. Because some of the items in the FAM scale are phrased with specific reference to the parental home and other itmes are much more vague, high scorers may be describing their parental homes, their current homes, or both. The examiner may find it useful to examine responses to individual items on the FAM scale to try to differentiate between the two home situations.

A low score on the FAM scale is indicative of a person who (is):

1. describes his/her home and family situation as pleasant
2. characterizes his/her home situation as loving and understanding
3. feels that his/her parents accept his/her friends and acquaintances
4. does not have significant marital conflicts

Poor Morale (MOR)

A high score on the MOR scale is indicative of an individual who (is):

1. lacks self-confidence
2. feels inadequate and inferior
3. feels like a failure in life
4. overwhelmed by feelings of uselessness and despair
5. pessimistic about the future; has given up hope
6. avoids facing up to difficulties and responsibilities
7. sensitive to reactions of other people
8. socially suggestible
9. feels misunderstood but does not express these feelings for fear of offending others
10. may become combative when intoxicated
11. if a psychiatric patient, more likely than other patients to show paranoid symptomatology including conceptual disorganization, suspiciousness, and hostility

A low score on the MOR scale is indicative of an individual who (is):

1. very self-confident
2. faces up to difficulties and responsibilities
3. not overly dependent on other people for reinforcements
4. at times may seem to be quite insensitive to feelings of others
5. appears to be inner-directed; not socially suggestible
6. feels successful in activities
7. optimistic about the future
8. if a psychiatric patient, less likely than other patients to manifest paranoid symptomatology or to feel fearful and depressed

Religious Fundamentalism (REL)

A high score on the REL scale is indicative of an individual who (is):

1. presents himself/herself as a very religious person who attends church regularly
2. subscribes to a number of fundamentalist religious beliefs, including literal

interpretation of the Bible, the second coming of Christ, and the existence of hell and the devil
3. believes his/her religion is the only true one; intolerant of persons whose religious beliefs are different
4. not likely to use alcohol excessively
5. if a psychiatric patient, more likely than other patients to display conceptual disorganization, unusual thought content, and religious delusions

A low score on the REL scale is indicative of an individual who (is):

1. may have strong religious convictions but does not subscribe to the fundamentalist religious beliefs characteristic of high scorers on this scale
2. tolerant of religious beliefs and practices that differ from his/her own
3. if a psychiatric patient, less likely than other patients to have delusions
4. if a psychiatric patient, less likely than other patients to feel depressed and fearful

Manifest Hostility (HOS)

A high score on the HOS scale is indicative of an individual who (is):

1. harbors intense hostile and aggressive impulses
2. often expresses negative impulses in passive, indirective ways such as teasing animals, poking fun at people, being uncooperative, and being very critical of the shortcomings of others
3. resentful of demands placed on him/her by other people
4. resents being taken advantage of
5. retaliatory in interpersonal relationships
6. cross, grouchy, and argumentative
7. competitive; socially aggressive

A low score on the HOS scale is indicative of an individual who (is):

1. does not admit to strong hostile or aggressive impulses
2. not critical and resentful in interpersonal relationships
3. seen by others as easygoing and somewhat passive

Phobias (PHO)

A high score on the PHO scale is indicative of an individual who (is):

1. admits to generalized fear, worry, or anxiety
2. admits to fear or anxiety associated with many different objects and/or situations including:
   a. animals (snakes, spiders, etc.)

   b. storms
   c. closed places
   d. open places
   e. heights
   f. darkness
   g. fire
   h. money
   i. blood
   j. disease
3. fearful of people, particularly groups or crowds
4. if T-score is greater than 70, experiences a generalized and incapacitating fear or anxiety that may be masking more serious psychopathology

A low score on the PHO scale is indicative of an individual who (is):

1. does not admit to the multiple fears characteristic of high scorers on the scale (although some specific fear(s) may be reported)
2. comfortable around groups of people

Hypomania (HYP)

A high score on the HYP scale is indicative of an individual who (is):

1. characterized by periods of excitement, happiness, or cheerfulness that often are unexplainable
2. tense, restless, high-strung
3. becomes bored easily
4. seeks out excitement and change
5. has broad interests, often undertaking more than he can handle
6. dislikes details and routine; often does not see things through to completion
7. immature
8. impulsive; makes quick decisions without carefully considering the consequences of the decisions
9. has poor tolerance for frustration; flies off the handle easily
10. does not harbor grudges; quick to forgive and forget

A low score on the HYP scale is indicative of an individual who (is):

1. has limited drive and energy level
2. may have difficulty getting started on things
3. reliable, persistent; likely to see a job through to completion
4. does not anger easily
5. seems satisfied with a life-style that others might judge to be boring and uneventful

Poor Health (HEA)

A high score on the HEA scale is indicative of an individual who (is):

1. expresses concern about health and physical functioning in general
2. admits to some physical preoccupation, often gastrointestinal in nature (eating, drinking, stomach discomfort, elimination, etc.)
3. presents other somatic complaints including:
   a. coughing
   b. pains in heart or chest
   c. hay fever; asthma
   d. breaking out of skin
   e. shortness of breath
   f. difficulties with sex organs
   g. tiredness, fatigue
4. does not complain of difficulties in motor activity or in cognitive functioning

A low score on the HEA scale is indicative of an individual who (is):

1. not preoccupied with health and physical functioning
2. does not admit to the somatic complaints characteristic of high scores on the scale

CRITICAL ITEMS

MMPI critical items are items whose content is judged to be indicative of serious psychopathology. The first set of MMPI critical items was identified by Grayson (1951) based on subjective clinical judgment. The 38 items dealt primarily with severe psychotic symptoms and overlapped considerably with scales F and 8. Grayson believed that responses in the scored direction to any of these items suggested potentially serious emotional problems that should be studied further. Caldwell (1969) also generated intuitively a more comprehensive set of critical items that he intended for use with computerized scoring and interpretive services. Koss, Butcher, and Hoffman (1976) investigated the validity of the Grayson and Caldwell critical items as indicators of crises, and they concluded that both sets of items performed poorly as indices of serious malfunctioning.

Koss, Butcher, and Hoffman (1976) asked clinicians to nominate MMPI items that seemed to be related to six crisis areas (acute anxiety state, depressed suicidal ideation, threatened assault, situational stress due to alcoholism, mental confusion, and persecutory ideas). The nominated items were then compared with criterion measures of the crises, resulting in a list of 73 valid critical items. The Koss-Butcher critical items are listed in Appendix J. Lachar and Wrobel (1979) used a similar approach in identifying 111 critical items related to 14 problem areas frequently encountered in inpatient and outpatient samples. The Lachar-Wrobel critical items also are listed in Appendix J. Although the Koss-Butcher and Lachar-Wrobel critical item sets overlap with the earlier sets developed by Grayson and Caldwell, their content is much broader than that of the earlier sets.

Koss (1979, 1980) summarized the usefulness of the critical items. Research suggests that the Koss-Butcher and Lachar-Wrobel critical items are more valid than the Grayson and Caldwell critical items. Both of these newer sets of items overlap considerably with scales F and 8. In addition, most of the critical items are keyed in the true direction. These characteristics suggest that the critical item endorsements can be influenced greatly by persons using an acquiesence response set and those trying to exaggerate their problems. The critical items should not be interpreted unless the examiner is confident that neither of these response sets was operating when the subject responded to the MMPI items.

The critical items represent an additional source of hypotheses concerning test subjects. Because each item is in essence a single item scale, the reliability of each item is considerably less than that of the standard MMPI scales. Thus, the responses should not be overinterpreted. In a valid protocol, endorsement of critical items should lead the clinician to inquire further in the areas assessed by the items. No conclusions should be reached on the basis of critical item endorsements alone. It is not appropriate to count the number of critical item endorsements and use this count as one would use a score on an MMPI scale.

8

Supplementary Scales

In addition to its utilization in the construction of the standard validity and clinical scales, the MMPI item pool has been used to develop numerous other scales by variously recombining the 566 items using item analytic, factor analytic, and intuitive procedures. Dahlstrom, Welsh, and Dahlstrom (1972, 1975) presented more than 450 supplementary scales. Graham (1978) reviewed some of the more important of these scales. The supplementary scales have quite diverse labels, ranging from more traditional ones, such as Dominance and Suspiciousness, to more unusual ones, such as Success in Baseball and Yeshiva College Subcultural Scale. The scales vary considerably in terms of what they are supposed to measure, the manner in which they were constructed, their reliabilities, the extent to which they have been cross-validated, the availability of normative data, and the amount of additional validity data that has been generated. They also vary in terms of how frequently they have been utilized in clinical and research settings. Some scales appear to have been used only by their constructors, whereas others have been employed extensively in research studies and are used routinely in clinical interpretation of the MMPI.

The typical MMPI user cannot be aware of all of these additional scales and does not have the technical information required to evaluate their adequacy and potential utility. The purpose of this chapter is to review a relatively small number of the supplementary scales which, in the opinion of the author, have the greatest potential usefulness in clinical practice. Several criteria were used in deciding which scales to present. First, to be included a scale must be one intended to assess characteristics of interest to the practicing clinician. Second, there should be enough information available in the literature about the scale to permit meaningful conclusions about it. A few scales are included that do not meet the second criteria because the author's clinical experience suggests that they have potential utility even though adequate research concerning them does not yet exist.

Some readers may wonder why the subtle and obvious subscales that were developed by Wiener (1948) are not presented in this *Guide*. Wiener intuitively sorted items within some clinical scales into two categories. Obvious items were those whose content appeared to be related to psychopathology. Subtle items were those whose content did not seem to be related obviously to psychopathology. Wiener maintained that subtle items are of diagnostic importance because of their resistance to intentional response distortion. Interpretive information for the subtle and obvious subscales is not presented because subsequent research has indicated that the distinction between subtle and obvious items is not a meaningful or useful one. The obvious items within a scale are the most important ones in predicting nontest characteristics of subjects (Burkhart, Gynther, & Fromuth, 1980; Christian, Burkhart, & Gynther, 1978; Clayton, 1980; Gynther, Burkhart, & Hovanitz, 1979; Harper, 1981; Snyter & Graham, 1984). Most of the subtle items would not have remained in the clinical scales if Hathaway and McKinley had cross-validated the scales at the item level.

The format for discussing each scale is the same. Scale development information is presented, and, to the extent that they are available, reliability and validity data are reported. Interpretive information for high and low scores on each scale also is summarized. As with the clinical and validity scales, no absolute cutoffs for high and low scores can be determined. In general, T-scores greater than 70 should be considered as high scores, and T-scores below 40 should be considered as low scores. Whenever information about specific cutoff scores for a scale is available, such information is presented. The higher the scores are, the more likely it is that the interpretive information for high scores will apply. Similarly, the lower the scores are, the more likely it is that interpretive information for low scores will apply. Although an attempt was made to rely on research studies for interpretive information, in some cases so little research data are available that more subjective information, including analysis of item content and clinical impressions, is included. It should be emphasized that these supplementary scales are not intended to replace the standard validity and clinical scales. Rather, they are to be used in addition to the standard scales.

The composition and scoring of each supplementary scale are presented in Appendix K. It should be noted that the supplementary scales can be scored only if the entire 566-item MMPI is administered. The test publisher distributes scoring keys for the following supplementary scales: Anxiety (A), Repression (R), Ego Strength (Es), MacAndrew Alcoholism (MAC), Dependency (Dy), Dominance (Do), Social Responsibility (Re), Control (Cn), College Maladjustment (Mt), Overcontrolled-Hostility (O-H), Prejudice (Pr), Manifest Anxiety (MAS), and Social Status (St). The first four of these scales (A, R, Es, MAC) can be plotted as T-scores on the standard profile sheet. The test publisher offers a supplementary profile sheet for plotting the remaining scales listed above. A table for converting raw scores on the supplementary scales to T-scores is presented in Appendix L. The norm group used to calculate the T-score values was a subsample of the original Minnesota normal sample. The data in Appendixes K and L can be used to construct scoring keys and to transform raw scores to T-scores for scales for which the test publisher does not distribute scoring keys or profile sheets.

ANXIETY (A) AND REPRESSION (R) SCALES

Scale Development

Whenever the basic validity and clinical scales of the MMPI have been statistically factor-analyzed to reduce them to their most common denominators, two basic dimensions have emerged consistently (e.g., Block, 1965; Eichman, 1961, 1962; Welsh, 1956). Welsh (1956) developed the Anxiety (A) and Repression (R) scales to assess these two basic dimensions.

By factor-analyzing MMPI scores for male Veterans Administration patients, Welsh identified a factor which he originally labeled "general maladjustment." A scale was developed to assess this factor by identifying items that were most highly associated with the factor. This original scale was administered to new groups of psychiatric patients, and it was refined by utilizing internal consistency procedures. The 39 items that ultimately were statistically identified in this manner constitute the final A scale. Welsh suggested from an examination of these 39 items that the content of the A scale items falls into four categories: thinking and thought processes; negative emotional tone and dysphoria; lack of energy and pessimism; and malignant mentation. The items are keyed in such a way that high scores on the A scale are associated with more psychopathology.

The R scale was constructed by Welsh (1956) to measure the second major dimension emerging from factor analyses of the basic validity and clinical scales of the MMPI. A procedure similar to that used in developing the A scale also was employed with the R scale, and it resulted in a final scale that contained 40 items. Welsh suggested the following clusters based on the content of the R scale items: health and physical symptoms; emotionality, violence, and activity; reactions to other people in social situations; social dominance, feelings of personal adequacy, and personal appearance; and personal and vocational interests.

Reliability and Validity

Welsh (1956) reported reliability data for the A and R scales based on research by Kooser and Stevens. For 108 college undergraduates, the split-half reliability coefficients for A and R were .88 and .48, respectively. When 60 college sophomores were given the A and R scales on two occasions, separated by four months, test-retest reliability coefficients for A and R were .70 and .74, respectively. Test-retest coefficients for the A scale for college students with a six-week interval were .90 for men and .87 for women. Corresponding values for the R scale were .85 and .84, respectively (Moreland, 1985b). Gocka (1965) reported Kuder-Richardson 21 (internal consistency) values of .94 and .72 for the A and R scales, respectively, for 220 male Veterans Administration psychiatric patients.

It has been suggested by some writers that the major sources of variance in MMPI responses are associated with response sets. A response set exists when persons taking the test answer the items from a particular perspective or attitude about how they would like the items to show themselves to be. Edwards (1964) argued that the first factor of the MMPI, the one assessed by the A scale, simply assesses the examinees' willingness while describing themselves on the test to admit or endorse socially undesirable items. Messick and Jackson (1961) suggested that R scores simply indicate the extent to which examinees are willing to admit (acquiesce) on the test to all kinds of emotional difficulties. This interpretation appears to be supported by the fact that all of the items in the R scale are keyed in the false direction. Block (1965) refuted the response set or bias arguments by demonstrating that the same two major factor dimensions emerge even when the MMPI scales are altered to control for social desirability and acquiescence effects with the use of techniques developed by Edwards (1964) and others. Block also was able to identify through his research reliable extratest correlates for the two factor dimensions.

Welsh (1956) reported some unpublished data supplied by Gough for a group of normal subjects. Gough found that A scale scores correlated negatively with the K and L scales and with scale 1 of the MMPI, and correlated positively with the F scale and with scales 9 and 0. Gough also reported that high A scorers showed slowness of personal tempo, pessimism, vacillation, hesitancy, and inhibitedness. Sherriffs and Boomer (1954) found that high A scorers showed more self-doubt in examination situations. Welsh (1956) reported a study by Welsh and Roseman that indicated that patients who showed the most positive change during insulin shock therapy also showed marked decreases in A scale scores after such therapy. There also is evidence that A scores tend to decrease during psychiatric hospitalization (Lewinsohn, 1965). Duckworth and Duckworth (1975) suggested that a high A score indicates that a person is experiencing enough discomfort that he or she is likely to be motivated to change in psychotherapy. Block and Bailey (1955) reported reliable extratest correlates for high and low scores on the A scale. These correlates are presented below in the discussion of the interpretation of high and low A scores.

Welsh (1956) also reported that in the study by Welsh and Roseman the patients who were judged as most improved during their course of insulin shock therapy also showed some decreases in R scores in addition to the decrease in A scores. Lewinsohn (1965) found that only small changes were found in R scores during psychiatric hospitalization. Welsh (1956) reported data provided by Gough indicating that in a sample of normal subjects, R scale scores were positively correlated with the L and K scales and with scales 1 and 2 of the MMPI and negatively correlated with scale 9. Duckworth and Duckworth (1975) described high R scores as denying, rationalizing, and lacking self-insight. Block and Bailey (1955) identified extra-test correlates of high and low R scores. These correlates are included below in connection with the interpretation of high and low scores on the R scale. Below is summarized what these various studies on the A and R scales seem to have revealed.

Interpretation of High A Scores

A high score on the A scale is indicative of an individual who (is):

1. anxious, uncomfortable
2. has slow personal tempo
3. pessimistic
4. apathetic, unemotional, unexcitable
5. shy, retiring
6. lacks confidence in own abilities
7. hesitant, vacillating
8. inhibited, overcontrolled
9. influenced by diffuse personal feelings
10. defensive
11. rationalizes; blames others for difficulties
12. lacks poise in social situations
13. overly accepting of authority, conforming
14. submissive, compliant, suggestible
15. cautious
16. fussy
17. if male, has behavior that tends to be effeminate
18. cool, distant, uninvolved
19. becomes confused, disorganized, and maladaptive under stress
20. uncomfortable enough to be motivated to change in psychotherapy

In summary, high scoring A scale individuals, if from a normal population, are rather miserable and unhappy people. High scoring A scale individuals in a psychiatric setting fit such summarizing rubrics as neurotic, maladjusted, submissive, and overcontrolled. Because of their discomfort, high A scorers usually are highly motivated for psychotherapy or counseling.

Interpretation of Low A Scores

A low score on the A scale is indicative of an individual who (is):

1. does not feel anxious or uncomfortable
2. active, vigorous
3. expressive, colorful, verbally fluent
4. frank, outspoken
5. outgoing, sociable, friendly, informal
6. assumes ascendant role in relation to others
7. persuasive
8. ostentatious, exhibitionistic
9. efficient, capable, clear thinking

10. versatile, resourceful
11. self-confident
12. competitive; values success and achievement
13. interested in power, status, recognition
14. manipulates other people
15. unable to delay gratification of impulses
16. prefers action to thought; acts without considering consequences of actions

In summary, low A scale individuals are characterized as extroverted, competent, confident, and somewhat impulsive. Although such individuals are not likely to be experiencing serious psychological turmoil, they may or may not have adjustment problems.

Interpretation of High R Scores

A high score on the R scale is indicative of an individual who (is):

1. submissive
2. unexcitable
3. conventional, formal
4. clear thinking
5. slow; painstaking

In summary, a high R scorer is an internalizing individual who has adopted a rather careful and cautious life-style.

Interpretation of Low R Scores

A low score on the R scale is indicative of an individual who (is):

1. outgoing, outspoken, talkative
2. excitable, emotional
3. enthusiastic
4. spunky, daring
5. informal
6. robust, jolly
7. courageous
8. generous
9. dominant
10. impulsive
11. aggressive, bossy
12. sarcastic, argumentative
13. self-seeking, self-indulgent
14. shrewd, wary, guileful, deceitful

In summary, low R scorers tends to be rather outgoing, emotional, and spontaneous in their life-styles, and take an ascendant role in interpersonal relationships.

Conjoint Interpretation of A and R Scales

Welsh (1956, 1965) suggested that a more complete understanding of an examinee is possible if the A and R scores are considered conjointly. Welsh (1956) reported some preliminary work carried out by Welsh and Pearson in which protocols of Veterans Administration psychiatric inpatients were categorized as high A–low R, high A–high R, low A–low R, and low A–high R. Different psychiatric diagnostic labels were associated with cases in the four quadrants (e.g., depressive diagnoses most often occurring in the high A–high R quadrant and personality disorder diagnoses most often occurring in the low A–low R quadrant). Gynther and Brillant (1968) reported that Welsh's results were not replicated when the quadrant approach was utilized by them with their own sample of psychiatric outpatients.

Subsequently, Welsh (1965) suggested dividing each scale (A and R) into high, medium, and low levels to form nine categories or novants. Using male Veterans Administration patients, Welsh identified protocols that fit each of his novants. He then determined the typical profiles for the novants and inferred personality descriptions from the profile configurations (see Table 8.1). Welsh noted that the descriptions are biased toward patient groups rather than normal individuals, and that the descriptions are intended to lead to hypotheses for further investigation and should not be taken literally and should *not* be used for "cookbook" interpretation of profiles. Duckworth and Duckworth (1975) reported that they did not find Welsh's descriptions of the novants to be very accurate for college counselees, except for the high A–high R interpretation.

EGO STRENGTH (Es) SCALE

Scale Development

The Ego Strength (Es) scale was developed by Barron (1953) specifically to predict the response of neurotic patients to individual psychotherapy. The 68 Es scale items were identified empirically from the 566 MMPI item pool by comparing item response frequencies of 17 patients who were judged independently as clearly improved after six months of psychotherapy with response frequencies of 16 patients who were judged as unimproved after six months of psychotherapy. The Es scale items deal with physical functioning, seclusiveness, attitudes toward religion, moral posture, personal adequacy and ability to cope, phobias, and anxieties.

Table 8.1. Summary of clinical descriptors for each novant in Welsh's A and R scale schema

Novant	Descriptors
High A–low R	Subjects falling into this novant may be expected to be introspective, ruminative and overideational, with complaints of worrying and nervousness. There may be chronic feelings of inadequacy, inferiority, and insecurity which are often accompanied by rich fantasies with sexual content. Emotional difficulties may interfere with judgment, so that they are seen as lacking common sense. Patients in this novant do not use somatic defenses, and although they seem able to admit problems readily, the prognosis is poor.
High A–medium R	Severe personality difficulties may be expected, with loss of efficiency in carrying out duties. There may be periods of confusion, inability to concentrate, and other evidence of psychological deficit. Symptoms of depression, anxiety, and agitation predominate, although hysterical disorders sometimes appear. Subjects are often described as unsociable.
High A–high R	Depression is often encountered, with accompanying tenseness and nervousness as well as complaints of anxiety, insomnia, and undue sensitivity. Generalized neurasthenic features of fatigue, chronic tiredness, or exhaustion may be seen. These subjects are seen as rigid and worrying in a psychasthenic way, and suffer from feelings of inadequacy and a brooding preoccupation with their personal difficulties.
Medium A–low R	This novant profile represents a heterogeneous group of subjects, but often there are headaches and upper gastrointestinal tract symptoms after periods of tension and restlessness. Symptoms are often noted in response to frustration and situational difficulties, although subjects are reluctant to accept the psychogenic nature of their complaints. Patients tend to drop out of treatment quickly, so that a superficial approach is frequently all that is possible. Ambition is often noted, but the level of adjustment may be poor with excessive use of alcohol.
Medium A–medium R	Somatic symptomatology in this group tends to be specific rather than generalized, with epigastric and upper gastrointestinal pain predominating. In some cases there may be an active ulcer. Patients not showing somatic symptoms may complain of tension and depression. Frequently noted is the ability of these patients to tolerate discomfort rather than acting out.
Medium A–high R	Subjects are often described as inadequate or immature and tend to use illness as an excuse for not accomplishing more. Lack of insight is often noted, with mechanisms of repression and denial prominent in adjustment attempts. Patients give a chronic hypochondriacal history with somatic overconcern, particularly in the alimentary system; abdominal pain is common. Response to treatment is not often favorable, because they seem to have learned to use somatic complaints to solve emotional problems.
Low A–low R	Aggression and hostility may be noted in many subjects, and they are often described as arrogant, boastful, and self-centered; some are seen as dishonest and suspicious. Patients may show episodic attacks of acute distress in various organ systems, but these physical problems are not severe and generally yield to superficial treatment.

(*continued*)

Table 8.1. (*Continued*)

Novant	Descriptors
Low A–medium R	Although subjects in this novant are characterized by attempts at self-enhancement, they are not viewed favorably by others; they tend to be seen as irritable, immature, and insecure. Under stress they are prone to develop symptoms which are usually localized rather than diffuse. Patients suffer from complaints arrived at after protracted periods of mild tension; these are rarely incapacitating, although there is an indifferent response to treatment, and marginal adjustment is often noted.
Low A–high R	Lack of self-criticism with impunitive behavior may be found in subjects in this novant, and they are often self-centered, with many physical complaints. Occasionally there is mild anxiety and tension, but little depression occurs. Patients more often have pain in the extremities and the head rather than the trunk, but precordial and chest pain may be noted. They profit from reassurance, although insight is lacking into the nature of their symptoms.

Note: Welsh indicated that he viewed these descriptions as providing the basis for hypotheses for further investigation, and he warned against their literal interpretation or use for cookbook interpretation of profiles.

Source: W. G. Dahlstrom, G. S. Welsh, & L. E. Dahlstrom, *An MMPI Handbook,* Vol. I. The University of Minnesota Press, Minneapolis. Copyright 1960, 1972 by the University of Minnesota. Reproduced with permission.

Reliability and Validity

The Es scale was cross-validated by Barron (1953) using three different samples of neurotic patients for whom ratings of improvement during brief, psychoanalytically oriented psychotherapy were available. Because pretherapy Es scores were positively related to rated improvement for all three samples, Barron concluded that the Es scale is useful in predicting personality change during psychotherapy. Barron also reported that the odd-even reliability of the Es scale for a sample of 126 patients was .76 and that the test-retest reliability, using a three-month interval between testings, was .72 for a sample of 30 cases. Moreland (1985b) reported test-retest coefficients for male and female college students (with a six-week interval) of .80 and .82, respectively. Gocka (1965) reported a Kuder-Richardson 21 (internal consistency) value of .78 for the Es scale for 220 male Veterans Administration psychiatric patients.

Unfortunately, subsequent attempts by others to cross-validate the Es scale as a predictor of response to psychotherapy or other treatment approaches have yielded inconsistent findings. Some data indicate that psychiatric patients who change most during treatment have higher pretreatment Es scores than patients who show less change (e.g., Wirt, 1955, 1956), whereas other data suggest that change in treatment is unrelated to pretreatment Es scores (e.g., Ends & Page, 1957; Fowler, Teel, & Coyle, 1967; Getter & Sundland, 1962; Sullivan, Miller, & Smelser, 1958). Distler, May, and Tuma (1964) found that pretreatment Es scores were positively related to hospitalization outcome for male psychiatric patients and negatively related to hospitalization outcome for female psychiatric patients. Simmett (1962) reported that Veterans Administration psychiatric patients with higher pretreatment Es scores showed more personality growth during treatment, which included psychotherapy, than did patients with lower scores, but pretreatment Es scores were unrelated to rated symptomatic change for these same patients. It should be noted that many of the failures to replicate Barron's finding that Es scores were related to change after *psychotherapy* utilized change after *hospitalization* and therefore did not represent a true replication of his study.

Dahlstrom et al. (1975) tried to explain the inconsistent findings concerning the relationship between Es scores and treatment outcome. They suggested that when high Es scores occur for persons who obviously are having difficulties but who are denying them, the high Es scores may not be predictive of a favorable treatment outcome. However, high Es scores for persons who are admitting to emotional problems may suggest a favorable response to treatment. Clayton and Graham (1979) were not able to validate the Dahlstrom et al. hypothesis with a sample of hospitalized psychiatric patients. It is clear from the existing literature that the relationship between Es scores and treatment outcome is not a simple one and that factors such as kind of patients, type of treatment, and nature of the outcome measures must be taken into account. In general, however, high Es scores are predictive of positive personality change for neurotic patients who receive traditional, individual psychotherapy.

There also are research data indicating that the Es scale can be viewed as an indication of overall psychological adjustment. Higher scores on the Es scale are associated with more favorable adjustment levels as assessed by other MMPI indexes and extratest criteria. Es scores tend to be lower for psychiatric patients than for nonpatients and for people receiving psychiatric or psychological treatment than for people who are not involved in such treatment (Gottesman, 1959; Himelstein, 1964; Kleinmuntz, 1960; Quay, 1955; Spiegel, 1969; Taft, 1957). However, it has been reported that the Es scale fails to differentiate between delinquent and nondelinquent adolescents (Gottesman, 1959). Whereas Es scores tend to be higher for neurotic patients than for psychotic patients, the scale fails to discriminate among more specific diagnostic categories (Hawkinson, 1962; Rosen, 1963; Tamkin, 1957; Tamkin & Klett, 1957).

There are some data indicating that Es scores tend to increase as a result of psychotherapy or other treatment procedures. Lewinsohn (1965) reported that psychiatric patients showed an increase in level of Es scores from hospital admission to discharge. However, Barron and Leary (1955) found that Es scores did not change more for patients who received individual or group psychotherapy than for patients who remained on a waiting list for a similar period of time. It also was reported that psychotherapy patients who were self-referred scored higher on the Es scale than those who were referred by someone else (Himelstein, 1964), suggesting that high Es scorers are more aware of internal conflicts than are low Es scorers.

Scores on the Es scale are related positively to intelligence (Tamkin & Klett, 1957; Wirt, 1955) and to formal education (Tamkin & Klett, 1957). The relationship between Es scores and age is less clear. Tamkin and Klett (1957) found no relationship between Es scores and age, but Getter and Sundland (1962) reported that older persons tended to score lower on the Es scale. Consistent sex differences in Es scores have been reported, with males obtaining higher scores than females (Distler, May, & Tuma, 1964; Getter & Sundland, 1962; Taft, 1957). This sex difference originally was interpreted as reflecting the greater willingness of females to admit to problems and complaints (Getter & Sundland, 1962). However, a more reasonable explanation of the sex difference on the Es scale is that males score higher than females because the scale contains a number of items dealing with masculine role identification (Holmes, 1967).

Interpretation of High Es Scores

From the above discussion, it may be concluded that high scores on the Es scale generally tend to show more positive personality change during treatment than do low scorers. However, the relationship between Es scores and treatment prognosis is not a simple one, and patient and treatment variables must be taken into account. Also, high Es scorers tend to be better adjusted psychologically, and they are more able than low scorers to cope with problems and stresses in their life situations. Among psychiatric patients, high Es scores are likely to be associated with neurotic diagnoses and low Es scores are more likely to be found for psychotic patients.

In addition, published studies (e.g., Barron, 1953, 1956; Dahlstrom et al., 1975; Duckworth & Duckworth, 1975; Good & Brantner, 1961; Quay, 1955) reveal that a high Es score is indicative of an individual who (is):

1. lacks chronic psychopathology
2. stable, reliable, responsible
3. tolerant; lacks prejudice
4. alert, adventuresome
5. determined, persistent
6. self-confident, outspoken, sociable
7. intelligent, resourceful, independent
8. has a secure sense of reality
9. deals effectively with others
10. creates favorable first impressions
11. gains acceptance of others
12. opportunistic, manipulative
13. has strongly developed interests
14. if male, has appropriately masculine style of behavior
15. hostile, rebellious toward authority
16. competitive

17. sarcastic, cynical
18. seeks help because of situational problems
19. can tolerate confrontations in psychotherapy

In summary, people with high Es scores appear to be fairly well put together. In nonpsychiatric settings, such people are not likely to have serious emotional problems. Among persons with emotional problems, high Es scores suggest that problems are likely to be situational rather than chronic, that the individuals have psychological resources that can be drawn upon in helping them to solve the problems, and that the prognosis for positive change in psychotherapy or counseling is good.

Interpretation of Low Es Scores

In general, low Es scorers tend to be less well adjusted psychologically than high Es scorers, and they are not well equipped to deal with problems and stresses. In general, low scorers are likely to show less positive personality change during treatment. Among psychiatric patients, low Es scorers are more likely to be diagnosed as psychotic than as neurotic or personality disorder. In addition, Barron (1953, 1956), Dahlstrom and Welsh (1960), Dahlstrom et al. (1975), Duckworth and Duckworth (1975), and Good and Brantner (1961) suggested that a low score on the Es scale is indicative of an individual who (is):

1. has poor self-concept; feels worthless; broods
2. feels helpless
3. confused
4. has chronic physical complaints
5. has chronic fatigue
6. has fears, phobias
7. withdrawn, seclusive
8. inhibited, unadaptive
9. shows stereotyped, unoriginal approach to problems
10. mannerly, mild
11. has fundamental religious beliefs
12. rigid, moralistic
13. if male, has effeminate style of behavior
14. exaggerates problems as "cry for help"
15. has a poor work history
16. has problems that are characterological rather than situational in nature
17. expresses good intentions to change in psychotherapy but does not act on them

In summary, people with low Es scores do not seem to be very well put together. Such individuals are likely to be seriously maladjusted psychologically. Problems are likely to be long-standing in nature; personal resources for coping with problems are extremely limited; and the prognosis for positive change in psychotherapy is poor.

MACANDREW ALCOHOLISM SCALE (MAC)

Scale Development

The MacAndrew Alcoholism scale (MAC) (MacAndrew, 1965) was developed to differentiate alcoholic from nonalcoholic psychiatric patients. The scale was constructed by contrasting the MMPI responses of 200 male alcoholics seeking treatment at an outpatient clinic with those of 200 male nonalcoholic psychiatric patients from the same facility. These analyses identified 51 items that differentiated the two groups. Because MacAndrew was interested in developing a subtle scale, two of the 51 items that deal directly with excessive drinking behavior were eliminated from the scale. The items are scored in such a way that higher scores are more indicative of alcohol abuse. Schwartz and Graham (1979) reported that the major content dimensions of the MAC are cognitive impairment, school maladjustment, interpersonal competence, risk taking, extroversion and exhibitionism, and moral indignation.

Reliability and Validity

Moreland (1985b) reported test-retest reliability coefficients (six-week interval) for the MAC with samples of normal college men and women. The coefficients were .82 and .75, respectively. Several studies reported that MAC scores did not change significantly during treatment programs ranging in length from 69 to 90 days or during a one-year follow-up period after treatment (Chang, Caldwell, & Moss, 1973; Huber & Danahy, 1975; Rohan, 1972; Rohan, Tatro, & Rotman, 1969). Hoffman, Loper, and Kammeier (1974) compared the MMPIs of male alcoholics at the time of treatment to MMPIs taken 13 years earlier when they had entered college and found no differences in MAC scores over this extended period of time.

MacAndrew (1965) reported cross-validation data for his scale. A cutoff score of 24 correctly classified approximately 82 percent of the alcoholic and nonalcoholic subjects. Although classification rates have not been as high as those of MacAndrew, most subsequent research has indicated that the MAC effectively differentiates alcoholic from nonalcoholic patients in a variety of settings (Apfeldorf & Huntley, 1975; Rhodes, 1969; Rich & Davis, 1969; Rohan, 1972; Rosenberg, 1972; Schwartz & Graham, 1979; Uecker, 1970; Williams, McCourt, & Schneider, 1971). There also are data suggesting that drug addicts score higher than other psychiatric patients but not differently from alcoholics on the MAC (Fowler, 1975; Kranitz, 1972). Graham (1978) reported that pathological gamblers scored similarly to alcoholics and heroin addicts on the MAC.

In a longitudinal study, Hoffman, Loper, and Kammeier (1974) located MMPIs of alcoholic males in treatment; these MMPIs had been completed 13 years previously when they entered college. When the MAC scores of these men were compared with those of their classmates who did not become alcoholics, significant differences were found. There also are data suggesting that persons who drink excessively but who are not alcoholics score higher on the MAC than persons who do not drink excessively (Apfeldorf & Huntley, 1975; Williams, McCourt, & Schneider, 1971). The MAC also seems to be effective in identifying adolescents who have significant problems with alcohol and/or drug abuse (Wisniewski, Glenwick, & Graham, 1985; Wolfson & Erbaugh, 1984).

Several studies have suggested caution in using the MAC with black subjects (Graham & Mayo, 1985; Walters, Greene, & Jeffrey, 1984; Walters, Greene, Jeffrey, Kruzich, & Haskin, 1983). Although black alcoholics tend to obtain scores in the addictive range, classification rates are not very good because nonalcoholic black psychiatric patients also tend to have rather high MAC scores.

Interpretation

High scores on the MAC suggest the possibility of alcohol or other substance abuse. Obviously, it would not be responsible clinical practice to reach conclusions about substance abuse without obtaining corroborating information. In general, MAC raw scores of 28 and above strongly suggest substance abuse. Scores between 24 and 27 are somewhat suggestive of such abuse, but there will be many false positives (i.e., persons who are identified as abusers because of their scores who really are not abusers) at this level. Scores below 24 strongly contraindicate a substance abuse problem. Incorrect classification of nonabusers as abusers is especially likely to occur for individuals who have the extroverted, activity-oriented style commonly found among high MAC scorers but who do not abuse substances. Blacks who abuse substances are likely to obtain elevated MAC scores, but the tendency for black nonabusers to have elevated MAC scores will lead to more false positives than with white subjects.

In addition to the possibility of substance abuse, a high MAC score also is indicative of a person who (is):

1. socially extroverted
2. exhibitionistic
3. may experience blackouts
4. has difficulties in concentrating
5. may have history of behavior problems in school

6. self-confident, assertive
7. enjoys competition and risk taking

In addition to being contraindicative of substance abuse, a low MAC score also is indicative of a person who (is):

1. socially introverted
2. shy
3. conventional, conforming
4. lacking in self-confidence

DEPENDENCY (Dy) SCALE

Scale Development

The Dependency (Dy) scale was derived rationally by Navran (1954) to assess the strength of dependency needs. After an unsuccessful attempt to develop the scale empirically, Navran asked 16 judges independently to identify those MMPI items that, based on their own clinical experience, they felt were related to dependency. The initial 157 items identified by these 16 judges were administered to two samples of 50 psychiatric patients each, and internal consistency procedures were employed to identify further the items that had the most discriminability for both samples. The 57 items that resulted constitute the Dy scale. The items are keyed in such a way that higher scores are indicative of more dependency. The Dy scale items deal with problems such as feeling misunderstood, indecision, lack of self-confidence, excessive sensitivity to the reactions of others, somatic complaints, shyness in social situations, and religious concerns.

Reliability and Validity

Navran (1954) reported that the reliability (internal consistency) of the 57-item Dy scale for the 100 patients in the derivation samples was .91, and Gocka (1965) reported an identical Kuder-Richardson 21 (internal consistency) value based on 220 male Veterans Administration psychiatric patients. Button (1956), using a one-week interval between two testings, found a test-retest reliability coefficient of .85 for the Dy scale for a sample of 64 alcoholic patients in a state mental hospital. Moreland (1985b) reported test-retest coefficients (six-week interval) for male and female college students of .92 and .90, respectively.

In his original article on the development of the Dy scale, Navran (1954) reported that psychiatric patients scored significantly higher on Dy than did normals from the original MMPI standardization group utilized by Hathaway and McKinley, that the standardization group normals scored significantly higher than a group of graduate students, and that within the psychiatric patient samples nonparanoid schizophrenics scored significantly higher than paranoid schizophrenics. In another study, Button (1956) found that alcoholic patients did not score significantly differently on the Dy scale than did normal subjects, but both alcoholic and normal samples scored lower than psychiatric patient samples. Dahlstrom and Welsh (1960) reported a study by Warn which found that tuberculosis patients and epileptics scored higher than controls on the Dy scale, but paraplegics did not score differently from controls on the Dy scale. Zuckerman, Levitt, and Lubin (1961) combined items from the Dy scale with items from Gough's Dominance scale and found that a total score based on these two scales showed significant, but modest, relationships with peer ratings and self-ratings of dependency. Pruitt and Van deCastle (1962) found that higher Dy scores were associated with greater chronicity among welfare recipients. Pruitt and Van deCastle also reported the results of a study by Nelson (1959) which indicated that Dy scores were not predictive of length of therapy but that high Dy scorers were more likely to continue in therapy for at least one session after an initial intake interview. Button (1956) cited a personal communication in which Navran indicated that he viewed the Dy scale as a self-report of degree of dependency and not necessarily as an accurate measure of dependency. Conflict, in the sense of ambivalence, about dependency needs is suggested if scores on the Dy scale are not consistent with behavior or other evidence of dependency.

Interpretation of High Dy Scores

High scores on the Dy scale tend to be associated with general psychological maladjustment. A conflict about dependency needs is suggested when an individual has a high Dy score but behavior and other test data are not indicative of strong dependency needs. An examination of the content of the Dy scale items suggests that a high Dy score also is indicative of an individual who (is):

1. admits to strong dependency needs
2. feels misunderstood
3. feels dysphoric, unhappy
4. experiences somatic discomfort
5. lacks self-confidence
6. feels shy and embarrassed in social situations
7. excessively sensitive to the reactions of others
8. has traditional religious beliefs and may be worried about religious matters

In summary, a person with a high Dy score is likely to have very strong dependency needs that are not being fulfilled adequately. Such a person also may have serious emotional problems that lead to feelings of dysphoria and unhappiness.

Interpretation of Low Dy Scores

In general, low Dy scores are associated with satisfactory psychological adjustment. A conflict about dependency needs is suggested if a person has a low Dy score but behaves in a dependent manner. Examination of the content of the Dy scale items indicates that a low Dy score is indicative of an individual who (is):

1. does not admit to strong dependency needs
2. feels understood by others
3. feels happy
4. free of somatic discomfort
5. feels self-confident
6. comfortable and confident in social situations
7. not excessively sensitive to reactions of others
8. does not hold traditional religious beliefs and is not worried about religious matters

In summary, a person with a low Dy score is denying strong dependency needs and is not excessively sensitive to the reactions of others. Such a person is likely to be rather well adjusted psychologically and to feel happy and confident.

DOMINANCE (Do) SCALE

Scale Development

The Dominance (Do) scale was developed by Gough, McClosky, and Meehl (1951) as part of a larger project concerned with political participation. The 60-item scale includes a subscale of 28 MMPI items that can be scored separately from the total 60-item scale and for which normative data are available. The remaining 32 items are not MMPI items. High school and college students were given a definition of dominance ("strength" in fact-to-face personal situations; ability to influence others; not readily intimidated or defeated; feeling safe, secure, and confident in face-to-face situations) and were asked to nominate peers who were most dominant and least dominant. High- and low-dominance criterion groups were defined on the basis of these peer nominations, and both groups were given a 150-item questionnaire, which included some MMPI items. Item analyses of the responses identified 60 items, including 28 MMPI items, that differentiated between the high- and low-dominance criterion groups. The items are keyed in such a way that a high score on the Do scale is suggestive of high dominance. The 28 MMPI items included in the Do scale deal with a number of different content areas, including concentration, obsessive-compulsive behaviors, self-confidence, discomfort in social situations, concern about physical appearance, perseverance, and political opinions.

Reliability and Validity

Gough et al. (1951) reported a reliability coefficient (Kuder-Richardson 21) of .79 for the 60-item Do scale, and Gocka (1965) reported a Kuder-Richardson value of .60 for the 28-item Do scale for 220 male Veterans Administration psychiatric patients. A test-retest reliability coefficient of .86 for Marine Corps officers was reported by Knapp (1960). Moreland (1985b) reported test-retest coefficients (six-week interval) for male and female college students of .85 and .83, respectively. Knapp also reported correlations of .75 and .79 between Do scores based on the 28 MMPI items and Do scores on the total 60-item scale.

Gough et al. (1951) found that a raw score cutoff of 36 on the 60-item Do scale identified 94% of their high- and low-dominance high school subjects, whereas a raw score cutoff of 39 on the 60-item scale correctly identified 92% of high- and low-dominance college students. Correlations between Do scores based on the 28 MMPI items and peer ratings and self-ratings of dominance were .52 and .65, respectively, for college students and .60 and .41, respectively, for high school students.

Knapp (1960) found that Marine Corps officer pilots scored significantly higher on the 28-item Do scale than did enlisted men. The mean scores for the officers and enlisted men were quite similar to mean scores reported for high- and low-dominance high school and college students. Knapp interpreted his data as supporting the use of the Do scale as a screening device in selecting officers. However, Olmstead and Monachesi (1956) reported that the MMPI Do scale was not able to differentiate between firemen and fire captains. Eschenback and Dupree (1959) found that Do scores did not change as a result of situational stress (a realistic survival test). It would be interesting to know whether Do scores change as individuals change their dominance roles (e.g., when an enlisted person becomes an officer). Unfortunately, no data of this kind are available at this time.

Interpretation of High Do Scale Scores

High scorers on the Do scale see themselves and are seen by others as stronger in face-to-face personal situations, as not readily intimidated, and as feeling safe, secure, and self-confident. Although there is some limited evidence that high scores on the Do scale are more common among persons holding positions of greater responsibility and leadership, no data are available concerning the adequacy of performance in such positions as a function of Do scores. Also, a high Do score is indicative of an individual who (is):

1. appears poised and self-assured
2. self-confident
3. appears free to behave in straightforward manner
4. optimistic
5. resourceful, efficient
6. realistic, task-oriented
7. feels adequate to handle problems
8. persevering
9. has a dutiful sense of morality
10. has a strong need to face reality

In summary, high Do scorers are people who are confident of their abilities to cope with problems and stresses in their respective life situations.

Interpretation of Low Do Scale Scores

Low scorers on the Do scale see themselves and are seen by others as submissive, weaker in face-to-face contacts, unassertive, unable to stand up for their own rights and opinions, and easily influenced by other people. Low Do scorers are less likely than high Do scorers to be in positions of responsibility and leadership. Based on an examination of the content of the Do scale items, it appears that a low Do score is indicative of an individual who (is):

1. lacks self-confidence
2. pessimistic
3. inefficient, stereotyped in approach to problems
4. feels inadequate to handle problems
5. gives up easily
6. does not feel sense of duty to others
7. does not face up to the realities of his/her own life situation

In summary, low Do scorers tend to have difficulty in asserting themselves. In addition, they are not very effective in handling problems and stresses in their respective life situations.

SOCIAL RESPONSIBILITY (Re) SCALE

Scale Development

The Social Responsibility (Re) scale was developed by Gough, McClosky, and Meehl (1952) as part of a larger project concerning political participation. The original Re scale contained 56 items, with 32 items coming from the MMPI item pool. A score based on the 32 MMPI items can be obtained in addition to a score based on all 56 items, and normative data are available for the 32 MMPI item Re scale.

The four samples used in constructing the Re scale were 50 college fraternity men, 50 college sorority women, 123 social science students from a high school, and 221 ninth-grade students. In each sample, the most and least responsible individuals were identified empirically. The definition of responsibility utilized emphasized willingness to accept the consequences of one's own behavior, dependability, trustworthiness, integrity, and sense of obligation to the group. For the high school and college samples, high and low criterion ratings were based on peer nominations. Teachers provided ratings of responsibility for students in the ninth-grade sample. The responses of the most responsible and least responsible subjects so identified in each sample to the items in the MMPI item pool and to a questionnaire containing rationally generated items were examined. Items that revealed the best discrimination between most and least responsible subjects in all samples became the Re scale. The 32 MMPI items constituting the Re scale deal with concern for social and moral issues, disapproval of privilege and favor, emphasis on duties and self-discipline, conventionality versus rebelliousness, trust and confidence in the world in general, and poise, assurance, and personal security (Gough et al., 1952).

Reliability and Validity

Gough et al. (1952) reported an uncorrected split-half coefficient of .73 for the 56-item scale for a sample of ninth-grade students. Gocka (1965) reported a Kuder-Richardson 21 (internal consistency) value of .63 for the 32-item Re scale for 220 male Veterans Administration psychiatric patients. Moreland (1985b) reported test-retest coefficients (six-week interval) for male and female college students of .85 and .76, respectively. Gough and his colleagues also reported correlations of .84 and .88 between Re scores based on all 56 items and scores based on the 32 MMPI items in the Re scale for their college and high school samples.

Correlations between MMPI Re scale scores and criterion ratings of responsibility in the derivation samples were .47 for college students and .53 for high school students. For college students the correlation between MMPI Re scores and self-ratings of responsibility was .20, and the correlation between these two variables for the high school students was .23. Optimal cutting scores for the MMPI Re scale yielded correct classification of 78 to 87 percent of the most and least responsible individuals in the various derivation samples. Gough et al. (1952) reported some limited cross-validational data for the total (56-item) Re scale. They obtained a correlation of .22 between Re scores and ratings of responsibility for a sample of medical students. A correlation of .33 between Re scores and ratings of positive character integration was reported for a sample of fourth-year graduate students.

In two studies, persons with higher Re scores tended to have positions of leadership and responsibility. Knapp (1960) found that Marine Corps officers scored significantly higher on the MMPI Re scale than did enlisted men. Olmstead and Monachesi (1956) reported that fire captains scored higher on the MMPI Re scale than firemen, but the difference was not statistically significant.

Duckworth and Duckworth (1975) suggested that the Re scale measures acceptance (high score) or rejection (low score) of a previously held value system, usually that of one's parents. For persons above the age of 25, high Re scorers tend to accept their present value system and intend to continue using it, and low scorers may be questioning their current value system or rejecting their most recently held value system. For younger persons, high Re scores indicate that they accept the value system of their parents, whereas low Re scores indicate questioning or rejection of parental value systems. Duckworth and Duckworth also suggest that high Re scorers, regardless of age, are more rigid in acceptance of values and are less willing to explore other values. They also indicated that older persons tend to score higher than younger persons on the Re scale and that college students who are questioning parental values often receive quite low Re scores.

Interpretation of High Re Scores

High Re scorers tend to see themselves and are seen by others as willing to accept the consequences of their own behavior, as dependable and trustworthy, and as having integrity and a sense of responsibility to the group. They also are more likely than low Re scorers to be in positions of leadership and responsibility. High Re scorers are rigid in acceptance of values and are unwilling to explore other values. Younger persons with high Re scores tend to accept the values of their parents. Also, a high Re score is indicative of an individual who (is):

1. has deep concern over ethical and moral problems
2. has a strong sense of justice
3. sets high standards for self
4. rejects privilege and favor
5. has excessive emphasis on carrying his/her own share of burdens and duties
6. self-confident
7. has trust and confidence in the world in general

In summary, high Re scorers have incorporated societal and cultural values and are committed to behaving in a manner consistent with those values. In addition, they place high value on honesty and justice.

Interpretation of Low Re Scores

Low Re scorers do not see themselves and are not seen by others as willing to accept responsibility for their own behavior. They are lacking or deficient in dependability, trustworthiness, integrity, and sense of responsibility to the group. They are less likely than high Re scorers to be in positions of leadership and responsibility. Low Re scorers also are less rigid than high Re scorers in acceptance of values and are more willing to explore other values. Younger persons with low Re scores tend to deny the value system of their parents and to substitute another value system for the parental one. Older persons with low Re scores question or deny their most recently held value system and may have adopted new religious or political outlooks.

CONTROL (Cn) SCALE

Scale Development

Cuadra (1953) reasoned that the essential difference between persons with equal psychopathology who are hospitalized and those who are treated as outpatients is that the latter have more control over the expression of their pathology. The Cn scale was developed to assess this control dimension. Cuadra collected 30 pairs of MMPI profiles in which the members of a pair were similar in terms of age, sex, and profile elevation and configuration. However, in each pair one profile was of a person who was hospitalized for psychiatric treatment, and the other profile was of a person who was receiving outpatient psychiatric treatment. By comparing the MMPI item responses of the two groups of patients, 50 items were identified that were answered differently by two groups of patients. The items were keyed in such a way that high Cn scores indicate responses similar to those of the nonhospitalized patients. The content of the Cn scale items included awareness of one's own weaknesses, sensitivity to social criticism, religious beliefs, and involvement in exciting or risky activities.

Cuadra (1953) reported that scores on the Cn scale were significantly different for his two criterion groups, with nonhospitalized patients scoring higher, but he did not report any cross-validational data. Negative correlations between the Cn scale and the L and K scales of the MMPI and a positive correlation between Cn scores and F scale scores led Cuadra to conclude that one important dimension being tapped by the Cn scale is realistic self-appraisal.

Reliability and Validity

Gocka (1965) reported a Kuder-Richardson 21 (internal consistency) value of .58 for the Cn scale for 220 male Veterans Administration psychiatric patients. Moreland (1985b) reported test-retest coefficients (six-week interval) for male and female college students of .78 and .74, respectively. No additional validity studies of the Cn scale have been reported.

Interpretation of High Cn Scores

High Cn scorers who have serious psychological problems are not likely to exhibit problem behaviors to others and are more likely than low scorers to be able to handle their problems without being hospitalized. Duckworth and Duckworth (1975) indicated that the Cn scale must be interpreted in relation to the MMPI clinical scales. For persons with very elevated clinical scales, a high Cn score indicates an ability to control problems and to show only what they wish others to observe. Such control can be an asset, but it also can be a liability if the person chooses to hide problems from the psychotherapist and others who are involved in the treatment process. When a high Cn score occurs in the absence of marked elevations in the clinical scales, it is suggestive of an individual who is reserved and unemotional. Such persons may express a desire to be able to be more expressive of their emotions. In addition, a high Cn score is indicative of an individual who (is):

1. described by others as sophisticated and realistic
2. impatient with naive, moralistic, and opinionated people
3. aware of his/her own weaknesses
4. inwardly sensitive to social criticism
5. not accepting of traditional religious beliefs
6. rebellious toward authority
7. explores and experiments with the environment even though it may involve risk of social disapproval

In summary, high-scoring subjects on the Cn scale who have serious psychological problems tend to keep the problems to themselves rather than revealing them to others. Although this tendency allows such people to avoid hospitalization, it also may prevent them from admitting the need for help.

Interpretation of Low Cn Scores

When low Cn scores are found for persons with serious emotional problems, they indicate an inability to control problem behaviors and suggest that hospitalization may be required. Duckworth and Duckworth (1975) suggested that when low Cn scores are found in persons who do not have marked elevations on the clinical scales of the MMPI, they suggest the absence of serious psychological problems. In addition, a low Cn score is indicative of an individual who (is):

1. conventional
2. moralistic
3. not likely to experiment with or explore the environment
4. has traditional religious beliefs
5. has unrealistic self-appraisal

In summary, low Cn scorers having serious psychological problems cannot usually control their problem behaviors and may require hospitalization. Interestingly, low Cn scores also are found among persons who are free of serious psychological problems.

COLLEGE MALADJUSTMENT (Mt) SCALE

Scale Development

The college Maladjustment (Mt) scale was constructed to discriminate between emotionally adjusted and maladjusted college students (Kleinmuntz, 1960). Mt items were selected from the MMPI item pool by comparing responses of 40 adjusted male and female students and 40 maladjusted male and female students. The adjusted students had contacted a university clinic to arrange for a routine mental health screening examination as part of teacher certification procedures, and none of them admitted to a history of psychiatric treatment. The maladjusted students had contacted the same clinic for help with emotional problems and had remained in psychotherapy for three or more sessions. Item analytic procedures yielded 43 items that discriminated between the adjusted and maladjusted students. Items are keyed so that higher scores are more indicative of maladjustment. Kleinmuntz (1961) found that scores on the 43-item scale administered separately corresponded quite well to Mt scores derived from a standard MMPI administration.

Reliability and Validity

When Kleinmuntz (1961) administered the Mt scale to college students twice with an interval of three days, a test-retest reliability coefficient of .88 was obtained. Moreland (1985b) reported test-retest coefficients (six-week interval) for male and female college students of .89 and .86, respectively.

Kleinmuntz (1961) reported that college students who took the Mt scale when they entered school and later sought "emotional" counseling scored higher on the scale than did a similar group of students who sought out "vocational-academic" counseling. Using a Mt scale cutoff of 15, Parker (1961) was able to classify correctly 74 percent of maladjusted students who completed the Mt scale at the time that they sought counseling, but only 46 percent when the Mt scale was completed as part of a battery administered at the time of college admission. Parker's data and Kleinmuntz's own data led Kleinmuntz (1961) to conclude that the Mt scale is more accurate when it is used for identifying existing emotional problems than when it is used for predicting future emotional problems. Higher Mt scores for maladjusted than for adjusted students were subsequently reported in several different settings (Kleinmuntz, 1963). Wilderman (1984) found that within a college counseling sample higher Mt scores were associated with more elevated MMPI profiles and with more severe psychopathology as indicated by therapist ratings than were relatively lower Mt scores.

Female students tend to score higher than male students on the Mt scale. Mt scores of adjusted and maladjusted college students vary considerably from one college setting to another and among divisions within each college. This variation indicates that separate norms and cutoff scores should be established for each specific setting where the Mt scale is used.

Interpretation of High Mt Scores

Because of variations in Mt scores among college settings, it is not possible to identify an absolute cutoff score above which students should be considered to be maladjusted. However, among college students within a given setting, higher Mt scores are suggestive of greater maladjustment. Because the Mt scale has not been studied systematically in settings other than colleges and universities, it is not recommended for use with subjects who are not college students.

In addition to suggesting general maladjustment, a high Mt score for a college student is indicative of a person who (is):

1. ineffectual
2. pessimistic
3. procrastinating
4. anxious, worried
5. somatizes
6. feels that life is a strain much of the time

Interpretation of Low Mt scores

Within a given college setting, students with lower Mt scores generally are better adjusted emotionally than students with higher scores on the scale. In addition, a low score on the Mt scale for a college student is indicative of a person who (is):

1. optimistic
2. conscientious
3. relatively free of emotional discomfort

OVERCONTROLLED-HOSTILITY (O-H) SCALE

Scale Development

Megargee, Cook, and Mendelsohn (1967) suggested that there are two major types of persons who commit acts of extreme physical aggression. Habitually aggressive (undercontrolled) persons have not developed appropriate controls against the expression of aggression, so that when they are provoked they respond with aggression of an intensity proportional to the degree of provocation. Chronically overcontrolled persons have very rigid inhibitions against the expression of any form of aggression. Most of the time the overcontrolled individuals do not respond even with aggression appropriate to instigation, but occasionally, when the instigation is great enough, they may act out in an extremely aggressive manner. Megargee and his associates believed that the most aggressive acts typically are committed by the overcontrolled rather than the undercontrolled persons.

The O-H scale was constructed by identifying items that were answered differentially by extremely assaultive prisoners, moderately assaultive prisoners, prisoners convicted of nonviolent crimes, and men who had not been convicted of any crime. The 31 items are scored so that higher scores on O-H are indicative of more assaultive (overcontrolled) persons.

Reliability and Validity

Megargee, Cook, and Mendelsohn (1967) reported a coefficient of internal consistency (Kuder-Richardson 21) of .56 for the O-H scale for a combined group of criminals and college students. Moreland (1985b) reported test-retest coefficients for male and female college students of .72 and .56, respectively.

Although some studies (e.g., Megargee, Cook, and Mendelsohn, 1967; Deiker, 1974; Fredericksen, 1976) found that more violent criminals score higher on the O-H scale, other studies (e.g., Fisher, 1970) failed to find O-H differences between assaultive and nonassaultive prisoners. Lane (1976) suggested that some of the negative findings could be due to a confounding of race and the assaultiveness criterion and to the manner in which the O-H scale was administered. Although no data were presented to support the contention,

Lane stated that the O-H scale must be administered in the context of the entire MMPI. Data also suggest that when the O-H scale is used to identify assaultive prisoners cutoff scores should be identified individually for each setting in which the scale is used. There is little evidence to suggest that high O-H scores in groups other than prisoners are associated with violent acts.

Interpretation of High O-H Scores

In correctional settings, high O-H scores tend to be associated with aggressive and violent acts. However, the validity of the O-H scale is such that individual predictions of violence from O-H scores are not likely to be very accurate. In addition, cutoff scores for predicting violence should be established separately in each setting where the scale is used. The O-H scale has some potential use in other settings because it tells clinicians something about how subjects typically respond to provocation. Higher O-H scorers tend not to respond to provocation even appropriately most of the time, but occasional exaggerated responses of aggression may occur. A high O-H score also is indicative of a person who (is):

1. impunitive
2. reports fewer angry feelings
3. expresses less verbal hostility in reaction to frustration
4. more socialized and responsible
5. has strong needs to excel
6. dependent on others
7. trustful
8. describes nurturant and supportive family background

Interpretation of Low O-H Scores

Relatively little data exist concerning the interpretation of low scores on O-H. We do not expect the low scorers to display the overcontrolled-hostility syndrome described for high scorers. Low scorers may be either chronically aggressive persons or persons who are quite appropriate in the expression of their aggression.

PREJUDICE (Pr) SCALE

Scale Development

The Prejudice (Pr) scale was developed by Gough (1951a) to identify persons with anti-Semitic prejudices. The Levinsohn-Sanford Anti-Semitism Scale was administered to 271 high school seniors in a midwestern community, and the 40 highest scoring students (high prejudice) and the 40 lowest scoring students (low prejudice) were identified. The MMPI was administered to the students, and item analyses were conducted to compare the responses of high and low prejudice students to the MMPI items. The 47 items that discriminated significantly between the high and low prejudice groups were included in the Pr scale. The items in the Pr scale deal with such diverse things as intellectual interests, optimism versus pessimism, interpersonal trust, hostility and aggression, personal discontentment, self-assurance, inflexible thinking, and feelings of isolation and estrangement.

Reliability and Validity

Gocka (1965) reported a Kuder-Richardson 21 (internal consistency) value of .82 for the Pr scale for 220 male Veterans Administration psychiatric patients. Split-half reliability coefficients of .79 and .81 for college students were reported for the Pr scale (Gough, 1951a; Jensen, 1957). Jensen reported a test-retest reliability coefficient of .56 for the Pr scale for a sample of college freshmen, and Moreland (1985b) reported test-retest coefficients (six-week interval) of .81 and .87 for male and female college students, respectively.

After the scale was developed on a high school sample, correlations of .45 and .49 were reported between the Pr scale and the Levinsohn-Sanford Anti-Semitism Scale for college students (Gough, 1951ab). When Pr scores and scores on the California Ethnocentrism-Fascism Scale were correlated for high school and college students, coefficients ranging from .30 to .62 were obtained (Altus & Tafejian, 1953; Gough, 1951ab; Jensen, 1957; Sundberg & Bachelis, 1956; Tafejian, 1951). Pr scores also were found to correlate positively with Tafejian's 40-item prejudice scale (Stricker, 1961) and negatively with the Purdue Attitude Scale Toward Jews (Gough, 1951a; high scores on the Purdue scale indicate favorable attitudes).

Pr scores do not seem to be related to the sex of the respondent (Jensen, 1957). However, there is evidence that high Pr scorers are more likely to come from lower socioeconomic levels (Gough, 1951b), to have lower IQ scores (Gough, 1951b; Jensen, 1957), and to show poor academic achievement (Jensen, 1957). College students are more likely to score lower on Pr than high school students (Duckworth & Duckworth, 1975; Jensen, 1957). Also, students with different college majors differ in terms of Pr scores (Jensen, 1957). There also are data indicating that high Pr scorers are less well adjusted psychologically, as indicated by other MMPI indices of adjustment and faculty evaluations of student adjustment (Gough, 1951b; Jensen, 1957). Sundberg & Bachelis (1956) demonstrated that subjects can produce higher Pr scores when asked to respond as someone who was prejudiced and intolerant would respond, and lower Pr scores when asked to respond as someone who was tolerant and unprejudiced would respond.

Interpretation of High Pr Scores

Persons with high Pr scores are intolerant and prejudiced in their opinions and beliefs. They are extremely rigid in their beliefs, and they often will not even consider points of view different from their own. High Pr scorers are more common among persons of lower socioeconomic status, less intelligent persons, and persons with less formal education. High Pr scorers show poor academic performance and are less well adjusted psychologically than are low Pr scorers. In addition, a high Pr score is indicative of an individual who (is):

1. anti-intellectual
2. pessimistic; lacks hope and confidence in the future
3. cynical, distrustful, doubtful, suspicious
4. feels others cannot be trusted
5. fears exploitation by others
6. lacks self-regard, self-integrity
7. resentful of others; discredits achievements and abilities of others
8. hostile, bitter
9. discontented with current status
10. has a dogmatic style of thinking
11. lacks poise, self-assurance
12. feels isolated, estranged

In summary, high Pr scorers are very rigid and intolerant in their beliefs. Also, such people have a generally cynical, distrustful attitude toward other people and the world in general.

Interpretation of Low Pr Scores

Low Pr scorers tend to be tolerant and unprejudiced. They are flexible in their thinking and are open-minded and able to consider points of view different from their own. Low Pr scores are more common among persons from higher socioeconomic groups, with higher IQ scores, and with more formal education. College students often score very low on the Pr scale. Low Pr scorers tend to show high academic achievement, and they are well adjusted psychologically. In addition, a low Pr score is indicative of an individual who (is):

1. has intellectual interests
2. optimistic
3. can place trust in other people
4. self-confident, self-assured, poised
5. free of excessive hostility and bitterness
6. satisfied with current status

In summary, low Pr scorers tend to be open-minded and tolerant of attitudes and beliefs that differ from their own. They have a generally positive perception of the world and are effective in coping with their life situations.

MANIFEST ANXIETY SCALE (MAS)

Scale Development

The Manifest Anxiety scale (MAS) was developed originally by Taylor (1951, 1953) to select experimental subjects with high and low drive (anxiety) levels in order to study the effects of drive level on performance in a number of experimental situations. The scale was rationally constructed. Five clinicians were given a definition of manifest anxiety and were asked to designate items from the original MMPI item pool that were indicative of manifest anxiety. Sixty-five items on which there was 80 percent agreement among the judges and 135 additional buffer items constituted the original scale which was called the Biographical Inventory to disguise its intended purpose from examinees. After several subsequent revisions, a 225-item scale was developed. In addition to 50 of the original 65 items that showed the highest correlations with total anxiety scores, items from the MMPI L, F, and K scales and from a rigidity scale were included as buffer items.

Although subsequent revisions in the MAS have taken place, including attempts to simplify the vocabulary and sentence structure of items, the 50 anxiety items from the 225-item scale that constitute the MAS can be scored from the standard MMPI protocol. Although Taylor (1953) cautioned against scoring the MAS from a standard MMPI administration because of differences in buffer items, the scale typically is scored in this manner.

The 50 items in the MAS cover a rather wide variety of behaviors. Whereas many of the items clearly deal with overt signs of anxiety (e.g., sweating, blushing, shakiness, etc.), other items contain subjective reports of feeling nervous, tense, anxious, upset, etc. There also are many items that involve somatic complaints (e.g., nausea, headaches, diarrhea, stomach trouble, etc.). Difficulties in concentration and feelings of excitement and/or restlessness also are suggested by some of the items. Some items suggest lack of self-confidence, extreme sensitivity to the reactions of other people, and feelings of unhappiness and uselessness. The items are keyed in such a way that higher scores are indicative of greater anxiety.

Reliability and Validity

Hilgard, Jones, and Kaplan (1951) reported a split-half reliability coefficient of .92 for the MAS, and Gocka (1965) obtained a Kuder-Richardson 21 (internal consistency) value of .92 for 220 male Veterans Administration psychiatric patients. Taylor (1953), using a sample of college students, obtained test-retest reliability coefficients of .89, .82, and .81 over periods of 3 weeks, 5 months, and 7 to 19 months, respectively. Moreland (1985b) reported 6-week test-retest reliability of .90 for male and female subjects.

The MAS originally was developed to measure drive level in studies seeking to test Hullian predictions concerning the relationship between drive level and learning. Spence and Spence (1966) summarized these predictions and reviewed empirical evidence relevant to them. It was predicted that on simple learning tasks high scorers on the MAS would perform better than low scorers, whereas on more complex tasks high MAS scorers would perform worse than low scorers. Although the data relevant to these predictions are not completely consistent, in general they seem to support the predictions. However, it has become obvious that the relationship between anxiety and learning is not a simple one, and additional variables such as task difficulty, degree of perceived stress, etc., must be taken into account.

Byrne (1974) and Spielberger (1966ab) reviewed numerous studies conducted to clarify the relationship between anxiety, as assessed by the MAS, and many other extratest characteristics. They concluded that the relationship between anxiety and intelligence is not as strong as has been inferred from simple observation. Whereas most studies have reported small and often nonsignificant correlations between MAS scores and intelligence test scores, Spielberger (1966a) indicated that higher negative correlations are obtained with samples that include larger proportions of subjects of lower intellectual levels. The relationship between anxiety and academic achievement is generally insignificant across all ability levels. However, for subjects of middle level ability, higher MAS scores are negatively correlated with grades obtained and positively related to academic problems.

Byrne (1974) concluded from his literature review that MAS scores are positively correlated with other anxiety scale scores (e.g., separation anxiety, test anxiety) and to physiological measures of anxiety such as palmar sweating. Likewise, high MAS scorers tend to be rated high on manifest anxiety by observers. That MAS scores are related to general psychological maladjustment is suggested by data indicating that psychiatric patients achieve higher MAS scores than do medical patients or college students. In addition, high MAS scorers admit to more medical and psychiatric symptoms than low MAS scorers. MAS scores after psychotherapy tend to be lower than pretherapy scores. There also are data that suggest that high MAS scorers tend to perceive the environment as threatening and uncontrollable and that they are less able than low MAS scorers to control autonomic reactions to stress situations. High MAS scorers tend to focus on the present rather than the future and to rely on very recent past experiences in developing expectancies.

Spielberger (1966b) differentiated between trait and state anxiety. Trait anxiety refers to relatively stable, acquired tendencies to respond in an anxious manner in a stressful situation. State anxiety refers to temporary feelings of tension and apprehension and activation of the autonomic nervous system that fluctuate in response to situational changes. The MAS clearly assesses trait rather than state anxiety. MAS scores do not change in response to situational changes such as relaxation training or a stressful interview.

Interpretation of High MAS Scores

High MAS scorers are predisposed to experience great emotional discomfort in stressful situations. In such situations, they feel anxious, tense, and jumpy and are likely to experience some physiological changes such as excessive perspiration, increased pulse rate, etc. They perceive the environment as threatening and feel that they are at the mercy of forces beyond their control. They emphasize the present more than the future and develop expectancies on the basis of immediate past experiences. Whereas a high MAS scorer may do well on simple performance tasks, performance on more complex tasks, such as work or school performance, is likely to be impaired. In addition, a high MAS score is indicative of an individual who (is):

1. reports numerous physical or somatic complaints
2. feels excited or restless much of the time
3. has difficulties in concentrating
4. lacks self-confidence
5. overly sensitive to the reactions of others
6. feels unhappy and useless

Interpretation of Low MAS Scores

Low MAS scorers are not predisposed to experience extreme emotional discomfort in stressful situations. They remain calm and unruffled in such situations and feel in control of the situation. In complex learning situations, the low MAS scorer is expected to perform better than the high MAS scorer. In addition, a low MAS score indicates that an individual is self-confident and relatively free of physical or somatic complaints.

LOW BACK PAIN (Lb) SCALE

Scale Development

The Low Back Pain (Lb) scale was developed empirically by Hanvik (1949, 1951) to help with an important clinical challenge, namely, to differentiate between patients with chronic low back pain but with no evidence of organic disease and patients with similar pain but with clear evidence of organic disease. The 25 items in the Lb scale were identified from the total MMPI item pool by comparing the response frequencies of two groups of patients with low back pain (Dahlstrom & Welsh, 1960). One group consisted of 30 patients whose pain was diagnosed independently by other clinical criteria as due to protruding intervertebral disk, and the other group included 30 patients for whom comparable pain was diagnosed as quite likely not resulting from organic disease. The 25 items are keyed in such a way that high Lb scores are suggestive of functional pain (i.e., pain in which psychological factors are believed to be preeminent) and low Lb scores are suggestive of pain resulting from organic disease. The content of the Lb items includes multiple physical complaints, denial of social anxiety and negative feelings about people, lack of some traditional religious beliefs, restlessness, dysphoria, and failure to express one's attitudes and beliefs to others. Hanvik recommended that a raw score cutoff of 11 be used to discriminate between patients with functional versus organic pain.

Reliability and Validity

Gocka (1965) reported a Kuder-Richardson 21 (internal consistency) value of .22 for the Lb scale of 220 male Veterans Administration psychiatric patients. Dahlstrom (1954) reported that the Lb scale was useful in identifying patients with chronic low back pain for which no physical explanation could be found. He also indicated that recovery after surgery for known physical defects was poorer for patients with higher Lb scores. Lewinsohn (1965) found that Lb scores of psychiatric patients were lower at the time of hospital discharge than at admission.

Interpretation of High Lb Scores

In persons who are reporting chronic low back pain, high scores on the Lb scale indicate that the pain may be functional in nature, particularly if no medical evidence of an organic defect can be found. Whereas Hanvik (1949, 1951) found that a raw score cutoff of 11 yielded the best discrimination between functional and organic patient groups, Good and Brantner (1961) suggested using a T-score cutoff of 70. Although an optimal cutoff score quite likely should be established separately in each clinical setting where the scale is used, the higher the Lb scores are, the more likely it is that chronic low back pain is functional in nature. Although no other research data are available concerning other extratest correlates of high Lb scores, an examination of the content of the Lb scale items suggests that a high Lb score may be indicative of an individual who (is):

1. experiences physical discomfort in addition to the back pain (headaches, heart pounding, shortness of breath)
2. restless
3. denies getting angry or irritated with other people
4. somewhat dysphoric
5. does not express his/her opinions or beliefs to others
6. comfortable in interacting in social situations
7. does not have traditional religious beliefs
8. tries to cover up inadequacies and insecurities

In summary, when used along with other appropriate clinical criteria, a high Lb score suggests that psychological factors may be preeminent in reported low back pain. A person with a high Lb score tends to direct feelings and problems inwardly, where they may find expression in somatic symptoms.

Interpretation of Low Lb Scores

Among persons who report chronic low back pain, low scores on the Lb scale may be contraindicative of a functional disorder. Some medical evidence of an organic cause for their discomfort usually is available. As with high scores, no additional research data other than those cited above are available concerning other extratest correlates of low Lb scores. However, a reading of the content of the Lb scale items indicates that a low Lb score may be indicative of an individual who (is):

1. does not report physical or somatic discomfort other than the low back pain
2. happy and contented
3. admits getting angry and irritated with other people
4. expresses his/her opinions or beliefs to others
5. uncomfortable and shy in social situations
6. has traditional religious beliefs
7. rather open about his/her inadequacies and insecurities

In summary, when used along with other appropriate clinical criteria, a low Lb score suggests that organic rather than psychological factors may be preeminent in reported low back pain. A person with a low Lb score tends to be rather open and honest about his/her feelings and insecurities.

CAUDALITY (Ca) SCALE

Scale Development

Although the differential diagnosis of frontal versus parietal lobe damage has been and should continue to be made primarily on the basis of neurological and other medical evidence, there have been several efforts to develop MMPI scales to help in this important clinical problem. Although no responsible clinician would use a paper-and-pencil test for making a clinical diagnosis as important as frontal versus nonfrontal cortical damage, such scales may offer an additional item of information if and when they are adequately validated.

The present Caudality (Ca) scale is a revision and extension of an earlier scale developed by Friedman (1950) in an attempt to discriminate between patients with frontal lobe and parietal lobe brain damage. In developing the present Ca scale, Williams (1952) cross-validated Friedman's scale on new samples of frontal and parietal lobe cases, identified new items from the MMPI item pool that differentiated patients with frontal lobe damage from patients with parietal lobe damage, and combined some of the new items with some items from the Friedman scale to form the 36-item Ca scale. The items are keyed in such a way that high Ca scores are believed to be predictive of nonfrontal damage, and low Ca scores are alleged to be indicative of frontal damage. The 36 Ca scale items deal with anxiety, depression, somatic complaints, social introversion, problems in emotional control, and fear of loss of control of thought processes.

Reliability and Validity

Gocka (1965) reported a Kuder-Richardson 21 (internal consistency) value of .86 for the Ca scale for 220 male Veterans Administration psychiatric patients. Williams (1952) reported that when a raw score of 11 on the Ca scale was used as a cutoff, 78 percent accuracy was achieved in separating patients with frontal lobe damage from those with parietal lobe damage (as compared with a 50 percent base rate in the samples utilized). Williams's data also indicated that scores on the Ca scale are positively related to scores on scale 7 of the MMPI and negatively related to the MMPI K scale.

Meier and French (1964) found that a T-score cutoff of 50 led to accurate identification of patients with temporal lobe abnormalities. One year after surgery to remove the tissue generating the electrographic focus, Ca scores were lower than the presurgery scores, and the T-score cutoff of 50 no longer accurately identified the patients who previously had manifested temporal lobe abnormalities. Meier and French concluded that when used along with other appropriate clinical evidence the Ca scale may be effective in helping to localize temporal lobe abnormalities, and that the higher Ca scores among patients with temporal lobe involvement may turn out to be the result of personality changes (anxiety, guilt, feelings of inadequacy, etc.) associated with the temporal lobe damage.

Interpretation of High Ca Scores

When dealing with patients with focalized organic brain pathology as determined by standard neurological and related indices, high Ca scores may be suggestive of posterior localization of damage. Although the Ca scale should not be used alone in localizing brain damage, it can be a useful addition to other data. Whereas no research data are available concerning other extratest correlates of high Ca scores, study of the content of the Ca scale items suggests that a high Ca score is indicative of an individual who (is):

1. feels anxious, guilty, depressed
2. reports multiple physical complaints
3. feels inadequately equipped to handle stresses in his/her life situation
4. worries excessively
5. socially extroverted
6. has problems in controlling emotional expression
7. fears losing control of his/her thought processes

In summary, although the Ca scale should be viewed primarily as a research tool that is not yet adequately validated, when it is used in conjunction with other appropriate clinical evidence, high Ca scores may be suggestive of parietal localization of cortical damage. High Ca scorers tend to have problems in emotional and cognitive control, which is consistent with clinical observations of patients with parietal damage.

Interpretation of Low Ca Scores

When dealing with patients with focalized brain damage as identified by the usual neurological criteria, low Ca scores may be indicative of frontal lobe involvement. Whereas research data are not available concerning the other extratest correlates of low Ca scores, the content of the Ca scale items suggests that a low Ca score describes an individual who (is):

1. denying anxiety, complaints and discomfort
2. free of somatic complaints and discomfort
3. presents self as comfortable and confident in social situations
4. feels in control of emotions and thought processes

In summary, although the Ca scale should be viewed primarily as a research tool which as yet has not been adequately validated, when it is used in conjunction with other appropriate clinical evidence, low Ca scores may be suggestive of frontal localization of cortical damage. Low Ca scorers appear to be in control of emotions and cognitive processes.

A FINAL CAUTION

The reader again is reminded that the scales discussed in this chapter are supplementary ones. They are intended for use along with the standard MMPI scales. The reliability and validity for many of these scales have not been adequately demonstrated. If they are used in clinical interpretation of the MMPI, any inferences derived from them should be viewed as tentative and should be validated against other clinical and test data.

9

A General Interpretive Strategy

In 1956, Paul Meehl made a strong plea for a "good cookbook" for psychological test interpretation. Meehl's proposed cookbook was to include detailed rules for categorizing test responses and was to provide empirically determined extratest correlates for each category of test responses. The rules could be applied automatically by a nonprofessional worker (or by a computer), and the interpretive statements could be selected for a particular type of protocol from a larger library of statements. Although some efforts have been made to construct such a cookbook (e.g., Gilberstadt & Duker, 1965; Marks & Seeman, 1963; Marks et al., 1974), the current status of psychological test interpretation is far from Meehl's ideal automatic process. All tests, including the MMPI, provide opportunities for standardized observation of current behavior of examinees. On the basis of these test behaviors, inferences are made about other extratest behaviors of the examinees. The clinician serves as an information processor and as a clinical judge in the assessment process. The major purpose of this chapter is to suggest one approach (but by no means the only one) that clinicians can utilize in translating MMPI protocols into meaningful inferences about examinees.

It should be clearly understood that the MMPI should be used to generate *hypothesis* or *inferences* about an examinee. The interpretive data presented in earlier chapters of this *Guide* will not apply completely and unfailingly to each and every person with a specified MMPI protocol. In interpreting MMPI's, one must deal in probabilities. Some particular extratest characteristic is *more likely* than some other characteristic to hold true for a person with a particular type of MMPI protocol, but one can never be completely sure that the more likely characteristic will in fact be found for that person. The inferences generated from an individual's MMPI protocol should be validated against other test and nontest information available about that person. The MMPI is most valuable as an assessment tool when it is used in conjunction with other psychological tests, with interview and observational data, and with appropriate background information. Although blind interpretation of MMPI's is certainly possible, and in fact is the procedure involved in computerized interpretations of the MMPI, such interpretations should be used only to generate hypotheses, inasmuch as more accurate person-specific inferences are likely to occur when the MMPI is viewed in the context of all information available for an individual. This position is consistent with research findings by investigators such as Kostlan (1954) and Sines (1959).

In general, two kinds of interpretive inferences can be made on the basis of MMPI data. First, some characteristics of an examinee with a particular kind of MMPI protocol are ones that, with better than chance probability, differentiate that examinee from other persons in a particular setting (e.g., hospital, clinic, etc.). For example, one might infer from a hospitalized patient's MMPI profile that he or she is likely to be a serious suicidal risk. Because most patients are not actually suicidal, this inference clearly differentiates this particular patient from other patients. A second kind of inference is one that involves a characteristic that is common to many individuals in a particular setting. For example, the inference that a hospitalized psychiatric patient does not know how to handle stress in an effective manner is one that probably is true for most patients in that setting. Although the differential, patient-specific inferences tend to be more useful than the more general ones, the latter are important in understanding an individual case, particularly for clinicians and others involved in the treatment process who might not have a clear understanding of what behaviors are shared by most persons in a particular setting.

Whereas Meehl envisioned the assessment process as dealing exclusively with nontest behaviors that are directly and empirically tied to specific aspects of test performance, the current status of the assessment field is such that only limited relationships of this sort have been identified. Often it is possible and/or necessary to make higher order inferences about examinees based on a conceptualization of their personalities. For example, there currently are no hard data indicating that a particular MMPI profile is predictive of a future suicide attempt. However, if we have inferred from an individual's MMPI that he or she is extremely depressed, agitated, and emotionally uncomfortable, is impulsive, and shows poor judgment much of the time, the higher order inference that such a person has a higher risk of suicide than patients in general is a logical one. Although it is legitimate to rely on such higher order inferences in interpreting MMPI's, one should probably have greater confidence in the inferences that are less inferentially and more directly related to MMPI performance.

A GENERAL STRATEGY

In his clinical work the author utilizes an approach to MMPI interpretation which involves trying to answer the following questions about each MMPI protocol:

1. What was the test-taking attitude of the examinee, and how should this attitude be taken into account in interpreting the protocol?
2. What is the general level of adjustment of the person who produced the protocol?

3. What kinds of behaviors (symptoms, attitudes, defenses, etc.) can be inferred about or expected from the person who produced the protocol?
4. What etiology or set of psychological dynamics underlies the behaviors described above?
5. What are the most appropriate diagnostic labels for the person who produced the protocol?
6. What are the implications for the treatment of the person who produced the protocol?

Test-Taking Attitude

The ideal examinee is one who approaches the task of completing the MMPI in a serious and cooperative manner. This individual reads each MMPI item and responds to the item in an honest, direct manner. When such an ideal situation is realized, the examiner can feel confident that the test responses are a representative sample of the examinee's behavior and can proceed with the interpretation of the protocol. However, as suggested in Chapter 3, for various reasons examinees may approach the test-taking task with an attitude that deviates from the ideal situation described above. Specification of test-taking attitude for each individual examinee is important because such differential attitudes must be taken into account in generating inferences from the MMPI protocol. In addition, such attitudes may be predictive of similar approaches to other nontest aspects of the examinee's life situation.

Qualitative aspects of an examinee's test behavior often serve to augment inferences based on the more quantitative scores and indices. One such factor is the amount of time required to complete the MMPI. As stated in Chapter 2, the typical examinee takes between 1 and 1½ hours to complete the test. Excessively long testing times may be indicative of indecisiveness, psychomotor retardation, confusion, or passive resistance to the testing procedures. Extremely short times suggest that either examinees were quite impulsive in responding to the test items or they did not read and consider each individual item.

Examinees occasionally become very tense, agitated, or otherwise upset in the MMPI test-taking situation. Such behavior may be predictive of similar responses in other stressful situations. Some examinees, who are obsessive in their thinking and/or indecisive, write qualifications to their true-false responses in the margins of the answer sheet. This author is even aware of one case in which the examinee attempted to eat the box form cards. Needless to say, such behavior has important diagnostic significance.

Although the qualitative features of test performance discussed above can offer important information about an examinee, the four validity indicators (?, L, F, K) are the primary objective sources of inferences about test-taking attitude. The Cannot Say (?) scale indicates the number of items omitted by the examinee. A large number of omitted items may indicate indecisiveness, ambivalence, or an attempt to avoid admitting negative things about oneself without deliberately lying. Examinees who answer all or most of the items are not availing themselves of this simplistic way of attempting to present a positive picture of themselves.

In judging test-taking attitude from the L scale, the examinee's educational or socioeconomic status must be taken into account (see Chapter 3). If the L scale is higher than what is expected for an individual when these factors are considered, one should consider the possibility that the examinee is using a rather naive and global denial of problems and shortcomings in an attempt to present himself/herself in a favorable light.

Scores on the F scale reflect the extent to which an examinee's responses to a finite pool of deviant items distributed throughout the MMPI compare to those of the Minnesota normal standardization groups, with a higher F scale score reflecting greater deviance. Scores that are considerably higher than average suggest that examinees are admitting to many clearly deviant behaviors and/or attitudes. Although there are several possible reasons for such an admission (see Chapter 3), one possibility is that the examinees are emotionally disabled and are using the MMPI as a vehicle to express a cry for help. Another possibility is that they are functioning in a healthy range but on the basis of subjective self-appraisal are using the test-taking task as a vehicle for being extremely self-critical and self-derrogatory. F scale scores that are considerably below average indicate that the examinees are admitting fewer than an average number of deviant attitudes and behaviors. They may be overly defensive and trying to create an unrealistically positive picture of themselves. F scale scores in the average range indicate that the examinees have been neither hypercritical of themselves nor overly defensive and denying in responding to the test items.

The K scale can serve as another index of defensiveness, but education and socioeconomic status must be taken into account in interpreting this scale (see Chapter 3). If scores on the K scale are significantly higher than one would expect from persons of a given educational and socioeconomic background, one should suspect that the examinees have been rather defensive in describing themselves. Scores lower than would be expected for a person with a given educational and socioeconomic background indicate a lack of defensiveness and a hypercritical attitude toward oneself. K scale scores in the middle range suggest that the examinees have been neither overly defensive nor overly self-critical in endorsing the MMPI items.

As discussed in Chapter 3, the profile configuration of the validity scales is important for understanding examinees' test-taking attitudes. In general, persons who are approaching the test with the intention of presenting themselves in an overly favorable way have L and K scale scores greater than the F scale score, producing a V-shape in the validity scale portion of the profile. On the other hand, persons who are using the test to be overly self-critical and/or to exaggerate their problems produce an inverted V-shape in the validity scales (i.e., the L and K scale scores will be significantly lower than the F scale score). In interpreting the clinical scales profile, therefore, clinicians must take into account the validity scales, adjusting the meanings of the profile as they feel necessary.

Adjustment Level

There are two important components to psychological adjustment level. First, there is the matter of how emotionally comfortable or uncomfortable individuals are. Second, there is the matter of how well the individuals carry out the responsibilities of their life situations irrespective of how conflicted they might be. For most people these two components are very much related. Persons who are psychologically comfortable tend to function well and vice versa. However, for some individuals (e.g., some neurotics), a great deal of discomfort and turmoil can be present, but adequate functioning continues. For other persons (e.g., chronic schizophrenics), quite serious impairment in coping with responsibilities can be found without an accompanying emotional discomfort. Clinical experience and some research findings suggest that the MMPI potentially can permit inferences about both of these aspects of adjustment level.

The F scale seems to be the single best MMPI index of degree of psychopathology. If one rules out the possibility of deviant response sets or styles that can invalidate the protocol (e.g., the angry adolescent who decides to answer true to all of the deviant items), high F scale scores suggest intense emotional turmoil and/or serious impairment in functioning. For example, most acutely psychotic subjects tend to obtain high scores on the F scale. However, some neurotic individuals and persons undergoing severe situational stress also achieve high F scale scores. On the other hand, some clearly psychotic (or neurotic) individuals, particularly those in whom the disorder has been present for quite some time, do not achieve very high F scale scores.

A second simple but meaningful index of adjustment has to do with the overall elevation of the clinical scales. In general, as more of the clinical scales are elevated (and as the degree of elevation increases), the greater is the probability that some serious psychopathology and poor levels of functioning are present. To obtain a crude, quantitative index of degree of this psychopathology, some clinicians find it useful to compute a mean T-score for eight clinical scales (excluding scales 5 and 0). Others simply count the number of clinical scales with T-scores above 70. Higher mean scores and more scores above 70 are indicative of greater psychopathology.

The *slope* of the profile also yields important inferences about adjustment level. If the clinical scales are elevated and a positive slope (left side low, right side high) is present, the likelihood of severe psychopathology, and perhaps even psychosis, should be considered. A negative slope (left side high, right side low) is more indicative of a neurotic individual or one who is internally conflicted and miserable but who still is able to function fairly well.

Scores on several of the standard clinical and special scales also can serve as indices of level of adjustment. Welsh's Anxiety (A) and Barron's Ego Strength

(Es) scales are measures of general maladjustment. High scorers on A and low scorers on Es tend to be rather disturbed emotionally. The A scale seems to be more sensitive to subjective emotional turmoil than to inability to cope behaviorally. Thus some hospitalized psychotics who cannot cope at all well are free of serious emotional distress and do not achieve elevated scores on the A scale. The Es scale indicates an individual's ability to cope with stresses and problems of everyday life, with high scorers generally better able to cope than low scorers. Scale 2 (Depression) is a good indicator of dissatisfaction with one's life situation. As scores on scale 2 become higher, greater dissatisfaction is suggested. Scale 7 (Psychasthenia) is perhaps the single best measure of feelings of anxiety and agitation. High scale 7 scorers usually are overwhelmed by anxiety, tension, fear, apprehension, etc.

Goldberg (1965) derived a linear regression equation for discriminating psychotic and neurotic MMPI profiles. In addition to serving this diagnostic function, the Goldberg index also seems to be related to level of maladjustment, with higher values indicating greater maladjustment. To compute the Goldberg index, one simply inserts T-score values into the following formula: L + Pa + Sc − Hy − Pt. Goldberg found for his samples that a cutoff of 45 on his index provided the best discrimination between psychotic and neurotic profiles. Whereas a considerable amount of experience in applying the formula to actual cases is necessary before the values yielded by the formula take on significance concerning adjustment level, in the author's own clinical experience, among psychiatric patients higher Goldberg values suggest greater psychopathology.

It may be helpful to check responses to the Koss-Butcher or Lachar-Wrobel critical items. These items deal with some blatantly psychotic behaviors and attitudes, sexual deviation, excessive use of alcohol, homicidal and/or suicidal impulses, and other manifestations of serious maladjustment. The critical item lists are reproduced in Appendix J of this *Guide*. As was discussed in Chapter 7, care should be taken not to overinterpret these individual item responses.

Characteristic Traits and Behaviors

At this point in the interpretive process, the clinician's goal is to describe the examinee's symptoms, traits, behaviors, attitudes, defenses, etc. in enough detail to allow an overall understanding of the person. Although not every protocol permits inferences about all of the points listed below, in general the author tries to make some statements or inferences about each of them:

1. symptoms
2. major needs (e.g., dependency, achievement, autonomy)
3. perceptions of the environment, particularly of significant other people in the examinee's life situation

4. reactions to stress (coping strategies, defenses)
5. self-concept
6. sexual identification
7. emotional control
8. interpersonal relationships
9. psychological resources

Inferences about the above features are based primarily on analysis of individual validity and clinical scales (high and low scores) and on two-point configurations of the clinical scales (see Chapters 3, 4, and 6). In addition, the special scales discussed in Chapters 7 and 8 often add important information about the examinee. One way for the beginner with the MMPI to utilize the standard and supplementary scales is to consider each high score, low score, and configuration of scores in turn, to consult the appropriate sections in earlier chapters of this *Guide,* and to write down appropriate hypotheses or inferences for each scale or configuration.

Initially there may appear to be some incongruencies among the various inferences that have been generated. The clinician should first consider the possibility that the apparent incongruencies are accurately reflecting different facets of the subject's personality and behavior. Consider, for example, a profile with elevations greater than 70 on both scales 2 and 4. The scale 2 elevation suggests sensitivity to the needs and feelings of other people, whereas the scale 4 elevation suggests insensitivity to the needs and feelings of others. It is possible that the same individual may show both characteristics at different times. In fact, research with the 24/42 profile type indicates that persons with this code tend to alternate between periods of great sensitivity to others and periods of gross insensitivity to others.

Sometimes incongruencies in inferences cannot be reconciled as easily as in the above example. In these instances the clinician must decide in which inferences to have the most confidence. In general, greater confidence should be placed in inferences that occur for several scales or configurations than in those that occur for a single scale. Inferences based on grossly elevated scales should receive greater emphasis than those based on moderate elevations. Inferences stemming from scale configurations typically will be more accurate than those based on a single scale. In most instances more confidence should be placed in inferences coming from the standard validity and clinical scales than from the supplementary scales, because there is a much more significant research base underlying the standard scale inferences.

As mentioned earlier in this chapter, some inferences about an examinee do not result directly from scores on a scale or configurations of scales. Rather, they are higher order inferences generated from a basic understanding of the examinee. For example, there are no data indicating that scores on particular MMPI scales are predictive of success as a real estate salesperson. However, one might predict that an examinee whose MMPI scores had led to inferences of strong achievement needs, competitiveness, and ability to create a good impression would be likely to be successful in real estate sales.

Dynamics and Etiology

In most assessment situations it is desirable to go beyond a description of an individual's behavior and to make inferences about the dynamics underlying the behavior or about the etiology of a particular problem or condition. For some MMPI scales and configurations of scales, the interpretive information presented in previous chapters of this *Guide* includes some statements about these underlying factors. In addition, it is possible and/or necessary to make some higher order inferences about dynamics. For example, if one infers from an examinee's MMPI protocol that he or she is afraid of becoming emotionally involved with other people because of a fear of being hurt or exploited, one might then speculate that the person has been hurt and/or exploited in earlier emotional relationships. Or if one interprets an MMPI protocol as indicating strong resentment of authority, it is reasonable to infer than the resentment has its origins in parent-child relationships. The higher order inferences often are based on MMPI data combined with other test and nontest (interview, history, etc.) data.

Diagnostic Impressions

Although the usefulness of psychiatric diagnosis per se has been questioned by many clinicians, referral sources often request information about diagnosis. In addition, it often is necessary to assign diagnostic labels for purposes such as insurance claims, disability status, competency status, etc. Many of the interpretive sections in earlier chapters of this *Guide* present diagnostic information for the individual clinical scales and for the two-point code types. In addition, it is useful to consider the slope of the MMPI profile. A negative slope (left side high, right side low) is suggestive of a nonpsychotic disorder, whereas a positive slope (left side low, right side high) is suggestive of a psychotic disorder. Scores on some of the supplementary MMPI scales discussed in Chapters 7 and 8 of this *Guide* also can be examined to add diagnostic information. For example, among psychiatric patients low Es scores tend to be associated with psychotic disorders. If scores on scales such as Persecutory Ideas (Pa1), Bizarre Sensory Experiences (Sc3), or Psychoticism (PSY) are high, the likelihood of a psychotic disorder becomes greater. The Goldberg index, which was discussed earlier in this chapter, can be helpful in differentiating between psychotic and nonpsychotic profiles. As with all other aspects of MMPI interpretation, other data (history, observation, etc.) must be taken into account in arriving at a diagnostic label for an individual.

Treatment Implications

A primary goal in most assessments is to be able to make meaningful recommendations about treatment. Sometimes, when demand for treatment exceeds the resources available, the decision simply is whether or not to accept a particular person for treatment. Such a decision may involve clinical judgment about how badly the person is in need of treatment as well as about how likely that person is to respond favorably to available treatment procedures. When differential treatment procedures are available, the assessment may be useful in deciding which procedures are likely to be most appropriate for a specific person. Even when the decision has been made before the assessment that a person will receive a particular treatment procedure, the assessment can be valuable by providing information about problem areas to be considered in treatment and by alerting the therapist (or others involved in treatment) to assets and liabilities that could facilitate or hinder progress in therapy.

The Ego Strength (Es) scale is the only scale discussed in this *Guide* that was designed specifically to predict response to psychotherapy (see Chapter 8). If one is dealing with a neurotic individual, a high Es score is likely to mean that such a person will benefit from traditional, individual psychotherapy. With other kinds of persons and/or treatment procedures the relationship between Es scores and treatment outcome is less clear, but in general, high Es scores can be interpreted as suggestive of psychological resources that can be tapped in treatment procedures.

The Control (Cn) scale (see Chapter 8) was designed to identify patients who, in spite of serious psychopathology, are able to be treated as outpatients rather than having to be hospitalized. High Cn scores indicate an ability to avoid displaying pathology to others. Whereas this ability may permit an individual to avoid hospitalization, it also can be a liability in treatment if the person chooses to conceal the pathology from the therapist or others involved in the treatment process.

As was discussed above in relation to characteristic traits and behaviors, many of the inferences about treatment will not come directly from scores on specific MMPI scales or configurations of scales. Rather, they are higher order inferences based on other inferences that have already been made about the examinee. For example, if one has inferred from the MMPI that an examinee is in a great deal of emotional turmoil, it can now be further inferred that this person is likely to be motivated enough to change in psychotherapy. On the other hand, if one has inferred that a person is very reluctant to accept responsibility for his or her own behavior and blames problems and shortcomings on other people, the prognosis for traditional psychotherapy is very poor. A person who is very suggestible is apt to respond more favorably to direct advice-giving than to insight-oriented therapy. A psychopathic individual (high scores on MMPI scales 4 and 9) who enters therapy rather than going to jail is likely to terminate therapy prematurely. Obviously, there are many other examples of higher order inferences related to treatment.

SPECIFIC REFERRAL QUESTIONS

The interpretive strategy that has just been discussed is intended to help the clinician generate as many meaningful inferences as possible about subjects' MMPIs. It should be recognized that very often persons are given the MMPI in an attempt to try to answer some very specific questions about them or to make some very specific predictions about their behavior. Unless these specific questions or predictions are dealt with directly, it is unlikely that the MMPI interpretation will be seen as having been useful.

Specific issues for which the MMPI may be useful include, but are not limited to, suicide potential, acting out behaviors, identification of psychotic disorders, detection of substance abuse problems, differentiating functional from organic somatic disorders, and predicting response to treatment. Sometimes there are MMPI data directly relevant to the issue of concern. For example, scores on the MacAndrew Alcoholism scale (MAC) permit accurate inferences about substance abuse. At other times, conclusions about issues of concern are dependent on clinical integration of many different kinds of MMPI data and second order inferences. The prediction of suicide attempts is a good example of this latter situation. There are no specific scales for predicting such behavior, and there are no actuarial formulas for this purpose. However, MMPI inferences about degree of clinical depression, energy level, impulsiveness, and similar characteristics can be integrated with history and observational data in helping clinicians to make this very difficult prediction.

AN ILLUSTRATIVE CASE

In order to help the reader understand the strategy discussed above, an actual case is now considered and a step-by-step analysis of the MMPI protocol is presented. As a practice exercise, readers can interpret the profile (Fig. 9.1) and supplementary scores (Table 9.1) and then compare their interpretations with the one that is presented below.

Background Information

This 27-year-old barber (J. A. K.) came to an outpatient psychological clinic complaining of depression, irritability, moodiness, lack of self-confidence, and extreme difficulty in making decisions. He dated the onset of his problems to five years earlier when he was discharged from military service and felt "on his own" for the first time in his life. J. A. K. was the older of two male children. He described his 25-year-old brother as being the opposite of him. Whereas J. A. K. was interested in art, literature, and other aesthetic things, his brother was

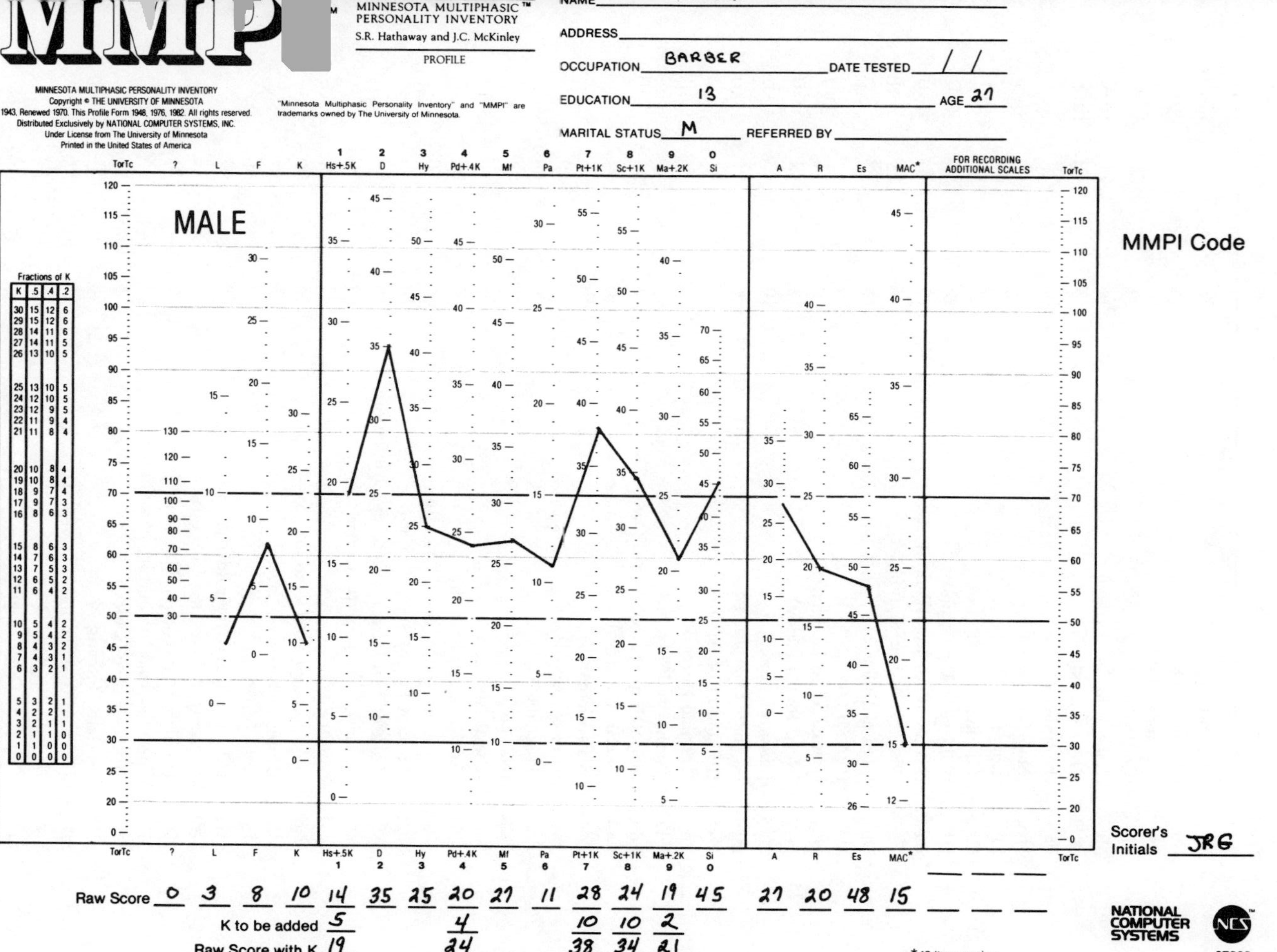

Fig. 9.1. MMPI profile for illustrative case (J.A.K.). (Minnesota Multiphasic Personality Inventory. Copyright © the University of Minnesota 1943, renewed 1970. This Profile Form 1948, 1982. Reproduced with permission.)

Table 9.1. Supplementary MMPI scores for illustrative case (J. A. K.)

Scale		Raw score	T-score
Dy	(Dependency)	35	67
Do	(Dominance)	13	45
Re	(Responsibility)	20	50
Cn	(Control)	29	61
Mt	(College Maladjustment)	32	71
O-H	(Overcontrolled Hostility)	13	52
Pr	(Prejudice)	13	52
MAS	(Manifest Anxiety)	31	73
Lb	(Low Back Pain)	13	66
Ca	(Caudality)	21	71
D1	(Subjective Depression)	22	93
D2	(Psychomotor Retardation)	10	76
D3	(Physical Malfunctioning)	4	56
D4	(Mental Dullness)	8	80
D5	(Brooding)	6	71
Hy1	(Denial of Social Anxiety)	0	31
Hy2	(Need for Affection)	3	42
Hy3	(Lassitude-Malaise)	10	83
Hy4	(Somatic Complaints)	7	67
Hy5	(Inhibition of Aggression)	3	53
Pd1	(Familial Discord)	2	51
Pd2	(Authority Problems)	6	61
Pd3	(Social Imperturbability)	4	35
Pd4A	(Social Alienation)	6	52
Pd4B	(Self-Alienation)	10	74
Pa1	(Persecutory Ideas)	1	46
Pa2	(Poignancy)	5	68
Pa3	(Naiveté)	2	41
Sc1A	(Social Alienation)	5	56
Sc1B	(Emotional Alienation)	4	66
Sc2A	(Lack of Ego Mastery, Cognitive)	4	66
Sc2B	(Lack of Ego Mastery, Conative)	10	94
Sc2C	(Lack of Ego Mastery, Defective Inhibition)	3	60
Sc3	(Bizarre Sensory Experiences)	5	60
Ma1	(Amorality)	4	67
Ma2	(Psychomotor Acceleration)	6	66
Ma3	(Imperturbability)	3	47
Ma4	(Ego Inflation)	2	46
Mf1	(Narcissism-Hypersensitivity)	8	67
Mf2	(Stereotypic Feminine Interests)	2	41
Mf3	(Denial of Stereotypic Masculine Interests)	7	81
Mf4	(Heterosexual Discomfort–Passivity)	1	33
Mf5	(Introspective-Critical)	3	46
Mf6	(Socially Retiring)	3	35
Si1	(Inferiority–Personal Discomfort)	19	96
Si2	(Discomfort with Others)	6	62
Si3	(Staid–Personal Rigidity)	10	55
Si4	(Hypersensitivity)	6	72

(continued)

Table 9.1. *(Continued)*

Scale		Raw score	T-score
Si5	(Distrust)	7	64
Si6	(Physical-Somatic Concerns)	2	53
SOC	(Social Maladjustment)	17	67
DEP	(Depression)	20	75
FEM	(Feminine Interests)	14	64
MOR	(Poor Morale)	15	64
REL	(Religious Fundamentalism)	6	49
AUT	(Authority Conflict)	12	56
PSY	(Psychoticism)	7	48
ORG	(Organic Symptoms)	11	63
FAM	(Family Problems)	3	47
HOS	(Manifest Hostility)	15	61
PHO	(Phobias)	12	67
HYP	(Hypomania)	11	48
HEA	(Poor Health)	7	55

interested in sports and other stereotypic masculine activities. J. A. K.'s father died about five years before he was seen in the clinic, and his mother had been dead for eight years. He described his childhood as pleasant. Although his parents did not show much affection toward him, neither did they make many demands of him. After graduation from high school, J. A. K. gave in to pressure from his father that he go to college. However, he could not concentrate on his studies, and he was dismissed after 1 year. He enlisted in the Army, where he served as a clerk for three years. He liked military life because "everything is laid out for you." After leaving the service, he became a partner in a barber shop with a boyhood friend. At the time that he was seen in the clinic, he expressed some ambivalence about barbering, and he talked about getting a job as a photographer. J. A. K. had been married for a little over one year, and his wife was pregnant with their first child. He was pleased at the prospect of being a father, but he also was afraid of the increased responsibility. At the time of the MMPI administration, he was described by the examiner as cooperative and friendly, and as eager to "do well" on the test. Few overt signs of anxiety, depression, or other emotional distress were observed. He completed the MMPI in about 1½ hours.

Test-Taking Attitude

J. A. K. completed the MMPI in about an average length of time, indicating that he was neither excessively indecisive nor impulsive in responding to the items. He omitted no items, suggesting that he was cooperative and did not use this rather simple way of avoiding unfavorable self-statements. His raw score of

3 on the L scale is what would be expected for someone of his educational and socioeconomic background, so we may infer that he was not blatantly defensive and denying in his approach to the test. J. A. K.'s F scale T-score of 62 suggests that he was admitting to more than an average number of deviant attitudes and behaviors, but it is not high enough to indicate some invalidating response set. In all likelihood he simply was being candid in describing himself on the MMPI.

For a person of his educational and socioeconomic level, we would expect a K scale score in a range of 55 to 60. J. A. K.'s score of 46 on the K scale indicates that he was somewhat self-critical in responding to the items. J. A. K.'s configuration on the validity scales resembles the inverted V-shape discussed above. Whereas it is possible that he was exaggerating his problems as a cry for help, the moderate level of the F scale and the position of the L and K scales near the mean indicate that more likely he was honestly describing a moderate discomfort and psychopathology. In summary, J. A. K. seems to have approached the MMPI in an honest and open manner, and although he was moderately self-critical in responding to the test items, there is no reason to believe that the test behavior is not a representative sample of his behavior.

Adjustment Level

J. A. K.'s F scale T-score of 62 indicates a moderate degree of emotional discomfort; it is at a level that indicates that he is able to cope with many aspects of his life situation, but at some great psychological cost to him. In general, his scores on the clinical scales are quite elevated. The mean T-score on the clinical scales (excluding scales 5 and 0) is about 70. Such a mean score indicates moderate to severe psychopathology and somewhat serious problems in functioning in everyday activities. He has four clinical scales equal to or greater than a T-score of 70, further supporting the inference of moderate to severe disturbance. Although the slope of his profile is not dramatic, it tends to be somewhat negative, suggesting internal conflict and discomfort but not severe impairment in functioning. His T-score of 69 on the Anxiety scale indicates that he is in a good deal of emotional turmoil. The rather extreme elevations on scales 2 and 7 further suggest turmoil, including anxiety, depression, and feeling overwhelmed and unable to cope. The critical items that he endorsed in the pathological direction deal with head discomfort, impulses to hurt himself or someone else, periods of activity that he later could not remember, peculiar odors, feelings of unreality, and wishing that he were dead. In summary, it appears that J. A. K. is in a great deal of personal discomfort. However, his discomfort level is somewhat greater than his actual inability to function in everyday activities. He is likely to feel terrible much of the time, but he continues to function in spite of how he feels.

Characteristic Traits and Behaviors

A first step in trying to generate inferences in this area is to examine each of J. A. K.'s validity scale scores and to consult Chapter 3 for appropriate hypotheses or inferences.

L (T = 46)

This score is about what is expected for someone of his educational and socioeconomic background; not particularly defensive or denying.

F (T = 62)

This score is somewhat higher than in most persons with his background; he admitted to some but not very many deviant behaviors and/or ideas; he endorsed items dealing with passivity, tendency to withdraw from problems, difficulties in sleeping, impulses to injure himself or other people, and periods of activity during which he was not aware of what he was doing; he functions adequately in many aspects of his life situation even though he is very unhappy and uncomfortable.

K (T = 46)

This score is somewhat lower than expected for someone who completed one year of college. He is self-critical and self-dissatisfied. He may be exaggerating his problems somewhat as a cry for help. He is somewhat ineffective in dealing with problems of everyday life; has little insight into his own motives and behaviors; is socially awkward; is socially conforming and overly compliant with authority; is inhibited, retiring, shallow; has a slow personal tempo; is critical of other people; is suspicious of motivations of others; is cynical, skeptical, and caustic, and has a disbelieving outlook.

Next, clinical scales on which J. A. K. achieved T-scores equal to or greater than 70 are identified, and appropriate sections of Chapter 4 are consulted for hypotheses.

Scale 2 (T = 94)

This is a very high score, suggestive of serious depression. He feels blue, depressed, unhappy, dysphoric; is pessimistic about the future, self-depreciatory; harbors guilt feelings. Depressive diagnosis is likely. He has somatic complaints, weakness, fatigue, loss of energy; is agitated, tense, irritable, high-strung, prone to worry; lacks self-confidence, feels useless and unable to function; feels like a failure on job; is introverted, shy, retiring, timid, seclusive, secretive, aloof;

maintains psychological distance; avoids interpersonal involvement. He is cautious and conventional in approach to problems; has difficulty in making decisions; is nonaggressive and overcontrolled; denies impulses, avoids unpleasantness, makes concessions to avoid confrontations, and is motivated for therapy because of intense discomfort.

Scale 7 (T = 81)

This score suggests a great deal of discomfort and turmoil. He is anxious, tense, agitated, worried, apprehensive, high-strung, jumpy; has difficulties concentrating; is introspective, ruminative, obsessive, compulsive. He feels insecure and inferior; lacks self-confidence; has self-doubts; is self-critical, self-conscious, self-derogatory; is rigid, moralistic; sets high standards for self and others; is perfectionistic, conscientious, guilty, depressed, neat, orderly, organized, meticulous, persistent, reliable. He lacks ingenuity in approach to problems; is dull, formal; he vacillates, is indecisive; distorts importance of problems, overreacts; does not interact socially; is hard to get to know; worries about popularity and acceptance; is sentimental, peaceable, softhearted, trustful, sensitive, kind, dependent, individualistic, unemotional, and immature. He has physical complaints (heart, gastrointestinal, genitourinary, fatigue, exhaustion, sleep disturbance). He is not responsive to brief psychotherapy; has some insight into problems but intellectualizes and rationalizes; is resistant to interpretations in therapy; will develop excessive hostility toward therapist; will remain in therapy longer than many patients, and make slow but steady progress. In therapy he will discuss difficulties with authority figures, poor work or study habits, and fear of homosexual impulses.

Scale 8 (T = 73)

At this level many of the blatantly psychotic items are not endorsed. He has a schizoid life-style; feels as if he is not part of social environment; feels isolated, alienated, misunderstood, unaccepted; is withdrawn, seclusive, secretive, inaccessible; avoids dealing with people and with new situations; is described by others as shy, aloof, uninvolved; has generalized anxiety; is resentful, hostile, aggressive, but unable to express such feelings; responds to stress by withdrawal into daydreams and fantasies; has self-doubts; feels inferior, incompetent, dissatisfied; has sexual preoccupation and sex role confusion. Others see him as nonconforming, unusual, unconventional, eccentric; his physical complaints are vague and long-standing; he is stubborn, moody, opinionated, generous, peaceable, sentimental, immature, impulsive, adventurous, sharp-witted, conscientious, high-strung. He has a wide range of interests, and is creative and imaginative. His goals are abstract and vague. He lacks basic information that is required for problem solving. His prognosis for therapy is poor because of long-standing problems and reluctance to relate in a meaningful way; he stays in therapy longer than most patients, and eventually may come to trust the therapist.

Scale 0 (T = 72)

He is socially introverted; insecure and uncomfortable in social situations; is shy, reserved, timid, retiring; feels more comfortable alone or with a few close friends; does not participate in many social activities; is especially uncomfortable around members of opposite sex; lacks self-confidence; is self-effacing; is hard to get to know; is seen by others as cold and distant; is sensitive to what others think of him; is troubled by lack of involvement with other poeple; is overcontrolled; does not display feelings openly; is submissive, compliant, overly accepting of authority; has a slow personal tempo; is reliable, dependable; is cautious, conventional, and unoriginal in approach to problems; is rigid and inflexible in attitudes and opinions; has difficulty in decision making; enjoys work; gets pleasure from personal achievement; worries; is irritable, anxious, moody; has guilt, depression.

Scale 1 (T = 70)

This score is indicative of bodily concern. He has vague, nonspecific physical complaints, epigastric complaints, chronic fatigue, pain, weakness. He is given a neurotic diagnosis. Acting out is unlikely. He is selfish, self-centered, narcissistic, pessimistic, defeatist, cynical, dissatisfied, unhappy. He makes others miserable and complains in a whiny manner; is critical and demanding; expresses hostility indirectly; is dull, unenthusiastic, unambitious; lacks ease of oral expression; does not manifest much anxiety; shows no signs of major incapacity; is functioning at reduced level of efficiency; has long-standing problems; is cynical; lacks insight; is not very responsive to traditional therapy; is critical of therapist.

Next, J. A. K.'s two-point code is identified. Chapter 6 is consulted and hypotheses appropriate for the 27/72 code are generated: He is anxious, nervous, tense, high-strung, jumpy; worries excessively; is vulnerable to real or imagined threat; anticipates problems before they occur; overreacts under stress; has somatic symptoms; has chronic fatigue, tiredness, exhaustion; is depressed, but may not feel especially sad; shows clinical signs of depression (slowed speech, weight loss, slow personal tempo, etc.); is pessimistic about the world in general and more specifically about the likelihood of overcoming his problems; broods, ruminates about his problems; has strong need for achievement and for recognition for accomplishments; has high expectancies for self; feels guilty because he has fallen short of his goals; is indecisive; feels inadequate, insecure, inferior; is intropunitive, blames self for problems; is rigid in thinking and problem solving; is meticulous, perfectionistic in daily activities; is excessively religious and moralistic; is docile and passive-dependent in relationships; has capacity for deep emotional ties; becomes clinging and dependent in times of stress; is not aggressive or belligerent; elicits nurturance and helping behavior in others; is motivated for therapy because of intense discomfort; remains in therapy and is likely to show considerable improvement; receives neurotic diagnosis.

J. A. K. has a 278 three-point code. Reference to Chapter 6 indicates that individuals with this code type tend to have symptoms of anxiety and depression. They are shy and introverted, and they feel inadequate and inferior. They set high standards for themselves and feel guilty when the standards are not met. In addition, this code type suggests a schizoid life-style and the possibility of brief psychotic episodes.

An examination of J. A. K.'s high and low scores on the supplementary scales discussed in Chapters 7 and 8 of this *Guide* leads to still more hypotheses about J. A. K.

MAC–MacAndrew Alcoholism Scale (T=30)

This low score contraindicates substance abuse problems. In addition, he is likely to be socially introverted, shy, conventional, and lacking in self-confidence.

MAS–Manifest Anxiety (T = 73)

He is predisposed to experience emotional discomfort in stressful situations; feels anxious, tense, jumpy; experiences physiological changes under stress (e.g., excessive perspiration, increased pulse rate, etc.); perceives his environment as threatening; feels at mercy of forces beyond his control; emphasizes present more than the future; bases expectations on immediate past experiences; has somatic complaints; feels excited, restless some of the time; has difficulties in concentrating; lacks self-confidence; is overly sensitive to reactions of others; feels unhappy, useless.

Do–Dominance (T = 45)

He is submissive, unassertive, unable to stand up for his own rights and opinions, easily influenced by others; he lacks self-confidence; is pessimistic, inefficient, and stereotyped in approach to problems; gives up easily; does not feel sense of duty to others; does not face up to realities of his life situation.

D1–Subjective Depression (T = 93)

He is unhappy, blue, depressed; lacks energy for coping with problems in his life situation; is not interested in what goes on around him; feels nervous, tense; has problems in concentrating and attending, poor appetite, sleep disturbance; broods, cries; lacks self-confidence; feels inferior, useless; is easily hurt by criticism; uneasy, shy, embarrassed in social situations; tends to avoid social interactions. Depressive disorder is the most likely diagnosis.

D4–Mental Dullness (T = 80)

He lacks energy to cope with problems of everyday life; is tense; has difficulty in concentrating, has poor memory and judgment; lacks self-confidence; feels inferior to others; gets little enjoyment out of life; feels life is no longer worth living.

D5–Brooding (T = 71)

He broods, ruminates, cries; lacks energy to cope with problems; feels that life is no longer worthwhile; feels inferior; is unhappy, easily hurt by criticism; feels he is losing control of his thought processes.

Hy1–Denial of Social Anxiety (T = 31)

He is socially introverted; is shy and bashful in social situations; finds it difficult to talk to people; is greatly influenced by social standards and customs.

Hy3–Lassitude-Malaise (T = 83)

He feels uncomfortable; says he is not in good health; is weak, tired, fatigued but may not report specific somatic symptoms; has difficulty concentrating, poor appetite, sleep disturbance; is unhappy, blue; sees home environment as unpleasant and uninteresting.

Pd3–Social Imperturbability (T = 35)

He feels uncomfortable in social situations; does not like to interact with other people; finds it difficult to talk with others; avoids being center of attention; does not express his opinions or defend them.

Pd4B–Self-Alienation (T = 74)

He is uncomfortable, unhappy; has problems in concentrating; finds daily life uninteresting; verbalizes regret, guilt, remorse for past misdeeds but is vague about nature of these misdeeds; finds it hard to settle down; may use alcohol excessively.

Sc2B–Lack of Ego Mastery, Conative (T = 94)

He feels that life is a strain; has depression, despair, difficulty in coping; worries excessively; withdraws into fantasy and daydreaming; finds daily life uninteresting; has given up hoping that things will get better; may wish that he were dead.

Mf3–Denial of Stereotypic Masculine Interests (T = 81)

He is not interested in culturally masculine occupations, does not enjoy culturally masculine activities and interests.

Mf4–Heterosexual Discomfort-Passivity (T = 33)

He denies being attracted to members of his own sex; is comfortable talking about sex; is assertive and aspiring.

DEP–Depression (T = 75)

He feels depressed, experiences guilt, regret, worry, and unhappiness. Life has lost its zest for him. He has little motivation to pursue things, has difficulties in concentration. He is anxious, apprehensive about the future; feels misunderstood; is convinced of his unworthiness; believes he deserves to be punished.

A careful examination of the numerous hypotheses generated about J. A. K. from his scores on the various scales reveals that there is remarkable overlap and agreement among the hypotheses generated from different scales. Only a few of the hypotheses are generated from a single scale. The reader will note a few inconsistencies among the hypotheses. Obviously, the greatest emphasis should be placed on those hypotheses that result from several or more scales. Hypotheses resulting from a single scale should be discarded or treated as very tentative. In dealing with the inconsistent hypotheses, several factors should be considered. If inconsistent hypotheses result from two scales and one of the scales has a more extreme score (higher or lower) than the other, greater emphasis should be placed on the hypotheses associated with the scale with the more extreme score. Also, one should consider whether the hypotheses resulted from empirical data or whether they were more subjectively generated (e.g., from item content). Greater weight should be given to those hypotheses that are of empirical origin.

The impression of J. A. K. as an anxious, depressed, insecure person was supported from several different sources within the MMPI. The inferences that J. A. K. is likely to be conventional and conforming were based on scores on several scales, including scales 2 and 7, and on the two-point and three-point codes. However, a relatively high score on scale 8 suggested that he might be unconventional and nonconforming. Because the inferences that he is conventional and conforming were based on several sources within the MMPI and the inference that he is unconventional and nonconforming was based only on scale 8, more confidence should be placed in the former rather than the latter inferences. Further, the scale 8 score was considerably lower than the scores on scales 2 and 7, suggesting that greater confidence should be placed in the inferences based on scales 2 and 7. The moderately high score on scale 8 and the 278 three-point code suggested the possibility of some psychotic episodes. However, no other aspects of the profile supported the inference about psychotic episodes. The Goldberg index, the overall elevation of the profile, the slope of the profile, and scores on supplementary scales, such as Psychoticism, Bizarre Sensory Experiences, and Lack of Ego Mastery, Cognitive, did not support an inference that J. A. K. is likely to be psychotic. Examination of the Harris Sc2B subscale on scale 8 suggested depression and other characteristics consistent with the impression of a nonpsychotic person.

After considering these matters, the next step in the interpretive process is to group the hypotheses into some meaningful categories (either those suggested earlier in this chapter or others that have meaning for the MMPI user).

Symptoms

There is rather clear agreement from various aspects of the MMPI protocol that J. A. K. is likely to be very depressed. He feels blue, unhappy, and dysphoric much of the time. Most of the time he is likely to be rather unemotional and unexcitable and to have a slow personal tempo, but he may also experience episodes of unexplainable excitement and restlessness. He tends to be very moody, and he may brood and ruminate over his problems. He is very pessimistic about the possibility that things will get better, and he may have concluded that life is no longer worthwhile. Although frequent suicidal thoughts are likely, he does not seem to be more likely to attempt suicide than other very depressed patients. He lacks energy to cope with everyday problems, and he is not very interested in or stimulated by his daily life. He may express guilt, remorse, or regret for past misdeeds, but he is vague about the nature of these misdeeds.

J. A. K. clearly also is experiencing a great deal of turmoil and discomfort. He is likely to feel tense, agitated, and anxious. He has a strong tendency to experience great emotional discomfort under stress, and at these times he may manifest physiological signs of anxiety (e.g., excessive perspiration, increased pulse rate, etc.). He tends to be very irritable, high-strung, jumpy, and apprehensive, and he is extremely vulnerable to real or imagined threat.

J. A. K. is likely to be quite concerned about bodily functioning, and may feel that he is in poor physical health. He may report a large number of very specific somatic symptoms, or his complaints may be very vague and nonspecific in nature. Chronic weakness, tiredness, fatigue, or exhaustion are probable. Sleep disturbances and poor appetite also may occur.

Difficulties with concentration and attention may also be reported by J. A. K. He is likely to complain of poor memory and judgment. Ruminative and obsessive thoughts and compulsive behaviors may be present. Decisions are especially difficult for him, and he appears to others to be indecisive much of the time. He may admit to having had periods during which he was unaware of what he was doing. These episodes, coupled with obsessive and intruding thoughts, may lead him to fear that he is losing his mind, but he is afraid to tell other people of this fear.

Major Needs

J. A. K. has very strong and unfulfilled dependency needs. He feels very inadequately prepared to handle problems and stresses on his own, and he is likely to turn to others for support and guidance. During periods of extreme stress he may display a rather infantile clinging behavior. He also has very strong needs for achievement and for recognition for his accomplishments. He sets high standards for himself, and he feels guilty when he fails to attain his goals, but his strong fear of failing keeps him from placing himself in directly competitive situations, and his goals are likely to be vague and poorly defined. Although he harbors strong hostile and aggressive impulses toward other people, particularly those who are perceived as not meeting his dependency needs, he is uncomfortable with these negative feelings and is not likely to express them directly. Rather, they are likely to gain expression in indirect passive-aggressive behaviors such as uncooperativeness, stubbornness, and hypercriticality of the behavior of others.

Perceptions of the Environment

J. A. K. views the world as a rather threatening and nonsupportive place. He feels that he is at the mercy of forces over which he has no control. His general outlook can be characterized as pessimistic, cynical, skeptical, caustic, and disbelieving. He tends to see other people as selfish, insensitive, unreasonable, and dishonest. He feels that he has been mistreated and misunderstood and that his needs have not been adequately met.

Reactions to Stress

J. A. K. feels inadequate and incompetent to cope with problems and stresses in his life situation. He feels that problems have been piling up so long that he no longer can cope with them. Although he may be able to cope with many aspects of his life situation, he does so at reduced efficiency and at great psychological cost to himself. His preferred reaction to problems is to deny their existence and to withdraw into fantasy and daydreaming. When these mechanisms fail, he may feel overwhelmed and his behavior may appear to be disorganized and maladaptive. He has a tendency to anticipate problems before they occur and to overreact to stress. He may develop somatic symptoms in reaction to stress. His approach to problem solving tends to be cautious, conventional, and unoriginal, and his thinking may be rigid and inflexible.

Self-concept

J. A. K.'s self-concept is extremely unfavorable. He sees himself as inferior to other people, and he feels inadequate to handle his own problems. He has set unrealistically high standards for himself, and he feels worthless and useless when he fails to live up to his goals. He is self-critical and self-depreciatory, and he feels unworthy and deserving of punishment. At times he is likely to harbor self-destructive impulses, but he does not appear to be more likely than other depressed patients to attempt suicide. His negative self-image is well integrated into his life-style and is likely to be very resistant to change. He may selectively attend to failures and shortcomings and ignore his past accomplishments.

Sexual Identification

J. A. K. harbors serious concerns about his sexual adequacy and may engage in rich sexual fantasies. Mature heterosexual relationships are difficult for him, and he probably feels uncomfortable around members of the opposite sex. Women are seen as sources of gratification for his intense dependency needs, and he may tend to cast them into the role of mother figures.

Emotional Control

J. A. K. is very constricted and overcontrolled most of the time. He is uncomfortable with his own feelings, both positive and negative ones, and he is not likely to express them directly. In fact, much of the time he may not even be aware of his own feelings. He harbors rather strong hostile and aggressive feelings, particularly toward parents and other authority figures, and these negative feelings find expression in rather indirect, passive-aggressive behaviors.

Interpersonal Relationships

Whereas J. A. K.'s strong needs for attention and recognition may drive him into some interpersonal relationships, they are likely to be shallow and superficial. He has the capacity for developing deep emotional ties, but he prevents people from getting too close to him because of fear of rejection and/or exploitation. He is uncomfortable around people unless he knows them very well, and he does not get involved in many social activities. He is timid, shy, and retiring around other people, and he tries to avoid being the center of attention. He finds it difficult to talk to others except for a few close relatives and friends. He does not make friends easily, and he is seen by other people as secretive, aloof, cool, distant, inaccessible, and hard to get to know. He worries a great deal about being accepted by peers, and he is bothered by his lack of meaningful involvement with other people. With the few people with whom he may be involved, he tends to be very passive, submissive, and compliant. He is easily influenced by the values and standards of others, and he is overly accepting of authority. He does not express or defend his opinions and values to other people. He is very sensitive to the reactions of others and is easily hurt by even minor criticism. He is intent on avoiding unpleasantness and makes many concessions in order to avoid confrontations.

Psychological Resources

J. A. K. is likely to have more resources and assets than his self-description suggests. In spite of his extreme discomfort, he is better able to cope with everyday problems than he thinks he is. Although he may not be closely involved with other people, he has the capacity for forming deep emotional ties. He has high standards for his own behavior. He tends to be neat, clean, and orderly, and he is reliable and conscientious. He is seen by others as sensitive, kind, peace-loving, and generous. He enjoys work and gets pleasure from personal achievement.

Dynamics and Etiology

Many of J. A. K.'s symptoms and problems are likely to be associated with his unrealistically high standards and goals for himself and his perceived failure to achieve them. The clinician should explore his family constellation to try to identify the sources of these unrealistic self-expectations. Often such attitudes are produced by demanding and perfectionistic parents who are almost impossible to please. As J. A. K. was the older of two male children, his parents may have had unrealistic expectations of him.

His feelings of inadequacy, dependency, and inability to cope could be related to overprotection and dominance on the part of his parents, particularly his mother. However, such insecurities also can result when an individual is not required, or at least encouraged, to accept increasing responsibilities as he is growing up. This latter inference is in keeping with J. A. K.'s report of his childhood.

One suspects that J. A. K.'s dependent, submissive style is directed at getting sympathy and support from other people. His attitudes and behaviors make it extremely difficult for people to react to him in negative or hostile ways. His avoidance of deep emotional involvement with other people ensures that he cannot be hurt seriously by them.

J. A. K.'s feeling of masculine inadequacy might be related to a faulty identification with his father. Although little is known about the father, except that he died when J. A. K. was 22, one might speculate that he might have been absent from the home a great deal, cool and aloof, very critical and demanding, or otherwise inaccessible as an acceptable male model for his son.

It is possible that J. A. K.'s anger and hostility stem from perceived failures on the part of other people to fulfill his strong dependency needs. Also, they might be related to demands placed on J. A. K. that he feels inadequately prepared to meet.

Diagnostic Impression

Persons with MMPI protocols similar to that of J. A. K. usually receive a diagnosis of depressive disorder or anxiety disorder. The level of his F scale score, the rather extreme elevations on scales 2 and 7, and the 27 two-point code all are consistent with such diagnoses. Occasionally, persons with this kind of protocol receive a diagnosis of schizoid personality or schizophrenic disorder, but based on the total data available about J. A. K., these latter diagnoses do not seem to fit in this case.

Implications for Treatment

Because of his intense turmoil and discomfort, J. A. K. is likely to be receptive to counseling or psychotherapy and highly motivated to change. His Es scale T-score is 56, suggesting only moderate resources that can be tapped in treatment. His T-score of 61 on the Control scale indicates that he is able selectively to avoid displaying his psychopathology and that he probably can be treated effectively as an outpatient. This same ability, however, may lead him to keep problems from his therapist.

From his scores on the clinical scales, we can infer that J. A. K. has some characteristics that could be obstacles to successful therapy. Although he seems to have some insight into his problems, he is likely to intellectualize and to rationalize excessively. He can be expected to be resistant to interpretations in therapy. Initially, he may have difficulty in relating to the therapist in a meaningful way. Later in therapy he may develop excessive anger and hostility toward the therapist. However, he is likely to remain in therapy longer than many patients, and eventually he may come to trust the therapist. Slow but steady changes in therapy can be expected.

An initial goal in therapy would be an examination and reevaluation of his self-expectations and development of more realistic standards and goals for himself. Recognition of his negative feelings, followed by development of more effective ways of expressing them, might also be accomplished in therapy. Through the development of a meaningful relationship with his therapist, J. A. K. can come to reassess his fear of becoming emotionally involved with other people.

Specific Referral Questions

Although it is unlikely that all of the referral questions considered earlier in this chapter would be asked for a single case, they all will be considered for J. A. K. for illustrative purposes.

Suicide

J. A. K.'s rather extreme elevations on scales 2 and 7 indicate that he is likely to feel that life is no longer worthwhile and may wish that he were dead. Whereas such suicidal ideas at times may be very intense, there is no indication from the MMPI that J. A. K. is more likely than other depressed patients to attempt suicide. Although scale 8 is moderately elevated, scales 4 and 9 are not very high. Obviously, other factors such as past history of suicide attempts or situational stresses, e.g., death of a family member, job loss, divorce, etc., could make the likelihood of suicide attempts greater.

Acting Out Behavior

Whereas there is some evidence that J. A. K. harbors some intense hostile and aggressive impulses, there is little reason to expect that he will act out these impulses. Quite to the contrary, he tends to be much too inhibited and overcontrolled. His mean T-score for the control scales (1, 2, 3, 5, 7) is about 75, whereas the mean T-score for the acting out scales (4, 8, 9) is about 62. Scales 4 and 9, which are indicative of acting out behavior, are among the lowest clinical scales in the profile. The 43 two-point code, which may suggest overcontrolled hostility and episodes of aggressive behavior, is not present. His score on the Hy5 subscale (Inhibition of Aggression) is somewhat above average. His score on the Wiggins Manifest Hostility (HOS) scale is not high enough to suggest problems with control. Finally, his score on the Sc2C subscale (Lack of Ego Mastery, Defective Inhibition) is not suggestive of acting out problems.

Psychosis

J. A. K.'s profile is not suggestive of psychosis. Although his scale 8 score is 75, it is not high enough to warrant a diagnosis of psychosis. Scale 7 is higher than scale 8, suggesting control of cognitive processes. The Persecutory Ideas subscale (Pa1), the Lack of Ego Mastery, Cognitive subscale (Sc2A), and the Bizarre Sensory Experiences subscale (Sc3) all are below 70, supporting the hypothesis that J. A. K. is not psychotic. When his T-scores are entered into Goldberg's index, a value of 22 is obtained. This value is considerably lower than the cutoff score of 45 that Goldberg found most effective in differentiating neurotic and psychotic profiles.

Functional Versus Organic Etiology

Whereas persons with profiles similar to that of J. A. K. tend to present somatic complaints, it is unlikely that he would have some specific conversion symptom (e.g., paralysis, blindness, etc.). The fact that scale 2 is much higher than scale 1 contraindicates a conversion reaction. If J. A. K. were complaining of low back pain, his score on the Lb scale would be considered borderline and not particularly helpful in determining whether the pain were functional or organic in nature.

Alcoholism and Addiction

Although persons with this kind of protocol may at times drink excessively, the MMPI protocol is not indicative of alcoholism or addiction. Scale 4, which is often elevated among persons with these problems, is relatively low in the profile. Also, the 27 two-point code is not one often found among alcoholics or addicts. J. A. K.'s raw score on the MacAndrew Alcoholism scale is 15, which is far below the cutoff score of 24 found by MacAndrew to be most effective in identifying alcoholics.

Summary

The above analysis of this single case is extremely lengthy in its presentation because it is meant as a teaching-learning tool for the beginning MMPI clinician. The experienced MMPI clinician would write a much briefer interpretation of the protocol. Specifically, the following is what the author would write about J. A. K. in a clinic chart, or to the referring source, or for his own psychotherapy notes, from the same MMPI protocol:

There is no indication that the protocol produced by J. A. K. is not valid. He was not overly defensive in answering the MMPI items, and, in fact, he tended to be somewhat self-critical.

J. A. K. appears to be in a great deal of psychological discomfort. He feels anxious, depressed, and overwhelmed by his problems. Although he continues to function adequately in most aspects of his life situation, he does so at great psychological cost to himself. Most of the time he is likely to be rather unemotional and unexcitable and to have a slow personal tempo, but he may also experience episodes of unexplainable excitement and restlessness. He ruminates over his problems; he is very pessimistic about the possibility that things might get better; and he may have concluded that life is no longer worthwhile. He feels very guilty about perceived misdeeds, and he may harbor suicidal ideas, but he does not seem to be more likely than other depressed patients to attempt suicide. He is likely to report somatic concerns, and they may be general and vague or very specific in nature. J. A. K. is likely to have problems with concentration, attention, memory, and judgment. Decisions are especially difficult for him. He may have experienced periods during which he was unaware of what he was doing, and these episodes, coupled with obsessive and intruding thoughts, may lead him to fear that he is losing his mind.

J. A. K. has very strong unfulfilled dependency needs. He feels very inadequately prepared to handle problems and stresses on his own, and he is likely to turn to others for support and guidance. He has very strong needs for achievement, and he feels guilty when he falls short of his goals. Although he harbors strong hostile and aggressive impulses toward other people, particularly those who are perceived as not meeting his dependency needs, he is uncomfortable with these negative feelings and is not likely to express them directly.

J. A. K. views the world as a rather threatening and nonsupportive place, and he feels that he is at the mercy of forces that are beyond his control. He has a very cynical, skeptical, and disbelieving attitude, and he feels mistreated and misunderstood by other people. His preferred reaction to problems is to deny their existence and to withdraw into fantasy and daydreaming. When these mechanisms fail, he may feel overwhelmed and his behavior may appear to be disorganized and maladaptive. He anticipates problems before they occur, and he overreacts to stress.

J. A. K. has an extremely unfavorable self-concept. It is well integrated into his life-style and is likely to be very resistant to change. J. A. K. is likely to have difficulty in establishing mature heterosexual relationships. He harbors doubts about his own masculinity and views women primarily as sources of gratification for his strong dependency needs. J. A. K. is very much constricted and overcontrolled most of the time, and he inhibits direct expression of negative feelings, but passive-aggressive behaviors may be expected. J. A. K.'s relationships with others tend to be very superficial and unrewarding. He needs other people and he has the capacity for developing deep emotional ties, but he is afraid of getting too involved with others because of fear of rejection and/or exploitation. He does not make friends easily, and other people see him as distant, aloof, and hard to get to know. He is very passive in interpersonal relationships, and he rarely expresses his true feelings. He is very sensitive to the reactions of others, and he is easily hurt by criticism. He makes many concessions to avoid confrontations. In spite of his extreme discomfort, he is better able to cope with everyday problems than he thinks he is. He tends to have high standards and is reliable and conscientious. He enjoys work and gets pleasure from personal achievement.

Many of J. A. K.'s problems stem from his unrealistically high standards and goals for himself and his perceived failure to achieve them. Such attitudes often are produced by demanding and perfectionistic parents who are almost impossible to please. J. A. K.'s dependent, submissive style is directed at getting sympathy and support from other people. His attitudes and behaviors make it very difficult for other people to react to him in negative or hostile ways. His avoidance of deep emotional ties ensures that he will not be seriously hurt by other people. One suspects that his feelings of masculine inadequacy stem from a faulty identification with his father. His anger probably comes from perceived failures on the part of other people to fulfill his strong dependency needs and from their placing of demands on him that he feels he cannot meet.

The most appropriate diagnostic label for J. A. K. is either depressive disorder or anxiety disorder. Because of his intense discomfort, he is likely to be receptive to counseling or psychotherapy. Initially, he might rationalize and intellectualize excessively and avoid relating to the therapist in a meaningful way. However, he is likely to remain in therapy, and slow but steady progress can be expected. An initial goal in therapy would be an examination and reevaluation of his self-expectations and development of more realistic goals for himself. Through the development of a meaningful relationship with the therapist, he can come to admit his fears and conflicts and acquire more effective ways of coping with them.

ADDITIONAL PRACTICE PROFILES

Brief interpretations of two additional MMPI profiles will now be presented. As a learning exercise, clinicians can write their own interpretations of each profile and then compare their interpretations with the ones presented below.

Figure 9.2 presents the MMPI profile of a 41-year-old male (D. A. V.) who was a patient in a psychiatric hospital when he completed the test. He was married, had completed 11 years of formal education, and was working as a truck driver at the time of his hospitalization.

D. A. V. was very frank and candid, and perhaps even self-critical, in his approach to the test, and he admitted to a large number of clearly deviant behaviors. He is likely to be quite disturbed emotionally. Although he does not experience disabling anxiety or depression, he does have problems in attending and concentrating, and he may admit to deficits in memory. He is likely to manifest signs of thinking disturbance. He may appear to be confused, disoriented, and disorganized. His thinking may be fragmented, autistic, and circumstantial, and bizarre thoughts and ideas are likely. A clearly paranoid orientation, including suspiciousness, hallucinations, delusions of persecution and/or grandeur, and feelings of unreality, may be present. Long-standing, vague somatic complaints also may be reported.

D. A. V. views the world as a very threatening and unsupportive place, and he feels quite unable to respond to the demands of his daily life. He feels very insecure and inferior, and he is guilty about his perceived failures in life. He reacts to stress by withdrawing into daydreaming and fantasy, and he may have difficulty in differentiating fantasy from reality.

D. A. V. has a rather cynical, pessimistic, and disbelieving attitude toward life. He is angry and resentful because of perceived mistreatment to others, but he is unable to express these negative feelings in modulated, adaptive ways. He is not emotionally involved with other people. He is distrustful and suspicious of their motives, and he keeps them at a psychological distance. Other people perceive him as cold, aloof, and hard to get to know. Whereas D. A. V. may have many interests, his goals are vague and abstract, and his achievement level is likely to be mediocre at best. He may be preoccupied with abstract and theoretical matters to the exclusion of specific, concrete aspects of his life situation.

The most appropriate diagnosis for D. A. V. is schizophrenia, paranoid type. He appears to have little insight into his problems and behaviors, and he is reluctant to accept responsibility for his difficulties. He blames others for his failures and shortcomings. Although his reluctance to relate to the therapist in a meaningful way would be a definite liability in psychotherapy, he probably would remain in therapy and eventually could come to trust the therapist. Antipsychotic medication may be useful in alleviating overt symptomatology.

Figure 9.3 presents the MMPI profile of M. A. R., a 28-year-old housewife with a high school education. She was given the MMPI while an outpatient at a community mental health center. It appears that M. A. R. was rather honest and straightforward in her approach to the MMPI. She was neither overly defensive nor excessively self-critical in her responses. The deviant behaviors to which she admitted are likely to be concentrated in some particular problem area (e.g., sexual concerns, marital difficulties, etc.). Although she may feel bored, restless, and dissatisfied with her life situation, she probably is free of disabling anxiety and depression, and she is unlikely to manifest frankly psychotic behaviors. She is likely to deny serious emotional problems, and she may structure difficulties in terms of marital incompatability.

M. A. R. is a very immature, narcissistic, and self-indulgent person who demands sympathy and attention from other people. However, she becomes very resentful when even mild demands are made on her. She appears to be overly identified with the stereotypic female role, and she is passive, dependent, and yielding in her relationships with men. At the same time, however, she is likely to be uncomfortable with this more traditional role, and she probably harbors strong desires to be more assertive. Her feminine identification may be quite weak, and she may resort to sexual promiscuity to try to demonstrate her feminine adequacy.

Although she is likely to be rather gregarious and outgoing and to make good first impressions, she really does not relate very well to other people, particularly males, and she is rather uncomfortable in social situations. She is guarded and suspicious about the motives of other people, and she avoids deep emotional ties. She is interested in others primarily because of what they can do for her. M. A. R. tends to be rather impulsive, and she acts without considering the consequences of her actions. She has a low tolerance for frustration, and she is impatient and irritable when things do not suit her. Periodic outbursts of anger and hostility can be expected.

The prognosis for traditional psychotherapy is poor. She does not admit to serious emotional problems, and therefore she is not likely to be receptive to treatment. She may agree to treatment if she is in trouble (e.g., legal difficulty, marital problems, etc.), but she is likely to terminate treatment prematurely when the situational stresses subside. She tends to intellectualize and to rationalize a great deal, and she blames others, particularly parents, for her problems. If situational stresses are prolonged, she may become motivated to try to change in therapy.

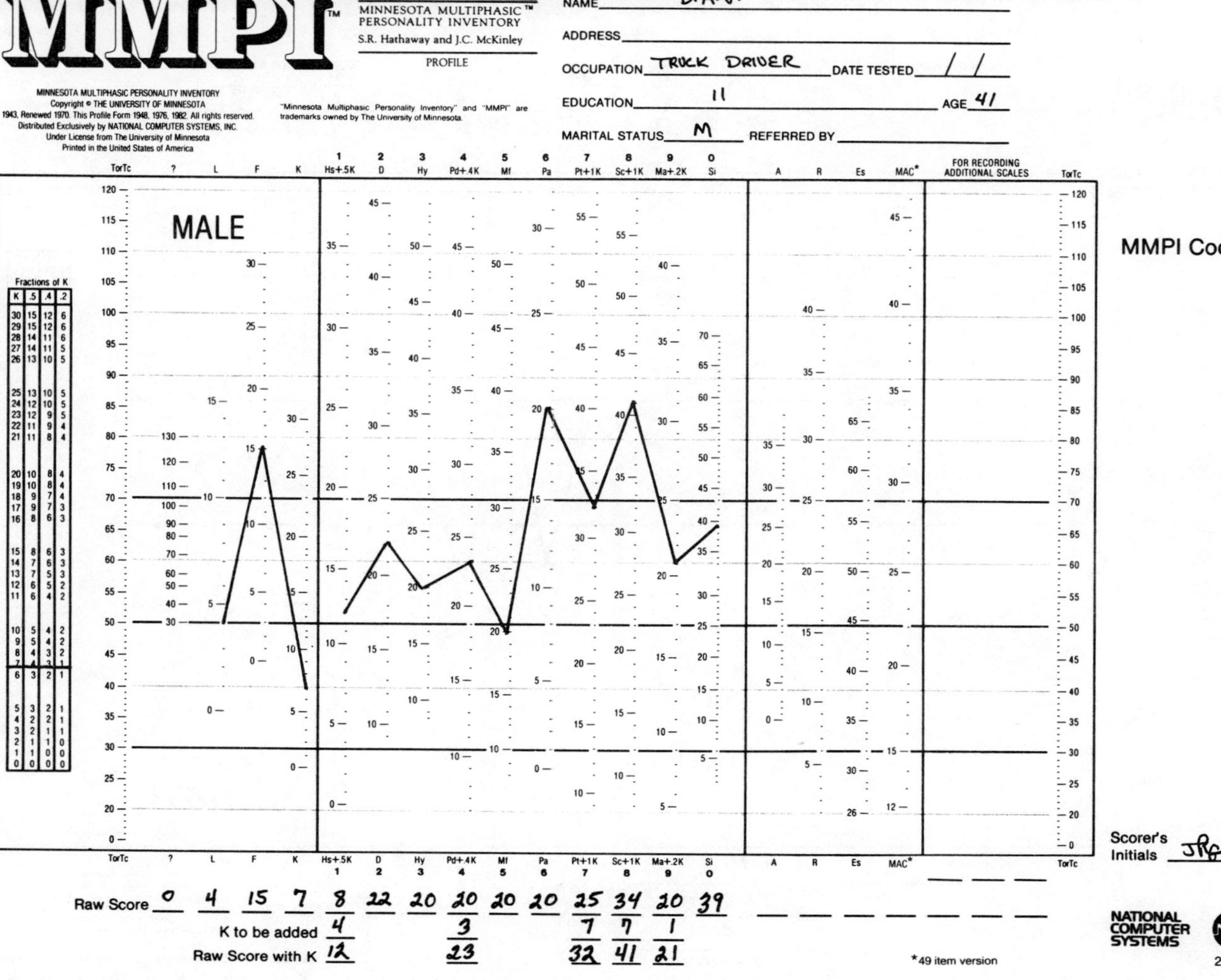

Fig. 9.2. MMPI profile for practice case (D. A. V.). (Minnesota Multiphasic Personality Inventory. Copyright © the University of

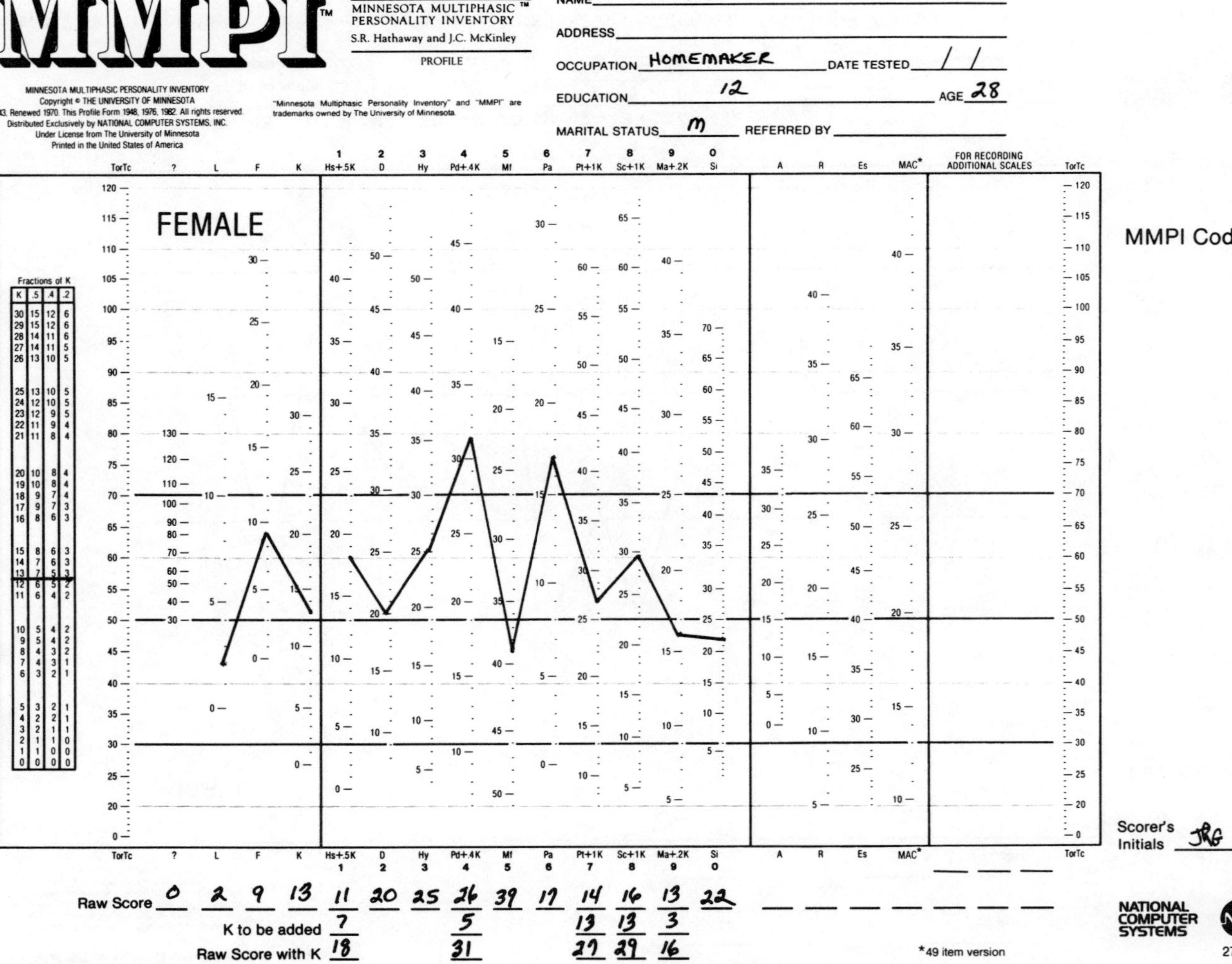

Fig. 9.3. MMPI profile for practice case (M. A. R.). (Minnesota Multiphasic Personality Inventory. Copyright © the University of Minnesota 1943, renewed 1970. This Profile Form 1948, 1982. Reproduced with permission.)

A FINAL COMMENT

The purpose of this chapter has been to present one strategy for organizing inferences from MMPI data into a meaningful understanding of a specific case. Although it is recognized that many MMPI users will find other strategies more to their liking, clinicians who are just starting to use the MMPI in clinical work may find the strategy suggested here to be helpful until they have gained enough experience and skill to develop strategies of their own.

10

Computerized Administration, Scoring, and Interpretation

In an era of almost unbelievable advances in computer technology, it is not at all surprising that there have been increasing efforts to automate the testing process. Automation in psychological testing occurs whenever a computer performs functions previously carried out by the human examiner. Computers can administer, score, and interpret tests. Although automation has been applied to a variety of psychological tests, objective personality inventories, such as the MMPI, lend themselves most readily to automation.

Computers have some definite advantages over human clinicians in the testing enterprise. First, they are fast. Operations that would take a person minutes, or even hours, to complete can be performed by computers in fractions of a second. Second, computers are accurate and reliable. Assuming that accurate information has been programmed into a computer, there is perfect reliability in the functions that it performs. Third, the computer has far greater storage capacity than the human clinician. A virtually infinite number of bits of information can be stored by the computer, to be called upon as needed in the testing process. Fourth, the flexibility provided by computer technology offers the possibility of developing tests or sets of test items tailored to the individual examinee. Programs can be written to interact with the examinee so that the answer to any specific item determines the next item to be given, skipping irrelevant data and/or exploring some areas in more depth. Although such computer-tailored assessment procedures have been employed in ability testing and diagnostic interviewing, this potential use of computer technology has not been widely exploited in personality testing (Butcher, Keller, & Bacon, 1985).

AUTOMATED ADMINISTRATION OF THE MMPI

Instead of using the traditional test booklets and answer sheets, subjects can complete the MMPI on a computer terminal, personal computer, or computer hardware dedicated specifically to the administration of the MMPI. The typical procedure is for subjects to sit at the machine while the MMPI items are individually displayed on a monitor. A response is made to each item by pressing designated keys on the machine or by touching a stylus to the desired response on the monitor. Each response is recorded automatically and saved in memory for later processing. Most programs permit subjects to change responses after they are made and to omit items and consider them again at the end of the test.

Automated administration has several advantages. First, many subjects find it more interesting than the traditional procedure and are more motivated to complete the task. Second, because subjects enter response data into the computer, no professional or clerical time is used for this purpose. However, a major disadvantage is that each administration consumes nearly an hour of valuable and costly computer time. Also, some subjects, particularly upset and confused clients or patients, may be overwhelmed by the task.

As discussed previously, the MMPI is a very robust instrument. Various forms of the test (e.g., booklet, audio tape recording) seem to yield essentially equivalent results. However, we must be concerned about the equivalence of the computer-administered and more traditional versions of the test. There are data suggesting that provision of an explicit Cannot Say option produces a greater number of omitted items than when the option is less obvious (Biskin & Kolotkin, 1977).

Some studies have found that subjects are more willing to admit to deviant behaviors when tests are computer-administered than when a standard administration is used (Evan & Miller, 1969; Koson, Kitchen, Kochen, & Stodolosky, 1970). However, at least one study found that patients produced more pathological profiles when the MMPI was administered in the usual fashion than when it was administered via computer (Bresolin, 1984).

Clearly, existing data are inadequate to permit us to conclude with confidence that standard and computer administrations of the MMPI produce equivalent results. However, after reviewing relevant research data, Moreland (1985a) concluded that the bulk of the evidence on computer adaptations of paper-and-pencil questionnaires points to the tentative conclusion that differences attributable to the type of administration typically are small and probably of little practical consequence.

The technology for on-line administration of the MMPI is rapidly changing. Because of copyright issues, at the present time persons wanting to use on-line administration of the MMPI must buy from the test distributor software that can be used with personal computers.

AUTOMATED SCORING OF THE MMPI

Programming a computer to score the MMPI is not a very difficult task. The computer's memory stores information that determines which items and which responses are scored for each scale. Dozens, and even hundreds, of scales can be scored in a matter of seconds. Because test norms also can be stored in the computer's memory, raw scores on the various scales can be converted easily to T-scores, and profiles based on these T-scores can be printed. This entire process can be accomplished in a fraction of the time that it would take to score and plot even the basic validity and clinical scales by hand.

Inputting test responses for scoring can be accomplished in a number of ways. If the MMPI has been administered on-line, the individual responses have been saved in the computer's memory and are ready for immediate scoring. If the subject uses a test booklet and answer sheet, an examiner or a clerk can enter the subject's responses from the answer sheet via a computer keyboard. With a little practice, the 566 items of the MMPI can be entered in a very short time (5 to 10 minutes). In either case the item responses can be scored by the personal computer on which they were entered, or they can be transmitted via teleprocessing equipment to Minneapolis where the scoring is done on a mainframe computer operated by the test distributor. The resulting scores are printed on the test user's computer printer, so they are available almost immediately. For large-volume users, special machine-scorable answer sheets can be used. These sheets can be mailed to Minneapolis for computer scoring, or they can be processed by the examiner using relatively inexpensive scanners that can be attached to personal computers.

AUTOMATED INTERPRETATON OF THE MMPI

Automated interpretations of the MMPI are not as simple and straightforward as are administration and scoring. Interpretive statements are written for various scores and patterns of scores that subjects might produce, and these statements are stored in the computer's memory. When an MMPI is administered to a specific subject and scored, the computer searches its memory to find interpretive statements that previously were judged to be appropriate for these particular scores and patterns of scores. These statements are then printed on the computer's printer.

It is important to distinguish between automated and actuarial interpretations (Graham & Lilly, 1984). Automation refers to the use of computers to store interpretive statements and to assign interpretive statements to particular scores and patterns of scores. The decisions about which statements are to be assigned to which scores may be based on research, actuarial tables, or clinical experience. Regardless of how the decisions were made initially, they are made automatically by the computer after the test is administered and scored.

Actuarial interpretations are ones in which the assignment of interpretive statements to scores and patterns of scores is based entirely on previously established empirical relationships between test scores and the behaviors included in the interpretive statements. Experience and intuition play no part in actuarial interpretation.

The MMPI interpretive services currently available are not actuarial in nature. They are what Wiggins (1973) called automated clinical prediction. On the basis of published research, clinical hypotheses, and clinical experience, a clinician generates interpretive statements judged to be appropriate for a particular set of MMPI scores. The statements are stored in the computer and called upon as needed. It should be made perfectly clear that the accuracy (validity) of these kinds of interpretations is dependent upon the knowledge and skill of the clinician who generated the interpretive statements. The validity of these interpretations should not be assumed and needs to be demonstrated every bit as much as the validity of a test needs to be demonstrated (Moreland, 1985c). Many different interpretive programs and services exist, and their validity has not been adequately established.

The number of MMPI interpretive programs and services changes rapidly. Some services go out of business or are acquired by other services, and new ones emerge. The apparent quality of the existing services varies considerably. Some of the interpretive programs have been written by persons with considerable knowlege of MMPI research and great clinical experience with the MMPI. Others programs appear to have been written by persons knowing very little about the MMPI. Because of the great difficulty in obtaining and maintaining adequate evaluative data for the various services, no attempt will be made here to include an exhaustive or even representative sampling of the services. Rather, to illustrate automated interpretation the MMPI answer sheet of the subject discussed in detail in Chapter 9 was sent to the test distributor, National Computer Systems, for processing, and the resulting Minnesota Report[1] is presented in its entirety.

The Minnesota Report was written almost entirely by one interpretive expert, incorporating both his knowledge of actuarial data and his personal clinical experience. The program is built hierarchically around code type interpretations (Butcher, Keller, & Bacon, 1985). If a profile fits an established code type, a standard report for that configural pattern is printed. Additions and modifications are based on elevations on other scales. If the profile does not fit an established code type, the report is based on a scale-by-scale analysis.

COMPARISON OF COMPUTERIZED AND CLINICIAN-GENERATED INTERPRETATIONS

A comparison of the Minnesota Report and the clinician-generated report for the same profile that was presented in Chapter 9 reveals considerable agreement between the interpretations. Both interpretations conclude that the MMPI is valid, that the subject is experiencing considerable emotional turmoil,

1. "The Minnesota Report" is a trademark owned by the University Press of the University of Minnesota. The sample report presented in this chapter has been reproduced with permission of the University Press.

THE MINNESOTA REPORT TM* Page 1

for the Minnesota Multiphasic Personality Inventory TM : Adult System

By James N. Butcher, Ph.D.

Client No. : 00000002985 Gender : Male
Setting : Mental Health Outpatient Age : 27
Report Date : 17-SEP-86
PAS Code Number : 00048040 563 0004

PROFILE VALIDITY

The client has responded to the items in a frank and open manner, producing a valid MMPI profile. He appears to be a relatively cooperative person who took the test seriously.

He has admitted to a number of psychological problems that warrant attention. He may be experiencing some difficulties managing his life situation and is seeking assistance at this time.

SYMPTOMATIC PATTERN

A pattern of chronic psychological maladjustment characterizes individuals with this MMPI profile. The client is overwhelmed by anxiety, tension, and depression. He feels helpless and alone, inadequate and insecure, and believes that life is hopeless and that nothing is working out right. He attempts to control his worries through intellectualization and unproductive self-analyses, but he has difficulty concentrating and making decisions.

He is functioning at a very low level of efficiency. He tends to overreact to even minor stress, and may show rapid behavioral deterioration. He also tends to blame himself for his problems. His life-style is chaotic and disorganized, and he has a history of poor work and achievement.

He may be preoccupied with occult ideas. Obsessive-compulsive and phobic behavior are likely to make up part of the symptom pattern. He has a wide range of interests, and appears to enjoy aesthetic and cultural activities. Interpersonally, he appears to be sensitive, concerned, and able to easily express his feelings toward others. He appears to have no sex-role conflict.

His response content indicates that he is preoccupied with feeling guilty and unworthy, and feels that he deserves to be punished for wrongs he has committed. He feels regretful and unhappy about life, complains about having no zest for life, and seems plagued by anxiety and worry about the future. He has difficulty managing routine affairs, and the item content he endorsed suggests a poor memory, concentration problems, and an inability to make decisions. He appears to be immobilized and withdrawn and has no energy for life. According to his response content, there is a strong possibility that he has seriously contemplated suicide. A careful evaluation of this possibility is suggested.

INTERPERSONAL RELATIONS

NOTE: This MMPI interpretation can serve as a useful source of hypotheses about clients. This report is based on objectively derived scale indexes and scale interpretations that have been developed in diverse groups of patients. The personality descriptions, inferences and recommendations contained herein need to be verified by other sources of clinical information since individual clients may not fully match the prototype. The information in this report should most appropriately be used by a trained, qualified test interpreter. The information contained in this report should be considered confidential.

Problematic personal relationships are also characteristic of his life. He seems to lack basic social skills and is behaviorally withdrawn. He may relate to others ambivalently, never fully trusting or loving anyone. Many individuals with this profile never establish lasting, intimate relationships. His marital situation is likely to be unrewarding and impoverished. He seems to feel inadequate and insecure in his marriage.

He is a rather introverted person who has some difficulties meeting other people. He is probably shy and may be uneasy and somewhat rigid and overcontrolled in social situations.

BEHAVIORAL STABILITY

This is a rather chronic behavioral pattern. Individuals with this profile live a disorganized and pervasively unhappy existence. They may have episodes of more intense and disturbed behavior resulting from an elevated stress level.

DIAGNOSTIC CONSIDERATIONS

Individuals with this profile show a severe psychological disorder and would probably be diagnosed as severely neurotic with an Anxiety Disorder or Dysthymic Disorder in a Schizoid Personality. The possibility of a more severe psychotic disorder, such as Schizophrenic Disorder, should be considered, however.

Individuals with this profile present some suicide risk and further evaluation of this possibility should be undertaken.

TREATMENT CONSIDERATIONS

Individuals with this MMPI profile often receive psychotropic medications for their depressed mood or intense anxiety. Many patients with this profile seek psychological treatment for their problems. Indeed, individuals with this profile usually require psychological treatment for their problems along with any medication that is given. Since many of their problems tend to be chronic ones, an intensive therapeutic effort might be required in order to bring about any significant change. Patients with this profile typically have many psychological and situational concerns; thus it is often difficult to maintain a focus in treatment.

He probably needs a great deal of emotional support at this time. His low self-esteem and feelings of inadequacy make it difficult for him to get energized toward therapeutic action. His expectancies for positive change in therapy may be low. Instilling a positive, treatment expectant attitude is important for him if treatment is to be successful.

Individuals with this profile tend to be overideational and given to unproductive rumination. They tend not to do well in unstructured, insight-oriented therapy and may actually deteriorate in functioning if they are asked to be introspective. He might respond more to supportive treatment of a directive, goal-oriented type.

Individuals with this profile present some suicide risk and precautions should be considered.

THE MINNESOTA REPORT Page 3

for the Minnesota Multiphasic Personality Inventory : Adult System

By James N. Butcher, Ph.D.

CLINICAL PROFILE

Client No. : 00000002985 Gender : Male
Setting : Mental Health Outpatient Age : 27
Report Date : 17-SEP-86

```
                      |  1   2   3   4   5   6   7   8   9   0
                      |
       ?   L   F   K  |  Hs  D   Hy  Pd  Mf  Pa  Pt  Sc  Ma  Si
                      |
110- ---------------- | ----------------------------------------- -110
   -                  |                                           -
   -                  |                                           -
   -                  |                                           -
   -                  |                                           -
100-                  |                                           -100
   -                  |                                           -
   -                  |                                           -
   -                  |      *                                    -
   -                  |                                           -
 90-                  |                                           -90
   -                  |                                           -
   -                  |                                           -
   -                  |                                           -
   -                  |                          *                -
 80-                  |                                           -80
   -                  |                                           -
   -                  |                                           -
   -                  |                              *            -
   -                  |                                      *    -
 70- ---------------- | -*-------------------------------------- -70
   -                  |                                           -
   -                  |          *                                -
   -                  |                  *                        -
   -          *       |              *                            -
 60-                  |                      *           *        -60
   -                  |                                           -
   -                  |                                           -
   -                  |                                           -
   -                  |                                           -
 50- ---------------- | ----------------------------------------- -50
   -                  |                                           -
   -      *       *   |                                           -
   -                  |                                           -
   -  *               |                                           -
 40-                  |                                           -40
   -                  |                                           -
   -                  |                                           -
   -                  |                                           -
   -                  |                                           -
 30- ---------------- | ----------------------------------------- -30
       ?   L   F   K  |  Hs  D   Hy  Pd  Mf  Pa  Pt  Sc  Ma  Si
                      |
                      |  1   2   3   4   5   6   7   8   9   0
```

Clinical Profile Scores:

	?	L	F	K	Hs	D	Hy	Pd	Mf	Pa	Pt	Sc	Ma	Si
Raw	0	3	8	10	14	35	25	20	27	11	28	24	19	45
K-Correction					5			4			10	10	2	
T	41	46	62	46	70	94	65	62	63	59	81	73	60	72

Percent True : 45 F - K (Raw) : -2

Profile Elevation : 70.5 Goldberg Index : 32
(Hs,D,Hy,Pd,Pa,Pt,Sc,Ma)

Welsh Code : 2*7"801'354 9-6/ F-LK?:

The Minnesota Multiphasic Personality Inventory

SUPPLEMENTAL PROFILE

Client No. : 00000002985 Report Date : 17-SEP-86 Page 4

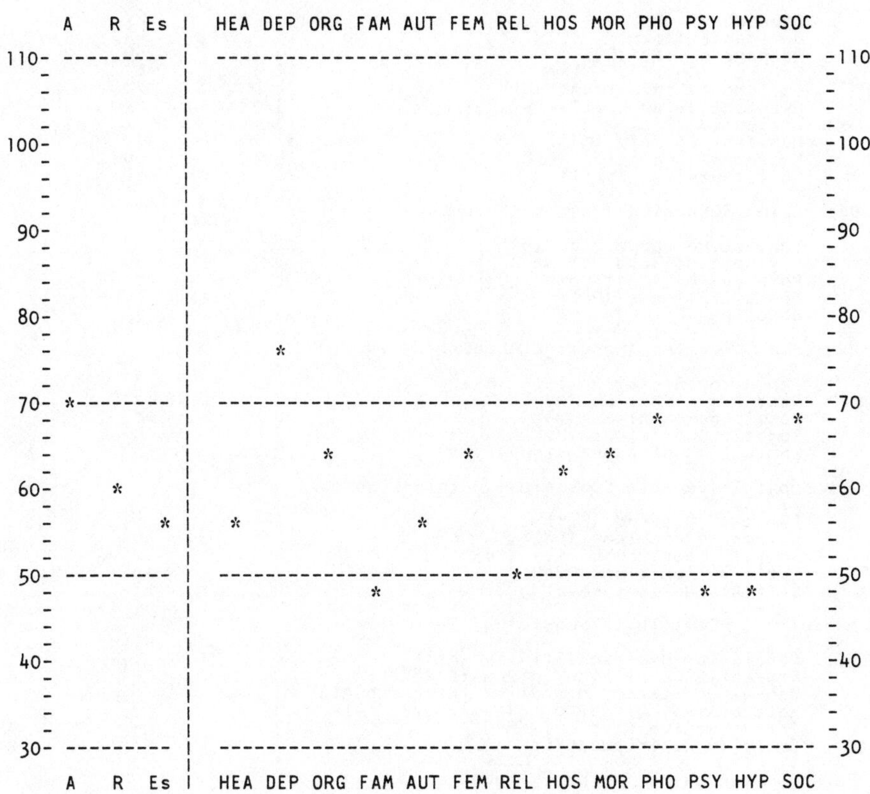

<u>Supplemental Profile Scores:</u>

	A	R	Es	HEA	DEP	ORG	FAM	AUT	FEM	REL	HOS	MOR	PHO	PSY	HYP	SOC
Raw	27	20	48	7	20	11	3	12	14	6	15	15	12	7	11	17
T	69	59	56	55	75	63	47	56	64	49	61	64	67	48	48	67

The Minnesota Multiphasic Personality Inventory

EXTENDED SCORE REPORT

Client No. : 00000002985 Report Date : 17-SEP-86 Page 5

Supplementary Scales:	Raw Score	T Score
Dependency (Dy)	35	67
Dominance (Do)	13	45
Responsibility (Re)	20	50
Control (Cn)	29	61
College Maladjustment (Mt)	32	78
Overcontrolled Hostility (O-H)	13	52
Prejudice (Pr)	13	52
Manifest Anxiety (MAS)	31	72
MacAndrew Addiction (MAC)	15	30
Social Status (St)	21	58
Depression Subscales (Harris-Lingoes):		
Subjective Depression (D1)	22	93
Psychomotor Retardation (D2)	10	76
Physical Malfunctioning (D3)	4	56
Mental Dullness (D4)	8	80
Brooding (D5)	6	71
Hysteria Subscales (Harris-Lingoes):		
Denial of Social Anxiety (Hy1)	0	31
Need for Affection (Hy2)	3	42
Lassitude-Malaise (Hy3)	10	83
Somatic Complaints (Hy4)	7	67
Inhibition of Aggression (Hy5)	3	53
Psychopathic Deviate Subscales (Harris-Lingoes):		
Familial Discord (Pd1)	2	51
Authority Problems (Pd2)	6	61
Social Imperturbability (Pd3)	4	35
Social Alienation (Pd4a)	6	52
Self Alienation (Pd4b)	10	74
Masculinity-Femininity Subscales (Serkownek):		
Narcissism-Hypersensitivity (Mf1)	8	67
Stereotypic Feminine Interests (Mf2)	2	41
Denial of Stereo. Masculine Interests (Mf3)	7	81
Heterosexual Discomfort-Passivity (Mf4)	1	33
Introspective-Critical (Mf5)	3	46
Socially Retiring (Mf6)	3	35
Paranoia Subscales (Harris-Lingoes):		
Persecutory Ideas (Pa1)	1	46
Poignancy (Pa2)	5	68
Naivete (Pa3)	2	41
Schizophrenia Subscales (Harris-Lingoes):		
Social Alienation (Sc1a)	5	56
Emotional Alienation (Sc1b)	4	66
Lack of Ego Mastery, Cognitive (Sc2a)	4	66
Lack of Ego Mastery, Conative (Sc2b)	10	94
Lack of Ego Mastery, Def. Inhib. (Sc2c)	3	60
Bizarre Sensory Experiences (Sc3)	5	60
Hypomania Subscales (Harris-Lingoes):		
Amorality (Ma1)	4	67
Psychomotor Acceleration (Ma2)	6	66
Imperturbability (Ma3)	3	47
Ego Inflation (Ma4)	2	46
Social Introversion Subscales (Serkownek):		
Inferiority-Personal Discomfort (Si1)	19	96
Discomfort with Others (Si2)	6	62
Staid-Personal Rigidity (Si3)	10	55
Hypersensitivity (Si4)	6	72
Distrust (Si5)	7	64
Physical-Somatic Concerns (Si6)	2	53

The Minnesota Multiphasic Personality Inventory

CRITICAL ITEM LISTING

Client No. : 00000002985 Report Date : 17-SEP-86 Page 6

The following Critical Items have been found to have possible significance in analyzing a client's problem situation. Although these items may serve as a source of hypotheses for further investigation, caution should be taken in interpreting individual items because they may have been inadvertently checked. Critical item numbers refer to The Group Form test booklet. Corresponding item numbers for Form R (only items 367-566 differ) can be found in the MMPI "Manual" or Volume I of "An MMPI Handbook." Corresponding item numbers for the Roche Testbook can be found in "The Clinical Use of the Automated MMPI."

ACUTE ANXIETY STATE (Koss-Butcher Critical Items)

3. I wake up fresh and rested most mornings. (F)
13. I work under a great deal of tension. (T)
29. I am bothered by acid stomach several times a week. (T)
43. My sleep is fitful and disturbed. (T)
230. I hardly ever notice my heart pounding and I am seldom short of breath. (F)
238. I have periods of such great restlessness that I cannot sit long in a chair. (T)
242. I believe I am no more nervous than most others. (F)
506. I am a high-strung person. (T)

DEPRESSED SUICIDAL IDEATION (Koss-Butcher Critical Items)

41. I have had periods of days, weeks, or months when I couldn't take care of things because I couldn't "get going". (T)
76. Most of the time I feel blue. (T)
84. These days I find it hard not to give up hope of amounting to something. (T)
88. I usually feel that life is worthwhile. (F)
107. I am happy most of the time. (F)
142. I certainly feel useless at times. (T)
259. I have difficulty in starting to do things. (T)
301. Life is a strain for me much of the time. (T)
318. My daily life is full of things that keep me interested. (F)
339. Most of the time I wish I were dead. (T)
379. I very seldom have spells of the blues. (F)
418. At times I think I am no good at all. (T)
526. The future seems hopeless to me. (T)

THREATENED ASSAULT (Koss-Butcher Critical Items)

39. At times I feel like smashing things. (T)
97. At times I have a strong urge to do something harmful or shocking. (T)
234. I get mad easily and then get over it soon. (T)

MENTAL CONFUSION (Koss-Butcher Critical Items)

328. I find it hard to keep my mind on a task or job. (T)
335. I cannot keep my mind on one thing. (T)
345. I often feel as if things were not real. (T)
356. I have more trouble concentrating than others seem to have. (T)

PERSECUTORY IDEAS (Koss-Butcher Critical Items)

265. It is safer to trust nobody. (T)

CHARACTEROLOGICAL ADJUSTMENT -- ANTISOCIAL ATTITUDE
(Lachar-Wrobel Critical Items)

28. When someone does me a wrong I feel I should pay him back if I can, just for the principle of the thing. (T)
38. During one period when I was a youngster, I engaged in petty thievery. (T)

Client No. : 00000002985 Report Date : 17-SEP-86 Page 7

250. I don't blame anyone for trying to grab everything he can get in this world. (T)

CHARACTEROLOGICAL ADJUSTMENT -- FAMILY CONFLICT
(Lachar-Wrobel Critical Items)

21. At times I have very much wanted to leave home. (T)

SOMATIC SYMPTOMS (Lachar-Wrobel Critical Items)

29. I am bothered by acid stomach several times a week. (T)
36. I seldom worry about my health. (F)
47. Once a week or oftener I feel suddenly hot all over, without apparent cause. (T)
55. I am almost never bothered by pains over the heart or in my chest. (F)
68. I hardly ever feel pain in the back of my neck. (F)
114. Often I feel as if there were a tight band about my head. (T)
189. I feel weak all over much of the time. (T)
190. I have very few headaches. (F)
243. I have few or no pains. (F)
281. I do not often notice my ears ringing or buzzing. (F)
544. I feel tired a good deal of the time. (T)

NCS Professional Assessment Services, P.O. Box 1416, Mpls, MN 55440 and that he seems to be asking for help with his problems. Both interpretations state that the subject is likely to be depressed and pessimistic about the future, but the automated report states more directly that suicide is a significant concern. Both interpretations also note that under stress the subject could become quite maladaptive and disorganized. There is agreement that interpersonal relations are likely to be strained because of the subject's distrust and fear of rejection. The two interpretations agree that the subject should be diagnosed as having an anxiety disorder or a depressive (dysthymic) disorder. Both interpretations mention the possibility of schizoid or schizophrenic features, but the clinician-generated interpretation more clearly states that schizoid personality disorder and schizophrenic disorder do not seem to fit this particular case.

There are some areas in which the two interpretations differ significantly. The automated interpretation states that the subject does not have sex-role conflict, whereas the clinician-generated interpretation suggests that he harbors doubts about his masculinity. Concerning treatment, both interpretations agree that the subject needs professional help and is likely to be receptive to such help because of his emotional turmoil. However, the automated interpretation suggests a rather negative prognosis for psychotherapy and emphasizes psychotropic medications and support. The clinician-generated interpretation offers a somewhat more positive prognosis, suggesting that the subject is likely to remain in therapy and to make slow but steady progress.

The overall agreement between the two interpretations is remarkable. Although there are some specific differences, the general pictures that emerge from the two interpretations are very similar. The agreement is not really unexpected. The clinician who developed the interpretive program for the Minnesota Report and the clinician who did the interpretation in Chapter 9 were basing their interpretations on the same research data.

This automated report would be very helpful to a clinician working with this subject. The inferences about the subject could be obtained efficiently and with little expenditure of professional time. However, it would be very important for the clinician to integrate the data from this report with other data about the subject. For example, the automated report makes inferences about poor work history, inadequacy and insecurity in the marriage, and potential for suicide. These inferences could be compared with data available from interview with the subject's wife, observations of the subject, and performance on other psychological tests.

EVALUATION OF AUTOMATED SERVICES

As the number of automated programs and services has increased in recent years, it has become increasingly difficult to evaluate their quality. This author is aware of some scoring programs that are using incorrect item numbers for some of the scales and inappropriate procedures for converting raw scores to

T-scores. The extent to which interpretive statements are based on adequate research is difficult to determine. For obvious reasons, programmers and services are reluctant to publish their statement libraries and the criteria according to which statements are selected for particular protocols. An exception is that Lachar (1974b) published his classification and interpretive rules in their entirety.

The decision to select the Minnesota Report as an illustration of an automated service was based on the author's confidence that the scoring in that report is accurate, that appropriate procedures have been used to convert raw scores to T-scores, and that the interpretive statements are based to a large extent on appropriate MMPI research data. It should not be concluded that services not specifically mentioned in this chapter are not good ones. The task of finding out enough about all of these services to make meaningful and informed evaluative statements was simply too great.

There are some important issues involved in the use of automated MMPI interpretations. One has to do with the extent to which the automated reports are integrated by adequately trained clinicians with other data available about test subjects. Although most of the services advise users that inferences in the test reports need to be verified by other data sources, in practice some clinicians use the automated reports instead of a comprehensive assessment. This is not good clinical practice.

Another concern is that because the automated reports are computer-generated, they are seen as being valid and questions rarely are asked about research demonstrating their validity. In fact, Ziskin (1981) recommends the use of automated reports in forensic cases because the computer-generated profiles and reports impress judges and jurors as more scientific. The validity of automated interpretations must be demonstrated empirically.

Qualifications of users of automated services are very important. Although all services purport to assess the qualifications of potential users to make sure that they use the interpretive reports appropriately, many users of the services are not qualified to use them. Some psychologists who are trained and licensed to practice psychology do not know enough about the MMPI to evaluate the appropriateness of the automated interpretations.

Almost all of the automated services list critical items that test subjects have endorsed in the scored direction. Although critical item endorsements represent an important additional source of hypotheses concerning test subjects, many users of the services overinterpret such endorsements. Each critical item is, in fact, a single item scale whose reliability is very questionable.

The automated interpretive systems often become fixated at a rather naive level (Butcher, 1978). Although the potential exists for modifying the systems as new interpretive data become available, there is a tendency not to change a system that is operating smoothly and producing a profit for the company. Butcher discussed several instances where, in response to critics, only minor cosmetic changes or no changes at all were made in existing interpretive programs.

In an effort to try to address some of the potential problems involved in the use of automated services, in 1966 the American Psychological Association developed some interim standards for such services (Fowler, 1969a). The standards made it clear that organizations offering the services have the primary responsibility for ensuring that the services are used by qualified persons and for demonstrating the reliability and validity of the interpretations included in the reports. More recently, the Committee on Professional Standards and the Committee on Psychological Tests and Assessment of the American Psychological Association (APA, 1986) published updated guidelines for computer-based tests and interpretations. These updated guidelines stated that it is the responsibility of developers of computer-based test services to demonstrate the equivalence of computerized and conventional versions of a test. Developers offering interpretations of test scores should describe how the interpretive statements are derived from the original scores and should make clear the extent to which interpretive statements are based on quantitative research versus clinical opinion. When statements in an interpretive report are based on expert clinical opinion, users should be given information that will allow them to weigh the credibility of the opinion. Developers also are expected to provide whatever information is needed to permit review by qualified professionals engaged in scholarly review of their interpretive services.

The updated guidelines make it very clear that professionals are responsible for any use they make of a computer-administered test or computer-generated interpretation. Users should be aware of the method employed in generating the scores and the interpretation and be sufficiently familiar with the test in order to be able to evaluate its applicability to the purpose for which it will be used. The user should judge for each test taker the validity of the computerized test report based on the user's professional knowledge of the total context of testing and the test taker's performance and characteristics.

Several different approaches have been used to try to determine the validity of automated MMPI interpretations (Moreland, 1985c). Early efforts involved asking users of the automated services to provide an overall rating of the accuracy of each automated report (e.g., Fowler, 1969b; Klett, 1971; Webb, 1970; Webb, Miller, & Fowler, 1969, 1970). Other studies have been a bit more sophisticated. Ratings have been made of the accuracy of individual paragraphs or individual statements within each report (e.g., Lachar, 1974c; Lushene & Gilberstadt, 1972). Not surprisingly, the users rated most reports as being accurate. A major problem with these studies is that judgments about what patients really were like and impressions from the MMPI-based reports were contaminated. In addition, it is not possible to judge to what extent reports were rated as accurate because of the inclusion of glittering generalities (Baillargeon & Danis, 1984) in the reports. In other words, the studies address convergent but not discriminant validity.

The most acceptable validity studies have been those in which external criterion information has been collected by persons who had no knowledge of MMPI results or of the automated reports. The interpretative statements within the reports were compared with the external criterion information about patients (e.g., Anderson, 1969; Hedlund, Morgan, & Master, 1972). The results of studies of this kind suggest at best moderate validity for the MMPI automated reports. However, the level of accuracy of the automated reports was not much different from that previously reported when clinicians examined MMPI profiles of subjects and generated descriptions of them (e.g., Graham, 1967; Little & Shneidman, 1959; Sines, 1959).

In a well-designed study, Moreland and Onstad (1985) attempted to overcome some of the problems of earlier studies. They asked clinicians to rate the accuracy of six sections of automated reports for 66 patients. To assess discriminant validity, clinicians also rated "bogus" reports that were not actually those of the patients indicated but were for other profiles of the same general code types and elevations as those of the patients. These investigators found that the genuine reports were rated as more accurate than the bogus reports overall and for five of the six sections of the reports.

All of the studies that have tried to establish the validity of interpretive systems have had serious shortcomings. Qualifications of raters and interrater reliabilities either have not been reported or have not been adequate. Typically only a limited number of interpretive reports have been studied. No study to date has evaluated an entire interpretive system. The external criterion measures used in most studies have been limited in scope and of questionable reliability.

With all of these problems, can any general conclusions be reached about the validity of automated interpretations? The validity of the automated services has not been demonstrated sufficiently to permit definite conclusions to be drawn about clients independently of other assessment data. The automated reports are intended to be used by qualified professionals to generate hypotheses about clients that can be compared with other data about clients. When used in this manner, the automated interpretive reports have considerable potential. However, the accuracy of statements made in automated interpretive reports probably vary considerably from service to service and from code type to code type within each service. The level of accuracy of the interpretive statements is at best modest, but in many cases it is no less than the accuracy of clinician-generated descriptions of clients based on MMPI data. Moreland (1984) suggested that clinicians be especially skeptical of automated reports when the profiles involved are rare ones. In these instances, authors of the automated systems have had to rely less on empirical data and more on clinical lore and individual experience in generating interpretive statements.

References

Alker, H. A. (1978). Minnesota Multiphasic Personality Inventory. In O. K. Buros (Ed.), *Eighth mental measurements yearbook* (pp. 931–935). Highland Park, NJ: Gryphon.

Altus, W. D., & Tafejian, T. T. (1953). MMPI correlates of the California E–F scale. *Journal of Social Psychology, 38,* 145–149.

American Psychological Association. (1986). *Guidelines for computer-based tests and interpretations.* Washington, DC: APA.

Anderson, B. N. (1969). *The utility of the Minnesota Multiphasic Personality Inventory in a private psychiatric hospital setting.* Unpublished master's thesis, Ohio State University, Columbus.

Apfeldorf, M., & Huntley, P. J. (1975). Application of MMPI alcoholism scales to older alcoholics and problem drinkers. *Journal of Studies on Alcohol, 37,* 645–653.

Archer, R. P. (in press). Using the MMPI with adolescents: Overview and recommendations. In C. D. Spielberger & J. N. Butcher (Eds.), *Advances in personality assessment: Vol. 7.* Hillsdale, NJ: Erlbaum.

Archer, R. P., Ball, J. D., & Hunter, J. A. (1985). MMPI characteristics of borderline psychopathology in adolescent inpatients. *Journal of Personality Assessment, 49,* 47–55.

Avery, R. D., Mussio, S. J., & Payne, G. (1972). Relationships between MMPI scores and job performance measures of fire fighters. *Psychological Reports, 31,* 199–202.

Baillargeon, J., & Danis, C. (1984). Barnum meets the computer: Critical test. *Journal of Personality Assessment, 48,* 415–419.

Ball, J. C. (1962). *Social deviancy and adolescent personality.* Lexington, KY: University of Kentucky Press.

Barker, H. R., Fowler, R. D., & Peterson, L. P. (1971). Factor analytic structure of the short form MMPI in a VA hospital population. *Journal of Clinical Psychology, 27,* 228–233.

Barron, F. (1953). An ego strength scale which predicts response to psychotherapy. *Journal of Consulting Psychology, 17,* 327–333.

Barron, F. (1956). Ego-strength and the management of aggression. In G. S. Welsh and W. G. Dahlstrom (Eds.), *Basic readings on the MMPI in psychology and medicine* (pp. 579–585). Minneapolis, MN: University of Minnesota Press.

Barron, F., & Leary, T. (1955). Changes in psychoneurotic patients with and without psychotherapy. *Journal of Consulting Psychology, 19,* 239–245.

Baughman, E. E., & Dahlstrom, W. G. (1968). *A psychological study in the rural south.* New York: Academic Press.

Bernstein, I. H. (1980). Security guards' MMPI profiles: Some normative data. *Journal of Personality Assessment, 44,* 377–380.

Biskin, B., & Kolotkin, R. L. (1977). Effects of computerized administration on scores on the Minnesota Multiphasic Personality Inventory. *Applied Psychological Measurement, 1,* 543–549.

Black, J. D. (1953). *The interpretation of MMPI profiles of college women.* Unpublished doctoral dissertation, University of Minnesota, Minneapolis.

Block, J. (1965). *The challenge of response sets: Unconfounding meaning, acquiescence, and social desirability in the MMPI.* New York: Appleton-Century-Crofts.

Block, J., & Bailey, D. Q. (1955). Q-sort item analyses of a number of MMPI scales. *Officer Education Research Laboratory, Technical Memorandum.* (OERL-TM-55-7).

Boerger, A. R. (1975). *The utility of some alternative approaches to MMPI scale construction.* Unpublished doctoral dissertation, Kent State University, Kent, OH.

Boerger, A. R., Graham, J. R., & Lilly, R. S. (1974). Behavioral correlates of single-scale MMPI code types. *Journal of Consulting and Clinical Psychology, 42,* 398–402.

Brayfield, A. H. (Ed.). (1965). Testing and public policy. *American Psychologist, 20,* 857–1005.

Bresolin, M. J., Jr. (1984). *A comparative study of computer administration of the Minnesota Multiphasic Personality Inventory in an inpatient psychiatric setting.* Unpublished doctoral dissertation, Loyola University, Chicago, IL.

Buechly, R., & Ball, H. (1952). A new test of "validity" for the group MMPI. *Journal of Consulting Psychology, 16,* 299–301.

Burkhart, B. R., Gynther, M. D., & Fromuth, M. E. (1980). The relative validity of subtle versus obvious items on the MMPI Depression scale. *Journal of Clinical Psychology, 36,* 748–751.

Butcher, J. N. (1978) Computerized scoring and interpreting services. In O. K. Buros (Ed.), *Eighth mental measurements yearbook* (pp. 942–945). Highland Park, NJ: Gryphon.

Butcher, J. N. (1979). Use of the MMPI in personnel selection. In J. N. Butcher (Ed.), *New developments in the use of the MMPI* (pp. 165–201). Minneapolis, MN: University of Minnesota Press.

Butcher, J. N. (1985a). Interpreting defensive profiles. In J. N. Butcher & J. R. Graham (Eds.), *Clinical applications of the MMPI* (No. 3). Minneapolis, MN: Department of Conferences, University of Minnesota.

Butcher, J. N. (1985b). Personality assessment in industry: Theoretical issues and illustrations. In H. J. Bernardin (Ed.), *Personality assessment in organizations* (pp. 277–310). New York: Praeger.

Butcher, J. N., Braswell, L., & Raney, D. (1983). A cross-cultural comparison of American Indian, black, and white inpatients on the MMPI and presenting symptoms. *Journal of Consulting and Clinical Psychology, 51,* 587–594.

Butcher, J. N., Keller, L. S., & Bacon, S. F. (1985). Current developments and future directions in computerized personality assessment. *Journal of Consulting and Clinical Psychology, 53,* 803–815.

Butcher, J. N., Kendall, P. C., & Hoffman, N. (1980). MMPI short forms: CAUTION. *Journal of Consulting and Clinical Psychology, 48,* 275–278.

Butcher. J. N., & Tellegen, A. (1966). Objections to MMPI items. *Journal of Consulting Psychology, 30,* 527–534.

Button, A. D. (1956). A study of alcoholics with the MMPI. *Quarterly Journal of Studies on Alcohol, 17,* 263–281.

Byrne, D. (1974). *An introduction to personality: Research, theory, and application.* Englewood Cliffs, NJ: Prentice-Hall.

Caldwell, A. B. (1969). *MMPI critical items.* Unpublished manuscript. (Available from Clinical Psychological Services, Inc., 3122 Santa Monica Blvd., Santa Monica, CA 90404).

Calvin, J. (1974). *Two dimensions or fifty: Factor analytic studies with the MMPI.* Unpublished materials, Kent State University, Kent, OH.

Calvin, J. (1975). *A replicated study of the concurrent validity of the Harris subscales for the MMPI.* Unpublished doctoral dissertation, Kent State University, Kent, OH.

Canter, A. H. (1951). MMPI profiles in multiple sclerosis. *Journal of Consulting Psychology, 15,* 253–256.

Carkhuff, R. R., Barnette, W. L., & McCall, J. N. (1965). *The counselor's handbook: Scale and profile interpretations of the MMPI.* Urbana, IL: Parkinson.

Carson, R. C. (1969). Interpretive manual to the MMPI. In J. N. Butcher (Ed.), *Research developments and clinical applications* (pp. 279–296). New York: McGraw-Hill.

Chang, A. F., Caldwell, A. B., & Moss, T. (1973). Stability of personality traits in alcoholics during and after treatment as measured by the MMPI: A one-year follow-up study.

Proceedings of the 81st Annual Convention of the American Psychological Association, 8, 387–388.

Chase, T. V., Chaffin, S., & Morrison, S. D. (1975). False positive adolescent MMPI profiles. *Adolescence, 40,* 507–519.

Christian, W. L., Burkhart, B. R., & Gynther, M. D. (1978). Subtle-obvious ratings of MMPI items: New interest in an old concept. *Journal of Consulting and Clinical Psychology, 46,* 1178–1186.

Chu, C. (1966). *Object cluster analysis of the MMPI.* Unpublished doctoral dissertation, University of California, Berkeley, CA.

Clayton, M. R. (1980). *The clinical utility of subtle and obvious MMPI items: Contributions of clinical configurations and predictive validity.* Unpublished doctoral dissertation, Kent State University, Kent, OH.

Clayton, M. R., & Graham, J. R. (1979). Predictive validity of Barron's Es scale: The role of symptom acknowledgment. *Journal of Consulting and Clinical Psychology, 47,* 424–425.

Cohler, B. J., Weiss, J. L., & Grunebaum, H. V. (1974). "Short-form" content scales for the MMPI. *Journal of Personality Assessment, 38,* 563–572.

Colligan, R. C., Osborne, D., & Offord, K. P. (1980). Linear transformation and the interpretation of MMPI T-scores. *Journal of Clinical Psychology, 36,* 162–165.

Comrey, A. L. (1957a). A factor analysis of items on the MMPI depression scale. *Educational and Psychological Measurement, 17,* 578–585.

Comrey, A. L. (1957b). A factor analysis of items on the MMPI hypochondriasis scale. *Educational and Psychological Measurement, 17,* 566–577.

Comrey, A. L. (1957c). A factor analysis of items on the MMPI hysteria scale. *Educational and Psychological Measurement, 17,* 586–592.

Comrey, A. L. (1958a). A factor analysis of items on the F scale of the MMPI. *Educational and Psychological Measurement, 18,* 621–632.

Comrey, A. L. (1958b). A factor analysis of items on the MMPI hypomania scale. *Educational and Psychological Measurement, 18,* 313–323.

Comrey, A. L. (1958c). A factor analysis of items on the MMPI paranoia scale. *Educational and Psychological Measurement, 18,* 99–107.

Comrey, A. L. (1958d). A factor analysis of items on the MMPI psychasthenia scale. *Educational and Psychological Measurement, 18,* 293–300.

Comrey, A. L. (1958e). A factor analysis of items on the MMPI psychopathic deviate scale. *Educational and Psychological Measurement, 18,* 91–98.

Comrey, A. L., & Marggraff, W. (1958). A factor analysis of items on the MMPI schizophrenia scale. *Educational and Psychological Measurement, 18,* 301–311.

Costello, R. M., Schoenfeld, L. S., & Kobos, J. (1982). Police applicant screening: An analogue study. *Journal of Clinical Psychology, 38,* 216–221.

Crovitz, E., Huse, M. N., & Lewis, D. E. (1973). Selection of physicians' assistants. *Journal of Medical Education, 48,* 551–555.

Cuadra, C. A. (1953). A scale for control in psychological adjustment (Cn). In G. W. Welsh and W. G. Dahlstrom (Eds.), *Basic readings on the MMPI in psychology and medicine.* (pp. 235–264). Minneapolis, MN: University of Minnesota Press.

Dahlstrom, W. G. (1954). Prediction of adjustment after neurosurgery. *American Psychologist, 9,* 353.

Dahlstrom, W. G. (1972). Whither the MMPI? In J. N. Butcher (Ed.), *Objective personality assessment: Changing perspectives* (pp. 85–115). New York: Academic Press.

Dahlstrom, W. G. (1980). Altered versions of the MMPI. In W. G. Dahlstrom & L. Dahlstrom (Eds.), *Basic readings on the MMPI: A new selection on personality measurement* (pp. 386–393). Minneapolis, MN: University of Minnesota Press.

Dahlstrom, W. G., & Dahlstrom, L. (Eds.). (1980). *Basic readings on the MMPI: A new selection on personality measurement.* Minneapolis, MN: University of Minnesota Press.

Dahlstrom, W. G., Lachar, D., & Dahlstrom, L. E. (1986). *MMPI patterns of American minorities.* Minneapolis, MN: University of Minnesota Press.

Dahlstrom, W. G., & Welsh, G. S. (1960). *An MMPI handbook: A guide to use in clinical practice and research.* Minneapolis, MN: University of Minnesota Press.

Dahlstrom, W. G., Welsh, G. S., & Dahlstrom, L. E. (1972). *An MMPI handbook: Vol. I. Clinical interpretation.* Minneapolis, MN: University of Minnesota Press.

Dahlstrom, W. G., Welsh, G. S., & Dahlstrom, L. E. (1975). *An MMPI handbook: Vol. II. Research Applications.* Minneapolis, MN: University of Minnesota Press.

Davis, K. R., & Sines, J. O. (1971). An antisocial behavior pattern associated with a specific MMPl profile. *Journal of Consulting and Clinical Psychology, 36,* 229–234.

Dean, E. F. (1972). A lengthened mini: The Midi–Mult. *Journal of Clinical Psychology, 28,* 68–71.

Deiker, T. E. (1974). A cross-validation of MMPI scales of aggression on male criminal criterion groups. *Journal of Consulting and Clinical Psychology, 42,* 196–202.

Distler, L. S., May, P. R., & Tuma, A. H. (1964). Anxiety and ego strength as predictors of response to treatment in schizophrenic patients. *Journal of Consulting Psychology, 28,* 170–177.

Drake, L. E. (1946). A social I.E. scale for the MMPI. *Journal of Applied Psychology, 30,* 51–54.

Drake, L. E., & Oetting, E. R. (1959). *An MMPI codebook for counselors.* Minneapolis, MN: University of Minnesota Press.

Duckworth, J. C., & Duckworth, E. (1975). *MMPI interpretation manual for counselors and clinicians.* Muncie, IN: Accelerated Development, Inc.

Dunnette, M. D., Bownas, D. A., & Bosshardt, M. J. (1981). *Electric power plant study: Prediction of inappropriate, unreliable or aberant job behavior in nuclear power plant settings.* Minneapolis, MN: Personnel Decisions Research Institute.

Edwards, A. L. (1957). *The social desirability variable in personality assessment and research.* New York: Dryden.

Edwards, A. L. (1964). Social desirability and performance on the MMPI. *Psychometrika, 29,* 295–308.

Ehrenworth, N. V. (1984). A comparison of the utility of interpretive approaches with adolescent MMPI profiles. Unpublished doctoral dissertation, Virginia Consortium for Professional Psychology, Norfolk, VA.

Ehrenworth, N. V., & Archer, R. P. (1985). A comparison of clinical accuracy ratings of interpretive approaches for adolescent MMPI responses. *Journal of Personality Assessment, 49,* 413–421.

Eichman, W. J. (1961). Replicated factors on the MMPI with female NP patients. *Journal of Consulting Psychology, 25,* 55–60.

Eichman, W. J. (1962). Factored scales for the MMPI: A clinical and statistical manual. *Journal of Clinical Psychology, 18,* 363–395.

Ends, E. J., & Page, C. W. (1957). Functional relationships among measures of anxiety, ego strength and adjustment. *Journal of Clinical Psychology, 13,* 148–150.

Eschenback, A. E., & Dupree, L. (1959). The influence of stress on MMPI scale scores. *Journal of Clinical Psychology, 15,* 42–45.

Evan, W. M., & Miller, J. R. (1969). Differential effects on response bias of computer vs. conventional administration of a social science questionnaire. *Behavior Science, 14,* 216–227.

Evans, D. R. (1977). Use of the MMPI to predict effective hotline workers. *Journal of Clinical Psychology, 33,* 1113–1114.

Faschingbauer, T. R. (1974). A 166-item written short form of the group MMPI: The FAM. *Journal of Consulting and Clinical Psychology, 42,* 645–655.

Fisher, G. (1970). Discriminating violence eminating from over-controlled versus under-controlled aggressivity. *British Journal of Social and Clinical Psychology, 9,* 54–59.

Fordyce, W. E. (1979). *Use of the MMPI in the assessment of chronic pain* (Clinical Notes on the MMPI No. 3). Minneapolis, MN: National Computer Systems.

Fowler, R. D. (1969a). Automated interpretation of personality test data. In J. N. Butcher (Ed.), *MMPI: Research developments and clinical applications* (pp. 105–126). New York: McGraw-Hill.

Fowler, R. D. (1969b). The current status of computer interpretation of psychological tests. *American Journal of Psychiatry, 125,* 21–27.

Fowler, R. D. (1975). *A method for the evaluation of the abuse prone patient.* Paper presented at the meeting of the American Academy of Family Physicians, Chicago, IL.

Fowler, R. D., & Coyle, F. A. (1968). Overlap as a problem in atlas classification of MMPI profiles. *Journal of Clinical Psychology, 24,* 435.

Fowler, R. D., & Coyle, F. A. (1969). Collegiate normative data on MMPI content scales. *Journal of Clinical Psychology, 25,* 62–63.

Fowler, R. D., Teel, S. K., & Coyle, F. A. (1967). The measurement of alcoholic response to treatment by Barron's ego strength scale. *Journal of Psychology, 67,* 65–68.

Fox, J., Gould, E., & André, J. (1965). *Crime classification and personality patterns.* Unpublished manuscript.

Fredericksen, S. J. (1976, March). *A comparison of selected personality and history variables in highly violent, mildly violent, and nonviolent female offenders.* Paper presented at 11th Annual MMPI Symposium, Minneapolis, MN.

Friedman, S. H. (1950). *Psychometric effects of frontal and parietal lobe brain damage.* Unpublished doctoral dissertation, University of Minnesota.

Garb, H. N. (1984). The incremental validity of information used in personality assessment. *Clinical Psychology Review, 4,* 641–655.

Garetz, F. K., & Anderson, R. W. (1973). Patterns of professional activities of psychiatrists: A follow-up of 100 psychiatric residents. *American Journal of Psychiatry, 130,* 981–984.

Getter, H., & Sundland, D. M. (1962). The Barron ego strength scale and psychotherapy outcome. *Journal of Consulting Psychology, 26,* 195.

Gilberstadt, H. (1970). *Comprehensive MMPI code book for males.* Minneapolis, MN: MMPI Research Laboratory, Veterans Administration Hospital. (Report No. 1B 11-5).

Gilberstadt, H., & Duker, J. (1965). *A handbook for clinical and actuarial MMPI interpretation.* Philadelphia: Saunders.

Gocka, E. (1965). *American Lake norms for 200 MMPI scales.* Unpublished materials, Veterans Administration Hospital, American Lake, WA.

Gocka, E., & Holloway, H. (1963). *Normative and predictive data on the Harris and Lingoes subscales for a neuropsychiatric population* (Report No. 7). American Lake, WA: Veterans Administration Hospital.

Goldberg, L. R. (1965). Diagnosticians vs. diagnostic signs: The diagnosis of psychosis vs. neurosis for the MMPI. *Psychological Monographs, 79* (9, Whole No. 602).

Goldberg, L. R. (1968). Simple models or simple processes. *American Psychologist, 23,* 483–496.

Goldberg, L. R. (1972). Parameters of personality inventory construction: A comparison of prediction strategies and tactics. *Multivariate Behavioral Research Monographs, 7,*(2).

Good, P. K., & Brantner, J. P. (1961). *The physician's guide to the MMPI.* Minneapolis, MN: University of Minnesota Press.

Gottesman, I. I. (1959). More construct validation of the ego-strength scale. *Journal of Consulting Psychology, 23,* 342–346.

Gough, H. G. (1948). A new dimension of status: I. Development of a personality scale. *American Sociological Review, 13,* 401–409.

Gough, H. G. (1950). The F minus K dissimulation index for the MMPI. *Journal of Consulting Psychology, 14,* 408–413.

Gough, H. G. (1951a). Studies of social intolerance: II. A personality scale for anti-Semitism. *Journal of Social Psychology, 33,* 247–255.

Gough, H. G. (1951b). Studies of social intolerance: III. Relationship of the Pr scale to other variables. *Journal of Social Psychology, 33,* 257–262.

Gough, H. G. (1954a). *Brief descriptive and interpretational summary of scales of the Minnesota Multiphasic Personality Inventory.* Unpublished materials.

Gough, H. G. (1954b). Some common misconceptions about neuroticism. *Journal of Consulting Psychology, 18,* 287–292.

Gough, H. G., McClosky, H., & Meehl, P. E. (1951). A personality scale for dominance. *Journal of Abnormal and Social Psychology, 46,* 360–366.

Gough, H. G., McClosky, H., & Meehl, P. E. (1952). A personality scale for social responsibility. *Journal of Abnormal and Social Psychology, 47,* 73–80.

Gough, H. G., McKee, M. G., & Yandell, R. J. (1955). *Adjective check list analyses of a number of selected psychometric and assessment variables.* Officer Education Research Laboratory. (Technical Memorandom No. OERL-TM-5S-10)

Graham, J. R. (1967). A Q-sort study of the accuracy of clinical descriptions based on the MMPI. *Journal of Psychiatric Research, 5,* 297–305.

Graham, J. R. (1977a). *Stability of MMPI configurations in a college setting.* Unpublished manuscript, Kent State University, Kent, OH.

Graham, J. R. (1977b). *The MMPI: A practical guide.* New York: Oxford.

Graham, J. R. (1978). A review of some important MMPI special scales. In P. McReynolds (Ed.), *Advances in psychological assessment, Vol. IV* (pp. 311–331). San Francisco, CA: Jossey-Bass.

Graham, J. R., & Lilly, R. S. (1984). *Psychological testing.* Englewood Cliffs, NJ: Prentice Hall.

Graham, J. R., & Lilly, R. S. (1986, March). *Linear T-scores versus normalized T-scores: An empirical study.* Paper presented at the 21st Annual Symposium on Recent Developments in the Use of the MMPI, Clearwater Beach, FL.

Graham, J. R., & Mayo, M. A. (1985, March). *A comparison of MMPI strategies for identifying black and white male alcoholics.* Paper presented at the 20th Annual Symposium on Recent Developments in the Use of the MMPI, Honolulu, HI.

Graham, J. R., & McCord, G. (1985). Interpretation of moderately elevated MMPI scores for normal subjects. *Journal of Personality Assessment, 49,* 477–484.

Graham, J. R., Schroeder, H. E., & Lilly, R. S. (1971). Factor analysis of items on the Social Introversion and Masculinity-Femininity scales of the MMPI. *Journal of Clinical Psychology, 27,* 367–370.

Graham, J. R., Smith, R. L., & Schwartz, G. F. (1986). Stability of MMPI configurations for psychiatric inpatients. *Journal of Consulting and Clinical Psychology, 54,* 375–380.

Grayson, H. M. (1951). *A psychological admissions testing program and manual.* Los Angeles, CA: Veterans Administration Center, Neuropsychiatric Hospital.

Greene, R. L. (1978). An empirically derived MMPI carelessness scale. *Journal of Clinical Psychology, 34,* 407–410.

Greene, R. L. (1980). *The MMPI: An interpretive manual.* New York: Grune & Stratton.

Greene, R. L. (in press). Etiological influences and issues in clinical assessment: Use of the MMPI. *Journal of Consulting and Clinical Psychology.*

Guthrie, G. M. (1949). *A study of the personality characteristics associated with the disorders encountered by an internist.* Doctoral dissertation, University of Minnesota, Minneapolis.

Guthrie, G. M. (1952). Common characteristics associated with frequent MMPI profile types. *Journal of Clinical Psychology, 8,* 141–145.

Gynther, M. D., Altman, H., & Sletten, I. W. (1973). Replicated correlates of MMPI two-point types: The Missouri Actuarial System. *Journal of Clinical Psychology* (Suppl. 39).

Gynther, M. D., Altman, H., & Warbin, W. (1973). Interpretation of uninterpretable Minnesota Multiphasic Personality Inventory profiles. *Journal of Consulting and Clinical Psychology, 40,* 78–83.

Gynther, M. D., & Brillant, P. J. (1968). The diagnostic utility of Welsh's A–R categories. *Journal of Projective Techniques and Personality Assessment, 32,* 572–574.

Gynther, M. D., Burkhart, B. R., & Hovanitz, C. (1979). Do face-valid items have more predictive validity than subtle items? The case of the MMPI Pd scale. *Journal of Consulting and Clinical Psychology, 47,* 295–300.

Gynther, M. D., & Green, S. B. (1980). Accuracy may make a difference, but does a difference make for accuracy? A response to Pritchard and Rosenblatt. *Journal of Consulting and Clinical Psychology, 48,* 268–272.

Hanvik, L. J. (1949). *Some psychological dimensions of low back pain.* Doctoral dissertation, University of Minnesota, Minneapolis.

Hanvik, L. J. (1951). MMPI profiles in patients with low back pain. *Journal of Consulting Psychology, 15,* 250–253.

Harper, L. R. (1981). *The relative contribution of subtle, neutral, and obvious items to clinical profiles.* Unpublished master's thesis, Kent State University, Kent, OH.

Harrell, T. W., & Harrell, M. S. (1973). The personality of MBAs who reach general management early. *Personnel Psychology, 26,* 127–134.

Harris, R., & Christiansen, C. (1946). Prediction of response to brief psychotherapy. *Journal of Psychology, 21,* 269–284.

Harris, R., & Lingoes, J. (1955). *Subscales for the Minnesota Multiphasic Personality Inventory.* Mimeographed materials, The Langley Porter Clinic.

Harris, R., & Lingoes, J. (1968). *Subscales for the Minnesota Multiphasic Personality Inventory.* Mimeographed materials, The Langley Porter Clinic.

Hase, H. D., & Goldberg, L. R. (1967). Comparative validity of different strategies of constructing personality inventory scales. *Psychological Bulletin, 67,* 231–248.

Hathaway, S. R. (1947). A coding system for MMPI profiles. *Journal of Consulting Psychology, 11,* 334–337.

Hathaway, S. R. (1956). Scales 5 (Masculinity-Femininity), 6 (Paranoia), and 8 (Schizophrenia). In G. S. Welsh & W. G. Dahlstrom (Eds.), *Basic readings on the MMPI in psychology and medicine* (pp. 104–111). Minneapolis, MN: University of Minnesota Press.

Hathaway, S. R. (1965). Personality inventories. In B. B. Wolman (Ed.), *Handbook of clinical psychology* (pp. 451–476). New York: McGraw-Hill.

Hathaway, S. R., & Briggs, P. F. (1957). Some normative data on new MMPI scales. *Journal of Clinical Psychology, 13,* 364–368.

Hathaway, S. R., & McKinley, J. C. (1940). A multiphasic personality schedule (Minnesota): I. Construction of the schedule. *Journal of Psychology, 10,* 249–254.

Hathaway, S. R., & McKinley, J. C. (1942). A multiphasic personality schedule (Minnesota): III. The measurement of symptomatic depression. *Journal of Psychology, 14,* 73–84.

Hathaway, S. R., & McKinley, J. C. (1983). *The Minnesota Multiphasic Personality Inventory manual.* New York: Psychological Corporation.

Hathaway, S. R., & Meehl, P. E. (1952). *Adjective check list correlates of MMPI scores.* Unpublished materials, University of Minnesota.

Hathaway, S. R., & Monachesi, E. D. (Eds.). (1953). *Analyzing and predicting juvenile delinquency with the MMPI.* Minneapolis, MN: University of Minnesota Press.

Hathaway, S. R., & Monachesi, E. D. (1963). *Adolescent personality and behavior: MMPI patterns of normal, delinquent, dropout, and other outcomes.* Minneapolis, MN: University of Minnesota Press.

Hawkinson, J. R. (1961). A study of the construct validity of Barron's Ego Strength scale with a state mental hospital population. Unpublished doctoral dissertation, University of Minnesota, Minneapolis.

Hedlund, J. L. (1977). MMPI clinical scale correlates. *Journal of Consulting and Clinical Psychology, 45,* 739–750.

Hedlund, J. L., Morgan, D. W., & Master, F. D. (1972). The Mayo Clinic automated MMPI program: Cross-validation with psychiatric patients in an army hospital. *Journal of Clinical Psychology, 28,* 505–510.

Henrichs, T. F. (1964). Objective configural rules for discriminating MMPI profiles in a psychiatric population. *Journal of Clinical Psychology, 20,* 157–159.

Henrichs, T. F. (1966). A note on the extension of MMPI configural rules. *Journal of Clinical Psychology, 22,* 51–52.

Henrichs, T. F. (1981). *Using the MMPI in medical consultation* (Clinical Notes on the MMPI, No. 6). Minneapolis, MN: National Computer Systems.

Henrichs, T. F., & Waters, W. F. (1972). Psychological adjustment and responses to open-heart surgery: Some methodological considerations. *British Journal of Psychiatry, 120,* 491–496.

Hilgard, E. R., Jones, L. V., & Kaplan, S. J. (1951). Conditioned discrimination as related to anxiety. *Journal of Experimental Psychology, 42,* 94–99.

Himelstein, P. (1964). Further evidence of the Ego Strength scale as a measure of psychological health. *Journal of Consulting Psychology, 28,* 90–91.

Hoffman, H., & Jackson, D. N. (1976). Substantive dimensions of psychopathology derived from MMPI content scales and the Differential Personality Inventory. *Journal of Consulting and Clinical Psychology, 44,* 862.

Hoffman, H., Loper, R. G., & Kammeier, M. L. (1974). Identifying future alcoholics with MMPI alcoholism scales. *Quarterly Journal of Studies on Alcohol, 35,* 490–498.

Holmes, D. S. (1967). Male-female differences in MMPI Ego Strength: An artifact. *Journal of Consulting Psychology, 31,* 408–410.

Hovey, H. B. (1953). MMPI profiles and personality characteristics. *Journal of Consulting Psychology, 17,* 142–146.

Hovey, H. B., & Lewis, E. G. (1967). *Semiautomatic interpretation of the MMPI.* Brandon, VT: Clinical Psychology Publishing Co.

Hsu, L. M. (1984). MMPI T-scores: Linear versus normalized. *Journal of Consulting and Clinical Psychology, 52,* 821–823.

Huber, N. A., & Danahy, S. (1975). Use of the MMPI in predicting completion and evaluating changes in a long-term alcoholism treatment program. *Journal of Studies on Alcohol, 36,* 1230–1237.

Huff, F. W. (1965). Use of actuarial description of abnormal personality in a mental hospital. *Psychological Reports, 17,* 224.

Jackson, D. N. (1971). The dynamics of structured tests: 1971. *Psychological Review, 78,* 239–249.

Jansen, D. G., & Garvey, F. J. (1973). High-, average-, and low-rated clergymen in a state hospital clinical program. *Journal of Clinical Psychology, 29,* 89–92.

Jensen, A. R., (1957). Authoritarian attitudes and personality maladjustment. *Journal of Abnormal and Social Psychology, 54,* 161–170.

Johnson, J. R., Null, C., Butcher, J. N., & Johnson, K. N. (1984). Replicated item level factor analysis of the full MMPI. *Journal of Personality and Social Psychology, 47,* 105–114.

Kammeier, M. L., Hoffman, H., & Loper, R. G. (1973). Personality characteristics of alcoholics as college freshmen and at times of treatment. *Quarterly Journal of Studies on Alcohol, 34,* 390–399.

Kelly, W. L. (1974). Psychological prediction of leadership in nursing. *Nursing Research, 23,* 38–42.

Kent, G. H. (1946). *Series of emergency scales.* New York: Psychological Corporation.

Kincannon, J. C. (1968). Prediction of the standard MMPI scale score from 71 items: The Mini-Mult. *Journal of Consulting and Clinical Psychology, 32,* 319–325.

King, G. D. (1978). Minnesota Multiphasic Personality Inventory. In O. K. Buros (Ed.), *Eighth mental measurements yearbook* (pp. 935–938). Highland Park, NJ: Gryphon.

Kleinmuntz, B. (1960). An extension of the construct validity of the Ego Strength scale. *Journal of Consulting Psychology, 24,* 463–464.

Kleinmuntz, B. (1961). The college maladjustment scale (MT): Norms and predictive validity. *Educational and Psychological Measurement, 21,* 1029–1033.

Kleinmuntz, B. (1963). MMPI decision rules for the identification of college maladjustment: A digital computer approach. *Psychological Monographs, 77* (14, Whole No. 577).

Klett, W. (1971). The utility of computer interpreted MMPIs at St. Cloud VA Hospital. *Newsletter of Research in Psychology, 13,* 45–47.

Knapp, R. R. (1960). A reevaluation of the validity of MMPI scales of dominance and responsibility. *Educational and Psychological Measurement, 20,* 381–386.

Koson, D., Kitchen, C., Kochen, M., & Stodolosky, D. (1970). Psychological testing by computer: Effect on response bias. *Educational and Psychological Measurement, 30,* 803–810.

Koss, M. P. (1979). MMPI item content: Recurring issues. In J. N. Butcher (Ed.), *New developments in the use of the MMPI* (pp. 3–38). Minneapolis, MN: University of Minnesota Press.

Koss, M. P. (1980). Assessing psychological emergencies with the MMPI. In J. Butcher, G. Dahlstrom, M. Gynther, & W. Schofield (Eds.), *Clinical notes on the MMPI* (No. 4). Minneapolis, MN: National Computer Systems.

Koss, M. P., & Butcher, J. N. (1973). A comparison of psychiatric patients' self-report with other sources of clinical information. *Journal of Research in Personality, 7,* 225–236.

Koss, M. P., Butcher, J. N., & Hoffman, N. (1976). The MMPI critical items: How well do they work? *Journal of Consulting and Clinical Psychology, 44,* 921–928.

Kostlan, A. (1954). A method for the empirical study of psychodiagnosis. *Journal of Consulting Psychology, 18,* 83–88.

Kranitz, L. (1972). Alcoholics, heroin addicts and non-addicts: Comparisons on the MacAndrew Alcoholism scale on the MMPI. *Quarterly Journal of Studies on Alcohol, 33,* 807–809.

Lachar, D. (1974a). Accuracy and generalization of an automated MMPI interpretation system. *Journal of Consulting and Clinical Psychology, 42,* 267–273.

Lachar, D. (1974b). *The MMPI: Clinical assessment and automated interpretation.* Los Angeles, CA: Western Psychological Services.

Lachar, D. (1974c). Prediction of early U.S. Air Force cadet adaptation with the MMPI. *Journal of Counseling Psychology, 21,* 404–408.

Lachar, D., & Alexander, R. S. (1978). Veridicality of self-report: Replicated correlates of the Wiggins MMPI content scales. *Journal of Consulting and Clinical Psychology, 46,* 1349–1356.

Lachar, D., Klinge, V., & Grisell, J. L. (1976). Relative accuracy of automated MMPI narratives generated from adult norm and adolescent norm profiles. *Journal of Consulting and Clinical Psychology, 44,* 20–24.

Lachar, D., & Wrobel, T. A. (1979). Validation of clinicians' hunches: Construction of a new MMPI critical item set. *Journal of Consulting and Clinical Psychology, 47,* 277–284.

Lane, P. J. (1976). *Annotated bibliography of the Megargee et al.'s Overcontrolled-Hostility (O-H) scale and the overcontrolled personality literature.* Unpublished materials, Florida State University, Tallahassee, FL.

Lanyon, R. I. (1968). *A handbook of MMPI group profiles.* Minneapolis, MN: University of Minnesota Press.

Lauber, M., & Dahlstrom, W. G. (1953). MMPI findings in the rehabilitation of delinquent girls. In S. R. Hathaway & E. D. Monachesi (Eds.), *Analyzing and predicting juvenile delinquency with the MMPI* (pp. 61–69). Minneapolis, MN: University of Minnesota Press.

Lewandowski, D., & Graham, J. R. (1972). Empirical correlates of frequently occurring two-point code types: A replicated study. *Journal of Consulting and Clinical Psychology, 39,* 467–472.

Lewinsohn, P. M. (1965). Dimensions of MMPI change. *Journal of Clinical Psychology, 21,* 37–43.

Lichtenstein, E., & Bryan, J. H. (1966). Short-term stability of MMPI profiles. *Journal of Consulting Psychology, 30,* 172–174.

Lingoes, J. (1960). MMPI factors of the Harris and Wiener subscales. *Journal of Consulting Psychology, 24,* 74–83.

Little, K. B., & Shneidman, E. S. (1959). Congruencies among interpretations of psychological test and anamnestic data. *Psychological Monographs, 73,* (6, Whole No. 476).

Loper, R. G., Kammeier, M. L., & Hoffman, H. (1973). MMPI characteristics of college freshmen males who later became alcoholics. *Journal of Abnormal Psychology, 82,* 159–162.

Lubin, B., Larsen, R. M., & Matarazzo, J. D. (1984). Patterns of psychological test usage in the United States: 1935–1982. *American Psychologist, 39,* 451–454.

Lushene, R. E. (1967). *Factor structure of the MMPI item pool.* Unpublished master's thesis, Florida State University, Tallahassee.

Lushene, R. E., & Gilberstadt, H. (1972, March). *Validation of VA MMPI computer-generated reports.* Paper presented at the Veterans Administration Cooperative Studies Conference, St. Louis, MO.

MacAndrew, C. (1965). The differentiation of male alcoholic out-patients from nonalcoholic psychiatric patients by means of the MMPI. *Quarterly Journal of Studies on Alcohol, 26,* 238–246.

Marks, P. A., & Seeman, W. (1963). *Actuarial description of abnormal personality.* Baltimore, MD: Williams & Wilkins.

Marks, P. A., Seeman, W., & Haller, D. L. (1974). *The actuarial use of the MMPI with adolescents and adults.* Baltimore, MD: Williams & Wilkins.

Matarazzo, J. D. (1972). *Wechsler's measurement and appraisal of adult intelligence.* Baltimore, MD: Williams & Wilkins.

McKinley, J. C., & Hathaway, S. R. (1940). A multiphasic personality schedule (Minnesota): II. A differential study of hypochondriasis. *Journal of Psychology, 10,* 255–268.

McKinley, J. C., & Hathaway, S. R. (1944). The MMPI: V. Hysteria, hypomania, and psychopathic deviate. *Journal of Applied Psychology, 28,* 153–174.

McKinley, J. C., Hathaway, S. R., & Meehl, P. E. (1948). The MMPI: VI. The K scale. *Journal of Consulting Psychology, 12,* 20–31.

Meehl, P. E. (1951). *Research results for counselors.* St. Paul, MN: State Department of Education.

Meehl, P. E. (1956). Wanted—a good cookbook. *American Psychologist, 11,* 263–272.

Meehl, P. E., & Dahlstrom, W. G. (1960). Objective configural rules for discriminating psychotic from neurotic MMPI profiles. *Journal of Consulting Psychology, 24,* 375–387.

Meehl, P. E., & Hathaway, S. R. (1946). The K factor as a suppressor variable in the MMPI. *Journal of Applied Psychology, 30,* 525–564.

Megargee, E. I. (1979). Development and validation of an MMPI-based system for classifying criminal offenders. In J. N. Butcher (Ed.), *New developments in the use of the MMPI* (pp. 303–324). Minneapolis, MN: University of Minnesota Press.

Megargee, E. I., Bohn, M. J., Meyer, J. E., Jr., & Sink, F. (1979). *Classifying criminal offenders: A new system based on the MMPI.* Beverly Hills, CA: Sage.

Megargee, E. I., Cook, P. E., & Mendelsohn, G. A. (1967). The development and validation of an MMPI scale of assaultiveness in overcontrolled individuals. *Journal of Abnormal Psychology, 72,* 519–528.

Meier, M. J., & French, L. A. (1964). Caudality scale change following unilateral temporal lobectomy. *Journal of Clinical Psychology, 20,* 464–467.

Meikle, S., & Gerritse, R. (1970). MMPI cookbook pattern frequencies in a psychiatric unit. *Journal of Clinical Psychology, 26,* 82–84.

Messick, S., & Jackson, D. N. (1961). Acquiescence and the factorial interpretation of the MMPI. *Psychological Bulletin, 58,* 299–304.

Mezzich, J. E., Damarin, F. L., & Erickson, J. R. (1974). Comparative validity of strategies and indices of differential diagnosis of depressive states from other psychiatric conditions using the MMPI. *Journal of Consulting and Clinical Psychology, 42,* 691–698.

Moore, D. D., & Handal, P. J. (1980). Adolescents' MMPI performance, cynicism, estrangement, and personal adjustment. *Psychology, 36,* 932–936.

Moreland, K. L. (1984). Intelligent use of automated psychological reports. *Critical Items, 1,* 4–5. (Distributed by National Computer Systems, Minneapolis, MN)

Moreland, K. L. (1985a). Computer-assisted psychological assessment in 1986: A practical guide. *Computers in Human Behavior, 1,* 221–233.

Moreland, K. L. (1985b). *Test-retest reliability of 80 MMPI scales.* Unpublished materials. (Available from NCS Professional Assessment Services, P.O. Box 1416, Minneapolis, MN 55440)

Moreland, K. L. (1985c). Validation of computer-based test interpretations: Problems and prospects. *Journal of Consulting and Clinical Psychology, 53,* 816–825.

Moreland, K. L., & Onstad, J. A. (1985, March). *Validity of the Minnesota Clinical Report, I: Mental health outpatients.* Paper presented at the 20th Annual Symposium on Recent Developments in the Use of the MMPI, Honolulu, HI.

Navran, L. A. (1954). A rationally derived MMPI scale to measure dependence. *Journal of Consulting Psychology, 18,* 192.

Nelson, J. W. (1959). Dependency as a construct: An evaluation and some data. *Dissertation Abstracts, 19,* 2149–2150.

Newmark, C. S., Gentry, L., & Whitt, J. K. (1983). Utility of MMPI indices of schizophrenia with adolescents. *Journal of Clinical Psychology, 39,* 170–172.

Olmstead, D. W., & Monachesi, E. D. (1956). A validity check on MMPI scales of responsibility and dominance. *Journal of Abnormal and Social Psychology, 53,* 140–141.

Osborne, D. (1979). Use of the MMPI with medical patients. In J. N. Butcher (Ed.), *New developments in the use of the MMPI* (pp. 141–163). Minneapolis, MN: University of Minnesota Press.

Overall, J. E., & Gomez-Mont, F. (1974). The MMPI-168 for psychiatric screening. *Educational and Psychological Measurement, 34,* 315–319.

Panton, J. H. (1958). MMPI profile configurations among crime classification groups. *Journal of Clinical Psychology, 14,* 305–308.

Panton, J. (1959). The response of prison inmates to MMPI subscales. *Journal of Social Therapy, 5,* 233–237.

Parker, C. A. (1961). The predictive use of the MMPI in a college counseling center. *Journal of Counseling Psychology, 8,* 154–158.

Pauker, J. D. (1966). Stability of MMPI profiles of female psychiatric inpatients. *Journal of Clinical Psychology, 22,* 209–212.

Payne, F. D., & Wiggins, J. S. (1972). MMPI profile types and the self-report of psychiatric patients. *Journal of Abnormal Psychology, 79,* 1–8.

Pepper, L. J., & Strong, P. N. (1958). *Judgmental subscales for the Mf scale of the MMPI.* Unpublished materials, Hawaii Department of Health, Honolulu, HI.

Persons, R. W., & Marks, P. A. (1971). The violent 4-3 MMPI personality type. *Journal of Consulting and Clinical Psychology, 36,* 189–196.

Peterson, D. R. (1954). Predicting hospitalization of psychiatric outpatients. *Journal of Abnormal and Social Psychology, 49,* 260–265.

Pritchard, D. A., & Rosenblatt, A. (1980). Racial bias in the MMPI: A methodological review. *Journal of Consulting and Clinical Psychology, 48,* 263–267.

Pruitt, P. W., & Van deCastle, R. L. (1962). Dependency measures and welfare chronicity. *Journal of Consulting Psychology, 26,* 559–560.

Quay, H. (1955). The performance of hospitalized psychiatric patients on the ego-strength scale of the MMPI. *Journal of Clinical Psychology, 11,* 403–405.

Rhodes, R. J. (1969). The MacAndrew Alcoholism scale: A replication. *Journal of Clinical Psychology, 25,* 189–191.

Rich, C. C., & Davis, H. G. (1969). Concurrent validity of MMPI alcoholism scales. *Journal of Clinical Psychology, 25,* 425–426.

Rohan, W. P. (1972). MMPI changes in hospitalized alcoholics: A second study. *Ouarterly Journal of Studies on Alcohol, 33,* 65–76.

Rohan, W. P., Tatro, R. L., & Rotman, S. R. (1969). MMPI changes in alcoholics during hospitalization. *Quarterly Journal of Studies on Alcohol, 30,* 389–400.

Rosen, A. (1963). Diagnostic differentiation as a construct validity indication for the MMPI ego-strength scale. *Journal of General Psychology, 69,* 65–68.

Rosenberg, N. (1972). MMPI alcoholism scales. *Journal of Clinical Psychology, 28,* 515–522.

Rutter, M., Graham, P., Chadwick, O. F. D., & Yule, W. (1976). Adolescent turmoil: Fact or fiction? *Journal of Child Psychology, 17,* 35–56.

Schubert, H. J. P. (1973). *A wide-range MMPI manual.* Unpublished materials.

Schwartz, G. F. (1977). *An investigation of the stability of single scale and two-point MMPI code types for psychiatric patients.* Unpublished doctoral dissertation, Kent State University, Kent, OH.

Schwartz, M. F., & Graham, J. R. (1979). Construct validity of the MacAndrew Alcoholism scale. *Journal of Consulting and Clinical Psychology, 47,* 1090–1095.

Serkownek, K. (1975). *Subscales for Scales 5 and 0 of the Minnesota Multiphasic Personality Inventory.* Unpublished materials, 3134 Whitehorn Rd., Cleveland Hts., OH.

Sherriffs, A. C., & Boomer, D. S. (1954). Who is penalized by the penalty for guessing? *Journal of Educational Psychology, 45,* 81–90.

Simmett, E. R. (1962). The relationship between the Ego Strength scale and rated in-hospital improvement. *Journal of Clinical Psychology, 18,* 46–47.

Sines, L. K. (1959). The relative contribution of four kinds of data to accuracy in personality assessment. *Journal of Consulting Psychology, 23,* 483–492.

Sivanich, G. (1960). *Test-retest changes during the course of hospitalization among some frequently occurring MMPI profiles.* Unpublished doctoral dissertation, University of Minnesota.

Snyter, C. M., & Graham, J. R. (1984). The utility of subtle and obvious MMPI subscales. *Journal of Clinical Psychology, 40,* 981–985.

Sobel, H. J., & Worden, W. (1979). The MMPI as a predictor of psychosocial adaptation to cancer. *Journal of Consulting and Clinical Psychology, 47,* 716–724.

Solway, K. S., Hays, J. R., & Zieben, M. (1976). Personality characteristics of juvenile probation officers. *Journal of Community Psychology, 4,* 152–156.

Spence, J. T., & Spence, K. W. (1966). The motivational components of manifest anxiety: Drive and drive stimuli. In C. D. Spielberger (Ed.), *Anxiety and behavior* (pp. 291–326). New York: Academic Press.

Spiegel, D. E. (1969). SPI and MMPI predictors of psychopathology. *Journal of Projective Techniques and Personality Assessment, 33,* 265–273.

Spielberger, C. D. (1966a). The effects of anxiety on complex learning and academic achievement. In C. D. Spielberger (Ed.), *Anxiety and behavior* (pp. 361–398). New York: Academic Press.

Spielberger, C. D. (1966b). Theory and research on anxiety. In C. D. Spielberger (Ed.), *Anxiety and behavior* (pp. 3–20). New York: Academic Press.

Stein, K. B. (1968). The TSC scales: The outcome of a cluster analysis of the 550 MMPI items. In P. McReynolds (Ed.), *Advances in psychological assessment, Vol. I* (pp. 80–104). Palo Alto, CA: Science and Behavior Books.

Stone, L. A., Bassett, G. R., Brosseau, J. D., Demers, J., & Stiening, J. A. (1972). Psychological test scores for a group of MEDEX trainees. *Psychological Reports, 31,* 827–831.

Stricker, G. (1961). A comparison of two MMPI prejudice scales. *Journal of Clinical Psychology, 17,* 43.

Strupp, H. H., & Bloxom, A. L. (1975). An approach to defining a patient population in psychotherapy research. *Journal of Counseling Psychology, 22,* 231–237.

Sue, S., & Sue, D. W. (1974). MMPI comparisons between Asian-American and non-Asian students utilizing a student health psychiatric clinic. *Journal of Counseling Psychology, 21,* 423–427.

Sullivan, D. L., Miller, C., & Smelser, W. (1958). Factors in length of stay and progress in psychotherapy. *Journal of Consulting Psychology, 22,* 1–9.

Sundberg, N. D., & Bachelis, W. D. (1956). The fakability of two measures of prejudice: The California F scale and Gough's Pr scale. *Journal of Abnormal and Social Psychology, 52,* 140–142.

Swenson, W. M., Pearson, J. S., & Osborne, D. (1973). *An MMPI source book: Basic item, scale, and pattern data for 50,000 medical patients.* Minneapolis, MN: University of Minnesota Press.

Swenson, W. M., Rome, H. P., Pearson, J. S., & Brannick, T. L. (1965). A totally automated psychological test: Experience in a medical center. *Journal of the American Medical Association, 191,* 925–927.

Tafejian, T. R. (1951). The E-F scale, the MMPI, and Gough's Pr scale. *American Psychologist, 6,* 501.

Taft, R. (1957). The validity of the Barron Ego Strength scale and the Welsh Anxiety index. *Journal of Consulting Psychology, 21,* 247–249.

Tamkin, A. S. (1957). An evaluation of the construct validity of Barron's Ego-Strength scale. *Journal of Consulting Psychology, 13,* 156–158.

Tamkin, A. S., & Klett, C. J. (1957). Barron's Ego Strength scale: A replication of an evaluation of its construct validity. *Journal of Consulting Psychology, 21,* 412.

Taulbee, E. S., & Sisson, B. D. (1957). Configural analysis of MMPI profiles of psychiatric groups. *Journal of Consulting Psychology, 21,* 413–417.

Taylor, J. A. (1951). The relationship of anxiety to the conditioned eyelid response. *Journal of Experimental Psychology, 41,* 81–92.

Taylor, J. A. (1953). A personality scale of manifest anxiety. *Journal of Abnormal and Social Psychology, 48,* 285–290.

Taylor, J. B., Ptacek, M., Carithers, M., Griffin, C., & Coyne, L. (1972). Rating scales as measures of clinical judgment: III. Judgments of the self on personality inventory scales and direct ratings. *Educational and Psychological Measurement, 32,* 543–557.

Terman, L. M., & Miles, C. C. (1936). *Sex and personality: Studies in masculinity and femininity.* New York: McGraw-Hill.

Tisdale, M. J. (1982). *Descriptors associated with low T-scores on scale 5 of the MMPI for graduate and undergraduate females.* Unpublished master's thesis, Kent State University, Kent, OH.

Tryon, R. C. (1966). Unrestricted cluster and factor analysis, with application to the MMPI and Holzinger-Harman problems. *Multivariate Behavioral Research, 1,* 229–244.

Tryon, R. C., & Bailey, D. (Eds.). (1965). *Users' manual of the BC TRY system of cluster and factor analysis* (Taped version). Berkeley, CA: University of California Computer Center.

Uecker, A. E. (1969). Comparability of two methods of administering the MMPI to brain-damaged geriatric patients. *Journal of Clinical Psychology, 25,* 196–198.

Uecker, A. E. (1970). Differentiating male alcoholics from other psychiatric inpatients: Validity of the MacAndrew scale. *Quarterly Journal of Studies on Alcohol, 31,* 379–383.

Uecker, A. E., Boutilier, L. R., & Richardson, E. H. (1980). "Indianism" and MMPI scores of men alcoholics. *Journal of Studies on Alcohol, 41,* 357–362.

Walters, G. D., Greene, R. L., & Jeffrey, T. B. (1984). Discriminating between alcoholic and nonalcoholic blacks and whites on the MMPI. *Journal of Personality Assessment, 48,* 486–488.

Walters, G. D., Greene, R. L., Jeffrey, T. B., Kruzich, D. J., & Haskin, J. J. (1983). Racial variations on the MacAndrew Alcoholism scale of the MMPI. *Journal of Consulting and Clinical Psychology, 51,* 947–948.

Warman, R. E., & Hannum, T. E. (1965). MMPI pattern changes in female prisoners. *Journal of Research in Crime and Delinquency, 2,* 72–76.

Webb, J. T. (1970). Validity and utility of computer-produced reports with Veterans Administration psychiatric populations. *Proceedings of the 78th Annual Convention of the American Psychological Association, 5,* 541–542.

Webb, J. T., Miller, M. L., & Fowler, R. D. (1969). Validation of a computerized MMPI interpretation system. *Proceedings of the 77th Annual Convention of the American Psychological Association, 4,* 523–524.

Webb, J. T., Miller, M. L., & Fowler, R. D. (1970). Extending professional time: A computerized MMPI interpretation service. *Journal of Clinical Psychology, 26,* 210–214.

Welsh, G. S. (1948). An extension of Hathaway's MMPI profile coding system. *Journal of Consulting Psychology, 12,* 343–344.

Welsh, G. S. (1956). Factor dimensions A and R. In G. S. Welsh & W. G. Dahlstrom (Eds.), *Basic readings on the MMPI in psychology and medicine* (pp. 264–281). Minneapolis, MN: University of Minnesota Press.

Welsh, G. S. (1965). MMPI profiles and factors A and R. *Journal of Clinical Psychology, 21,* 43–47.

Welsh, G. S., & Dahlstrom, W. G. (Eds.). (1956). *Basic readings on the MMPI in psychology and medicine.* Minneapolis, MN: University of Minnesota Press.

Wiener, D. N. (1948). Subtle and obvious keys for the MMPI. *Journal of Consulting Psychology, 12,* 164–170.

Wiggins, J. S. (1966). Substantive dimensions of self-report in the MMPI item pool. *Psychological Monographs, 80* (22, Whole No. 630).

Wiggins, J. S. (1969). Content dimensions in the MMPI. In J. N. Butcher (Ed.), *MMPI: Research developments and clinical applications* (pp. 127–180). New York: McGraw-Hill.

Wiggins, J. S. (1971). *Content scales: Basic data for scoring and interpretation.* Unpublished materials.

Wiggins, J. S. (1973). *Personality and prediction: Principles of personality assessment.* Reading, MA: Addison-Wesley.

Wiggins, J. S., Goldberg, L. R., & Applebaum, M. (1971). MMPI content scales: Interpretive norms and correlations with other scales. *Journal of Consulting and Clinical Psychology, 37,* 403–410.

Wiggins, J. S., & Vollmar, J. (1959). The content of the MMPI. *Journal of Clinical Psychology, 15,* 45–47.

Wilderman, J. E. (1984). *An investigation of the clinical utility of the College Maladjustment scale.* Unpublished master's thesis, Kent State University, Kent, OH.

Williams, A. F., McCourt, W. F., & Schneider, L. (1971). Personality self-descriptions of alcoholics and heavy drinkers. *Quarterly Journal of Studies on Alcohol, 32,* 310–317.

Williams, C. L. (1986). MMPI profiles from adolescents: Interpretive strategies and treatment considerations. *Journal of Child and Adolescent Psychotherapy, 3,* 179–193.

Williams, H. L. (1952). The development of a caudality scale for the MMPI. *Journal of Clinical Psychology, 8,* 293–297.

Wimbish, L. G. (1984). *The importance of appropriate norms for the computerized interpretation of adolescent MMPI profiles.* Unpublished doctoral dissertation, Ohio State University, Columbus.

Wirt, R. D. (1955). Further validation of the Ego-Strength scale. *Journal of Consulting Psychology, 19,* 444.

Wirt, R. D. (1956). Actuarial prediction. *Journal of Consulting Psychology, 20,* 123–124.

Wisniewski, N. M., Glenwick, D. S., & Graham, J. R. (1985). MacAndrew scale and sociodemographic correlates of adolescent alcohol and drug use. *Addictive Behaviors, 10,* 55–67.

Wolfson, K. P., & Erbaugh, S. E. (1984). Adolescent responses to the MacAndrew Alcoholism scale. *Journal of Consulting and Clinical Psychology, 52,* 625–630.

Ziskin, J. (1981). Use of the MMPI in forensic settings (*Clinical Notes on the MMPI,* No. 9). Minneapolis, MN: National Computer Systems.

Zuckerman, M., Levitt, E. E., & Lubin, B. (1961). Concurrent and construct validity of direct and indirect measures of dependency. *Journal of Consulting Psychology, 25,* 316–323.

Appendices

Appendix A. Composition of Standard Validity and Clinical Scales

L Scale
- True: NONE
- False: 15, 30, 45, 60, 75, 90, 105, 120, 135, 150, 165, 195, 225, 255, 285

F Scale
- True: 14, 23, 27, 31, 34, 35, 40, 42, 48, 49, 50, 53, 56, 66, 85, 121, 123, 139, 146, 151, 156, 168, 184, 197, 200, 202, 205, 206, 209, 210, 211, 215, 218, 227, 245, 246, 247, 252, 256, 269, 275, 286, 291, 293
- False: 17, 20, 54, 65, 75, 83, 112, 113, 115, 164, 169, 177, 185, 196, 199, 220, 257, 258, 272, 276

K Scale
- True: 96
- False: 30, 39, 71, 89, 124, 129, 134, 138, 142, 148, 160, 170, 171, 180, 183, 217, 234, 267, 272, 296, 316, 322, 374, 383, 397, 398, 406, 461, 502

Scale 1–Hypochondriasis (Hs)
- True: 23, 29, 43, 62, 72, 108, 114, 125, 161, 189, 273
- False: 2, 3, 7, 9, 18, 51, 55, 63, 68, 103, 130, 153, 155, 163, 175, 188, 190, 192, 230, 243, 274, 281

Scale 2–Depression (D)
- True: 5, 13, 23, 32, 41, 43, 52, 67, 86, 104, 130, 138, 142, 158, 159, 182, 189, 193, 236, 259
- False: 2, 8, 9, 18, 30, 36, 39, 46, 51, 57, 58, 64, 80, 88, 89, 95, 98, 107, 122, 131, 145, 152, 153, 154, 155, 160, 178, 191, 207, 208, 233, 241, 242, 248, 263, 270, 271, 272, 285, 296

Scale 3–Hysteria (Hy)
- True: 10, 23, 32, 43, 44, 47, 76, 114, 179, 186, 189, 238, 253
- False: 2, 3, 6, 7, 8, 9, 12, 26, 30, 51, 55, 71, 89, 93, 103, 107, 109, 124, 128, 129, 136, 137, 141, 147, 153, 160, 162, 163, 170, 172, 174, 175, 180, 188, 190, 192, 201, 213, 230, 234, 243, 265, 267, 274, 279, 289, 292

Scale 4–Psychopathic Deviate (Pd)
- True: 16, 21, 24, 32, 33, 35, 38, 42, 61, 67, 84, 94, 102, 106, 110, 118, 127, 215, 216, 224, 239, 244, 245, 284
- False: 8, 20, 37, 82, 91, 96, 107, 134, 137, 141, 155, 170, 171, 173, 180, 183, 201, 231, 235, 237, 248, 267, 287, 289, 294, 296

Scale 5–Masculinity-Femininity (Mf), Male
- True: 4, 25, 69, 70, 74, 77, 78, 87, 92, 126, 132, 134, 140, 149, 179, 187, 203, 204, 217, 226, 231, 239, 261, 278, 282, 295, 297, 299
- False: 1, 19, 26, 28, 79, 80, 81, 89, 99, 112, 115, 116, 117, 120, 133, 144, 176, 198, 213, 214, 219, 221, 223, 229, 249, 254, 260, 262, 264, 280, 283, 300

Scale 5–Masculinity-Femininity (Mf), Female
- True: 4, 25, 70, 74, 77, 78, 87, 92, 126, 132, 133, 134, 140, 149, 187, 203, 204, 217, 226, 239, 261, 278, 282, 295, 299
- False: 1, 19, 26, 28, 69, 79, 80, 81, 89, 99, 112, 115, 116, 117, 120, 144, 176, 179, 198, 213, 214, 219, 221, 223, 229, 231, 249, 254, 260, 262, 264, 280, 283, 297, 300

Source: W. G. Dahlstrom, G. S. Welsh, & L. E. Dahlstrom, *An MMPI Handbook,* Vol. I. The University of Minnesota Press, Minneapolis. Copyright 1960, 1972 by the University of Minnesota. Reproduced with permission.

Scale 6–Paranoia (Pa)
True: 15, 16, 22, 24, 27, 35, 110, 121, 123, 127, 151, 157, 158, 202, 275, 284, 291, 293, 299, 305, 317, 338, 341, 364, 365
False: 93, 107, 109, 111, 117, 124, 268, 281, 294, 313, 316, 319, 327, 347, 348

Scale 7–Psychasthenia (Pt)
True: 10, 15, 22, 32, 41, 67, 76, 86, 94, 102, 106, 142, 159, 182, 189, 217, 238, 266, 301, 304, 305, 317, 321, 336, 337, 340, 342, 343, 344, 346, 349, 351, 352, 356, 357, 358, 359, 360, 361
False: 3, 8, 36, 122, 152, 164, 178, 329, 353

Scale 8–Schizophrenia (Sc)
True: 15, 16, 21, 22, 24, 32, 33, 35, 38, 40, 41, 47, 52, 76, 97, 104, 121, 156, 157, 159, 168, 179, 182, 194, 202, 210, 212, 238, 241, 251, 259, 266, 273, 282, 291, 297, 301, 303, 305, 307, 312, 320, 324, 325, 332, 334, 335, 339, 341, 345, 349, 350, 352, 354, 355, 356, 360, 363, 364
False: 8, 17, 20, 37, 65, 103, 119, 177, 178, 187, 192, 196, 220, 276, 281, 306, 309, 322, 330

Scale 9–Hypomania (Ma)
True: 11, 13, 21, 22, 59, 64, 73, 97, 100, 109, 127, 134, 143, 156, 157, 167, 181, 194, 212, 222, 226, 228, 232, 233, 238, 240, 250, 251, 263, 266, 268, 271, 277, 279, 298
False: 101, 105, 111, 119, 120, 148, 166, 171, 180, 267, 289

Scale 0–Social Introversion (Si)
True: 32, 67, 82, 111, 117, 124, 138, 147, 171, 172, 180, 201, 236, 267, 278, 292, 304, 316, 321, 332, 336, 342, 357, 377, 383, 398, 411, 427, 436, 455, 473, 487, 549, 564
False: 25, 33, 57, 91, 99, 119, 126, 143, 193, 208, 229, 231, 254, 262, 281, 296, 309, 353, 359, 371, 391, 400, 415, 440, 446, 449, 450, 451, 462, 469, 479, 481, 482, 505, 521, 547

Appendix B. T-Score Conversions for Standard Validity and Clinical Scales

	Males														Females														
Raw score	?	L	F	K	1 (Hs) + .5 K	2 (D)	3 (Hy)	4 (Pd) + .4 K	5 (Mf)	6 (Pa)	7 (Pt) + 1 K	8 (Sc) + 1 K	9 (Ma) + .2 K	0 (Si)	?	L	F	K	1 (Hs) + .5 K	2 (D)	3 (Hy)	4 (Pd) + .4 K	5 (Mf)	6 (Pa)	7 (Pt) + 1 K	8 (Sc) + 1 K	9 (Ma) + .2 K	0 (Si)	Raw score
60	58													87	58										107	107		87	**60**
59														86											106	106		86	**59**
58												119		85											104	104		85	**58**
57											120	117		84											102	103		84	**57**
56											118	115		83											101	101		83	**56**
55											116	113		82											99	100		82	**55**
54							118				114	111		81						117	112				98	98		81	**54**
53							116				112	109		80						115	110				96	97		80	**53**
52							115				110	107		79						113	109				94	95		79	**52**
51							113		110		107	105		78						111	107		20		93	94		78	**51**
50	56						111		108		105	103		77	56					109	105		22		91	92		77	**50**
49							109		106		103	101		76						107	103		24		89	91		76	**49**
48							107	119	104		101	99		75						105	101	119	26		88	89		75	**48**
47							106	116	102		99	97		74						103	100	116	28		86	87		74	**47**
46						120	104	114	100		97	96		73						102	98	114	30		84	86		73	**46**
45						118	102	111	98		95	94		72						100	96	111	32		83	84		72	**45**
44						116	100	109	96		93	92		71						98	94	109	34		81	83		71	**44**
43						113	98	107	94		91	90		70					111	96	93	107	37		79	81		70	**43**
42						111	96	104	92		89	88		69					109	94	91	104	39		78	80		69	**42**
41						108	95	102	90		87	86		68					107	92	89	102	41		76	78		68	**41**
40	53					106	93	110	88		85	84	108	67	53				105	90	87	100	43		74	77	108	67	**40**
39						104	91	97	86		83	82	106	66					103	88	86	97	45		73	75	106	66	**39**
38					118	101	89	95	84		81	80	103	65					101	86	84	95	47		71	74	103	65	**38**
37					116	99	87	93	82		79	78	101	64					99	84	82	93	49		69	72	101	64	**37**
36					113	96	86	90	80		77	76	98	63					97	82	80	90	51		68	71	98	63	**36**
35					111	94	84	88	78		75	74	96	62					95	80	79	88	53		66	69	96	62	**35**
34					108	92	82	86	76		73	73	93	61					93	78	77	86	55		65	67	93	61	**34**
33					106	89	80	83	74		71	71	91	60					91	76	75	83	57		63	66	91	60	**33**
32					103	87	78	81	73	120	69	69	88	58					89	75	73	81	59	120	61	64	88	58	**32**
31			110		100	84	76	79	71	117	66	67	86	56			110		87	73	72	79	61	117	60	63	86	56	**31**

30	50		108	83	98	82	75	76	69	114	64	65	83	55	50		108	83	85	71	70	76	63	114	58	61	83	55	**30**
29			106	81	95	80	73	74	67	111	62	63	81	54			106	81	82	69	68	74	66	111	56	60	81	54	**29**
28			104	79	93	77	71	71	65	108	60	61	78	53			104	79	80	67	66	71	68	108	55	58	78	53	**28**
27			102	77	90	75	69	69	63	105	58	59	75	52			102	77	78	65	64	69	70	105	53	57	75	52	**27**
26			100	75	88	72	67	67	61	102	56	57	73	51			100	75	76	63	63	67	72	102	51	55	73	51	**26**
25			98	74	85	70	65	64	59	100	54	55	70	50			98	74	74	61	61	64	74	100	50	54	70	50	**25**
24			96	72	82	68	64	62	57	97	52	53	68	49			96	72	72	59	59	62	76	97	48	52	68	49	**24**
23			94	70	80	65	62	60	55	94	50	51	65	48			94	70	70	57	57	60	78	94	46	51	65	48	**23**
22			92	68	77	63	60	57	53	91	48	50	63	47			92	68	68	55	56	57	80	91	45	49	63	47	**22**
21			90	66	75	60	58	55	51	88	46	48	60	46			90	66	66	53	54	55	82	88	43	47	60	46	**21**
20	47		88	64	72	58	56	53	49	85	44	46	58	45	47		88	64	64	51	52	53	84	85	41	46	58	45	**20**
19			86	62	70	56	55	50	47	82	42	44	55	44			86	62	62	49	50	50	86	82	40	44	55	44	**19**
18			84	61	67	53	53	48	45	79	40	42	53	43			84	61	60	47	49	48	88	79	38	43	53	43	**18**
17			82	59	65	51	51	46	43	76	38	40	50	42			82	59	58	46	47	46	90	76	36	41	50	42	**17**
16			80	57	62	48	49	43	41	73	36	38	48	41			80	57	56	44	45	43	92	73	35	40	48	41	**16**
15		86	78	55	59	46	47	41	39	70	34	36	45	40		86	78	55	54	42	43	41	95	70	33	38	45	40	**15**
14		83	76	53	57	44	45	39	37	67	32	34	43	39		83	76	53	52	40	42	39		67	32	37	43	39	**14**
13		80	73	51	54	41	44	36	35	65	30	32	40	38		80	73	51	50	38	40	36		65	30	35	40	38	**13**
12		76	70	49	52	39	42	34	34	62	28	30	38	37		76	70	49	48	36	38	34		62	28	34	38	37	**12**
11		73	68	48	49	36	40	32	32	59	26	28	35	36		73	68	48	46	34	36	32		59	27	32	35	36	**11**
10	44	70	66	46	47	34	38	29	30	56	23	26	33	35	44	70	66	46	44	32	34	29		56	25	31	33	35	**10**
9		66	64	44	44	32	36	27	28	53	21	25	30	34		66	64	44	42	30	33	27		53	23	29	30	34	**9**
8		63	62	42	41	29	35	24	26	50		23	28	33		63	62	42	39	28	31	24		50	22	27	28	33	**8**
7		60	60	40	39			22		47		21	26	32		60	60	40	37		29	22		47	20	26	26	32	**7**
6		56	58	38	36			20		44			23	30		56	58	38	35		27	20		44		24	23	30	**6**
5		53	55	36	34					41			21	29		53	55	36	33		26			41		23	21	29	**5**
4		50	53	35	31					38				28		50	53	35	31		24			38				28	**4**
3		46	50	33	29					35				27		46	50	33	29					35				27	**3**
2		44	48	31	26					33				26		44	48	31	27					33				26	**2**
1		40	46	29	23					30				25		40	46	29	25					30				25	**1**
0	41	36	44	27	21					27					41	36	44	27	23					27					**0**

Source: W. G. Dahlstrom, G. S. Welsh, & L. E. Dahlstrom, *An MMPI Handbook,* Vol. I. The University of Minnesota Press, Minneapolis. Copyright 1960, 1972 by the University of Minnesota. Reproduced with permission.

Appendix C. T-Score Conversions for Adolescents

T-SCORE CONVERSIONS WITHOUT K CORRECTIONS FOR ADOLESCENT MALES AGE 14 AND BELOW

Raw score	T-scores													Raw score
	L	F	K	1	2	3	4	5	6	7	8	9	0	
0	32	36	23	34	9	10	10	0	23	30	32	15	11	**0**
1	37	38	25	37	12	13	12	3	25	32	33	17	12	**1**
2	42	40	27	40	15	16	14	5	27	33	35	19	14	**2**
3	46	42	29	43	17	18	16	8	30	34	36	21	15	**3**
4	51	44	31	46	19	20	18	10	33	36	37	23	16	**4**
5	56	46	33	49	21	22	21	12	35	37	38	25	18	**5**
6	61	48	35	52	23	25	23	15	38	38	39	27	19	**6**
7	66	50	37	55	26	27	25	17	41	40	40	29	20	**7**
8	71	52	39	58	28	29	28	20	44	41	41	31	22	**8**
9	76	54	41	61	30	31	30	22	46	43	42	33	23	**9**
10	80	56	43	64	32	33	32	24	49	44	43	35	24	**10**
11	85	58	45	67	35	36	35	27	52	45	44	37	26	**11**
12	90	60	48	70	37	38	37	29	55	47	45	39	27	**12**
13	95	62	50	73	39	40	39	31	57	48	46	41	28	**13**
14	100	64	52	76	41	42	42	34	60	49	47	43	30	**14**
15	105	66	54	79	43	44	44	36	63	51	48	45	31	**15**
16		68	56	82	46	47	46	38	65	52	50	47	33	**16**
17		70	58	84	48	49	49	41	68	54	51	49	34	**17**
18		71	60	87	50	51	51	43	71	55	52	50	35	**18**
19		73	62	90	52	53	53	46	74	56	53	52	37	**19**
20		75	64	93	55	56	56	48	76	58	54	54	38	**20**
21		77	66	96	57	58	58	50	79	59	55	56	39	**21**
22		79	68	99	59	60	60	53	82	60	56	58	41	**22**
23		81	70	102	61	62	62	55	84	62	57	60	42	**23**
24		83	72	105	63	64	65	57	87	63	58	62	43	**24**
25		85	74	108	66	67	67	60	90	65	59	64	45	**25**
26		87	76	111	68	69	69	62	93	66	60	66	46	**26**
27		89	79	114	70	71	72	65	95	67	61	68	47	**27**
28		91	81	117	72	73	74	67	98	69	62	70	49	**28**
29		93	83	120	75	75	76	69	101	70	63	72	50	**29**
30		95	85	123	77	78	79	72	104	71	65	74	51	**30**
31		97		126	79	80	81	74	106	73	66	76	53	**31**
32		99		129	81	82	83	76	109	74	67	78	54	**32**
33		101		132	83	84	86	79	112	75	68	80	56	**33**
34		103			86	87	88	81	114	77	69	82	57	**34**
35		105			88	89	90	83	117	78	70	84	58	**35**
36		107			90	91	93	86	120	80	71	86	60	**36**
37		109			92	93	95	88	123	81	72	88	61	**37**
38		111			95	95	97	91	125	82	73	90	62	**38**

Raw score	T-scores													Raw score
	L	F	K	1	2	3	4	5	6	7	8	9	0	
39		113			97	98	100	93	128	84	74	92	64	**39**
40		115			99	100	102	95	131	85	75	94	65	**40**
41		117			101	102	104	98		86	76	96	66	**41**
42		119			103	104	106	100		88	77	98	68	**42**
43		121			106	107	109	102		89	78	100	69	**43**
44		123			108	109	111	105		91	80	101	70	**44**
45		125			110	111	113	107		92	81	103	72	**45**
46		127			112	113	116	109		93	82	105	73	**46**
47		129			115	115	118	112		95	83		75	**47**
48		131			117	118	120	114		96	84		76	**48**
49		133			119	120	123	117			85		77	**49**
50		135			121	122	125	119			86		79	**50**
51		137			123	124		121			87		80	**51**
52		139			126	126		124			88		81	**52**
53		141			128	129		126			89		83	**53**
54		143			130	131		128			90		84	**54**
55		145			132	133		131			91		85	**55**
56		147			135	135		133			92		87	**56**
57		149			137	138		135			93		88	**57**
58		151			139	140		138			95		89	**58**
59		153			141	142		140			96		91	**59**
60		155			143	144		143			97		92	**60**
61		157									98		93	**61**
62		159									99		95	**62**
63		161									100		96	**63**
64		163									101		98	**64**
65											102		99	**65**
66											103		100	**66**
67											104		102	**67**
68											105		103	**68**
69											106		104	**69**
70											107		106	**70**
71											108			**71**
72											110			**72**
73											111			**73**
74											112			**74**
75											113			**75**
76											114			**76**
77											115			**77**
78											116			**78**

Source: W. G. Dahlstrom, G. S. Welsh, & L. E. Dahlstrom, *An MMPI Handbook,* Vol. I. The University of Minnesota Press, Minneapolis. Copyright 1960, 1972 by the University of Minnesota. Reproduced with permission.

T-SCORE CONVERSIONS WITHOUT K CORRECTIONS FOR ADOLESCENT MALES AGE 15

Raw score	T-scores													Raw score
	L	F	K	1	2	3	4	5	6	7	8	9	0	
0	32	37	22	36	9	12	10	06	27	29	33	15	10	**0**
1	37	38	24	39	11	15	13	8	29	31	34	17	12	**1**
2	42	40	26	41	13	17	15	10	31	32	35	19	13	**2**
3	46	41	28	44	15	20	17	12	33	34	36	21	15	**3**
4	50	43	30	46	18	22	19	14	35	35	37	22	16	**4**
5	55	45	32	48	20	24	22	16	37	37	38	24	17	**5**
6	59	46	34	51	22	26	24	18	40	38	39	26	19	**6**
7	63	48	37	53	24	28	26	20	42	39	40	28	20	**7**
8	67	50	39	55	27	30	28	22	44	41	41	30	21	**8**
9	72	52	41	58	29	32	30	24	46	42	42	32	23	**9**
10	76	53	43	60	31	34	32	26	48	44	43	34	24	**10**
11	80	55	45	62	33	36	34	28	50	45	44	36	25	**11**
12	85	57	47	65	36	38	37	31	52	46	45	38	27	**12**
13	89	58	49	67	38	40	39	33	54	48	46	40	28	**13**
14	93	60	51	69	40	42	41	35	56	49	47	42	30	**14**
15	98	62	53	72	43	44	43	37	58	51	48	43	31	**15**
16		63	55	74	45	46	45	39	60	52	49	45	32	**16**
17		65	58	76	47	48	47	41	63	54	50	47	34	**17**
18		67	60	79	49	50	49	43	65	55	51	49	35	**18**
19		68	62	81	52	52	52	45	67	56	52	51	36	**19**
20		70	64	84	54	54	54	47	69	58	53	53	38	**20**
21		72	66	86	56	57	56	49	71	59	54	55	39	**21**
22		73	68	88	58	59	58	51	73	61	55	57	40	**22**
23		75	70	91	61	61	60	53	75	62	56	59	42	**23**
24		77	72	93	63	63	62	56	77	64	57	61	43	**24**
25		78	74	95	65	65	64	58	79	65	58	63	44	**25**
26		80	76	98	67	67	66	60	81	66	59	65	46	**26**
27		82	78	100	70	69	69	62	83	68	60	66	47	**27**
28		83	81	102	72	71	71	64	86	69	61	68	48	**28**
29		85	83	105	74	73	73	66	88	71	62	70	50	**29**
30		87	85	107	77	75	75	68	90	72	63	72	51	**30**
31		88		109	79	77	77	70	92	73	64	74	52	**31**
32		90		112	81	79	79	72	94	75	65	76	54	**32**
33		92		114	83	81	81	74	96	76	66	78	55	**33**
34		93			86	83	84	76	98	78	67	80	56	**34**
35		95			88	85	86	79	100	79	68	82	58	**35**
36		97			90	87	88	81	102	81	69	84	59	**36**
37		98			92	89	90	83	104	82	70	86	60	**37**
38		100			95	91	92	85	106	83	71	87	62	**38**
39		102			97	94	94	87	109	85	72	89	63	**39**
40		103			99	96	96	89	111	86	73	91	64	**40**
41		105			101	98	99	91		88	74	93	66	**41**
42		107			104	100	101	93		89	75	95	67	**42**

Raw score	L	F	K	1	2	3	4	5	6	7	8	9	0	Raw score
	T-scores													
43		108			106	102	103	95		90	76	97	69	**43**
44		110			108	104	105	97		92	77	99	70	**44**
45		112			111	106	107	99		93	78	101	71	**45**
46		114			113	108	109	101		95	79	103	73	**46**
47		115			115	110	111	104		96	80		74	**47**
48		117			117	112	114	106		98	81		75	**48**
49		119			120	114	116	108			82		77	**49**
50		120			122	116	118	110			83		78	**50**
51		122			124	118		112			84		79	**51**
52		124			126	120		114			85		81	**52**
53		125			129	122		116			86		82	**53**
54		127			131	124		118			87		83	**54**
55		129			133	126		120			88		85	**55**
56		130			135	128		122			89		86	**56**
57		132			138	131		124			90		87	**57**
58		134			140	133		127			91		89	**58**
59		135			142	135		129			92		90	**59**
60		137			145	137		131			93		91	**60**
61		139									94		93	**61**
62		140									95		94	**62**
63		142									96		95	**63**
64		144									97		97	**64**
65											98		98	**65**
66											99		99	**66**
67											100		101	**67**
68											101		102	**68**
69											102		103	**69**
70											103		105	**70**
71											104			**71**
72											105			**72**
73											106			**73**
74											107			**74**
75											108			**75**
76											109			**76**
77											110			**77**
78											111			**78**

T-SCORE CONVERSIONS WITHOUT K CORRECTIONS FOR ADOLESCENT MALES AGE 16

Raw score	L	F	K	1	2	3	4	5	6	7	8	9	0	Raw score
0	31	35	20	33	8	10	10	0	34	28	30	11	8	**0**
1	35	37	22	36	11	12	12	3	35	30	32	13	10	**1**
2	40	39	24	39	13	15	15	5	36	31	33	15	11	**2**
3	44	40	27	42	15	17	17	8	37	33	35	17	12	**3**
4	49	42	29	45	18	19	19	10	39	34	36	19	14	**4**
5	53	44	31	47	20	21	21	12	40	36	37	21	15	**5**
6	58	46	33	50	22	23	23	15	42	37	38	23	17	**6**
7	62	47	36	53	24	26	25	17	43	39	39	25	18	**7**
8	67	49	38	56	27	28	28	20	45	40	40	28	20	**8**
9	71	51	40	59	29	30	30	22	46	42	41	30	21	**9**
10	76	53	42	62	31	32	32	24	48	43	42	32	22	**10**
11	80	54	45	64	33	34	34	27	49	45	43	34	24	**11**
12	85	56	47	67	36	37	36	29	51	46	44	36	25	**12**
13	89	58	49	70	38	39	38	31	52	48	45	38	27	**13**
14	94	60	51	73	40	41	41	34	54	49	46	40	28	**14**
15	99	61	54	76	42	43	43	36	55	51	48	43	29	**15**
16		63	56	78	45	45	45	39	57	52	49	45	31	**16**
17		65	58	81	47	47	47	41	58	54	50	47	32	**17**
18		66	60	84	49	50	49	43	60	55	51	49	34	**18**
19		68	63	87	51	52	51	46	61	56	52	51	35	**19**
20		70	65	90	54	54	53	48	63	58	53	53	37	**20**
21		72	67	93	56	56	56	50	64	59	54	55	38	**21**
22		73	70	95	58	58	58	53	66	61	55	58	39	**22**
23		75	72	98	60	61	60	55	67	62	56	60	41	**23**
24		77	74	101	63	63	62	57	68	64	57	62	42	**24**
25		79	76	104	65	65	64	60	70	65	58	64	44	**25**
26		80	79	107	67	67	66	62	71	67	59	66	45	**26**
27		82	81	109	69	69	69	65	73	68	61	68	46	**27**
28		84	83	112	71	71	71	67	74	70	62	70	48	**28**
29		86	85	115	74	74	73	69	76	71	63	73	49	**29**
30		87	88	118	76	76	75	72	77	73	64	75	51	**30**
31		89		121	78	78	77	74	79	74	65	77	52	**31**
32		91		124	80	80	79	76	80	76	66	79	54	**32**
33		92		126	83	82	82	79	82	77	67	81	55	**33**
34		94			85	85	84	81	83	79	68	83	56	**34**
35		96			87	87	86	84	85	80	69	85	58	**35**
36		98			89	89	88	86	86	82	70	88	59	**36**
37		99			92	91	90	88	88	83	71	90	61	**37**
38		101			94	93	92	91	89	85	72	92	62	**38**
39		103			96	96	95	93	91	86	74	94	63	**39**
40		105			98	98	97	95	92	87	75	96	65	**40**
41		106			101	100	99	98		89	76	98	66	**41**
42		108			103	102	101	100		90	77	100	68	**42**

Raw score	L	F	K	1	2	3	4	5	6	7	8	9	0	Raw score
	T-scores													
43		110			105	104	103	103		92	78	103	69	**43**
44		112			107	106	105	105		93	79	105	71	**44**
45		113			110	109	107	107		95	80	107	72	**45**
46		115			112	111	110	110		96	81	109	73	**46**
47		117			114	113	112	112		98	82		75	**47**
48		118			116	115	114	114		99	83		76	**48**
49		120			119	117	116	117			84		78	**49**
50		122			121	120	118	119			85		79	**50**
51		124			123	122		121			86		81	**51**
52		125			125	124		124			88		82	**52**
53		127			128	126		126			89		83	**53**
54		129			130	128		129			90		85	**54**
55		131			132	130		131			91		86	**55**
56		132			134	133		133			92		88	**56**
57		134			137	135		136			93		89	**57**
58		136			139	137		138			94		90	**58**
59		138			141	139		140			95		92	**59**
60		139			143	141		143			96		93	**60**
61		141									97		95	**61**
62		143									98		96	**62**
63		144									99		98	**63**
64		146									101		99	**64**
65											102		100	**65**
66											103		102	**66**
67											104		103	**67**
68											105		105	**68**
69											106		106	**69**
70											107		107	**70**
71											108			**71**
72											109			**72**
73											110			**73**
74											111			**74**
75											112			**75**
76											114			**76**
77											115			**77**
78											116			**78**

T-SCORE CONVERSIONS WITHOUT K CORRECTIONS FOR ADOLESCENT MALES AGES 17 AND 18

Raw score	T-scores													Raw score
	L	F	K	1	2	3	4	5	6	7	8	9	0	
0	30	32	20	35	16	13	6	05	19	27	31	12	6	**0**
1	34	34	23	38	17	15	9	7	22	28	32	14	8	**1**
2	38	36	25	40	19	17	11	9	25	30	33	16	9	**2**
3	43	39	27	43	21	19	13	11	28	32	34	18	11	**3**
4	47	41	29	45	23	21	16	13	31	33	35	20	12	**4**
5	51	43	31	48	24	23	18	16	34	35	36	22	14	**5**
6	55	45	34	50	26	25	20	18	37	36	37	24	15	**6**
7	59	47	36	53	28	27	23	20	40	38	38	26	17	**7**
8	63	50	38	55	30	29	25	22	43	39	39	28	18	**8**
9	68	52	40	58	32	30	27	24	46	41	40	31	20	**9**
10	72	54	42	60	34	32	29	26	49	42	41	33	21	**10**
11	76	56	45	63	35	34	32	29	52	44	43	35	23	**11**
12	80	58	47	65	37	36	34	31	55	45	44	37	24	**12**
13	84	60	49	68	39	38	36	33	58	47	45	39	26	**13**
14	88	63	51	70	41	40	39	35	61	48	46	41	27	**14**
15	93	65	53	73	43	42	41	37	64	50	47	43	29	**15**
16		67	56	75	44	44	43	40	67	52	48	45	30	**16**
17		69	58	78	46	46	46	42	70	53	49	48	32	**17**
18		71	60	80	48	48	48	44	72.	55	50	50	33	**18**
19		73	62	83	50	49	50	46	75	56	51	52	35	**19**
20		76	64	85	52	51	52	48	78	58	52	54	36	**20**
21		78	67	88	54	53	55	50	81	59	53	56	38	**21**
22		80	69	90	55	55	57	53	84	61	55	58	39	**22**
23		82	71	93	57	57	59	55	87	62	56	60	41	**23**
24		84	73	95	59	59	62	57	90	64	57	62	42	**24**
25		87	75	98	61	61	64	59	93	65	58	65	44	**25**
26		89	78	100	63	63	66	61	96	67	59	67	45	**26**
27		91	80	103	64	65	69	63	99	69	60	69	47	**27**
28		93	82	105	66	67	71	66	102	70	61	71	49	**28**
29		95	84	108	68	68	73	68	105	72	62	73	50	**29**
30		97	86	110	70	70	75	70	108	73	63	75	52	**30**
31		100		113	72	72	78	72	111	75	64	77	53	**31**
32		102		115	73	74	80	74	114	76	66	79	55	**32**
33		104		118	75	76	82	77	117	78	67	82	56	**33**
34		106			77	78	85	79	120	79	68	84	58	**34**
35		108			79	80	87	81	123	81	69	86	59	**35**
36		110			81	82	89	83	126	82	70	88	61	**36**
37		113			83	84	91	85	128	84	71	90	62	**37**
38		115			84	86	94	87	131	86	72	92	64	**38**
39		117			86	87	96	90	134	87	73	94	65	**39**
40		119			88	89	98	92	137	89	74	96	67	**40**
41		121			90	91	101	94		90	75	99	68	**41**
42		124			92	93	103	96		92	77	101	70	**42**

Raw score	T-scores													Raw score
	L	F	K	1	2	3	4	5	6	7	8	9	0	
43		126			93	95	105	98		93	78	103	71	**43**
44		128			95	97	108	100		95	79	105	73	**44**
45		130			97	99	110	103		96	80	107	74	**45**
46		132			99	101	112	105		98	81	109	76	**46**
47		134			101	103	114	107		99	82		77	**47**
48		137			102	105	117	109		101	83		79	**48**
49		139			104	107	119	111			84		80	**49**
50		141			106	108	121	114			85		82	**50**
51		143			108	110		116			86		83	**51**
52		145			110	112		118			88		85	**52**
53		147			112	114		120			89		86	**53**
54		150			113	116		122			90		88	**54**
55		152			115	118		124			91		89	**55**
56		154			117	120		127			92		91	**56**
57		156			119	122		129			93		92	**57**
58		158			121	124		131			94		94	**58**
59		161			122	126		133			95		95	**59**
60		163			124	127		135			96		97	**60**
61		165									97		98	**61**
62		167									99		100	**62**
63		169									100		101	**63**
64		171									101		103	**64**
65											102		104	**65**
66											103		106	**66**
67											104		107	**67**
68											105		109	**68**
69											106		110	**69**
70											107		112	**70**
71											108			**71**
72											109			**72**
73											111			**73**
74											112			**74**
75											113			**75**
76											114			**76**
77											115			**77**
78											116			**78**

T-SCORE CONVERSIONS WITHOUT K CORRECTIONS FOR ADOLESCENT FEMALES AGE 14 AND BELOW

Raw score	T-scores													Raw score
	L	F	K	1	2	3	4	5	6	7	8	9	0	
0	31	36	19	36	11	7	14	126	28	29	32	16	13	**0**
1	36	39	22	39	13	9	16	124	30	30	34	18	15	**1**
2	41	41	24	41	15	11	19	122	32	32	35	20	16	**2**
3	46	44	27	44	17	13	21	120	34	33	36	22	18	**3**
4	50	46	29	46	20	15	23	118	36	34	37	24	19	**4**
5	55	49	31	49	22	18	25	115	38	36	38	26	20	**5**
6	59	51	33	51	24	20	27	113	40	37	40	28	21	**6**
7	64	54	35	54	26	22	29	111	43	39	41	30	23	**7**
8	69	56	38	56	28	24	31	109	45	40	42	32	24	**8**
9	73	59	40	59	30	27	34	107	47	42	43	35	25	**9**
10	78	61	42	61	32	29	36	104	49	43	45	37	26	**10**
11	83	64	44	64	34	31	38	102	51	44	46	39	28	**11**
12	87	66	47	66	36	33	40	100	54	46	47	41	29	**12**
13	92	69	49	69	38	35	42	99	56	47	48	43	30	**13**
14	97	71	51	71	41	38	44	97	58	49	49	45	32	**14**
15	101	74	53	74	43	40	46	95	60	50	51	47	33	**15**
16		76	56	76	45	42	49	92	62	52	52	49	34	**16**
17		79	58	79	47	44	51	90	65	53	53	51	35	**17**
18		81	60	81	49	46	53	88	67	54	54	54	37	**18**
19		84	62	84	51	49	55	86	69	56	56	56	38	**19**
20		86	65	86	53	51	57	84	71	57	57	58	39	**20**
21		89	67	89	55	53	59	81	73	59	58	60	40	**21**
22		91	69	91	57	55	61	79	75	60	59	62	42	**22**
23		94	71	94	59	58	64	77	78	62	60	64	43	**23**
24		96	73	96	62	60	66	75	80	63	62	66	44	**24**
25		99	76	99	64	62	68	73	82	64	63	68	45	**25**
26		101	78	101	66	64	70	70	84	66	64	70	47	**26**
27		104	80	104	68	66	72	68	86	67	65	72	48	**27**
28		106	82	106	70	69	74	66	89	69	67	75	49	**28**
29		109	85	109	72	71	76	64	91	70	68	77	51	**29**
30		111	87	111	74	73	79	62	93	72	69	79	52	**30**
31		114		113	76	75	81	59	95	73	70	81	53	**31**
32		116		116	78	78	83	57	97	74	71	83	54	**32**
33		119		118	80	80	85	55	99	76	73	85	56	**33**
34		121			83	82	87	53	102	77	74	87	57	**34**
35		124			85	84	89	51	104	79	75	89	58	**35**
36		126			87	86	92	48	106	80	76	91	59	**36**
37		129			89	89	94	46	108	82	77	94	61	**37**
38		131			91	91	96	44	110	83	79	96	62	**38**
39		134			93	93	98	42	113	84	80	98	63	**39**
40		136			95	95	100	40	115	86	81	100	64	**40**
41		139			97	98	102	37		87	82	102	66	**41**
42		141			99	100	104	35		89	84	104	67	**42**

Raw score	T-scores													Raw score
	L	F	K	1	2	3	4	5	6	7	8	9	0	
43		144			102	102	107	33		90	85	106	68	**43**
44		146			104	104	109	31		92	86	108	69	**44**
45		149			106	106	111	29		93	87	110	71	**45**
46		151			108	109	113	26		94	88	113	72	**46**
47		154			110	111	115	24		96	90		73	**47**
48		156			112	113	117	22		97	91		75	**48**
49		159			114	115	119	20			92		76	**49**
50		161			116	118	122	18			93		77	**50**
51		164			118	120		15			95		78	**51**
52		166			120	122		13			96		80	**52**
53		169			123	124		11			97		81	**53**
54		172			125	126		9			98		82	**54**
55		174			127	129		7			99		83	**55**
56		177			129	131		4			101		85	**56**
57		179			131	133		2			102		86	**57**
58		182			133	135					103		87	**58**
59		184			135	138		−2			104		88	**59**
60		187			137	140		−4			106		90	**60**
61		189									107		91	**61**
62		192									108		92	**62**
63		194									109		94	**63**
64		197									110		95	**64**
65											112		96	**65**
66											113		97	**66**
67											114		99	**67**
68											115		100	**68**
69											117		101	**69**
70											118		102	**70**
71											119			**71**
72											120			**72**
73											121			**73**
74											123			**74**
75											124			**75**
76											125			**76**
77											126			**77**
78											128			**78**

T-SCORE CONVERSIONS WITHOUT K CORRECTIONS FOR ADOLESCENT FEMALES AGE 15

Raw score	T-scores													Raw score
	L	F	K	1	2	3	4	5	6	7	8	9	0	
0	31	36	21	37	9	9	13	120	26	29	32	19	13	**0**
1	36	38	23	39	11	11	15	118	29	31	34	20	14	**1**
2	40	41	25	41	13	13	17	115	31	32	35	22	15	**2**
3	45	43	27	43	15	15	19	113	33	33	36	24	17	**3**
4	49	45	29	46	17	17	21	111	36	35	37	26	18	**4**
5	53	47	32	48	19	19	23	109	38	36	39	28	19	**5**
6	58	50	34	50	21	21	25	107	40	37	40	29	21	**6**
7	62	52	36	52	24	23	27	105	42	39	41	31	22	**7**
8	66	54	38	55	26	25	30	103	44	40	42	33	23	**8**
9	70	57	40	57	28	27	32	101	47	41	43	35	24	**9**
10	75	59	42	59	30	29	34	100	49	43	44	37	26	**10**
11	79	61	45	61	32	31	36	98	51	44	45	39	27	**11**
12	83	63	47	64	34	33	38	96	53	45	46	41	28	**12**
13	88	66	49	66	37	35	40	94	55	47	47	42	30	**13**
14	92	68	51	68	39	37	42	92	58	48	48	44	31	**14**
15	96	70	53	70	41	39	44	90	60	49	49	46	32	**15**
16		73	56	72	43	42	46	88	62	51	50	48	33	**16**
17		75	58	75	45	44	48	86	64	52	51	50	35	**17**
18		77	60	77	47	46	51	84	66	53	53	52	36	**18**
19		79	62	79	49	48	53	82	68	55	54	54	37	**19**
20		82	64	81	52	50	55	79	71	56	55	56	39	**20**
21		84	67	84	54	52	57	77	73	58	56	57	40	**21**
22		86	69	86	56	54	59	75	75	59	57	59	41	**22**
23		89	71	88	58	56	61	73	77	60	58	61	42	**23**
24		91	73	90	60	58	63	71	79	62	59	63	44	**24**
25		93	75	93	62	60	65	69	82	63	60	65	45	**25**
26		95	77	95	65	62	67	67	84	64	61	67	46	**26**
27		98	80	97	67	64	69	65	86	66	62	69	48	**27**
28		100	82	99	69	66	71	63	88	67	63	70	49	**28**
29		102	84	102	71	68	74	61	90	68	64	72	50	**29**
30		104	86	104	73	70	76	59	93	70	65	74	52	**30**
31		107		106	75	72	78	57	95	71	66	76	53	**31**
32		109		108	78	74	80	55	97	72	68	78	54	**32**
33		111		110	80	76	82	53	99	74	69	80	55	**33**
34		114			82	79	84	51	101	75	70	82	57	**34**
35		116			84	81	86	49	103	76	71	83	58	**35**
36		118			86	83	88	47	106	78	72	85	59	**36**
37		120			88	85	90	45	108	79	73	87	61	**37**
38		123			90	87	92	42	110	80	74	89	62	**38**
39		125			93	89	95	40	112	82	75	91	63	**39**
40		127			95	91	97	38	114	83	76	93	64	**40**
41		130			97	93	99	36		85	77	95	66	**41**
42		132			99	95	101	34		86	78	96	67	**42**

Raw score	T-scores													Raw score
	L	F	K	1	2	3	4	5	6	7	8	9	0	
43		134			101	97	103	32		87	79	98	68	**43**
44		136			103	99	105	30		89	80	100	70	**44**
45		139			106	101	107	28		90	82	102	71	**45**
46		141			108	103	109	26		91	83	104	72	**46**
47		143			110	105	111	24		93	84		73	**47**
48		146			112	107	113	22		94	85		75	**48**
49		148			114	109	115	20			86		76	**49**
50		150			116	111	118	18			87		77	**50**
51		152			119	113		16			88		79	**51**
52		155			121	115		14			89		80	**52**
53		157			123	118		12			90		81	**53**
54		159			125	120		10			91		82	**54**
55		162			127	122		8			92		84	**55**
56		164			129	124		6			93		85	**56**
57		166			131	126		3			94		86	**57**
58		168			134	128		1			95		88	**58**
59		171			136	130		−1			97		89	**59**
60		173			138	132		−3			98		90	**60**
61		175									99		92	**61**
62		178									100		93	**62**
63		180									101		94	**63**
64		182									102		95	**64**
65											103		97	**65**
66											104		98	**66**
67											105		99	**67**
68											106		101	**68**
69											107		102	**69**
70											108		103	**70**
71											109			**71**
72											110			**72**
73											112			**73**
74											113			**74**
75											114			**75**
76											115			**76**
77											116			**77**
78											117			**78**

T-SCORE CONVERSIONS WITHOUT K CORRECTIONS FOR ADOLESCENT FEMALES AGE 16

Raw score	T-scores													Raw score
	L	F	K	1	2	3	4	5	6	7	8	9	0	
0	29	35	22	35	8	10	11	127	21	27	32	12	10	**0**
1	34	37	24	37	10	12	14	125	24	29	33	14	12	**1**
2	38	39	26	40	12	14	16	122	27	30	34	17	13	**2**
3	42	41	28	42	14	16	18	120	29	32	35	19	15	**3**
4	47	44	30	44	16	18	20	118	32	33	36	21	16	**4**
5	51	46	33	47	18	20	23	116	35	34	38	23	17	**5**
6	56	48	35	49	20	22	25	113	37	36	39	26	18	**6**
7	60	50	37	51	22	24	27	111	40	37	40	28	20	**7**
8	64	53	39	54	24	26	29	109	42	38	41	30	21	**8**
9	69	55	41	56	26	28	31	106	45	40	42	32	22	**9**
10	73	57	44	58	28	30	33	104	48	41	43	35	23	**10**
11	78	59	46	61	30	32	36	102	50	42	44	37	24	**11**
12	82	62	48	63	32	34	38	100	53	44	45	39	26	**12**
13	86	64	50	65	34	36	40	98	55	45	46	41	27	**13**
14	91	66	52	67	36	38	42	96	58	46	47	44	28	**14**
15	95	68	55	70	38	40	44	94	61	48	48	46	29	**15**
16		71	57	72	40	42	47	91	63	49	49	48	31	**16**
17		73	59	74	43	44	49	89	66	50	50	50	32	**17**
18		75	61	77	45	46	51	87	68	52	51	53	33	**18**
19		77	63	79	47	48	53	84	71	53	52	55	34	**19**
20		80	66	81	49	50	55	82	74	54	53	57	36	**20**
21		82	68	84	51	52	57	80	76	56	54	59	37	**21**
22		84	70	86	53	54	60	77	79	57	55	62	38	**22**
23		86	72	88	55	56	62	75	81	58	56	64	39	**23**
24		89	74	91	57	57	64	73	84	60	58	66	41	**24**
25		91	77	93	59	59	66	70	87	61	59	68	42	**25**
26		93	79	95	61	61	68	68	89	62	60	71	43	**26**
27		95	81	98	63	63	71	66	92	64	61	73	44	**27**
28		98	83	100	65	65	73	64	94	65	62	75	46	**28**
29		100	85	102	67	67	75	61	97	66	63	77	47	**29**
30		102	88	105	69	69	77	59	99	67	64	80	48	**30**
31		104		107	71	71	79	57	102	69	65	82	49	**31**
32		107		109	73	73	82	54	105	70	66	84	51	**32**
33		109		112	75	75	84	52	107	71	67	86	52	**33**
34		111			77	77	86	50	110	73	68	89	53	**34**
35		113			79	79	88	47	112	74	69	91	54	**35**
36		116			81	81	90	45	115	75	70	93	55	**36**
37		118			83	83	92	43	118	77	71	95	57	**37**
38		120			85	85	95	40	120	78	72	98	58	**38**
39		122			87	87	97	38	123	79	73	100	59	**39**
40		125			89	89	99	36	125	81	74	102	60	**40**
41		127			92	91	101	34		82	75	104	62	**41**
42		129			94	93	103	31		83	77	106	63	**42**

Raw score	T-scores													Raw score
	L	F	K	1	2	3	4	5	6	7	8	9	0	
43		131			96	95	106	29		85	78	109	64	**43**
44		134			98	97	108	27		86	79	111	65	**44**
45		136			100	99	110	24		87	80	113	67	**45**
46		138			102	101	112	22		89	81	115	68	**46**
47		140			104	103	114	20		90	82		69	**47**
48		143			106	105	116	17		91	83		70	**48**
49		145			108	107	119	15			84		72	**49**
50		147			110	109	121	13			85		73	**50**
51		149			112	111		10			86		74	**51**
52		152			114	113		8			87		75	**52**
53		154			116	115		6			88		77	**53**
54		156			118	117		4			89		78	**54**
55		158			120	119		1			90		79	**55**
56		161			122	121		−1			91		80	**56**
57		163			124	123		−3			92		82	**57**
58		165			126	124		−6			93		83	**58**
59		167			128	126		−8			94		84	**59**
60		170			130	128		−10			95		85	**60**
61		172									97		86	**61**
62		174									99		88	**62**
63		176									100		89	**63**
64		178									101		90	**64**
65											102		91	**65**
66											103		93	**66**
67											104		94	**67**
68											105		95	**68**
69											106		96	**69**
70											107		98	**70**
71											108			**71**
72											109			**72**
73											110			**73**
74											111			**74**
75											112			**75**
76											113			**76**
77											114			**77**
78														**78**

T-SCORE CONVERSIONS WITHOUT K CORRECTIONS FOR ADOLESCENT FEMALES AGES 17 AND 18

Raw score	T-scores													Raw score
	L	F	K	1	2	3	4	5	6	7	8	9	0	
0	28	32	18	31	5	7	7	125	21	25	29	15	7	**0**
1	33	35	21	34	7	9	10	122	24	27	31	17	9	**1**
2	37	37	23	36	9	11	12	120	27	28	32	19	10	**2**
3	41	40	26	38	11	13	14	117	30	30	33	22	11	**3**
4	45	42	28	41	13	15	17	115	33	31	35	24	13	**4**
5	49	45	31	43	15	17	19	113	35	33	36	26	14	**5**
6	54	47	33	45	17	19	21	111	38	34	37	28	15	**6**
7	58	49	36	48	20	21	24	108	41	36	38	30	17	**7**
8	62	52	38	50	22	23	26	106	44	37	39	32	18	**8**
9	66	54	41	52	24	25	28	104	47	39	40	34	19	**9**
10	70	57	44	55	26	27	31	102	50	40	41	37	21	**10**
11	74	59	46	57	28	29	33	100	53	42	43	39	22	**11**
12	79	62	49	59	30	31	35	98	56	43	44	41	23	**12**
13	83	64	51	61	32	33	37	96	59	44	45	43	25	**13**
14	87	67	54	64	35	35	40	94	61	46	46	45	26	**14**
15	91	69	56	66	37	37	42	92	64	47	47	47	27	**15**
16		72	59	68	39	39	44	89	67	49	48	50	29	**16**
17		74	61	71	41	41	47	87	70	50	49	52	30	**17**
18		77	64	73	43	43	49	85	73	52	50	54	31	**18**
19		79	66	75	45	45	51	83	76	53	52	56	33	**19**
20		81	69	77	47	47	54	80	79	55	53	58	34	**20**
21		84	71	80	50	49	56	78	82	56	54	60	35	**21**
22		86	74	82	52	51	58	76	84	58	55	63	37	**22**
23		89	76	84	54	53	61	74	87	59	56	65	38	**23**
24		91	79	87	56	55	63	71	90	60	57	67	39	**24**
25		94	81	89	58	57	65	69	93	62	58	69	41	**25**
26		96	84	91	60	59	67	67	96	63	60	71	42	**26**
27		99	86	93	62	61	70	65	99	65	61	73	43	**27**
28		101	89	96	65	63	72	62	102	66	62	76	45	**28**
29		104	91	98	67	65	74	60	105	68	63	78	46	**29**
30		106	94	100	69	67	77	58	108	69	64	80	47	**30**
31		109		103	71	69	79	56	110	71	65	82	49	**31**
32		111		105	73	71	81	53	113	72	66	84	50	**32**
33		113		107	75	73	84	51	116	74	68	86	51	**33**
34		116			78	75	86	49	119	75	69	89	53	**34**
35		118			80	77	88	47	122	77	70	91	54	**35**
36		121			82	79	91	44	125	78	71	93	55	**36**
37		123			84	81	93	42	128	79	72	95	57	**37**
38		126			86	83	95	40	131	81	73	97	58	**38**
39		128			88	85	98	38	134	82	74	99	59	**39**
40		131			90	87	100	36	136	84	76	101	61	**40**
41		133			93	89	102	33		85	77	104	62	**41**
42		136			95	91	104	31		87	78	106	63	**42**

Raw score	T-scores													Raw score
	L	F	K	1	2	3	4	5	6	7	8	9	0	
43		138			97	93	107	29		88	79	108	65	**43**
44		141			99	95	109	27		90	80	110	66	**44**
45		143			101	97	111	24		91	81	112	67	**45**
46		145			103	99	114	22		93	82	114	69	**46**
47		148			105	101	116	20		94	84		70	**47**
48		150			108	103	118	18		95	85		71	**48**
49		153			110	105	121	15			86		73	**49**
50		155			112	107	123	13			87		74	**50**
51		158			114	109		11			88		75	**51**
52		160			116	111		9			89		77	**52**
53		163			118	113		6			90		78	**53**
54		165			120	115		4			92		79	**54**
55		168			123	117		2			93		81	**55**
56		170			125	119					94		82	**56**
57		173			127	121		−3			95		83	**57**
58		175			129	123		−5			96		85	**58**
59		177			131	125		−7			97		86	**59**
60		180			133	127		−9			98		87	**60**
61		182									100		89	**61**
62		185									101		90	**62**
63		187									102		91	**63**
64		190									103		93	**64**
65											104		94	**65**
66											105		95	**66**
67											106		97	**67**
68											108		98	**68**
69											109		99	**69**
70											110		101	**70**
71											111			**71**
72											112			**72**
73											113			**73**
74											114			**74**
75											116			**75**
76											117			**76**
77											118			**77**
78											119			**78**

Appendix D. Composition of Harris Subscales

Scale 2–Depression

D_1–Subjective Depression
- True: 32, 41, 43, 52, 67, 86, 104, 138, 142, 158, 159, 182, 189, 236, 259
- False: 2, 8, 46, 57, 88, 107, 122, 131, 152, 160, 191, 207, 208, 242, 272, 285, 296

D_2–Psychomotor Retardation
- True: 41, 52, 182, 259
- False: 8, 30, 39, 57, 64, 89, 95, 145, 207, 208, 233

D_3–Physical Malfunctioning
- True: 130, 189, 193, 288
- False: 2, 18, 51, 153, 154, 155, 160

D_4–Mental Dullness
- True: 32, 41, 86, 104, 159, 182, 259, 290
- False: 8, 9, 46, 88, 122, 178, 207

D_5–Brooding
- True: 41, 67, 104, 138, 142, 158, 182, 236
- False: 88, 107

Scale 3–Hysteria

Hy_1–Denial of Social Anxiety
- True: None
- False: 141, 172, 180, 201, 267, 292

Hy_2–Need for Affection
- True: 253
- False: 26, 71, 89, 93, 109, 124, 136, 162, 234, 265, 289

Hy_3–Lassitude-Malaise
- True: 32, 43, 76, 189, 238
- False: 2, 3, 8, 9, 51, 107, 137, 153, 160, 163

Hy_4–Somatic Complaints
- True: 10, 23, 44, 47, 114, 186
- False: 7, 55, 103, 174, 175, 188, 190, 192, 230, 243, 274

Hy_5–Inhibition of Aggression
- True: None
- False: 6, 12, 30, 128, 129, 147, 170

Scale 4–Psychopathic Deviate

Pd_1–Familial Discord
- True: 21, 42, 212, 216, 224, 245
- False: 96, 137, 235, 237, 527*

Pd_2–Authority Problems
- True: 38, 59, 118, 520*
- False: 37, 82, 141, 173, 289, 294, 429*

Pd_3–Social Imperturbability
- True: 64, 479,* 520,* 521*
- False: 82, 141, 171, 180, 201, 267, 304,* 352*

Pd_{4A}–Social Alienation
- True: 16, 24, 35, 64, 67, 94, 110, 127, 146, 239, 244, 284, 305,* 368,* 520*
- False: 20, 141, 170

Pd_{4B}–Self-Alienation
- True: 32, 33, 61, 67, 76, 84, 94, 102, 106, 127, 146, 215, 368*
- False: 8, 107

Scale 6–Paranoia

Pa_1–Persecutory Ideas
- True: 16, 24, 35, 110, 121, 123, 127, 151, 157, 202, 275, 284, 291, 293, 338, 364
- False: 347

Pa_2–Poignancy
- True: 24, 158, 299, 305, 317, 341, 365
- False: 111, 268

Pa_3–Naiveté
- True: 15
- False: 93, 109, 117, 124, 313, 316, 319, 348

Source: W. G. Dahlstrom, G. S. Welsh, & L. E. Dahlstrom, *An MMPI Handbook,* Vol. I. The University of Minnesota Press, Minneapolis. Copyright 1960, 1972 by the University of Minnesota. Reproduced with permission.

*Although these items were included in Pd subscales by Harris & Lingoes, they are not in the Pd scale. Because they have been included in past scoring and research with the subscales, it is this author's recommendation that they be retained in the subscales.

Scale 8–Schizophrenia

Sc_{1A}–Social Alienation
True: 16, 21, 24, 35, 52, 121, 157, 212, 241, 282, 305, 312, 324, 325, 352, 364
False: 65, 220, 276, 306, 309

Sc_{1B}–Emotional Alienation
True: 76, 104, 202, 301, 339, 355, 360, 363
False: 8, 196, 322

Sc_{2A}–Lack of Ego Mastery, Cognitive
True: 32, 33, 159, 168, 182, 335, 345, 349, 356
False: 178

Sc_{2B}–Lack of Ego Mastery, Conative
True: 32, 40, 41, 76, 104, 202, 259, 301, 335, 339, 356
False: 8, 196, 322

Sc_{2C}–Lack of Ego Mastery, Defective Inhibition
True: 22, 97, 156, 194, 238, 266, 291, 303, 352, 354, 360
False: None

Sc_3–Bizarre Sensory Experiences
True: 22, 33, 47, 156, 194, 210, 251, 273, 291, 332, 334, 341, 345, 350
False: 103, 119, 187, 192, 281, 330

Scale 9–Hypomania

Ma_1–Amorality
True: 143, 250, 271, 277, 298
False: 289

Ma_2–Psychomotor Acceleration
True: 13, 97, 100, 134, 181, 228, 238, 266, 268
False: 111, 119

Ma_3–Imperturbability
True: 167, 222, 240
False: 105, 148, 171, 180, 267

Ma_4–Ego Inflation
True: 11, 59, 64, 73, 109, 157, 212, 232, 233
False: None

Appendix E. T-Score Conversions for Harris Subscales

Raw score	D1	D2	D3	D4	D5	Hy1	Hy2	Hy3	Hy4	Hy5	Pd1	Pd2	Pd3	Pd4A	Pd4B
								Males							
32	122														
31	119														
30	117														
29	114														
28	111														
27	108														
26	105														
25	102														
24	99														
23	96														
22	93														
21	91														
20	88														
19	85														
18	82													95	
17	79								106					91	
16	76								102					88	
15	73	103		114				104	98					84	93
14	70	98		109				100	94					81	89
13	67	92		104				95	91					77	85
12	65	87		100			79	91	87				68	74	81
11	62	81	104	95			75	87	83		103	92	64	70	77
10	59	76	98	90	92		71	83	79		98	86	60	66	74
9	56	70	91	85	87		66	79	75		92	80	56	63	70
8	53	65	84	80	82		62	74	71		86	74	52	59	66
7	50	59	77	75	76		58	70	67	82	80	67	48	56	62
6	47	54	70	70	71	64	54	66	63	75	74	61	44	52	58
5	44	48	63	65	65	59	50	62	59	68	69	55	40	49	54
4	41	43	56	60	60	53	46	57	55	60	63	49	35	45	51
3	39	37	49	55	54	47	42	53	51	53	57	43	31	42	47
2	36	32	42	50	49	42	38	49	47	46	51	37	27	38	43
1	33	26	35	45	44	36	34	45	43	39	45	30	23	35	39
0	30	21	29	40	38	31	30	41	39	31	39	24	19	31	35

Source: W. G. Dahlstrom, G. S. Welsh, & L. E. Dahlstrom, *An MMPI Handbook*, Vol. I. The University of Minnesota Press, Minneapolis. Copyright 1960, 1972 by the University of Minnesota. Reproduced with permission.

Raw score	D1	D2	D3	D4	D5	Hy1	Hy2	Hy3	Hy4	Hy5	Pd1	Pd2	Pd3	Pd4A	Pd4B
Females															
32	109														
31	106														
30	104														
29	101														
28	99														
27	96														
26	94														
25	91														
24	89														
23	86														
22	84														
21	81														
20	79														
19	76														
18	74													96	
17	71								93					92	
16	69								89					89	
15	66	97		110				97	86					85	93
14	64	92		106				93	83					81	90
13	61	86		101				90	79					78	86
12	59	81		96			81	86	76				69	74	82
11	56	76	99	91			77	82	73		103	106	66	70	78
10	54	71	93	87	88		73	78	69		98	98	62	67	74
9	51	66	87	82	83		69	74	66		92	91	58	63	70
8	49	61	80	77	77		64	70	63		86	84	54	59	67
7	46	56	74	72	72		60	67	59	74	80	76	50	56	63
6	44	51	67	68	66	65	56	63	56	67	74	69	47	52	59
5	41	45	61	63	61	59	51	59	53	60	69	62	43	49	55
4	39	40	55	58	55	54	47	55	49	54	63	54	39	45	51
3	36	35	48	54	50	48	43	51	46	47	57	47	35	41	47
2	34	30	42	49	45	43	39	47	43	41	51	40	31	38	44
1	31	25	36	44	39	38	34	44	39	34	45	32	28	34	40
0	29	20	29	39	34	32	30	40	36	27	39	25	24	30	36

Appendix E. *(Continued)*

Raw score	Pa1	Pa2	Pa3	Sc1A	Sc1B	Sc2A	Sc2B	Sc2C	Sc3	Ma1	Ma2	Ma3	Ma4
							Males						
32													
31													
30													
29													
28													
27													
26													
25													
24													
23													
22													
21													
20				120					121				
19				116					117				
18				111					113				
17	117			107					109				
16	113			103					105				
15	108			99					101				
14	104			94			115		97				
13	99			90			110		93				
12	95			86			105		89				
11	90			82			99	112	85		102		
10	86			77	118	103	94	106	81		95		
9	82	95	76	73	109	97	88	99	77		87		89
8	77	88	71	69	101	91	83	93	73		80	77	83
7	73	81	66	65	92	85	77	86	69		73	71	77
6	68	75	61	60	83	78	72	80	65	81	66	65	71
5	64	68	56	56	74	72	66	73	60	74	59	59	65
4	59	62	51	52	66	66	61	67	56	67	52	53	58
3	55	55	46	48	57	60	55	60	52	59	45	47	52
2	50	49	41	44	48	53	50	54	48	52	38	42	46
1	46	42	36	39	39	47	45	47	44	45	31	36	40
0	41	36	31	35	31	41	39	41	40	37	24	30	34

Raw score	Pa1	Pa2	Pa3	Sc1A	Sc1B	Sc2A	Sc2B	Sc2C	Sc3	Ma1	Ma2	Ma3	Ma4
						Females							
32													
31													
30													
29													
28													
27													
26													
25													
24													
23													
22													
21													
20				117					118				
19				113					114				
18				109					110				
17	124			105					106				
16	119			101					102				
15	114			97					98				
14	110			93			110		94				
13	105			88			105		91				
12	100			84			100		87				
11	95			80			95	102	83		98		
10	90			76	120	104	90	96	79		92		
9	85	97	78	72	111	98	85	91	75		85		88
8	80	90	73	68	103	91	80	85	71		79	81	82
7	75	83	68	64	94	85	74	80	67		73	75	76
6	71	76	62	60	85	79	69	74	63	89	66	69	70
5	66	69	57	55	76	72	64	69	59	81	60	63	64
4	61	62	52	51	67	66	59	63	55	72	53	57	58
3	56	55	47	47	58	60	54	58	51	64	47	51	52
2	51	49	42	43	50	53	49	52	47	55	41	45	46
1	46	42	37	39	41	47	44	46	43	47	34	39	40
0	41	35	32	35	32	41	39	41	39	38	28	33	34

Appendix F. Composition of Scale 5 and Scale 0 Subscales

Mf1–Narcissism-Hypersensitivity
True: 25, 89, 117, 179, 217, 226, 239, 278, 282, 297, 299
False: 79, 133, 187, 198, 214, 262, 264

Mf2–Stereotypic Feminine Interests
True: 4, 70, 74, 77, 78, 87, 92, 132, 140, 149, 204, 261, 295
False: 300

Mf3–Denial of Stereotypic Masculine Interests
True: None
False: 1, 81, 144, 176, 219, 221, 223, 283

Mf4–Heterosexual Discomfort-Passivity
True: 69
False: 19, 80, 231

Mf5–Introspective-Critical
True: 204
False: 92, 99, 115, 249, 254, 264

Mf6–Socially Retiring
True: None
False: 89, 99, 112, 116, 117, 126, 140, 203, 229

Si1–Inferiority-Personal Discomfort
True: 32, 67, 82, 138, 147, 171, 172, 180, 201, 236, 267, 278, 292, 304, 321, 336, 359, 377, 383, 411, 455, 549, 564
False: 57, 309, 353, 371

Si2–Discomfort with Others
True: 357, 377, 427, 469, 473, 487, 505
False: 449, 450, 462, 479, 481, 521, 547

Si3–Staid-Personal Rigidity
True: None
False: 33, 91, 99, 143, 208, 229, 231, 254, 400, 415, 440, 446, 449, 450, 469, 505

Si4–Hypersensitivity
True: 25, 32, 126, 138, 236, 278, 391, 427, 487, 549
False: None

Si5–Distrust
True: 117, 124, 147, 278, 316, 359, 383, 398, 411, 436, 481, 482
False: None

Si6–Physical-Somatic Concerns
True: 33, 236, 332
False: 119, 193, 262, 281, 309, 449, 451

Source: K. Serkownek, *Subscales for Scales 5 and 0 of the Minnesota Multiphasic Personality Inventory*. Unpublished materials, Cleveland, OH.

Appendix G. T-Score Conversions for Scale 5 and Scale 0 Subscales

Raw score	Males						Females					
	Si1	Si2	Si3	Si4	Si5	Si6	Si1	Si2	Si3	Si4	Si5	Si6
27	131						126					
26	127						122					
25	123						118					
24	118						114					
23	114						109					
22	110						105					
21	105						101					
20	101						97					
19	96						92					
18	92						88					
17	88						84					
16	83		88				80		82			
15	79		82				76		76			
14	75	113	77				71	110	70			
13	70	106	72				67	104	64			
12	66	100	66		97		63	97	58		99	
11	61	94	61		90		59	91	53		92	
10	57	87	55	103	84	122	54	85	47	91	86	119
9	53	81	50	95	77	114	50	79	41	84	79	110
8	48	75	45	88	71	105	46	73	35	77	73	102
7	44	68	39	80	64	96	42	66	29	70	66	94
6	40	62	34	72	58	87	37	60	23	63	60	85
5	35	55	28	65	52	79	33	54	17	56	53	77
4	31	49	23	57	45	70	29	48	12	49	47	69
3	26	43	18	50	39	62	25	42	6	42	41	60
2	22	36	12	42	32	53	20	35	0	35	34	52
1	18	30	7	35	26	44	16	29	0	28	28	44
0	13	24	1	28	20	36	12	23	0	21	21	35

Appendix G. *(Continued)*

Raw score	Males						Females					
	Mf1	Mf2	Mf3	Mf4	Mf5	Mf6	Mf1	Mf2	Mf3	Mf4	Mf5	Mf6
18	122						115					
17	116						108					
16	111						103					
15	105						97					
14	100	121					92	84				
13	94	115					86	78				
12	89	108					81	72				
11	83	101					75	66				
10	78	95					70	60				
9	72	88				77	64	54				81
8	67	81	88			70	59	48	66			73
7	61	74	81		81	63	53	42	58		82	66
6	56	68	73		73	56	48	36	49		73	58
5	50	61	66		64	49	43	30	40		64	52
4	45	54	58	70	55	42	37	24	31	68	55	44
3	39	48	51	58	46	35	32	18	22	53	46	37
2	34	41	43	46	37	28	26	12	13	38	37	30
1	28	34	35	33	29	21	21	6	5	23	29	22
0	23	27	28	21	20	14	15	0	0	8	20	15

Source: K. Serkownek, *Subscales for Scales 5 and 0 of the Minnesota Multiphasic Personality Inventory.* Unpublished materials, Cleveland, OH.

Appendix H. Composition of Wiggins Content Scales

SOC–Social Maladjustment
- True: 52, 171, 172, 180, 201, 267, 292, 304, 377, 384, 453, 455, 509
- False: 57, 91, 99, 309, 371, 391, 449, 450, 479, 482, 502, 520, 521, 547

DEP–Depression
- True: 41, 61, 67, 76, 94, 104, 106, 158, 202, 209, 210, 217, 259, 305, 337, 338, 339, 374, 390, 396, 413, 414, 487, 517, 518, 526, 543
- False: 8, 79, 88, 207, 379, 407

FEM–Feminine Interests
- True: 70, 74, 77, 78, 87, 92, 126, 132, 140, 149, 203, 261, 295, 463, 538, 554, 557, 562
- False: 1, 81, 219, 221, 223, 283, 300, 423, 434, 537, 552, 563

MOR–Poor Morale
- True: 84, 86, 138, 142, 244, 321, 357, 361, 375, 382, 389, 395, 397, 398, 411, 416, 418, 431, 531, 549, 555
- False: 122, 264

REL–Religious Fundamentalism
- True: 58, 95, 98, 115, 206, 249, 258, 373, 483, 488, 490
- False: 491

AUT–Authority Conflict
- True: 59, 71, 93, 116, 117, 118, 124, 250, 265, 277, 280, 298, 313, 316, 319, 406, 436, 437, 446
- False: 294

PSY–Psychoticism
- True: 16, 22, 24, 27, 33, 35, 40, 48, 50, 66, 73, 110, 121, 123, 127, 136, 151, 168, 184, 194, 197, 200, 232, 275, 278, 284, 291, 293, 299, 312, 317, 334, 341, 345, 348, 349, 350, 364, 400, 420, 433, 448, 476, 511, 551
- False: 198, 347, 464

ORG–Organic Symptoms
- True: 23, 44, 108, 114, 156, 159, 161, 186, 189, 251, 273, 332, 335, 541, 560
- False: 46, 68, 103, 119, 154, 174, 175, 178, 185, 187, 188, 190, 192, 243, 274, 281, 330, 405, 496, 508, 540

FAM–Family Problems
- True: 21, 212, 216, 224, 226, 239, 245, 325, 327, 421, 516
- False: 65, 96, 137, 220, 527

HOS–Manifest Hostility
- True: 28, 39, 80, 89, 109, 129, 139, 145, 162, 218, 269, 282, 336, 355, 363, 368, 393, 410, 417, 426, 438, 447, 452, 468, 469, 495, 536
- False: None

PHO–Phobias
- True: 166, 182, 351, 352, 360, 365, 385, 388, 392, 473, 480, 492, 494, 499, 525, 553
- False: 128, 131, 169, 176, 287, 353, 367, 401, 412, 522, 539

HYP–Hypomania
- True: 13, 134, 146, 181, 196, 228, 234, 238, 248, 266, 268, 272, 296, 340, 342, 372, 381, 386, 409, 439, 445, 465, 500, 505, 506
- False: None

HEA–Poor Health
- True: 10, 14, 29, 34, 72, 125, 279, 424, 519, 544
- False: 2, 18, 36, 51, 55, 63, 130, 153, 155, 163, 193, 214, 230, 462, 474, 486, 533, 542

Source: J. S. Wiggins, Substantive dimensions of self-report in the MMPI item pool. *Psychological Monographs,* 1966, *80* (22, Whole No. 630).

Appendix I. T-Score Conversions for Wiggins Content Scales

Raw score	SOC	DEP	FEM	MOR	REL	AUT	PSY	ORG	FAM	HOS	PHO	HYP	HEA
							Females						
43							120						
42							118						
41							116						
40							114						
39							112						
38							110						
37							108						
36							106	114					
35							104	112					
34							102	109					
33		98					100	107					
32		96					98	105					
31		94					96	103					
30		92	80				94	101					
29		90	77				92	98					
28		88	74				90	96					106
27	83	86	71				88	94		90	91		104
26	81	84	68				86	92		87	89		101
25	79	82	65				84	90		85	86	82	99
24	77	80	62				82	87		83	84	79	96
23	75	78	59	76			80	85		81	82	76	94
22	73	76	56	74			78	83		79	80	74	91
21	71	74	53	72			76	81		77	77	71	89
20	69	72	51	70		82	74	79		75	75	69	86
19	67	70	48	68		79	72	77		72	73	66	83
18	65	68	45	66		77	70	74		70	70	63	81
17	63	66	42	64		74	68	72		68	68	61	78
16	61	64	39	62		71	66	70	98	66	66	58	76
15	59	62	36	60		69	64	68	94	64	64	56	73
14	57	60	33	58		66	63	66	90	62	61	53	71
13	55	58	30	56		63	61	63	86	59	59	50	68
12	53	56	27	54	68	61	59	61	82	57	57	48	65
11	52	54	24	52	64	58	57	59	78	55	55	45	63
10	50	53	21	50	60	55	55	57	74	53	52	43	60
9	48	51	18	48	57	53	53	55	70	51	50	40	58
8	46	49	15	46	53	50	51	52	66	49	48	37	55

Raw score	SOC	DEP	FEM	MOR	REL	AUT	PSY	ORG	FAM	HOS	PHO	HYP	HEA
							Females						
7	44	47	13	44	49	47	49	50	62	47	45	35	53
6	42	45	10	42	46	45	47	48	58	44	43	32	50
5	40	43	07	40	42	42	45	46	54	42	41	30	48
4	38	41	04	38	38	39	43	44	50	40	39	27	45
3	36	39	01	36	35	36	41	42	46	38	36	24	42
2	34	37		34	31	34	39	39	42	36	34	22	40
1	32	35		32	27	31	37	37	38	34	32	19	37
0	30	33		30	24	28	35	35	34	31	30	17	35

Source: J. S. Wiggins, Content scales: Basic data for scoring and interpretation. Unpublished materials, 1971. Reproduced by permission.

Raw score	SOC	DEP	FEM	MOR	REL	AUT	PSY	ORG	FAM	HOS	PHO	HYP	HEA
							Males						
48							119						
47							117						
46							116						
45							114						
44							112						
43							110						
42							109						
41							107						
							105						
40							104						
39							102						
37							100						
36							98						
35							97	120					
34							95	117					
33		101					93	115					
32		99					91	113					
31		97					90	110					
30		95	108				88	108					
29		93	105				86	106					
28		91	102				85	103					110
27	88	89	100				83	101		86	107		107
26	86	87	97				81	98		84	104		105

Appendix I. *(Continued)*

Raw score	SOC	DEP	FEM	MOR	REL	AUT	PSY	ORG	FAM	HOS	PHO	HYP	HEA
						Males							
25	84	85	94				79	96		82	102	80	102
24	82	83	91				78	94		79	99	77	99
23	80	81	89	80			76	91		77	96	75	97
22	78	79	86	78			74	89		75	94	73	94
21	76	77	83	76			72	87		73	91	71	92
20	74	75	80	74		76	71	84		71	88	68	89
19	72	73	77	72		74	69	82		69	86	66	87
18	70	71	75	70		71	67	80		67	83	64	84
17	67	69	72	68		69	65	77		65	80	62	81
16	65	68	69	66		66	64	75	103	63	78	59	79
15	63	66	66	64		64	62	73	99	61	75	57	76
14	61	64	64	62		61	60	70	94	59	72	55	74
13	59	62	61	60		59	59	68	90	57	70	53	71
12	57	60	58	58	69	56	57	66	86	55	67	50	68
11	55	58	55	56	65	54	55	63	81	53	64	48	66
10	53	56	52	54	62	51	53	61	77	51	62	46	63
9	51	54	50	52	59	49	52	59	73	49	59	44	61
8	49	52	47	50	56	46	50	56	68	47	56	41	58
7	47	50	44	48	52	44	48	54	64	45	54	39	55
6	45	48	41	46	49	41	46	52	60	43	51	37	53
5	43	46	39	44	46	39	45	49	56	41	48	34	50
4	40	44	36	42	42	36	43	47	51	39	46	32	48
3	38	42	33	40	39	34	41	45	47	37	43	30	45
2	36	40	30	38	36	31	40	42	43	35	40	28	42
1	34	38	27	36	32	29	38	40	38	33	38	25	40
0	32	36	25	34	29	26	36	37	34	31	35	23	37

Appendix J. Critical Item Lists

KOSS-BUTCHER CRITICAL ITEMS

Acute Anxiety State

2. I have a good appetite. (F)
3. I wake up fresh and rested most mornings. (F)
5. I am easily awakened by noise. (T)
9. I am about as able to work as I ever was. (F)
13. I work under a great deal of tension. (T)
29. I am bothered by acid stomach several times a week. (T)
43. My sleep is fitful and disturbed. (T)
72. I am troubled by discomfort in the pit of my stomach every few days or oftener. (T)
152. Most nights I go to sleep without thoughts or ideas bothering me. (F)
186. I frequently notice my hand shakes when I try to do something. (T)
230. I hardly ever notice my heart pounding and I am seldom short of breath. (F)
238. I have periods of such great restlessness that I cannot sit long in a chair. (T)
242. I believe I am no more nervous than most others. (F)
290. I work under a great deal of tension. (T)
337. I feel anxiety about something or someone almost all the time. (T)
506. I am a high-strung person. (T)
543. Several times a week I feel that something dreadful is going to happen. (T)
555. I sometimes feel that I am about to go to pieces. (T)

Depressed Suicidal Ideation

41. I have periods of days or weeks when I couldn't get going. (T)
76. Most of the time I feel blue. (T)
84. These days I find it hard not to give up hope of amounting to something. (F)
88. I usually feel that life is worthwhile. (F)
104. I don't seem to care what happens to me. (T)
107. I am happy most of the time. (F)
142. I certainly feel useless at times. (T)
158. I cry easily. (T)
236. I brood a great deal. (T)
252. No one cares much what happens to you. (T)
259. I have difficulty starting to do things. (T)
301. Life is a strain for me much of the time. (T)
318. My life is full of things that keep me interested. (F)
339. Most of the time I wish I were dead. (T)
379. I very seldom have spells of the blues. (F)
418. At times I feel I am no good at all. (T)
526. The future seems hopeless to me. (T)

Threatened Assault

39. At times I feel like smashing things. (T)
97. At times I have a strong urge to do something harmful or shocking. (T)

145. At times I feel like picking a fist fight with someone. (T)
234. I get mad easily and get over it soon. (T)
381. I am often said to be hotheaded. (T)

Situational Stress Due to Alcoholism

137. I believe that my home life is as pleasant as that of most people I know. (F)
215. I have used alcohol excessively. (T)
460. I have used alcohol moderately (or not at all). (F)

Mental Confusion

27. Evil spirits possess me at times. (T)
33. I have had strange and peculiar experiences. (T)
50. My soul sometimes leaves my body. (T)
66. I see things or animals or people around me that others do not see. (T)
168. There is something wrong with my mind. (T)
184. I commonly hear voices without knowing where they come from. (T)
323. I have had very peculiar and strange experiences. (T)
328. I find it hard to keep my mind on a task or job. (T)
335. I cannot keep my mind on one thing. (T)
345. I often feel as if things were not real. (T)
349. I have strange and peculiar thoughts. (T)
356. I have more trouble concentrating than others seem to have. (T)

Persecutory Ideas

16. I am sure I get a raw deal from life. (T)
35. If people had not had it in for me I would have been much more successful. (T)
110. Someone has it in for me. (T)
121. I believe I am being plotted against. (T)
123. I believe I am being followed. (T)
136. I commonly wonder what hidden reason another person may have for doing something nice for me. (T)
151. Someone has been trying to poison me. (T)
157. I feel I have often been punished without cause. (T)
197. Someone has been trying to rob me. (T)
200. There are persons who are trying to steal my thoughts and ideas. (T)
265. It is safer to trust nobody. (T)
278. I have often felt that strangers were looking at me critically. (T)
284. I am sure I am being talked about. (T)
293. Someone has been trying to influence my mind. (T)
315. I am sure I get a raw deal from life. (T)
331. If people had not had it in for me I would have been much more successful. (T)
347. I have no enemies who really wish to harm me. (F)
364. People say insulting and vulgar things about me. (T)

LACHAR-WROBEL CRITICAL ITEMS

Anxiety and Tension

13. I work under a great deal of tension. (T)
16. I am sure I get a raw deal from life. (T)
186. I frequently notice my hand shakes when I try to do something. (T)
238. I have periods of such great restlessness that I cannot sit long in a chair. (T)
242. I believe I am no more nervous than most others. (F)
287. I have very few fears compared to my friends. (F)

335. I cannot keep my mind on one thing. (T)
337. I feel anxiety about something or someone almost all the time. (T)
352. I have been afraid of things or people that I knew could not hurt me. (T)
407. I am usually calm and not easily upset. (F)
543. Several times a week I feel as if something dreadful is about to happen. (T)

Depression and Worry

2. I have a good appetite. (F)
3. I wake up fresh and rested most mornings. (F)
9. I am about as able to work as I ever was. (F)
76. Most of the time I feel blue. (T)
86. I am certainly lacking in self-confidence. (T)
88. I usually feel that life is worthwhile. (F)
139. Sometimes I feel as if I must injure either myself or someone else. (T)
142. I certainly feel useless at times. (T)
168. There is something wrong with my mind. (T)
178. My memory seems to be all right. (F)
301. Life is a strain for me much of the time. (T)
339. Most of the time I wish I were dead. (T)
397. I have sometimes felt that difficulties were piling up so high that I could not overcome them. (T)
418. At times I think I am no good at all. (T)
431. I worry quite a bit over possible misfortune. (T)
526. The future seems hopeless to me. (T)

Sleep Disturbance

5. I am easily awakened by noise. (T)
31. I have nightmares every few nights. (T)
43. My sleep is fitful and disturbed. (T)
152. Most nights I go to sleep without thoughts or ideas bothering me. (F)
359. Sometimes some unimportant thought will run through my mind and bother me for days. (T)
559. I have often been frightened in the middle of the night. (T)

Deviant Beliefs

110. Someone has it in for me. (T)
119. My speech is the same as always (not faster or slower, or slurring; no hoarseness). (F)
121. I believe I am being plotted against. (T)
123. I believe I am being followed. (T)
151. Someone has been trying to poison me. (T)
197. Someone has been trying to rob me. (T)
200. There are persons who are trying to steal my thoughts and ideas. (T)
275. Someone has control over my mind. (T)
284. I am sure I am being talked about. (T)
291. At one or more times in my life I felt that someone was making me do things by hypnotizing me. (T)
293. Someone has been trying to influence my mind. (T)
331. If people had not had it in for me I would have been much more successful. (T)
347. I have no enemies who really wish to harm me. (F)
364. People say insulting and vulgar things about me. (T)

Source for MMPI item numbers (group form) is Lachar and Wrobel (1979). Item numbers are reproduced with permission of American Psychological Association. The actual MMPI items are copyrighted by the University of Minnesota (1943, 1970) and are reproduced with permission of the University of Minnesota Press.

551. Sometimes I am sure that other people can tell what I am thinking. (T)

Deviant Thinking and Experiences

33. I have had very peculiar and strange experiences. (T)
48. When I am with people, I am bothered by hearing very queer things. (T)
66. I see things or animals or people around me that others do not see. (T)
134. At times my thoughts have raced ahead faster than I could speak them. (T)
184. I commonly hear voices without knowing where they come from. (T)
334. Peculiar odors come to me at times. (T)
341. At times I hear so well that it bothers me. (T)
349. I have strange and peculiar thoughts. (T)
350. I hear strange things when I am alone. (T)
420. I have had some very unusual religious experiences. (T)
464. I have never seen a vision. (F)

Substance Abuse

156. I have had periods in which I carried on activities without knowing later what I had been doing. (T)
215. I have used alcohol excessively. (T)
460. I have used alcohol moderately (or not at all). (F)
466. Except by a doctor's orders I never take drugs or sleeping powders. (F)

Antisocial Attitude

28. When someone does me a wrong, I feel I should pay him/her back if I can, just for the principle of the thing. (T)
38. During one period when I was a youngster I engaged in petty thievery. (T)
56. As a youngster I was suspended from school one or more times for cutting up. (T)
118. In school I was sometimes sent to the principal for cutting up. (T)
205. At times it has been impossible for me to keep from stealing or shoplifting something. (T)
250. I don't blame anyone for trying to grab everything he/she can get in this world. (T)
269. I can easily make other people afraid of me, and sometimes do for the fun of it. (T)
280. Most people make friends because friends are likely to be useful to them. (T)
294. I have never been in trouble with the law. (F)

Family Conflict

21. At times I have very much wanted to leave home. (T)
96. I have very few quarrels with members of my family. (F)
137. I believe that my home life is as pleasant as that of most people I know. (F)
245. My parents and family find more fault with me than they should. (T)

Problematic Anger

97. At times I have a strong urge to do something harmful or shocking. (T)
145. At times I feel like picking a fist fight with someone. (T)
234. I get mad easily and then get over it soon. (T)
381. I am often said to be hotheaded. (T)

Sexual Concern and Deviation

20. My sex life is satisfactory. (F)
37. I have never been in trouble because of my sex behavior. (F)
69. I am very strongly attracted by members of my own sex. (T)

74. I have often wished I were a girl. (Or, if you are a girl): I have never been sorry that I am a girl. (T/F)
133. I have never endulged in any unusual sex practices. (F)
179. I am worried about sex matters. (T)
297. I wish I were not bothered by thoughts about sex. (T)
519. There is something wrong with my sex organs. (T)

Somatic Symptoms

23. I am troubled by attacks of nausea and vomiting. (T)
29. I am bothered by acid stomach several times a week. (T)
36. I seldom worry about my health. (F)
44. Much of the time my head seems to hurt all over. (T)
47. Once a week or oftener, I feel suddenly hot all over, without apparent cause. (T)
55. I am almost never bothered by pains over the heart or in my chest. (F)
62. Parts of my body often have feelings like burning, tingling, crawling, or like "going to sleep." (T)
68. I hardly ever feel pain in the back of my neck. (F)
72. I am troubled by discomfort in the pit of my stomach every few days or oftener. (T)
114. Often I feel as if there were a tight band about my head. (T)
125. I have a great deal of stomach trouble. (T)
154. I have never had a fit or convulsion. (F)
174. I have never had a fainting spell. (F)
175. I seldom or never have dizzy spells. (F)
189. I feel weak all over much of the time. (T)
190. I have very few headaches. (F)
194. I have had attacks in which I could not control my movements or speech but in which I knew what was going on around me. (T)
243. I have few or no pains. (F)
251. I have had blank spells in which my activities were interrupted and I did not know what was going on around me. (T)
273. I have numbness in one or more regions of my skin. (T)
281. I do not often notice my ears ringing or buzzing. (F)
330. I have never been paralyzed or had any unusual weakness of any of my muscles. (F)
544. I feel tired a good deal of the time. (T)

Appendix K. Composition of Supplementary Scales

A–Anxiety (Welsh, 1956)
- True: 32, 41, 67, 76, 94, 138, 147, 236, 259, 267, 278, 301, 305, 321, 337, 343, 344, 345, 356, 359, 374, 382, 383, 384, 389, 396, 397, 411, 414, 418, 431, 443, 465, 499, 511, 518, 544, 555
- False: 379

R–Repression (Welsh, 1956)
- True: None
- False: 1, 6, 9, 12, 39, 51, 81, 112, 126, 131, 140, 145, 154, 156, 191, 208, 219, 221, 271, 272, 281, 282, 327, 406, 415, 429, 440, 445, 447, 449, 450, 451, 462, 468, 472, 502, 516, 529, 550, 556

Es–Ego Strength (Barron, 1953)
- True: 2, 36, 51, 95, 109, 153, 174, 181, 187, 192, 208, 221, 231, 234, 253, 270, 355, 367, 380, 410, 421, 430, 458, 513, 515
- False: 14, 22, 32, 33, 34, 43, 48, 58, 62, 82, 94, 100, 132, 140, 189, 209, 217, 236, 241, 244, 251, 261, 341, 344, 349, 359, 378, 384, 389, 420, 483, 488, 489, 494, 510, 525, 541, 544, 548, 554, 555, 559, 561

MAC–MacAndrew Alcoholism (MacAndrew, 1965)
- True: 6, 27, 34, 50, 56, 57, 58, 61, 81, 94, 116, 118, 127, 128, 140, 156, 186, 224, 235, 243, 251, 263, 283, 309, 413, 419, 426, 445, 446, 477, 482, 483, 488, 500, 507, 529, 562
- False: 86, 120, 130, 149, 173, 179, 278, 294, 320, 335, 356, 378

Dy–Dependency (Navran, 1954)
- True: 19, 21, 24, 41, 63, 67, 70, 82, 86, 98, 100, 138, 141, 158, 165, 180, 189, 201, 212, 236, 239, 259, 267, 304, 305, 321, 337, 338, 343, 357, 361, 362, 375, 382, 383, 390, 394, 397, 398, 408, 443, 487, 488, 489, 509, 531, 549, 554, 564
- False: 9, 79, 107, 163, 170, 193, 264, 369

Do–Dominance (Gough, McClosky, & Meehl, 1951)
- True: 64, 229, 255, 270, 368, 432, 523
- False: 32, 61, 82, 86, 94, 186, 223, 224, 240, 249, 250, 267, 268, 304, 343, 356, 395, 419, 483, 558, 562

Re–Social Responsibility (Gough, McClosky, & Meehl, 1952)
- True: 58, 111, 173, 221, 294, 412, 501, 552
- False: 6, 28, 30, 33, 56, 116, 118, 157, 175, 181, 223, 224, 260, 304, 419, 434, 437, 468, 469, 471, 472, 529, 553, 558

Cn–Control (Cuadra, 1953)
- True: 6, 20, 30, 56, 67, 105, 116, 134, 145, 162, 169, 181, 225, 236, 238, 285, 296, 319, 337, 382, 411, 418, 436, 446, 447, 460, 529, 555
- False: 58, 80, 92, 96, 111, 167, 174, 220, 242, 249, 250, 291, 313, 360, 378, 439, 444, 483, 488, 489, 527, 548

Mt–College Maladjustment (Kleinmuntz, 1961)
- True: 13, 29, 32, 41, 84, 86, 93, 94, 124, 142, 236, 238, 259, 298, 301, 314, 335, 336, 356, 361, 397, 414, 418, 442, 455, 516, 544, 555, 560
- False: 2, 3, 8, 9, 18, 46, 63, 107, 143, 152, 160, 163, 242, 407

Source: W. G. Dahlstrom, G. S. Welsh, & L. E. Dahlstrom, *An MMPI Handbook:* Vol. II. *Research Applications.* The University of Minnesota Press, Minneapolis.

O-H–Overcontrolled Hostility
(Megargee, Cook, & Mendelsohn, 1967)
True: 78, 91, 229, 319, 338, 373, 394, 425, 488, 559
False: 1, 30, 81, 90, 102, 109, 129, 130, 141, 165, 181, 183, 290, 329, 382, 396, 439, 446, 475, 501, 534

Pr–Prejudice (Gough, 1951a)
True: 47, 84, 93, 106, 117, 124, 136, 139, 157, 171, 186, 250, 280, 304, 307, 313, 319, 323, 338, 349, 373, 395, 406, 411, 435, 437, 469, 485, 543
False: 78, 176, 221

MAS–Manifest Anxiety scale (Taylor, 1953)
True: 13, 14, 23, 31, 32, 43, 67, 86, 125, 142, 158, 186, 191, 217, 238, 241, 263, 301, 317, 321, 322, 335, 337, 340, 352, 361, 397, 418, 424, 431, 439, 442, 499, 506, 530, 549, 555
False: 7, 18, 107, 163, 190, 230, 242, 264, 287, 371, 407, 523, 528

Lb–Low Back Pain (Hanvik, 1949)
True: 67, 111, 127, 238, 346
False: 3, 45, 98, 109, 148, 153, 180, 190, 230, 267, 321, 327, 378, 394, 429, 483, 502, 504, 516, 536

Ca–Caudality (Williams, 1952)
True: 28, 39, 76, 94, 142, 147, 159, 180, 182, 189, 236, 239, 273, 313, 338, 343, 361, 389, 499, 512, 544, 549, 551, 560
False: 8, 46, 57, 69, 163, 188, 242, 407, 412, 450, 513, 523

Appendix L. T-Score Conversions for Supplementary Scales

Raw score	A	R	Es	MAC	Dy	Do	Re	Cn	Mt	O-H	Pr	MAS	Lb	Ca	A	R	Es	MAC	Dy	Do	Re	Cn	Mt	O-H	Pr	MAS	Lb	Ca	Raw score
	Males														*Females*														
68			87														94												**68**
67			86														92												**67**
66			85														91												**66**
65			83														89												**65**
64			82														87												**64**
63			80														86												**63**
62			78														84												**62**
61			77														83												**61**
60			75														81												**60**
59			74														80												**59**
58			72														78												**58**
57			70		91												76		84										**57**
56			69		90												75		83										**56**
55			67		89												73		82										**55**
54			66		88												72		81										**54**
53			64		87												70		80										**53**
52			62		86												69		79										**52**
51			61		85												67		78										**51**
50			59		84			115				96					65		77			113				88			**50**
49			58		83			112				94					64		76			111				87			**49**
48			56		81			109				93					62		75			108				86			**48**
47			54		80			107				92					61		74			106				84			**47**
46			53	119	79			104				91					59		73			103				83			**46**

Raw score	A	R	Es	MAC	Dy	Do	Re	Cn	Mt	O-H	Pr	MAS	Lb	Ca	A	R	Es	MAC	Dy	Do	Re	Cn	Mt	O-H	Pr	MAS	Lb	Ca	Raw score
								Males														***Females***							
45			51	116	78			102				90					58		72			100				82			**45**
44			49	113	77			99				88					56	120	71			98				81			**44**
43			48	110	76			97	94			87					54	117	69			95	88			80			**43**
42			46	107	75			94	92			86					53	114	68			92	86			79			**42**
41			45	104	74			91	91			85					51	111	67			90	85			78			**41**
40		101	43	101	73			89	89			83				102	50	109	66			87	84			76			**40**
39	84	99	41	99	72			86	88			82			78	100	48	106	65			85	82			75			**39**
38	82	97	40	96	70			84	87			81			77	98	47	103	64			82	81			74			**38**
37	81	95	38	93	69			81	85			80			76	95	45	100	63			79	80			73			**37**
36	80	93	37	90	68			79	84			78		99	75	93	43	97	62			77	78			72		95	**36**
35	79	91	35	87	67			76	82			77		98	74	91	42	94	61			74	79			71		93	**35**
34	77	89	33	84	66			73	81			76		96	73	88	41	91	60			72	76			69		91	**34**
33	76	86	32	81	65			71	79			75		94	71	86	39	89	59			69	74			68		89	**33**
32	75	84	30	79	64		78	68	78		88	73		92	70	84	37	86	58		78	66	73		88	67		87	**32**
31	74	82	29	76	63		76	66	76		86	72		90	69	81	36	83	57		75	64	72		86	66		85	**31**
30	72	80	27	73	62		74	63	75		84	71		89	68	79	34	80	56		72	61	70		84	65		84	**30**
29	71	78	25	70	61		71	61	73		82	70		86	67	76	32	77	55		70	58	69		82	64		82	**29**
28	70	76	24	67	59	87	69	58	72		80	68		84	66	74	31	74	54	87	67	56	68		80	62		80	**28**
27	69	74	22	64	58	85	66	55	70	101	78	67		83	64	72	29	71	53	85	64	53	66	91	78	61		78	**27**
26	67	72	20	61	57	82	64	53	69	98	76	66	120	81	63	69	28	69	51	82	62	51	65	88	76	60	120	76	**26**
25	66	70	19	59	56	79	62	50	68	95	75	65	116	79	62	67	26	66	50	79	59	48	64	85	75	59	116	74	**25**
24	65	68	17	56	55	76	59	48	66	92	73	63	112	77	61	65	24	63	49	76	57	45	62	82	73	58	112	72	**24**
23	64	66	16	53	54	73	57	45	65	88	71	62	108	75	60	62	23	60	48	73	54	43	61	78	71	57	108	71	**23**
22	62	63	14	50	53	70	54	43	63	84	69	61	104	73	58	60	21	57	47	70	51	40	60	75	69	55	104	69	**22**
21	61	61	12	47	52	68	52	40	62	81	67	60	99	71	57	58	20	54	46	68	49	38	58	72	67	54	99	67	**21**

Appendix L. *(Continued)*

Raw score	A	R	Es	MAC	Dy	Do	Re	Cn	Mt	O-H	Pr	MAS	Lb	Ca	A	R	Es	MAC	Dy	Do	Re	Cn	Mt	O-H	Pr	MAS	Lb	Ca	Raw score
							Males														***Females***								
20	60	59		44	51	65	50	38	60	77	65	58	95	69	56	55	18	51	45	65	46	35	57	69	65	53	95	65	**20**
19	59	57		41	50	62	47	35	59	73	63	57	91	68	55	53	17	49	44	62	43	32	56	66	63	52	91	63	**19**
18	57	55		39	48	59	45	32	57	70	62	56	87	66	54	51	15	46	43	59	41	30	54	63	62	51	87	61	**18**
17	56	53		36	47	56	42	30	56	66	60	55	83	64	53	48	14	43	42	56	38	27	53	59	60	50	83	60	**17**
16	55	51		33	46	53	40	27	54	63	58	53	78	62	51	46	12	40	41	53	35	25	52	56	58	49	78	58	**16**
15	54	49		30	45	51	37	25	53	59	56	52	74	60	50	44		37	40	51	33	22	50	53	56	47	74	56	**15**
14	52	47		27	44	48	35	22	51	56	54	51	70	58	49	41		34	39	48	30	19	49	50	54	46	70	54	**14**
13	51	45		24	43	45	33	20	50	52	52	50	66	56	48	39		31	38	45	28	17	48	47	52	45	66	52	**13**
12	50	43		21	42	42	30	17	49	50	51	48	62	55	47	36		29	37	42	25	14	46	44	51	44	62	50	**12**
11	49	40			41	39	28	14	47	45	49	47	57	53	46	34		26	36	39	22	11	45	41	49	43	57	49	**11**
10	47	38			40	37	25	12	46	42	47	46	53	51	44	32		23	35	37	20	9	44	37	47	42	53	47	**10**
9	46	36			39	34	23	9	44	38	45	45	49	49	43	29		20	34	34		6	42	34	45	40	49	45	**9**
8	45	34			37	31	21	7	43	35	43	43	45	47	42	27			32	31		4	41	31	43	39	45	43	**8**
7	44	32			36	28	18	4	41	31	41	42	41	45	41	25			31	28		1	40	28	41	38	41	41	**7**
6	42	30			35	25		2	40	28	39	41	36	43	40	22			30	25			38	25	39	37	36	36	**6**
5	41	28			34	22			38	24	38	40	32	41	38	20			29	22			37	22	38	36	32	32	**5**
4	40	26			33	20			37	20	36	38	28	40	37	18			28	20			36	18	36	35	28	28	**4**
3	38	24			32				35		34	37	24	38	36	15			27				34		34	33	24	24	**3**
2	37	22			31				34		32	36	20	36	35	13			26				33		32	32	20	20	**2**
1	36	20			30				33		30	35		34	34	11			25				32		30	31			**1**
0	35	17			29				31		28	33		32	33				24				30		25	30			**0**

Source for A, R, Es, Dy, Do, Re, Cn, Pr, Lb, Ca: W. G. Dahlstrom, G. S. Welsh, and L. E. Dahlstrom, *An MMPI Handbook,* Vol. I, The University of Minnesota Press, Minneapolis. Copyright 1960, 1972 by the University of Minnesota. Reproduced with permission.
Source for MAC, Mt, O-H, MAS: Materials provided by National Computer Systems. Reproduced with permission of the University of Minnesota Press.

Author Index

Subject Index